Historical Materia

research in critical marxist

No.2 Summer 1998

Articles

China Miéville
The Conspiracy of Architecture: Notes on a Modern Anxiety   **1**

Gregory Elliott
Velocities of Change: Perry Anderson's Sense of an Ending   **33**

Andrew Chitty
Recognition and Social Relations of Production   **57**

Michael Neary & Graham Taylor
Marx and the Magic of Money: Towards an Alchemy of Capital   **99**

Paul Burkett
A Critique of Neo-Malthusian Marxism: Society, Nature, and
Population   **118**

Intervention

Slavoj Zizek
Risk Society and its Discontents   **143**

Reviews

Ben Watson on Adorno and Music   **165**
Mike Haynes on Popular Violence and the Russian Revolution   **185**
Esther Leslie on Walter Benjamin   **215**
Elmar Altvater on David Harvey   **225**
Martin Jenkins on Althusser and Psychoanalysis   **236**
Geoffrey Kay on Freeman & Carchedi   **240**
Henning Teschke on the Amsterdam Benjamin Conference   **245**

Notice of future articles   **250**

Subscription details   **251**

Notes on contributors   **252**

The Conspiracy of Architecture: Notes on a Modern Anxiety[1]

China Miéville

Introduction

We, the residents of modernity, live in an unquiet house.

This essay examines the relationship between human subjects and their built environment, but it does so less by focusing on architecture than on what one might call 'architecture once removed'. It is less concerned with the built environment itself than with a prevalent *image* of that environment in 'high' and 'popular' culture, in literature, in film and painting. It is my contention that a particular unsettling image of buildings has gained increasing currency in the modern epoch. I will attempt to show that such an image – and a concomitant anxiety – exists, and to offer an explanation for its provenance.

In historically locating this conception of architecture I will argue for an inextricable linkage of the aesthetic and sociological. Thus I am directly concerned with the actual, lived relationship between humans and buildings but my approach is rather different from that of most writers in this area. In my emphasis on literature and art, on *representations* of architecture, I may appear more circuitous.[2]

The image at the centre of this investigation is that of the *animate, alien building*.

By animate I mean that the buildings are projected as *active* and even *conscious agents*, able to intervene in the world. They are seen as alien in that their agendas, their motivations, are utterly *non-human*.

The essay is divided into six sections. First I try to show through example that the architectural anxiety I have identified is widespread. I then evaluate Bachelard's phenomenological analysis of the poetic image of the house. That analysis is rejected, but an important element of the phenomenological approach is retained. There follows a brief examination of some of the vast literature on the sociology of architecture. I then evaluate the arguments surrounding Marx's concept of commodity fetishism. The theoretical usefulness and validity of this concept have come under sustained attack, from Marxist as well as non-Marxist critics. The phenomenon of commodity fetishism is central to my analysis, however, and this section is therefore a brief attempt to

[1] I would like to thank Max Schaefer, Daphne Berdahl and especially the *HM* editorial board for their invaluable comments on an earlier draft of this essay.
[2] Exemplary of what one might term the more mainstream, 'direct' approach to the question are Rapoport 1976 and 1977. Rapoport is cited more or less at random from the voluminous literature.

respond to the critiques and rehabilitate the notion. I then offer a theoretical synthesis of the previous two sections, and finally an extended analysis of an extraordinary example of the image of architecture under examination.

I attempt to show that the image of the animate, alien building is explicable as an aesthetic response to the peculiar alienated relation between humanity and architecture under capitalism.

1. The house-creature

> "The house," Marsha said faintly, shutting off the flow. In the white enamel sink, an ugly pool of blood sluggishly dribbled reluctantly down the drain. "The house itself is alive."
> "Absolutely," Hamilton agreed. "And we're inside it."[3]

Freed from the constraints of 'realism', the image of the house-as-alien can be indulged openly. It is for this reason that the cultural anxiety over the autonomous agency of architecture is most obvious in what one might term paraliterary genres; science fiction, fantasy and horror.

Philip K. Dick's extraordinary, hallucinatory sequence quoted above represents probably the *ne plus ultra* of this concern in literature.[4] The house becomes a terrifying beast as the boundary between the organic and the built becomes utterly confused. 'Down in the basement the furnace was breathing' as 'the house-creature inhaled and exhaled'. The electrical wiring becomes a neurological system, the water pipes veins, the ivy on the roof hair. The walls yield 'like human flesh'. When the characters attempt to escape the carpet licks them back, and the walls drip with 'an avid, leaking sheet of anticipatory saliva'.

The relationship between the humans and the house is made unpleasantly clear: '[t]he house-creature was getting ready to feed.'

Floor and ceiling meet as the house chews up an unlucky inhabitant.

> [T]hey stood watching the creature methodically contract and expand. Digestive processes were taking place. Finally, the movement ebbed away. A last ripple of spasmodic activity passed through it, and then the creature was silent.
> With a dull whir, the window shades came down, forming opaque shadows that remained in place.
> "It's sleeping," Marsha said...

In this sequence the alien nature of the house is radically highlighted. The agenda of the house-creature is so at odds with that of humans that the inhabitants are nothing more than food. Architecture here is *its own end*, and humans, far from being the purpose of architecture's existence, become the *means* to keep the house alive.

---

[3] Dick 1979, p. 207.
[4] All references Dick 1979, pp. 207–12.

A similar vision of house as consumer of its inhabitants (if less literal and grotesquely organic) is found in Robert Marasco's 1973 novel *Burnt Offerings*. The Allardyce house in which the Rolfe family are staying regenerates itself at their expense, healing cracks and structural flaws as it draws energy from them. 'The house is, in fact, a living entity, a psychic vampire, and it is sucking the Rolfe family dry, as it has untold families before.'[5]

Dick returned to the theme of the house-creature, if less dramatically expressed, in *A Maze of Death*. The source of the conspiracy which is killing the characters one by one is to be found in The Building, which we first see thus: '[p]ounding, vibrating, the wall creaked as if alive...' The building is able to change its location at will. It sends out tiny mobile replicas of itself, in an analogy with birth that is made explicit. At first sight these miniature buildings are believed to be harmless; it transpires that they are able to attack to devastating effect.[6]

All the forces which conspire against the settlers in the novel are directed by The Building and its spawn. In the final realisation that the entire scenario was a shared illusion conjured up by computer, we learn that the motivations of The Building were literally unknowable and unthinkable in human terms. This use of the computer to symbolise the alien-ness of architecture's consciousness is also evident in the borderline SF thriller *Gridlock*.[7] A giant computerised office building turns against its human inhabitants, killing them in a variety of inventive ways using a myriad of moving parts (lifts, robots etc.). The building's motivation is explained as follows:

> "I ought to have known better than to anthropomorphize like that," said Beech. "... Ishmael [the computer controlling the building] has no subjective feelings at all. Revenge is a human motive."
>
> "... A computer isn't just an enlarged human brain. We can attribute human qualities to Ishmael, we can even imagine something as fanciful as a ghost in the machine, but of course all we're doing is referring to the various aspects of his behavior that are human-like, which is not the same thing as human at all..."[8]

Ishmael's aim, its motivations, its agenda, is so alien to human consciousness that its sole *raison d'être* has become to kill its inhabitants.

In Scott Bradfield's story 'The Secret Life of Houses' the house is less aggressive, but no less animate and no less alien. In the mind of the child Margaret the house moves.

---

[5] King 1988, p. 218.
[6] Dick 1970. p. 124, p. 116, p. 84, p. 87.
[7] The American edition, referenced here, was published as *The Grid*.
[8] Kerr 1997, p. 353.

> Rooted in the deep earth like a tree, the house articulated with
> and overgrew other roots, the secret passages of other houses
> ... The house was trying to pull Mother back into the world
> where Margaret lived. ... Somewhere she seemed to touch on
> the periphery of other dreams, and realized, drifting to the
> surface of her own, that somewhere she converged with the
> dreams of her own house. The house dreamed fantastic
> dreams of self-fulfillment, overwhelming pride, spontaneous
> transformations. The house dreamed it was an ocean liner, a
> vast white iceberg, a right whale boiling with plankton and
> animalcula, a duplex shopping center with multiple cinemas.
> The house heaved up on its concrete legs, ripping at the
> earth, pulling out long, dwindling complexes of nerve and
> tissue. The house moved. The house walked.[9]

The image of the house as active agent is amply demonstrated here in
the house's perambulatory dreams and perceived attempts to reclaim
Mother. Also present in an elliptical and lyrical form is the alien-ness of
the house. The passage of the house's dream represents a journey
further and further from human consciousness. The ocean is an
environment completely alien to humans, and the house initially
transposes its traditional role of maintaining human safety to this
environment: it becomes a liner, a house upon the water. Then a
reaction and the house moves to an antithetical position, becomes the
liner's nemesis, the iceberg, destroyer of liners and hence of human
safety. Remaining in the sea, the house's ambition undergoes a
dialectical movement beyond the poles of pro- and anti-human: it
becomes a whale, a creature popularly seen as sentient but which is
quintessentially non-human. In the whale are the plankton from which it
derives sustenance, living creatures now means for the whale's survival.
We too are small creatures in the body of the house: if the house wants
to be a whale, we, clearly, become plankton, stripped of our agency by
that of the house, for the house's benefit.

Having set in motion this passage further and further from human
consciousness, human agendas, Bradfield's extraordinary segue from
whale to mall – separated only by a comma, very much part of that
same journey from liner to iceberg to whale – renders the shopping
centre itself alien. The mall, defined by the myriad of commodities it
contains and its spectacles to hold people in thrall, is made the final
destination of an alien consciousness. Architecture is deftly made
alien(ating/ated) by making it the culmination of its own dream of
difference. Ultimately, the architecture alleges, *I* am the most alien thing
I can think of. At the moment when I seem most at your service, when I
act as repository of all your commodities, that is when I am further
from your human agenda than if I were your friend (the liner), your
enemy (the iceberg) or a consciousness on which you do not impinge at

---

[9] Bradfield 1990, p. 223.

all (the whale). In the dream of the house, Bradfield makes architecture profoundly unsafe.

The theme of the animate, alien building can easily be unearthed even where the architecture at first sight appears only to be the *locus* for an inhuman force, rather than the force itself. The dividing line is not sharply drawn.

This is clear in modern treatments of the haunted house. 'The Whistling Room' investigated by Hodgson's ghost-finder Carnacki is the *repository* of the spirit of an evil jester, and yet it is the room *itself* which malevolently whistles, in a literal and grotesque way.

> The floor in the middle of the huge, empty room, was puckered upwards in the centre into a strange, soft-looking mound, parted at the top into an everchanging hole, that pulsated to that great, gentle hooning. At times, as I watched, I saw the heaving of the indented mound, gap across with a queer, inward suction, as with the drawing of an enormous breath; then the thing would dilate and pout once more to the incredible melody. ... [I]t came to me that the thing was living. I was looking at two enormous, blackened lips, blistered and brutal, there in the pale moonlight...[10]

As Carnacki himself puts it, 'I had come across one of those rare and horrible cases of the *Inanimate* reproducing the functions of the *Animate*'.[11]

This unclear distinction between buildings as loci and buildings as *agents* can be seen in the opening (also, with very slight changes, the closing) paragraph of Shirley Jackson's *The Haunting of Hill House*.

> No live organism can continue for long to exist sanely under conditions of absolute reality; even larks and katydids are supposed, by some, to dream. Hill House, not sane, stood by itself against its hills, holding darkness within; it had stood so for eighty years and might stand for eighty more. Within, walls continued upright, bricks met neatly, floors were firm, and doors were sensibly shut; silence lay steadily against the wood and stone of Hill House, and whatever walked there, walked alone.[12]

The tension is clear. The house is a repository of darkness, something walks within it, but it is also seen as 'live' and, crucially, 'not sane'. It is a commonplace to remark that Hill House itself is more than a setting. The house 'from the very first paragraph, is attributed a personality, and given the status of antagonist'.[13] But while it is quite true that Jackson's houses 'exerted a mysterious force of their own', Lenemaja Friedman is quite wrong to assert that they 'reflected the egos and foibles of their

---

[10] Hodgson 1913, p. 170.
[11] Hodgson 1913, p. 158.
[12] Jackson 1959, p. 3.
[13] Tuttle 1988, p. 132.

original owners'.[14] At least in the case of Hill House, the building is emphatically *not* a reflection of human characteristics. Indeed, it 'reared its great head back against the sky without concession to humanity'.[15] And as the book's opening makes clear, the house is not sane.

Neither, however, is it *insane*. Sanity and insanity are polar opposites, but they are both defined by human criteria. Hill House is 'not sane'. This is a far more radical other than 'insane'. Human terms here simply do not apply.

Hill House 'seemed somehow to have formed itself, flying together into its own powerful pattern under the hands of its builders'.[16] Like Dick's house in *Eye in the Sky*, and Marasco's in *Burnt Offerings*, Hill House uses humans as mere means. The builders here are merely the conduit for the self-creation of the house. The house has become its own end.

The anxiety surrounding alien architecture can be found in nearly as overt a form in surrealist art, which shares with SF and horror the fact that it, as Philip K. Dick has put it (talking about his own work), has 'never had too high a regard for what is generally called "reality"'.[17] Thus surrealism, like genre literature, is not constrained from expressing its anxieties more or less openly, whether or not they are 'possible'.

In an interstice between surrealism and 'mainstream' film-making, a work such as Roman Polanski's *The Tenant* hints at the theme of the building as alien agent: rubbish disappears from stairs where it has been spilled, as if consumed by the building as an offering; church doors stick fast, trapping Polanski's character within; much is made of the immobility of furniture, as rooms resist attempts to change their layout; the pipes of the house complain in an absurdly obstreperous manner at the slightest attempt to put them to their (human) 'use'.

In a more overtly surreal vein, the films of Jan Svankmajer represent one of the most stunning example of this architectural concern. Svankmajer himself has spoken of his interest in 'the unquiet house', and the theme can be ascertained in much of his work, most obviously in *A Quiet Week in a House* (1969) and *The Fall of the House of Usher* (1980). The paradigmatic example remains *The Flat* (1968).[18]

---

[14] Friedman 1975, p. 104.
[15] Jackson 1959, p. 35.
[16] Jackson 1959, p. 35.
[17] Dick 1979. p. v.
[18] Svankmajer has always lived in what was until recently Czechoslovakia, now the Czech republic. For most of his life, then, the film-maker worked under 'actually existing socialism'. As is made clear later in this piece I argue that the architectural anxiety under question – including that in Svankmajer's work – is explicable in terms of the phenomenon of commodity fetishism. I follow Marx in arguing that this is a result of capitalist social relations. Although the debate ranges substantially beyond the scope of this essay, it is worth pointing out, therefore, that my argument lends indirect support to the school which characterises the erstwhile Eastern Bloc as state capitalist. Unless, of course, commodity fetishism can leak across borders leaving capitalism behind – a dubious notion.

The Flat is the story of a man in a room. 'The man ... comes from nowhere and goes nowhere; his life is reduced to a brief time spent in a room in which the world of objects ... attacks and menaces him.'[19] The rebellion of objects is the rebellion of the flat itself. The mirror will only reflect the back of his head,[20] the bed decomposes into shreds when he lies on it, a glass from which he attempts to drink shrinks to a useless size. As in many of the examples of the unquiet house, the architecture's agency extends to the objects within: a knife turns on its wielder in *Eye in the Sky* as the first signal that the house is sentient; for Bradfield's house, the zenith of its agency occurs at the moment it is replete with commodities.

In *The Flat*, the shrinking of the glass is depicted by a rapid succession of progressively smaller glasses: it is the *sheer multitude* of commodities that is the conspiracy of the house. Here, as in Bradfield, the theme of the sentient house and the concomitant alienation of the human are explicitly linked to the condition of commodification under capitalism.

So far I have focused on works which do little to hide the central image of unquiet architecture. Often, however, a task of decoding must be undertaken to show that such an anxiety exists in a work. Thus for example, in Jean Dubuffet's 1946 painting 'Apartment Buildings, Paris', the wan, flat humans who populate the buildings are signalled by their absence, sketched with very thin white paint, featureless and crudely executed. The buildings, by contrast, are rendered in thick, organic daubs of browns and reds that almost ooze off the canvas. The paint, the medium of agency, the stuff with which *presence* can be asserted, all belongs to the architecture. The paint wells up around the flat human inhabitants like mud between toes, threatening to efface them in an oily wash. Like a photograph of lava eructations, we see the paint caught momentarily in mid-flow. As spectators we feel that if we turn our backs for a moment time will start again: the surface tension which – just – keeps the buildings from breaking their banks and inscribing themselves on the bodies of the humans will not hold. The picture captures the moment of the crisis of human agency and the ascendance of architecture.

Having turned away from surrealist or 'fantastic' art, I will offer as a final example of the trope a hugely popular film which seems to obey all the rules of 'realism'. Nothing we know to be impossible – such as animate architecture – is ever overtly depicted. And yet, I will argue, architecture's agency is signalled as *the* driving force behind the events which shake the human characters. The film is concerned with a conspiracy of architecture. The film is Hitchcock's *Vertigo* (1958).

Architecture dominates the film: it is a neurotic concern.

---

[19] O'Pray 1995, p. 57.
[20] The reference is to 'La Reproduction Interdite' (1937–39), Magritte's well-known 'portrait' of Edward James.

Setting is exact: the film makes repeated, extended use of San Francisco's streets. But the built environment is more than just a locus. Indeed, the obsessive foregrounding of the city undermines its actual historical/spatial specificity: in Jameson's words, '[t]he hallucinatory San Francisco of *Vertigo* is undateable, out of time'.[21] Hallucinatory in its aggressive presence yet removed from time, the 'San Francisco' of *Vertigo* carves out its own spatial/temporal moment. In their oneiric now-ness, the buildings undermine their own apparent reality. In the very act of recognising the city the viewer is made uneasy by the continual hallucinatory looming presence of the supposedly real place.

Zizek has suggested that Hitchcock's films often contain a 'stain of the Real', 'a non-symbolised stain, a hole in reality which designates the ultimate limit where 'the word fails''.[22] The Real is that which 'eludes the symbolic grasp' of representation, that which by definition is beyond the reach of human representation, and hence human agency. In the case of *Vertigo*, the stain has spread, and ruptured reality, and replaced it. The real is made hallucinatory, too-real, and becomes the Real. The 'stain' in *Vertigo* is the buildings (which are the city, which is the setting, which – for the purposes of the film – is the whole world). The too-real depiction of the buildings invests them with agency, with the power to create a world, the world of San Francisco-as-Real.

The buildings are 'non-symbolized': it is in their very 'realness', their excess of recognisability, that they become Real. 'The word' – human representation – cannot contain them. To submit to the word would be to submit to the agency of humans, to admit that humans have the power symbolically to define them. It is precisely that which the 'hallucinatory San Francisco' denies: it symbolically defines *itself as itself*.

The humans in *Vertigo* are suffered to live in the Real, a world which they do not symbolically control. Their agency counts for nothing. [23]

From the opening sequence when Scottie (James Stewart) and a police colleague are chasing someone across the roofs of the city, architecture is *made strange*. We see the city from an angle not designed for human aesthetic consumption, a strange and dangerous landscape of peaks and crests that defy easy resolution as part of a building's

---

[21] Jameson 1992. p. 59.
[22] Zizek 1992. p. 239.
[23] In Scottie's (James Stewart's) dream, Zizek locates a point at which the Thing (that is of the Real) gazes on the subject. This, he says, 'marks the moment when the subject is immediately entrapped in, caught into, the dream of the Other-Thing'. The moment is when Scottie 'stares at his own head, depicted as a kind of psychotic partial object located in the point of convergence of the running lines in the background' (Zizek 1992, p. 252). This is convincing, but neglects to mention that the converging lines are graphic representations of the film's repeated shot down a sheer drop in or between buildings: they are a study in perspective looking down a yawning architectural gap. The dream does nothing more than point the finger at the architecture. Thus, while it is possible that this moment represents Scottie's *realisation* of his own disempowerment at the hands of the Real, the buildings, it is not true that it represents the moment of disempowerment itself, as Zizek alleges. The disempowerment has been there from the start.

supposed use-value. Humans are no longer self-evidently the ends or buildings the means. At several points throughout the film this making strange is repeated: Madeleine's (Kim Novak's) use of a dark, grey, *unused* back passageway to enter a bright shop emphasises that the non-human side of architecture impinges on the human. This point is reinforced by the contrast between the dark and decrepit (non-human) tower and the bright, obviously frequented church of which it is an annex.

This disorientation is vastly increased with the early appearance of the film's most potent visual effect. 'If there is one element that crystallizes the impact, ingenuity, and sheer strangeness of *Vertigo* ... it is the repeated shot representing Scottie/James Stewart's troubled gaze into an abyss far below.' The shot, which appears at key crisis moments throughout the film, is an extraordinary effect 'of merciless disorientation' achieved 'by tracking away from the subject of the shot while simultaneously zooming toward it'. In his discussion of the shot, Sterritt omits one salient point: how it appears to the viewer.[24]

The shot is always straight down, either the length of a single tower or into a chasm between buildings. And it appears to the viewer as if the buildings in shot grow suddenly taller.

Scottie's vertigo, in other words, is signified by sudden and extraordinary *physical action* on the part of the built environment.

This is the most dramatic, but by no means an isolated instance of the decisive interference of architecture in the human world.

Throughout the film scenes open on a building, holding still until the human characters enter shot and then the building. The camera does not follow them: it remains fixed as it was, the composition of the shot dictated by the architecture, as if the important characters in *Vertigo* are not the humans at all. Their appearance in the camera's lens is incidental.

No one in the film ever draws curtains or blinds at night. The effect of this is to present shot after shot of characters, especially Scottie and Midge (Barbara Bel Geddes), being watched from behind by the city. There is almost a pantomimic sense of unease as the characters blithely fail to *look behind* them, at the enemy silently watching. When Midge accidentally upsets Scottie, she vents her rage by defacing her art and throwing the dirty brush at the window, to where the camera cuts just in time to see the brush hit and a spot of paint obscure one of the hundreds of city lights which have watched the scene. The sense of the watching city as enemy, as *responsible*, is thus highlighted: Midge's rage is directed against it. But hers is a hollow victory. One light is obscured but a thousand remain.

Architecture in *Vertigo* is 'always already there'. In the painting of Carlotta Valdes, at the site of Madeleine's attempted suicide, lurking in shot behind the shoulder of Scottie in the city, to one side of the canvas

---

[24] Sterritt 1993, pp. 82–3.

or screen lurks the vast *corner* of a building or a pillar, a detail signalling the enormity of the architecture off-screen, locating it as *out of shot*, beyond human ken, but jutting into human affairs.

After Scottie's breakdown, he discovers Judie/Madeleine living in a hotel. We first see its awning, which reads 'Empire Hotel'. But the huge neon sign which extends vertically the height of the building inverts this, and tells the truth: 'Hotel Empire'. The hotel is the most paradoxical of buildings, a home to hundreds in which humans are utterly transitory. The hotel is permanent, its inhabitants ephemeral. And as Judy's dwelling declares, in buildings' terms (signalled by the verticality of the writing, verticality opposed throughout the film to the 'horizontality' of human affairs[25]) the city is a Hotel Empire, the Kingdom of buildings become their own ends. At the significant moment of Judy's (re)transformation into Madeleine, the door by which she leaves into a liminal state and re-enters is suffused in a highly unnatural green glow, ostensibly from the 'Hotel Empire' sign just outside her window. The light has become a spot, pointing her way in and out of the transformation which will ultimately lead to her death. It is the buildings which dictate the human action, just as when Madeleine's first suicide attempt in San Francisco bay saw her leap into the water in exactly the spot to which the bridge, looming enormously in the left of the screen, pointed.

Vertigo may pretend to be a 'realistic' film, in which only the possible (if highly unlikely) occurs. This does not stop it from representing an extraordinarily fraught example of the conspiracy of architecture, the maleficient intervention into human affairs of the built environment.

2. Bachelard and the image before thought

The multitude of examples above is intended to show that the anxiety over the unquiet house, alien architecture, is prevalent at all levels of modern cultural production. But something is still missing: an analysis of what, in each case, the image of the autonomous building might *mean*.

This omission is deliberate. I am concerned with the *fact* and the social foundation of this peculiar image. I do not concern myself with what this image means because the image functions as a *trope*, able to signify different things (sometimes wildly different things) in different works. My project is an examination of what Bachelard calls 'detached images'[26] – images *in themselves*, rather than images as conveyors of meaning. Like Bachelard, I focus on 'poetic' images of architecture.

---

[25] Cf: 'A house is imagined as a vertical being. it rises upward. It differentiates itself in terms of its verticality. It is one of the appeals to our consciousness of verticality.' Bachelard 1964, p. 17.
[26] Bachelard 1964, p. xxv.

Despite this shared project, however, the problems of Bachelard for a Marxist analysis are enormous, and should be made clear.

Bachelard's *The Poetics of Space* is an exercise in 'topophilia', an investigation of 'images of *felicitous space*'.[27] Linking its various dignified little sermons on poetic images of the house, shells, wardrobes and the like is an implicit assumption about the thinking of space. 'Bachelard links representational spaces, which he travels through as he dreams ... , with ... intimate and absolute space'.[28] The intimate and absolute space is the nostalgic recollection of the House as timeless sanctuary from history.

Two notions are intertwined here. One is that the house (or, more accurately, House) is the indivisible, basic mental unit of architecture, the experienced space through which we think all space: 'all really inhabited space bears the essence of the notion of home'.[29] It is certainly true that the House is an image of great importance for societal self-conception: it is a piece of efficacious mental capital. Given this social-symbolic centrality of the House, the idea that all architecture is ultimately a derivation of the social theme of 'House' is persuasive, at least at the level of symbolism. As Lefebvre points out, speaking of the 'historico-poetic reality' of the house, '[t]his memory ... has an obsessive quality: it persists in art, poetry, drama and philosophy'.[30] Bachelard is right, then, about the *poetic usefulness* of the trope of the house.

However, Bachelard's second assertion, the reason he posits for that poetic usefulness, is idealist and unsustainable. It is that the House can defeat history.

> An entire past comes to dwell in a new house ... And the daydream deepens to the point where an immemorial domain opens up for the dreamer of a home beyond man's earliest memory ... [T]he house is not experienced from day to day only, on the thread of a narrative, or in the telling of our own story. Through dreams, the various dwelling-places in our lives co-penetrate and retain the treasures of former days. And after we are in the new house, when memories of other places we have lived in come back to us, we travel to the land of Motionless Childhood, motionless the way all Immemorial things are. We live fixations...[31]

> At times we think we know ourselves in time, when all we know is a sequence of fixations in the spaces of the being's stability ... In its countless alveoli space contains compressed time. That is what space is for.[32]

---

[27] Bachelard 1964, p. xxxv.
[28] Lefebvre 1991, p. 121.
[29] Bachelard 1964, p. 5.
[30] Lefebvre 1991, p. 120.
[31] Bachelard 1964, pp. 5–6.
[32] Bachelard 1964, p. 8.

Both Lefebvre and Bachelard acknowledge that the House is an invaluable trope with which to think, but here the difference is clear. Where Lefebvre (and I) would see an 'obsessive' memory, Bachelard precisely sees a gateway to 'a home *beyond* man's earliest memory'. This is a transcendantly idealist – indeed quasi-religious – conception of history as essentially inimicable to human-ness, which seeks refuge in the prelapsarian House. The centrality of timelessness to human experience is stressed over that of change/history/time. 'Being, suffused with immemorial spatial memory, transcends becoming'.[33] In Bachelard's own words, 'Being is already [ie: before human time] a value'.[34] Thus Bachelard's model is ahistorical, and must be rejected as an explanation for the power of the House-image.

So what is the use of Bachelard's writings for a Marxist analysis of poetic images of architecture? It lies in the focus of his phenomenological concern, the units of his analysis.

At the start of this section, I made it clear that the various 'meanings' of the image under investigation in various works of art is not my concern. I have alleged two things about the image of the unquiet house: one is that it is very peculiar; the other is that it exists nevertheless. Bachelard is surely right in his contention that '[t]he communicability [rather than the 'meaning'] of an unusual image is a fact of great ontological significance'.[35]

Even when we reject Bachelard's own explanation for the communicability of the house-image, in his assertion that 'the image comes *before* thought'[36] there is an important truth. If we see as the *meaning* of an image the result of the application of thought to it, then my analysis is precisely concerned with the image 'before' thought, before that meaning. In Bachelard's terms, we are concerned not with what the image means but with *why it 'reverberates'*. In other words, I am asking not what thoughts the image is used to think, but why this image is apparently so good to think with.

It is my contention that the widespread adoption of this image for a massive variety of artistic purposes ('meanings') and in a variety of contexts is a result of the interaction between humans and buildings under capitalism.

3. Living in buildings

It would be extraordinary if the built environment had no effect on its inhabitants. There is, unfortunately, a tendency to express that relationship in egregiously reductive terms. Kupfer, for example, describes Speer's architecture in the Third Reich as helping

---

[33] Harvey 1990, p. 218.
[34] Bachelard 1964, p. 7.
[35] Bachelard 1964, p. xvii.
[36] Bachelard 1964, p. xx.

'incapacitate the people for real political action by implementing totalitarian modes of interaction and undermining the people's power', and claims that it 'fostered the political relationship of command and obedience'.[37] Despite some lip-service to a more nuanced view, his basic thesis is that architecture has 'direct political influence'.[38]

This determinist and reductionist model does not argue for an interaction between people and architecture, but for a mechanistic model wherein individuals merely 'reflect' the politics embedded in architecture. This kind of architectural determinism is unsustainable. Its 'simple behaviourist model of environment-person relationship' 'patently overestimates the effect of the layout of the environment on behavior' '[g]iven the fantastic diversity of behavior in similar environments'.[39]

There is another, equally unsustainable, view. Based on the idealist separation of 'art' and 'society', this argument holds that the coincidence of social concerns and architecture is horribly stultifying to architecture's 'artistic' nature. Sinclair Gauldie, for example, wrings his hands at the 'grave outlook' facing architecture. As art, its 'function' is 'to help man master these inner confusions by enriching his cognitive-imaginative experience'.[40]

The absolute separation of architecture and social context is evident in Gauldie's snobbish irritation at the 'frustration' of architecture's development as an 'art' which *celebrates* its transcendence of social concerns. He sees this 'development' being hamstrung by

> [t]he increasing complexity and rigidity of the legislative and economic framework within which the architect has to operate: it is not possible to build high art out of the hopes and fears of the sanitary inspector, the fire-prevention officer and the chartered accountant.[41]

Gauldie's paeans to the disappearing world of 'high art' are a quintessentially English aristocratic outrage at the ascendancy of bourgeois culture, deflected onto the petty bourgeois inspectorate able, to the aristocracy's profound distaste, to dictate terms for its masters.[42] They are the death cries of a moribund class.[43] By lambasting social concerns as vulgarian Gauldie articulates the disquiet of a class that, in positing itself as the repository of 'taste', clings to tattered dreams of its own importance. This class is appalled that some ghastly oik has final say over its 'art', based on narrow obssessions about details such as the

---

[37] Kupfer 1985, p. 265.
[38] Kupfer 1985, p. 266.
[39] Lang 1980, p. 151.
[40] Gauldie 1966, p. 27.
[41] Gauldie 1966, pp. 28–9.
[42] Gauldie's sanitary inspector and fire-prevention officer are representatives of that great British whipping boy, the officious minor functionary.
[43] Although given the tenacious longevity of the aristocracy in England it might be more apt to describe it as undead, rather than moribund.

fact that its sewage outlet will overflow, or that a fire will kill all of its tenants.

Gauldie's admission that architecture is 'a social art'[44] is misleading. He has no understanding of any *organic* connection between architecture and individual. His plea for a society 'which not merely allows ... [the architect] but clearly asks him to enrich its aesthetic experience'[45] is a plea to lift the social constraints on the architect *as artist*. Society is connected to architecture only insofar as it stultifies it, holds it back from being 'high art'. In an ideal world, that constraining connection will be broken.

There is clearly some connection between social behaviour and architectural form. As Lang has noted, '[a]nyone who ... walks down one street rather than another simply because it is cheerier, or who selects a home in one neighbourhood rather than another because it is more attractive knows that the quality of the built environment affects one's perceptions of the quality of personal life'[46] – and more simply, affects behaviour. The challenge is to express this connection in a sufficiently nuanced form.

> Houses, once solidly built, tend to perpetuate the patterns of behavior that they were originally designed to accommodate. Similarly, the spatial relations between one house and another, between each house and its source of food and water (as well as markets, churches, and inns), and between an entire group of dwellings and its highways and environs, represent a way of life which they at once acknowledge, symbolize, and reinforce.[47]

Sparshott's model is rather clumsily rendered. He wrestles unsuccessfully with the problem of expressing the dialectical nature of cultural practice (simultaneously based on, reproducing and potentially transformative of social norms) and falls back on an unconvincing two-stage temporal model of that interaction. However, his formulation goes some way to improving things, precisely in its explicit recognition of an *interaction* between buildings and human agents,[48] what Berleant calls 'the complementary relation between building and site and between both of these and the human user'.[49]

These formulations represent ever-closer approximations to a sufficiently sensitive view of the relationship. What is missing so far is the consideration of the socio-economic backdrop against which the

---

[44] Gauldie 1966, p. 29.
[45] Gauldie 1966, p. 29.
[46] Lang 1980, p. 147. Not, of course, that most of us can 'select a home' based primarily on such blithe aesthetic criteria.
[47] Sparshott 1994, p. 5.
[48] Why Sparshott should choose to express the social role of architecture with what appears to be a vaguely mediaeval example is entirely unclear. The interaction, one presumes, does not stop with the onset of industrialisation.
[49] Berleant 1988, p. 97.

interaction of human and built environment takes place.[50] For this we can turn to the vastly influential work of Henri Lefebvre. He shows how not only architectural production, but space itself – experienced space – changes with social structures. Thus, for example, he sees the façade under capitalism, 'made to be seen and to be seen from' as 'a measure of social standing and prestige' and paradigmatic of 'bourgeoisified space' which degrades the three-dimensionality of space with its focus on the visual.[51] The social nature of architectural production and the particular form of the interaction of humans and architecture in this model are *functions* of the wider social structure.

A critical understanding of the social context is crucial in considering the mutual constitution of human agency and the built environment, and the efficacy of architectural change in ameliorating or worsening people's lived conditions. Callinicos has said of human agency – and the same is true of the interaction of architecture and human agency – that it 'involves the exercise of powers determined at least in part by the social relations prevailing at the time they were performed'.[52] Lefebvre's insistence on the salience of capitalist relations to modern architectural form is no less than the application of that understanding to the particular form of human agency which is architectural production. The fruits of that production then act to help create a constraining and enabling environment within which humans can exercise their agency, part of which, of course, will be devoted to the maintenance of the built environment which helped to condition it.

With this formulation we can see both the mutual interaction of environment and agency and, what is often ignored, the vital constitutive role of wider social relations. 'However far one pushes back the story, action-explanation [including, we can add, the explanation of the particular 'actions' which make up humans' lived interaction with architecture] will still involve both individuals' beliefs and desires and the structures on which their powers partly depend.'[53]

In an attempt to suggest a nuanced theory of human-architecture interaction I have dismissed reactionary witterings about 'high art', moved beyond architectural determinism and away from simplistic, non-dialectical models of interaction. I have tried to integrate the 'always-already-thereness' of social structures.

It is in this light that we must consider those analyses of buildings which view them as embodying (a) culture. In a particularly nebulous formulation[54] this thematic has been expressed by Langer. According to

---

[50] One can – charitably – see the germ of this understanding in Berleant's inclusion of 'site' as well as building and human in the relationship, or in Sparshott's concern with 'environs', or more obviously Lang's mention of the 'sociophysical system' (p. 147). None of these, however, represents more than a cursory and inchoate understanding of the problematic.

[51] Lefebvre 1991, p. 361.

[52] Callinicos 1988, p. 38.

[53] Callinicos 1988, p. 38.

[54] Sparshott describes it as 'a notorious phrase, of which the general purport was clear but the precise interpretation proved hard to elucidate...' (Sparshott 1994, p. 6.)

her, 'the basic abstraction ... of architecture is *an ethnic domain*'.[55] Sparshott's suggestion that '[p]artly what she meant, certainly, was that in the buildings of a community its way of life found expression'[56] is doubtless true. This sense in which architecture embodies an 'ethnic domain' can be seen in Bourdieu's celebrated analysis of the Kabyle house.[57] In the relation of walls, inside and outside, house and garden, the sets of relations of the Kabyle society are mirrored, represented 'in reverse'. The house is invested with meaning in relation to the society of which it is part.

This sense of meaning is not, of course, *inherent* in the architecture but is invested in it by humans. Irrespective of whether it is part of the *discursive consciousness* of social agents, the embedding of social meaning in architecture is the result of human reflection, in terms of *practical consciousness* and lived experience. Humans are unique in their ascription of meaning to social forms. In other words, we do not merely interact with each other and with our environment, including our architecture, we *reflect* on that interaction. That reflection then becomes part of the interaction.

In Langer's discussion of the 'ethnic domain' we can see an epistemological result of this reflection.

> A Gypsy camp is a different place from an Indian camp, though it may be geographically where the Indian camp used to be.
> A place, in this non-geographical sense, is a created thing, an ethnic domain made visible, tangible, sensible.[58]

Langer's formulation veers towards essentialism, a Bachelardian poetics of space with an ethnic gloss. But in her acknowledgement that a place is 'created' she at least opens the door to an awareness that human agency is the generative force behind the power of the house-as-image, rather than any essential power of the 'House' itself. People, as material creatures existing, thinking and reflecting in space, think themselves through that space, and through what they do with it.

Inextricably linked to the fact that 'in the buildings of a community its way of life found expression' is a more profound epistemological fact. The 'place' in which such expression could take place is itself a 'created thing': it is not only the 'way' of life of a community which finds expression, but the *fact* of its life. That fact is always in part geographical. In this persuasive formulation, a society's self-conception, its very awareness of itself as *existing*, involves an awareness that it exists *somewhere*, in a particular place.[59]

---

[55] Langer 1953, pp. 94–5.
[56] Sparshott 1994, p. 6.
[57] Bourdieu 1990, pp. 271–83.
[58] Langer 1953, p. 95.
[59] This is true for nomadic, just as for sedentary societies. The 'place' in which such societies would locate themselves would be unfixed in space.

There are obvious analogies with Heidegger's notorious assertion that 'man *is* insofar as he *dwells*', that '[d]welling ... is *the basic character* of Being in keeping with which mortals exist'.[60]. This opaque conception, however, is the font of an egregious idealism which – in its eulogising of Being as an extra-historical ontology of things and people – denigrates space as 'nothing more than 'being-there''.[61] What Lefebvre identifies as Heidegger's 'obsession with absolute space presents obstacles on every side to the kind of history that we have been discussing ... for it stands opposed to any analytic approach'.[62]

There is a 'rational kernel' in Heidegger's model. Lefebvre's tart description of Heidegger's formulation as 'admirable if enigmatic' is quite right. It is admirable to the extent that it recognises that human self-awareness is always in part an awareness of human existence *in space*. It is enigmatic in its surfeit of obfuscatory nonsense 'explaining' dwelling as a being 'in the fourfold' of 'earth and sky, divinities and mortals',[63] and such-like. This kind of portentous musing boils down to Heidegger's idealist privileging of Being-that-dwells over historicised human agency. Heidegger acknowledges that we cannot but be geographical agents, and architectural ones, in our thinking. However, he does so based on quasi-religious idealist foundations. Without these foundations, the truth of our architectural agency remains but it is no longer what Heidegger thinks it is.

Heidegger is admirable to the extent that he is enigmatic. Without the enigma – uncovered and open to critique – his model is no longer admirable at all. We are left with the same conception of humans as beings that think themselves through space that we had arrived at without Heidegger's help.

I have attempted to construct a reasonably persuasive – dialectical, temporal, socially contextualised – view of the relationship between human agents and buildings, and I have stressed the *reflexivity* of humans. In stressing the centrality of experienced space to human self-perception I hope I have gone some way towards explaining the succulence of architecture as a trope with which to think socially.

In thinking through thinking about society through buildings, we turn to the cultural *conception* of architecture, 'architecture once removed'. In being reflected upon, the culture that is embedded in the architecture is brought to the forefront of social consciousness, made malleable.

'Memory transforms the house into the symbolic miniature of the Algerian social world. The remembered house is a sort of "centre of the world".'[64] The importance of Bahloul's analysis is that it concerns itself not with architecture but with *remembered* architecture. Thus the meanings embedded in the house are seen as the result of the *reflection*

---

[60] Heidegger 1971, p. 147, p. 160.
[61] Lefebvre 1991, p. 121.
[62] Lefebvre 1991, p. 122.
[63] Heidegger 1971, p. 149, p. 150.
[64] Bahloul 1996, p. 30.

on architecture and on society through architecture. In this sense memory in her analysis is analogous to 'artistic production' in mine. It is in the *act of reflecting* on architecture, through remembering it or through appropriating it as an image, that a particular meaning is made to inhere so strongly in it.

Architecture as an aesthetic/symbolic trope in artistic production will not be, of course, a simplistic reflection of the social experience of 'really existing architecture'. Neither, however, is it entirely random. This is where a phenomenological approach to artistic images is of particular value, ironically given its idealist pedigree, to a Marxist analysis. Phenomenology is concerned with the image *'before* thought', rather than with what we might call its 'artistic meaning', its meaning and role *in the work of art*. For a Marxist, therefore, the task becomes one of uncovering the *embedded* social meanings, the *assumptions about relations* on which the very *fact* of the shared reception of the image itself depends.

A 'Marxist phenomenology' is thus concerned to uncover the evidence of social relations that a shared image contains.

So far I have spoken in general terms about the relations between people and architecture. However, it is a tenet of my analysis that the image of the alien, autonomous building is a peculiarly *modern* anxiety. I must therefore turn my attention to the most salient feature of architecture under capitalism.

Most of the literature about the experience of architecture focuses almost entirely on the physicality of buildings. This is to ignore the profound experiential ramifications of living in a social system where 'land and housing are commodities to be ... [exchanged] for profit.'[65]

> [T]he poor man's basement dwelling is an uncongenial element, an "alien, restrictive power which only surrenders itself to him at the expense of his sweat and blood". He cannot look upon it as his home, as somewhere he can call his own. Instead he finds himself in someone else's house, in an *alien* house, whose owner lies in wait for him every day, and evicts him if he fails to pay the rent.[66]

The alienation of building from dweller is the result of the mediation of the market. Under capitalism, it is only through that mediation that humans interact with buildings at all, as Engels makes clear.

> In the housing question we have two parties confronting each other: the tenant and the landlord ... The former wishes to purchase from the latter the temporary use of a dwelling; he has money or credit ... It is a simple commodity sale; it is not a transaction between proletarian and bourgeois, between worker and capitalist.[67]

---

[65] Deutsche 1996, p. 54.
[66] Marx 1867, p. 366.
[67] Engels 1872, p. 19.

Under capitalism there are particular, socially specific mechanisms at work in the relations between people and the built environment. Most theories of 'human-environment interaction' are ahistorical, and fail to recognise this.

To understand the specific mechanisms at stake we must turn to Marx's later writings, and to the vexed question of commodity fetishism.

4. Commodity fetishism and its discontents

Commodity fetishism is often used as a stick with which to beat Marxists. It is derided as the 'conceptual fetish of vulgar social thought' which 'short-circuits analysis'.[68] Often this derision is linked to a postmodern sensibility which sees commodity fetishism as maintaining an 'outdated' adherence to 'grand narratives'. The very project, central to the theory of commodity fetishism, of distinguishing appearance from reality in social relations, is rejected.

This is not the place to argue at length against the *faux* radicalism that distinguishes postmodernist analysis. Suffice it to say here that the postmodern critique of commodity fetishism is a subset of the postmodern critique of the enlightenment project, of 'analysis' itself.

> Theory presupposes critical distance between its own categories and those of a naturalized mythology or commonsense system of assumptions. Simply to collapse that distance ... is to argue away the very grounds of rational critique.[69]

The grounds for critique are then perforce irrational – Derrida's 'unnameable' comes to mind. It is no surprise that postmodernism's much-vaunted project of subjecting 'metanarratives' to critique devolves, in its political prescriptions, into a wan liberalism at best, or Baudrillard's vacuous nihilism at worst.

A paradigmatic example of the postmodern critique of commodity fetishism is provided by Wigley.[70] In his discussion of Harvey's Marxist project to understand the social relations which underlie fetishism he dismisses the 'phallic pretension of this desire to penetrate the other'. The extraordinary equation of a belief that the appearance is not the whole story of social relations with a putative 'rejection of both the feminine surface and feminist discourse'[71] represents the very celebration of the surface which utterly undermines postmodernism's ability critically to theorise social relations, and a gendered essentialism so absurd (woman = surface) that it is difficult to believe the 'critique'

---

[68] Baudrillard 1981, p. 88.
[69] Christopher Norris quoted in Callinicos 1989, p94
[70] Wigley 1992.
[71] Wigley 1992, p. 98, p. 99.

is meant seriously. Let us be charitable and assume that Wigley is indulging a desire to *épater les Marxistes*.

In their abject failure to understand the place of commodity fetishism in Marx's total materialist theory, criticisms of this type. are based on readings of *Capital* as rhetoric (rather than as rigorous materialism) according to which 'the notion of fetishism can be interpreted as a rhetorician's theory of ideology'.[72] This, in Pietz's felicitous characterisation, is indicative of 'the postmodernist's magisterial incomprehension of what Marx was actually talking about'.[73]

But there are, to be sure, more serious criticisms of commodity fetishism. What is more, many of them come from Marxists. Callinicos, for example, believes that '[n]o great damage would be done to *Capital* by the excision of commodity fetishism'.[74] Rose asserts that 'attempts to develop ... theories [of ideology based on commodity fetishism] are possible only at the price of theoretical incoherence and political impotence'.[75]

Before addressing these and other questions and criticisms, it will clarify the argument substantially to reproduce an often-quoted section of Marx, wherein he lays out the core of the theory of commodity fetishism.

> The mysterious character of the commodity-form consists ... simply in the fact that the commodity reflects the social characteristics of men's own labour as objective characteristics of the products of labour themselves, as the socio-natural properties of these things. ... [T]he products of labour become commodities, sensuous things which are at the same time suprasensible or social. ... The commodity-form, and the value-relation of the products of labour within which it appears, have absolutely no connection with the physical nature of the commodity and the material relations arising out of this. It is nothing but the definite social relation between men themselves which assumes here, for them, the fantastic form of a relation between things. In order, therefore, to find an analogy we must take flight into the misty realm of religion. There the products of the human brain appear as autonomous figures endowed with a life of their own, which enter into relations both with each other and with the human race. So it is in the world of commodities with the products of men's hands. I call this the fetishism which attaches itself to the products of labour as soon as they are produced as commodities, and is therefore inseparable from the production of commodities.[76]

---

[72] Pietz 1993, p. 127.
[73] Pietz 1993, n. 25 p. 127.
[74] Callinicos 1983, p. 132.
[75] Rose 1977, p. 27.
[76] Marx 1876, pp. 164–65.

Although there are of course variations in tone, depth and details of analysis, the various Marxist critiques of commodity fetishism share a common concern. The fear is that commodity fetishism, as a theory of ideology, is *'reductionist*, the concept of the social formation evidently *essentialist* and *economistic.'*[77] As Eagleton puts it,

> if *The German Ideology* risks relegating ideological forms to a realm of unreality, the later work of Marx pulls them a little too close to reality for comfort. Have we not merely replaced a potential *idealism* of ideology with an incipient *economism* of it?[78]

This is 'a danger inherent in the notion of commodity fetishism, namely a tendency to see the operation of market as automatically inducing acceptance of capitalism'.[79]

One problem with this conception is that it too narrowly perceives commodity fetishism as a theory of ideology. We do not have to go so far as Jacques Rancière, who claims that 'fetishism is *not at all* a theory of ideology';[80] clearly in articulating the problematic of human subjectivity under capitalism, the question of perception and hence of ideology is at the very least implicit. However, we should move away from the limited notion that that is *all* that commodity fetishism is.

After all, Marx is clear that commodity fetishism makes social relations appear between people *'as what they are*, i.e. they do not appear as direct relations between persons in their work, but rather as material relations between persons and social relations between things'.[81] The question is clearly *not* one of mechanistic ideology, whereby capitalism produces its own misapprehension: 'relations between persons really do take the form of relations between things.'[82] The paradox of commodity fetishism is precisely that it is not 'ideological', narrowly defined. 'It [the value form which is the basis of commodity fetishism] is the absurdity not of an illusion, but of reality itself, and to this extent it is an absurdity which is true.'[83] Fetishism consists of 'the collapsing of social *facts* into natural ones'.[84]

Commodity fetishism is a logical corollary of Marx's theory of abstract labour and the commodification of labour power.[85] The

---

[77] Rose 1977, p. 47.
[78] Eagleton 1991, p. 87.
[79] Callinicos 1989, p. 151.
[80] Quoted in Pietz 1993, n. 27 p. 128.
[81] Marx 1876, p. 166. Emphasis mine.
[82] Geras 1971, p. 76.
[83] Geras 1971, p. 76.
[84] Geras 1971, p. 78. Emphasis mine.
[85] Ripstein's assertion that '[s]eparated from the labor theory of value, the charge of fetishism can still be leveled' is therefore wrong. He makes his claim based on the fact that 'exchangeability rests on human activities, rather than inherent properties of commodities' (Ripstein 1987, p. 736). For Ripstein, it is the *fact* of exchange that leads to fetishism, rather than the peculiar conditions of exchange under capitalism. In fact, the reification of social relations under commodity fetishism is a result of the commodification of labour power, presupposing the concept of abstract labour, the stuff of value in the labour

worker's only relation to 'society' is as a seller of labour power. Thus her own creative agency becomes a 'thing' to be bought and sold like other things. The 'subjugation of human relations to commodity exchange results in a reduction of human subjectivity to the status of an object'.[86] 'In this sense, relations between people *are* indeed relations between things.'[87] This experienced reification of a person's own labour power is one part of the story.

The subjugation of human relations by relations between things is inextricable from this, and explains why commodity fetishism is a *generalised condition*. It is realised in the exchange of commodities in the market, an activity faced by all in capitalist society. '[B]y equating their different products to each other in exchange as values, [people] ... equate their different kinds of labour as human labour. They do this without being aware of it.'[88] The act of exchange hides the various forms of socially specific concrete labour: this is to mystify the specific social relations embodied by the division of labour and depict the dynamics of the market which will alter these relations as driven by anarchic relations between abstract values in commodity form. Commodity fetishism understood as this dynamic process, then, represents the *actualisation of abstract labour*.

> Human economic relations are in fact grasped, by human self-consciousness, as relations between merchandise, since the social character of the independent labor of every producer in his private sphere is expressed in the exchange process.[89]

To focus on commodity fetishism as a theory of ideology rather than of *the constitution of the subject under capitalism* leaves one to explain the obvious signs of the phenomenon in *lived experience*, rather than in a nebulous realm of ideology.

Thus, for example, Callinicos jettisons the theory, as he understands it to be about 'ideology' and is uneasy (quite rightly) at the mechanistic relation between ideology and social reality that would posit. However, a brief look at the reality of life under capitalism leads him to mention that 'it is, in any case, evidently true that capitalism involves the rule of men by their products, as every economic crisis shows us'.[90] Callinicos cannot describe this as commodity fetishism (despite its startling similarity to Marx's description of the phenomenon), and we are left with the rather odd spectacle of the very lived reality of commodity

---

theory of value. '[O]nce a commodity plays the role of value equivalent to any other commodity [due to shared value-substance *as explicated by the labour theory of value*] it immediately seems as thought it possesses *in itself* the ability to measure the value of other commodities'. (Ellen 1988, p. 216.)

[86] Schott 1985, p. 70.
[87] De Angelis 1996, p. 24.
[88] Marx 1867, pp. 166-167.
[89] Balaban 1990, p. 7.
[90] Callinicos 1983, p. 132.

fetishism being cited as evidence for the untruth of a putative 'ideological' version of the formula.

Much simpler, surely, to accept that the theory does not describe the creation of ideology, but is a theory of *social process*. Balaban is clear on this point: '[T]he true essence of fetishism ... [lies] ... in the way the fetish is produced, since this ... characterizes ... *the fetishist self-conception of the subject*'.[91]

Pace, then, the often sophisticated attempts to debunk it, commodity fetishism is a reality under capitalism. It may seem paradoxical that consciousness under capitalism perceives 'absurd' relations, 'phenomenal forms' which are 'the direct opposite' of the actual relation, which are yet relations 'as they really are'. The *reality* of capitalism is its own utterly partial justification. Yet this is simply the manifestation of the paradoxical position into which the worker is forced by capitalism. In the exercise of her creative agency, because that agency has been commodified and sold, she maintains the very situation which disempowers her. There *are* contradictory realities in capitalism. The worker can only be disempowered by the appropriation of her own creative agency.

Geras is persuasive in arguing that despite the totalising nature of capitalism's mystificatory and self-naturalising discourses, there is room under capitalism for a burgeoning class consciousness, a standpoint outside that of commodity fetishism, in the political struggle of the working class, which ebbs and flows but is always part of capitalism.[92] That struggle involves a conceptualisation, be it utterly inchoate, of the worker as part of a class collective, a conception fundamentally at odds with the atomised seller of labour power projected under commodity fetishism. These two conceptions are always coexistent, and always at odds.

For the purposes of this essay, however, I am concerned not with class consciousness but with those relations which constitute and are constituted by commodity fetishism.

Commodity fetishism is usually explained as being the absolute naturalisation of the commodity form and its concomitant relations: the idea that value, for example, clearly a human function, inheres in the commodity itself *irrespective* of human agency.[93] This is quite true, and is the result of rendering human agency a commodity like any other, thus relinquishing human relations to capitalism's anarchic diktats. Commodity fetishism, then, is the naturalisation of the capitalist mode of production.

However, there is an older meaning of fetishism, and it was a meaning with which Marx was familiar. '[T]he attribution [to inanimate objects] of qualities of living organisms'.[94]

---

[91] Balaban 1990, p. 5.
[92] Geras 1971, p. 84.
[93] For example, Ellen 1988, p. 216.
[94] Ellen 1988, p. 219.

Marx had read de Brosses[95] – who first systematised the term 'fetishism'[96] – and his (Marx's) use of the word was informed by nineteenth century anthropological discourse. This conception of fetishism is prevalent throughout Marx. There is a recurrent trope – playful, perhaps – of investing inanimate objects, commodities, with agency.

> [I]n ... the misty realm of religion ... the products of the human brain appear as autonomous figures endowed with a life of their own, which enter into relations both with each other and with the human race. So it is in the world of commodities with the products of men's hands.[97]

The analogy could not be more explicit. Similarly, in the first paragraph of the section on commodity fetishism, Marx's analogy is with the inanimate becoming animate.

> As soon as ... [a table] emerges as a commodity, it changes into a thing which transcends sensuousness. It not only stands with its feet on the ground, but, in relation to all other commodities, it stands on its head, and evolves out of its wooden brain grotesque ideas, far more wonderful than if it were to begin dancing of its own free will.[98]

These pointed references cast in an interesting light the assertion that the things produced by humans 'far from being under their control, in fact control them'.[99] We can no longer simply make the assertion that capitalism is its own excuse, that commodity fetishism is the naturalisation of exchange-value. In addition to (and linked to) that, these passages pointedly render the 'relations between things' *exactly that*. The world picture is one of social interaction between *animate objects*, 'autonomous figures endowed with a life of their own', with humans under their control.

This is not to suggest, of course, that humans *literally* believe that commodities are alive. What I am arguing is that under conditions of commodity fetishism, wherein producers are ruled by their products, there is likely to be an anxiety surrounding the relation between commodities and the humans at their caprice. Just as Marx, at the level of rhetoric, expressed this anxiety, and posited the conception of animate commodities directly, so the anxiety may find cultural expression in art.

The link between this anxiety born of commodity fetishism and the 'conspiracy of architecture' under investigation is clear. The question, is, why should this anxiety be manifest so overwhelmingly in the case of

---

[95] Pietz 1993, p. 134.
[96] Zizek 1997, p. 98.
[97] Marx 1867, p. 165.
[98] Marx 1867, pp. 163–4.
[99] Marx 1867, pp. 167–8.

buildings, as opposed to other commodities? Because in terms of exchange value, all commodities are ontologically, if not quantitively, equal. Exchange value by its very definition is the same stuff that one finds in all commodities.

But in terms of social symbolic weight, some commodities are more equal than others.

5. When is a commodity not (just) a commodity?

£200,000 worth of chewing gum and a £200,000 house are quantitatively the same, but a house is simply a more symbolically fraught item than chewing gum, or a baseball trading card or a washing machine. I have tried to show that architecture is of fundamental social importance, that it represents an irreplaceable piece of 'mental capital' with which to think humanness.

Under capitalism, the built environment, and its most culturally important example, the house, has become an irresolvable paradox.

On the one hand the house is a repository of meaning. The house is the locus and embodiment of social values, and that function is increased dramatically on *reflection*, when we retrospectively or artistically use architecture as a mode in which to articulate our relationship with society. In this context, to think is indeed to dwell. There is nothing transcendent about the fact: it is rooted in human society. What is more, it is *particularly* rooted in bourgeois society. In the bourgeois distinctions between society and the individual, between work and life, the home becomes the locus for the 'individual', a place where they can leave 'society' behind and 'be themselves'. 'For the private citizen, for the first time the living-space became distinguished from the place of work. ... The private citizen ... required of the interior [living-space] that it should maintain him in his illusions.'[100]

Thus the house is a vital medium by which the modern individual thinks herself.

It is the modern, privatised sphere for the safe self-conception of the individual, the bourgeois variant of the trans-cultural use of architecture to locate the social being.[101]

---

[100] Benjamin 1935, pp. 557–8.
[101] On the essentially modern nature of the 'architectural uncanny' of which the alien architecture under discussion is a subset, see Vidler 1992, p. 3. Vidler is correct that the uncanny is 'the quintessential bourgeois kind of fear' (p. 4), if we understand bourgeois here to refer to a societal mode of articulation rather than to one confined to a group *within* capitalist society. But Vidler blurs this distinction, and his somewhat undiscerning pick-and-mix 'socio-psychoanalytical' approach (p. 6) leaves him unable to explain the generalisation of the anxiety beyond the minds of the bourgeoisie themselves: he talks of it being 'gradually generalized', 'disrespectful of class boundaries' (p. 6); he is descriptive but not explanatory. The theory of commodity fetishism as a processual theory of the constitution of the subject, outlined in section 4 above, addresses this shortcoming. Anxieties are no longer solely a product of class

And yet the house, and all architecture, is also a commodity, subject to the laws of commodity transactions. And it is in the sphere of such circulation that commodity fetishism projects the commodity as an alien being, an animate creation, a product that has turned on its creator and is in control of the social process.

The house is sanctuary. The house is despot. The house is the repository of all that is social and human. The house is animate, alienated dead labour, a product which spins forth 'grotesque ideas'.

These opposed conceptions coincide in one particular. The house is *powerful*.

In an effort to reconcile the irreconcilable in capitalism, a horrendously fraught image of the house is born. Animate, active and alien(ated), the tension between the house's inhuman commodity nature and its social/symbolic role result in the unstable image of the familiar, the safe, the home(ly) *as the* ne plus ultra *of the alien*, as in Bradfield. The relationship between humans and their creations is reversed. The house's role as repository of humans may be retained but it is *alienated*, gone bad, as in Marasco and Dick, where the house is a vampire or a hungry monster that *relies* on humans and contains them, but no longer as ends, only as means for its own perpetuation. They are not there to house us: we are there to feed them.

Autonomous. Marx's word is well chosen. However different the various houses and buildings I have examined, they are all *autonomous*, they all have their own ends.

The alien, animate house is a bastard image, the synthesis of two different truths.

6. 'Nemo has escaped!' Tafuri in Slumberland

Home, home, home. Three times in the first five frames of McCay's 'Little Nemo in Slumberland', Nemo and his belle tell us where they are going. The party is over, and the pair are returning to what should be their places of safety.

But by the fifth frame, and the final mention of Home, the putative safety of the built environment for which they are heading is cast into grave doubt.

In the fifth frame, we see the first house rise up off its knees. One of the most chilling aspects of this image is the fact that the house's legs *unbend*. They do not grow from nothing: the house has always had its legs, it could have stood at any time. The autonomy of the architecture is thus signalled as *not* pathological. There is no magic in the air tonight. The houses can stand any time they choose.

---

position, but of the kind of relationship capitalism imposes between its commodities and its human subjects.

For the first five frames of their animation, the buildings are not concerned with the two little humans. They have their own agenda. It is only in frame 10, long after the humans have begun to run in fear, that one of the walking houses sees them. It sticks its head up above the crowd and according to some unspoken signal it and its fellows suddenly give chase. The lateness of the attention paid to the pair increases the sense of *alien-ness* that surrounds the architecture.

As with all the Little Nemo comics, the strip concludes with the realisation that 'it was just a dream', that Nemo is at home in his bedroom. In this case, the realisation offers scant comfort. The strip's aesthetic undermines Nemo's escape from the Unquiet Houses. The 'unreal' nature of the dream is slyly called into question in frame five when the first house begins to stand and *neither Nemo nor his companion notice*. In the world of dreams, the only things that have any reality are those things that are perceived by the dreamer. And yet here, in what is ostensibly Nemo's dream, the readers can see something which he can not. The 'illusory' nature of the dreamworld is cast into immediate doubt.

Besides, Nemo's return home in the final frame is cold comfort given that the strip has radically undermined any notions we might have that home is where safety is. What has been chasing Nemo, after all, but a pack of solid New York town houses? But the triumph of the architecture is even more pointed than that.

The final, tiny frame is encased in the penultimate: frame 13 is a subset of frame 12. This is highlighted by the positioning of the girl in the bottom left hand corner of frame 12 and Nemo alone in frame 13. In all other frames Nemo and his charge have appeared together. In these two they each appear singly, side by side, still linked. There is a permeable membrane between frame 12 and frame 13. Nemo is still standing next to his friend, and although he has not fallen like her, and the houses are not chasing him as they are her, he is *inside* a house. We can see him as having escaped ... or as having been caught sooner, and swallowed.

And yet even in his escape (let us opt for the more cheerful of the two possibilities), the futility of running from the conspiracy of architecture is made plain. 'Nemo has escaped,' we can exclaim, and the uneasy realisation steals over us that Nemo means 'no one'. At the moment of his 'escape', standing uneasy in his house, what has happened is literally that 'no one has escaped'. Nemo is signified as an absence. His escape is no escape at all. There is no escaping the architecture that is out to get us.

Is this a kind of symbolic ultra-leftism? A poetic determinism which undermines localised resistance? It is no more than the inevitable truth about human-architecture relations – and images thereof – under capitalism.

The uncompromising Marxist architectural critic Manfredo Tafuri has made clear that *pace* the efforts of 'progressive' architects, '*one* cannot 'anticipate' a class architecture (an architecture 'for a liberated society')'.[102] He has come under attack for this, most notably from Fredric Jameson, who fervently if somewhat nebulously calls for a 'Gramscian' architectural criticism and architecture.[103] Jameson's critique, however, withers in the force of Tafuri's devastating work. With an enormous wealth of examples from throughout history, Tafuri examines the project of 'critical architecture' – the work of architects who in their creations attempt to criticize architecture itself, and by extension 'the structures that condition their planning ... the society that will use their architecture' in which critical architects have 'no trust'.[104]

Whatever such architecture's merits (and he is clear that it may be brilliant work), he unmasks 'the contradictory quality of this attempt to compromise a structure endowed with its own synthesis, through a criticism that cannot enter it'.[105] A building that embodied its own synthesis, the resolutions to the architectural and social contradictions it inevitably contains, would be a building built simultaneously *inside and outside its own history*. The language of architecture – produced, after all, 'as a discipline historically conditioned and [at this time] institutionally functional to ... the new perspectives of capitalist "Zivilisation",[106] if used to question itself 'does not know how or is not willing to expose itself ... to the dangerous test of an unprejudiced critical exploration'.

In arguing against Tafuri for 'Gramscian' (presumably 'counterhegemonic') architecture, Jameson implies that the liberating or oppressive qualities of architecture inhere in its design. Change the design – the social space created – and we change the embedded politics. However, there is nothing *spatially* determinist about Tafuri's belief. There are countless different buildings embodying countless different kinds of space in the built environment. It is, as Harvey puts it, 'a palimpsest of landscapes'.[107] Tafuri's point about the impossibility of creating 'architecture for a liberated society' is not based on space alone but on *history*. It is this social backdrop which, for Tafuri, explains 'how ineffectual are the brilliant gymnastics [of 'critical architecture'] carried out in the yard of the model prison'.[108]

Where so much progressive architectural criticism and architecture goes wrong is in the focus on the politics of space to the exclusion of all else. As Marx and Engels separately made clear more than a century ago, the alienation of dwellers from their houses under capitalism is not just about space (though good and bad building design doubtless affects the basic condition): humans are alienated from buildings because those buildings are *commodities*, and the condition of a capitalist economy is

---

[102] Tafuri 1980, p. xv. Italics his.
[103] Jameson 1985, p. 72, p. 87.
[104] Tafuri 1980, p. 235.
[105] Tafuri 1980, p. 116.
[106] Tafuri 1980, p. 235.
[107] Harvey 1982. p. 233.
[108] Tafuri 1980, p. xxii.

precisely the alienation of the producer and consumer from the mass of commodities which confront them.

What is more, under capitalism buildings *cannot* but be commodities. 'Under the social relations of capitalism ... all elements [of the built environment] assume a commodity form.'[109] There is, therefore, under capitalism *absolutely no* escaping the alienation of the commodified architecture which surrounds us.

And in the realm of 'art', the alienation of the human agent from the built environment – that peculiarly fraught form of commodity fetishism – manifests itself in the anxiety I have tried to uncover.

Of course, the specific historical conjunctures in which various works of art are created will lend unique nuances to their architectural anxieties. The peculiarly 'pure' and intense form of McCay's conspiracy of architecture must be considered in the context of its creation, during 'a building boom of unprecedented proportions', 'an architectural maelstrom', at the end of a decade of massive upheaval in New York's architecture.[110]

> As a whole section of the city like the Upper West Side changed its contours, it was like a great geological event – the collision of continents or the birth of mountain ranges. The territory literally erupted. Dynamite blasts rocked the neighborhood, shaking houses and scaring horses in the street. Broadway opened up like a fault. In almost every block of the grid, there were yawning pits in the bedrock, created by the vast excavations necessary for the foundations of the new, oversized buildings.[111]

Architecture was flexing, shifting, and reshaping the city. The sudden spread of the apartment building and its growing ascendancy over the traditional town-house led to nervous debates about the effect of various architectural forms on social life. Traditional values were under threat from the new architecture. 'We think ... that our national integrity and health and virtue are bound up in the Home, and that if it is taken from us we are lost,' wrote Charlotte Perkins Gilman in *Cosmopolitan*. 'We see our homes lifted clean off the ground ... we protest that this is not a home.'[112]

The enormous changes were the result of rapid economic expansion after the depression of the 1890s. All fixed, fast-frozen architectural relations were being swept away. All that was homely was profaned.

The sheer *nakedness* of McCay's architectural anxiety is born of these circumstances, a neurotic counterpoint to the boom. It is this context of heightened, generalised, *explicit* architectural anxiety which gives McCay's piece its meaning, a meaning to all intents and purposes

---

[109] Harvey 1982, p. 233.
[110] Hawes 1993, p. 153.
[111] Hawes 1993, p. 155.
[112] Cited in Hawes 1993, p. 175. Gilman is here describing the prevailing mood. She was herself entirely forward-looking about the new architecture.

indistinguishable from the 'fact' of the image of the animate, alien building. Uniquely among the works discussed, here the work is 'about' the image itself.

Svankmajer's, Hodgson's, Debuffet's visions are no less products of their time and location. To understand the specific form of the architectural trope in any detail we must understand the unique context of its creation. *But in its* general *form, it is an anxiety intrinsic to capitalism.* This is why we are all trapped.

Tafuri – along with Engels and Marx – gives theoretical voice to the plaintive cry that rises from the reader of *Little Nemo.* 'No one has escaped the conspiracy of architecture!' Indeed, and nor will anyone while we live in a commodity economy which allows – indeed thrives on – the grotesque coexistence of widespread homelessness and empty buildings in cities throughout the world. As long as we continue to live in a twisted slumberland where we, the human agents, are at the mercy of the dreams, the 'grotesque ideas' of the commodities that we create, the bastard image of the Unquiet House as despot, as vampiré, as alien enemy, will continue to reverberate throughout our culture.

References

Bachelard, Gaston [1964] 1994, *The Poetics of Space*, Boston: Beacon Press.

Bahloul, Joëlle 1996, *The Architecture of Memory*, Cambridge: Cambridge University Press.

Balaban, Oded 1990, 'Self-Consciousness and Fetishism', *Explorations in Knowledge*, 7, 1: 1–11.

Baudrillard, Jean 1981, *For a Critique of the Political Economy of the Sign*, St. Louis: Telos Press.

Benjamin, Walter [1935] 1979. 'Louis-Philippe, or, The Interior' in *Marxism and Art* edited by Maynard Solomon, Detroit: Wayne State University Press.

Berleant, Arnold 1988, 'The Environment as an Aesthetic Paradigm', *Dialectics and Humanism*, XV, 1–2: 95–106.

Bourdieu, Pierre, 1990, *The Logic of Practice*, Cambridge: Polity Press.

Bradfield, Scott 1990, 'The Secret Life of Houses' in *Dream of the Wolf*, New York: Alfred A. Knopf.

Callinicos, Alex 1983, *Marxism and Philosophy*, Oxford: Oxford University Press.

Callinicos, Alex 1988, *Making History*, New York: Cornell University Press.

Callinicos, Alex 1989, *Against Postmodernism*, Cambridge: Polity.

De Angelis, Massimo 1996, 'Social Relations, Commodity-Fetishism and Marx's Critique of Political Economy', *Review of Radical Political Economics*. 28, 4: 1–29

Deutsche, Rosalyn 1996, *Evictions*, Cambridge, MA.: MIT Press.

Dick, Philip K. 1970, *A Maze of Death*, New York: Doubleday.

Dick, Philip K. [1957] 1979 *Eye in the Sky*, Boston: Gregg Press.

Eagleton, Terry 1991, *Ideology: An Introduction*, London: Verso.

Ellen, Roy 1988, 'Fetishism', *Man N.S.*, 23, 2: 213–235.

Engels, Frederick [1872] 1954 *The Housing Question*, Moscow: Progress Publishers.

Friedman, Lenemaja 1975, *Shirley Jackson*, Boston: Twayne Publishers.

Gauldie, W. Sinclair 1966, 'Architecture and the Human Condition', *British Journal of Aesthetics*, 6, 1: 26–29

Geras, Norman 1971, 'Essence and Appearance: Aspects of Fetishism in Marx's *Capital*', *New Left Review*, 65: 69–85.

Harvey, David 1982, *The Limits to Capital*, Oxford: Blackwell.

Harvey, David 1990, *The Condition of Postmodernity*, Oxford: Blackwell.

Hawes, Elizabeth 1993, *New York, New York*, New York: Alfred A. Knopf.

Heidegger, Martin 1971, 'Building, Dwelling, Thinking' in *Poetry, Language, Thought*, New York: Harper and Row.

Hodgson, William Hope 1913, *Carnacki the Ghost-Finder*, London: Eveleigh Nash.

Jackson, Shirley 1959, *The Haunting of Hill House*, New York: The Viking Press.

Jameson, Fredric 1985, 'Architecture and the Critique of Ideology', in Ockman, Joan, et al (eds.). *Architecture, Criticism, Ideology*, Princeton: Princeton Architectural Press.

Jameson, Fredric 1992, 'Spatial Systems in *North by Northwest*' in *Everything You Always Wanted to Know about Lacan (But Were Afraid to Ask Hitchcock)* edited by Slavoj Zizek, London: Verso.

Kerr, Philip 1997, *The Grid*, New York: Warner.

King, Stephen 1988, 'Burnt Offerings' in *Horror: 100 Best Books*, edited by Steven Jones and Kim Newman, London: Xanadu Publications.

Kupfer, Joseph 1985, 'Building the Body Politic', *Social Theory and Practice*, 11, 3: 265–83.

Lang, John 1980, 'The Built Environment and Social Behavior: Architectural Determinism Reexamined', *VIA*, IV: 147–53.

Langer, Suzanne K. 1953, *Feeling and Form*, New York: Charles Scribner's Sons.

Lefebvre, Henri 1991 *The Production of Space*, Oxford; Blackwell

Marx, Karl [1844] 1975. 'The Economic and Philosophical Manuscripts' in *Early Writings*, London: Penguin.

Marx, Karl. [1867] 1976, *Capital* Volume 1, London: Penguin.

McCay, Winsor. 'Little Nemo in Slumberland' from the Sunday *New York Herald*, March 21 1909.

O'Pray, Michael 1995, 'Jan Svankmajer: a Mannerist Surrealist' in *Dark Alchemy* edited by Peter Hames, Westport, Connecticut: Greenwood Press.

Pietz, William 1993, 'Fetishism and Materialism: the Limits of Theory in Marx' in *Fetishism as Cultural Discourse*, edited by William Pietz and Emily Apter, New York: Cornell University Press.

Rapoport, Amos (ed.) 1976, *The Mutual Interaction of People and Their Built Environment*, The Hague: Mouton

Rapoport, Amos 1977, *Human Aspects of Urban Form*, Oxford: Pergamon Press.

Ripstein, Arthur 1987, 'Commodity Fetishism', *Canadian Journal of Philosophy*, 17, 4: 733–48.

Rose, Nikolas 1977, 'Fetishism and Ideology: a Review of Theoretical Problems', *Ideology and Consciousness*, 2: 27–54.

Schott, Robin 1985, 'Morality and Fetishism', *Cogito*, III, 4: 61–74.

Sparshott, Francis 1994, 'The Aesthetics of Architecture and the Politics of Space' in *Philosophy and Architecture* edited by Michael Mitias, Amsterdam: Rodopi.

Sterritt, David 1993, *The Films of Alfred Hitchcock*, Cambridge: Cambridge University Press.

Tafuri, Manfredo 1980, *Theories and History of Architecture* (2nd edition), New York: Harper and Row.

Tuttle, Lisa 1988, 'The Haunting of Hill House' in *Horror: 100 Best Books* edited by Steven Jones and Kim Newman, London: Xanadu Publications.

Vidler, Anthony 1992, *The Architectural Uncanny*, Cambridge, MA: MIT Press.

Wigley, Mark 1992, 'Theoretical Slippage', *Fetish: The Princeton Architectural Journal* 4: 88–129.

Williams, Raymond. 1977, *Marxism and Literature*, Oxford: Oxford University Press.

Zizek, Slavoj 1992, 'In His Bold Gaze My Ruin Is Writ Large' in *Everything You Always Wanted to Know about Lacan (But Were Afraid to Ask Hitchcock)* edited by Slavoj Zizek, London: Verso.

Zizek, Slavoj 1997, *The Plague of Fantasies*, London: Verso.

Velocities of Change: Perry Anderson's Sense of an Ending[1]

Gregory Elliott

In *Considerations on Western Marxism*, released in 1976, Perry Anderson stated and vindicated an affiliation to the Trotskyist tradition long apparent from the pages of *New Left Review* under his editorship.[2] Central to this tradition, in its orthodox forms, was a historico-political perspective which regarded the Soviet Union (and cognate regimes) as 'degenerate' or 'deformed' 'workers' states' – post-capitalist social formations whose complex character dictated rejection of Stalinism and anti-Sovietism alike. In Anderson's case, this orientation received a Deutscherite inflection: abroad, no less than at home, Soviet power was a contradictory phenomenon, by turns reactionary (Czechoslovakia) and progressive (Vietnam, Angola). The potential regeneration of the Russian Revolution and its sequels, whether via 'proletarian revolution' from below (Trotsky), or bureaucratic reformation from above (Deutscher), remained an article of faith among Marxists of this observance to the end. Accordingly, the *débâcle* of Gorbachevite *perestroika* proved a profoundly disorientating experience for many who lent little or no credence to the mendacious claims of 'actually existing socialism'. Amid capitalist euphoria at Communist collapse, what was to be said – and done? Anderson's displaced answer was forthcoming in 1992 in 'The Ends of History'.[3]

Mental fixtures

'A fideist of Enlightenment': such was John Gray's soubriquet for the author of *English Questions* and *A Zone of Engagement* in his review of them.[4] Taunting Anderson with the indeterminacy of his later work as regards the agency and goal of socialism, Gray acutely observed that he was 'strangely reticent on the fiasco of Gorbachev's reformist socialism', and moved to harpoon the 'bizarre collation' made in the concluding paragraph of 'A Culture in Contraflow': 'the collapse of the Communist

[1] This text is derived from a longer study, *Perry Anderson: The Merciless Laboratory of History*. It formed the basis of presentations to the *Historical Materialism* seminar at Linacre College, Oxford, in November 1997; and to a Modernity seminar at the LSE in February 1998. I am grateful to Matthew Beaumont and Justin Rosenberg for the respective invitations; and to Sebastian Budgen and Martin Jenkins for their editorial encouragement.
[2] See Elliott 1998, chapter 3.
[3] Anderson 1992a. pp. 279–375.
[4] Gray 1992.

order in Eastern Europe and the approach of federation in Western Europe have struck away mental fixtures of the Left and Right alike'.[5] On Gray's reading of this passage and others, 'transnational capitalist institutions double as placeholders for the international class solidarity that history has persistently mocked'. This would seem a precipitate extrapolation from the letter of Anderson's texts. But what the assertion in 'A Culture in Contraflow' does do, is to equate the regional modification of the inharmonic capitalist state-system with the elimination of an antagonistic socio-economic system. Moreover, if any 'mental fixtures of the Left' had been 'struck away' with 'the collapse of the Communist order in Eastern Europe', then an obvious candidate would be Anderson's own. Although no-one would have guessed it from his imperturbable postlapsarian writings, the Communist order had constituted a mental fixture of Anderson's Marxism and socialism. By his criteria, its implosion effected the zonal restoration, and ushered in the global dominion, of capitalism unbound.

By way of evidence, we may simply note that at the nadir of the second Cold War, in 1983, *New Left Review*'s revised Charter, drafted by Anderson and locating the journal in the 'political tradition' stemming from the Bolshevik Revolution, had maintained that the 'workers' states' 'represent a historic progress over the capitalist or pre-capitalist societies that preceded them, and a critical bulwark against imperialism'.[6] The stamp of such principles was firmly impressed upon Anderson's own writings of the period, whether *In the Tracks of Historical Materialism* or (especially) 'Trotsky's Interpretation of Stalinism', both published in 1983. Most significantly of all, perhaps, October 1917, whatever its subsequent degeneration, was said in *Arguments Within English Marxism* to have set in train an 'irreversible ... alteration of the potential of historical action, in the course of the 20th century'.[7] The political upshot? As a heterodox-Trotskyist critic of the Deutschero-Trotskyist position logically inferred, '[f]or a workers' state, however deformed or degenerate, to become a capitalist state must be a step back historically, a stage in a counter-revolutionary process which Marxists should oppose'.[8]

The *NLR* Charter had espoused 'the radical democratic reconstruction of all the post-capitalist states'.[9] Now, following the death of Brezhnev, and gerontocratic interludes, it seemed as if this scenario might come to pass: *ex oriente lux*. The fund of hope invested in the Gorbachev prospectus is not hard to imagine. In the event, however, *NLR* exhibited a certain reticence on the subject. Its editors abstained from analysis of reformist prospects in the pages of the

---

[5] Anderson 1992a, p. 301.
[6] Anderson 1983a, pp. 4–5.
[7] Anderson 1980, p. 21.
[8] Harman 1990, p. 80, responding to Ernest Mandel's reassertion of the 'post-capitalist economy'/'transitional society' analysis in Mandel 1990, (the quoted phrases appear on p. 47).
[9] Anderson 1983a, p. 5.

Review itself. Still, in a 1988 study dedicated to Boris Kagarlitsky and Boris Yeltsin, bearing the Deutscherite title *Revolution from Above*, Tariq Ali addressed the question of his Trotskyist sub-title: 'Where is the Soviet Union Going?' – and ventured the following response:

> Gorbachev represents a progressive, reformist current within the Soviet elite, whose programme, if successful, would represent an enormous gain for socialists and democrats on a world scale. The scale of Gorbachev's operation is ... reminiscent of the efforts of an American President of the nineteenth century ... In order to preserve the Union, Lincoln had to push through a second American revolution based on the abolition of slavery. In order to preserve the Soviet Union, Gorbachev needs to complete the political revolution ... but one based on an abolition of the whole nomenklatura system of privileges on which the power of the Soviet bureaucracy rests.

Ali specifically warned against the temptations of hindsight, which would be of nil benefit to the outcome of the 'debate taking place inside the USSR'. 'It is much easier to worship accomplished facts.'[10]

There is no reason to believe that Anderson would have endorsed Ali's outlook or analysis in all details. Even so, regardless of the felicity of the precise analogy with Lincoln's 'second revolution', it is safe to suppose a substantial measure of agreement, within a shared repertory. The one direct piece of evidence we possess suggests as much. In correspondence with Norberto Bobbio arising out of a 1988 article on the Italian philosopher's attempted liberal-socialist synthesis, Anderson regretted that he had omitted 'a vital issue for the whole topic'.

> That ... is the prospect for a liberal socialism in the post-revolutionary societies. ... For what else ... is the ... aim of perestroika in the USSR? The 'rule of law', 'guarantee of individual rights', and 'separation of powers' are all part ... of Gorbachev's own formal project. ... Of course, the outcome ... could not be less certain. Perestroika could miss a liberal socialism from either end ... that is, collapse back into the previous dictatorial regime, or flee forward into a *de facto* recreation of capitalism; possibly even combine these evils. But to use your own terms, a liberal socialism must now be reckoned – in the medium to long run – as one not unrealistic historical possibility, among others, in the USSR. It is difficult to see how any contemporary Marxist could fail to welcome that, however inadequate the legacy of Marxism

---

[10] Ali 1988, p. xiii. Having acknowledged fellow *NLR* editors Robin Blackburn and Peter Gowan, as well as Tamara Deutscher and Daniel Singer (p. vii), Ali confided that his 'own political formation had been greatly influenced by the writings of Isaac Deutscher, Leon Trotsky and Ernest Mandel (in that order)', (p. ix). For Mandel's own analysis, see Mandel 1989. The *Review's* first article on the subject was Medvedev 1986, preceded by cautious remarks in the 'Themes' of the same issue, *NLR*, 157, pp. 1–2.

> itself on these issues (about which I do not disagree). But if
> this were the case, the difference between our positions
> narrows greatly. ... [A] liberal socialism would be the
> common aim ... but reached by the *corsi e ricorsi* of a
> staggeringly illiberal historical process.[11]

The allusion is to a Viconian-cyclical, rather than Marxian-dialectical, philosophy of history ('corsi e ricorsi'); the time-frame extended ('the medium to long run'); the desired outcome denoted by a double negative ('one not unrealistic historical possibility'); and 'evils' – including capitalist restoration – entertained. But a duly qualified Deutscherite cunning of reason remains operative here.

No worshipper of accomplished facts, Anderson otherwise reserved public judgement, only pronouncing on the Gorbachev experiment – *fait inaccompli* – in an informative report on the 1991 Moscow coup for the *London Review of Books*.[12] The first thing to note about it is its ironic confirmation of a statement in conclusion to 'The Ends of History': '[h]istorical analogies are never more than suggestive'.[13] For the analogy via which Anderson sought to illuminate the summer's momentous events was, in a charming litotes, one which 'would not occur to most politically-conscious Russians':[14] Suharto's ouster of Sukarno in the aftermath of the October 1965 coup in Indonesia. It would not spring to the mind of most politically conscious previous readers of Anderson either. They would have anticipated some examination of the more canonical analogies with 1660 or 1815, and arbitration of whether what had transpired was adjacent to 1830 and 1848 or, alternatively, the 'new 1789' repudiated in 'Trotsky's Interpretation of Stalinism'.[15] But within what Anderson dubbed 'the larger certainties of the restoration', they too were 'in for some surprises'.[16]

A second striking feature of the reportage was the glacial accents of its assessment of Gorbachev. Credited with Soviet withdrawal from Afghanistan and the introduction of free elections at home, he was reckoned to have bestrode the world like some cross between a pale Colossus and an ingenuous Narcissus, while the lethal combination of *glasnost* without effective *perestroika* mined Soviet economy and Union: 'there is no other modern case of such a gap between external adulation and internal repudiation as eventually opened up in Gorbachev's government of the Soviet Union'.[17] Attendant upon Communist collapse in Eastern Europe, the end of the Cold War had been superinduced by 'the realities of all-round Soviet weakness' – the prevalence of the West

---

[11] Letter of 12 December 1988 in Anderson 1989.
[12] Anderson 1991.
[13] Anderson 1992b, p. 375.
[14] Anderson 1991, p. 5.
[15] Cf. Anderson 1984, pp.123–4.
[16] Anderson 1991, p. 8.
[17] Anderson 1991, p. 6.

in the 'great contest', not an accession of enlightened despotism in the East.[18] 'The central source of that weakness', Anderson observed,

> has steadily worsened under Gorbachev. Perestroika turned a declining economy into a disaster zone. Disrupting the old centralised planning system, it provided no coherent alternative, leading to a spiralling breakdown of supplies and accelerating fall in output. In material provision the majority of Soviet citizens now live worse, some much worse, than under Brezhnev. For many, their personal security has deteriorated too. For perestroika also undid the old centralised administrative system that kept ethnic differences under rigid control, without putting any effective federal framework in its place.[19]

Disabused of Gorbachev, Anderson was unintoxicated by Yeltsin, whose 'populism' was noted, even if he was exonerated of 'any deep-lying Russian chauvinism'; and whose 'brutish rule' was subsequently condemned in the context of the war in Chechnya.[20] The 'wider question of the future of Russian politics as capitalism settles in' was broached. The traditionally 'nationalist and expansionist bent' of Russian liberalism was the bane which its successors would have to disavow.[21] An independently organised working class was forecast as a protagonist, and given the lines of 'the central social question of the coming period – who are to become the proprietors of the factories and installations in which they work?'[22] But notwithstanding political ebullition and 'an extraordinary psychological liberation for its people', the future socio-economic course of Russia was set: 'restoration'.[23]

An inescapable terrain

The *coup de grâce* that succeeded *coup d'état* in Russia in 1991 prompted Anderson's co-signature of a death-certificate for Communism already issued in *NLR* by Ralph Miliband and Norberto

---

[18] In his obituary 'Diary' on E.P. Thompson (Anderson 1993), Anderson denied the laurels to the peace movement: '[Thompson] proved to be the prophet of [the Cold War's] end. That is remarkable enough. How far the peace movement contributed to the ending is another issue. ... On this we differed. Between the ideals of END and the realities of Soviet breakdown was a large gap. It is not a belittlement of the advocates of the end of the Cold War to distinguish them from its agents. The First World War was not terminated by the Zimmerwald Left or the Stockholm Appeal, but by the victory of the Entente. We do not honour them the less for that. Was the conclusion of the Cold War very different?' (p. 25). Cf. Halliday 1990a, Thompson 1990, and Halliday 1990b. These texts were reprinted in Blackburn (ed.) 1991. Anderson's subscription to the thrust of Halliday's inter-systemic analysis may be presumed.
[19] Anderson 1991, p. 6.
[20] Anderson 1991, p. 7, and 1996a, p. xii.
[21] Anderson 1991, p. 7.
[22] Anderson 1991, p. 8.
[23] Anderson 1991, p. 8.

Bobbio, following the bloody repression of the democracy movement in China in 1989. These texts were later reprinted in an impressive Verso symposium, edited by Blackburn – *After the Fall: The Failure of Communism and the Future of Socialism* (1991) – containing material from the *Review* and other sources. In his obituary of 'historical communism' (to which Anderson has referred approvingly),[24] Bobbio – a veteran opponent of the phenomenon – coincided, to a degree, with Hobsbawm – a comparably veteran proponent – in his forebodings about the capitalist consequences of Communist defeat.[25] In substance, these were extrapolated from what Anderson had himself identified as the 'external gains' – as opposed to the 'internal costs' – of 'the presence and performance' of Stalinism, however involuntary.[26]

A month after Bobbio's 'Upturned Utopia' was published in *La Stampa*, an article on the same subject appeared in *The National Interest*.[27] Francis Fukuyama's 'The End of History?' was not Panglossian. Yet if not all was for the best, liberal-democratic capitalism was apotheosised as the best possible – because practicable´– world, within the framework of an avowedly Hegelian philosophy of history. At the New School for Social Research in 1985, Anderson had suggested to his audience that whilst 'a much more consciously and lucidly philosophical history' was desirable, '[w]e do not need to revive a philosophy of history today'.[28] Fukuyama's essay in substantive, rather than analytical, philosophy of history, and its subsequent expansion in *The End of History and the Last Man*, stimulated revision of that judgement. It received diverse but respectful coverage in *NLR*,[29] in stark contrast to the virtual unanimity of negative response it elicited across the spectrum, from Huntington to Hobsbawm.[30] But in what is Anderson's principal postlapsarian statement to date – 'The Ends of History' (1992) – it was accorded privileged treatment, on the basis that its full measure had yet to be taken. 'The charge heard on the Right, of an inverted Marxism, is', Anderson wrote, 'grounds for tribute on the Left.'[31]

In thus dissenting from numerous critics, including Lutz Niethammer, who had reconstructed Fukuyama's antecedents in 1989 unaware of their impending afterlife, Anderson was guided by the general consideration that Niethammer's

> critique of the Franco-German tradition in effect concludes,
> not with an alternative to its diagnosis of the age, contesting
> its substantive theses, but with a call to eschew such ventures

---

[24] Anderson 1998.
[25] Cf. Bobbio 1989 with Hobsbawm 1990 in Blackburn (ed.) 1991, especially p. 5 and pp. 122–3 respectively.
[26] Anderson 1984, p. 126.
[27] Fukuyama 1989.
[28] Anderson 1986a, p. 34.
[29] See *NLR* 193, May/June 1992, pp. 89–113, for reactions from Fred Halliday, Michael Rustin, and Ralph Miliband; and McCarney 1993.
[30] Cf., for example, Hobsbawm's off-hand dismissal in Hobsbawm 1990, p. 124.
[31] Anderson 1992b, p. 345.

altogether – rejecting any macro-historical narrative as
intellectually and politically overweening. Currently, the effect
of such a withdrawal would be to leave the American variant
in possession of the field. If this is to be questioned, it can
only be on its own – legitimate, even inescapable – terrain.[32]

Anderson's contestation of a terrain vacated as the preserve of
speculative metaphysics, whether by Anglo-Saxon empiricism or Gallic
post-structuralism, began by following Niethammer in his identification
of the vision of *posthistoire* as an 'inversion' of Enlightenment
teleology.[33] Fukuyama had reverted both this inversion (substituting
optimism for pessimism), and Marx's *renversement* of Hegel (restoring
idealism in place of materialism), while relocating the goal of the
historical process (capitalism rather than communism). 'End-times'
were, on balance, 'quality-time'; and (contrary to cheap critical
victories) the purposive culmination of history was expressly not the
sheer cessation of events.[34] Where Niethammer had been concerned
with the twentieth-century mutation of a nineteenth-century topos at
the hands of *Kulturkritiker*, in an equally imposing exercise in
intellectual history Anderson reached back to Hegel and recovered
Cournot. This served to demonstrate what Fukuyama had anyway
acknowledged: to borrow Régis Debray's acid remark on Michel
Rocard's proclamation of the 'end of ideology' in 1989, that the 'end of
history' represented a 'scoop' that was 'only two hundred years old'.[35]
But no mere display of antiquarian erudition, it detailed what other
commentators had complained of: Fukuyama's Procrustean operation
to fit Hegel to a Kojèvian frame. Moreover, it rescued from oblivion a
strikingly contemporary Cournot, responsible for a 'remarkable ...
prevision of the fate of communism',[36] were it to be confined to a
national economic autarky which no amount of political autarchy could
insulate against international pressures; and a no less remarkable
divination of the imperilment of life on Earth were capitalism to hold
unregulated sway over the planet.

The ghost missing from this philosophical banquet was Marx, for
whom (*pace* Fukuyama) communism did not consummate history, but
did terminate 'the prehistory of human society'; and who had observed
that, according to 'bourgeois' political economy, 'there has been history,
but there is no longer any'.[37] Only mentioned in passing thus far, Marx
– or, rather, Stalinist Marxism – assumed greater relief as Anderson
proceeded to Kojève's pre-war lectures on the *Phenomenology*, and
post-war second thoughts, which had inducted the Nietzschean motifs

---

[32] Anderson 1992b, p. 284, cf. Niethammer 1992.
[33] Anderson 1992b, p. 280.
[34] Anderson 1992b, pp. 282, 333.
[35] Debray 1989, p. 118.
[36] Anderson 1992b, p. 307.
[37] 'Preface to A Contribution to the Critique of Political Economy' (1859), in
Marx and Engels 1969, p. 108; 'The Poverty of Philosophy' (1847), in Marx and
Engels 1976, p. 174.

encapsulated in the title of Fukuyama's book. As for Hegel, 'world history' remained the relevant tribunal: *Die Weltgeschichte ist das Weltgericht*.[38] However, the goal of its finalisation altered, from the differentiated freedom of the constitutional state to the 'universal and homogeneous State'. And the locus of its realisation shifted, from revolutionary France to revolutionary Russia (the spirit of Napoleon, the spectre of Stalin), and thence, via an evolutionary EEC (shades of Monnet), back again – albeit that an incipiently classless, consumerist USA afforded the paradigm of homogeneity.[39]

Having explored 'the three major speculations on the end of history'[40] – Hegel, Cournot, Kojève – and glanced at some sequels – De Man, Gehlen, Habermas – Anderson returned to Fukuyama's conjugation of Hegel and the late Kojève. 'The resultant synthesis', he concluded, 'is an original one, tying liberal democracy and capitalist prosperity together in an emphatic terminal knot.'[41] Now, Anderson did not exactly propose to play Alexander to Fukuyama's Gordius. Indeed, he largely aligned himself with the essayist against his critics. Those who had taxed him with a utopianism that envisioned a liberal-capitalist paradise where purgatory or inferno persisted, were guilty of interpretative myopia. However complacent in several respects, Fukuyama's

> schema did not require the suppression of every significant social conflict or the solution of every major institutional problem. It simply asserted that liberal capitalism is the *ne plus ultra* of political and economic life on earth. The end of history is not the arrival of a perfect system, but the elimination of any better alternatives to this one.[42]

Accordingly, his detractors were put on notice 'to show that there are powerful systemic alternatives he has discounted.'[43]

Of the possible contenders, the first – contemporary nationalism – was devoid of the requisite universal scope, rendering Fukuyama's deflation of the bombast with which America's (last) Gulf War was infused apt. The second – religious fundamentalism, even (or especially) the Islamic variety latched on to by superannuated Cold Warriors – was a sublimation of nationalism.[44] And the third – a

---

[38] Kojève 1980, p. 185: '"Weltgeschichte ist Weltgericht" ("World History is a tribunal that judges the world"). History is what judges men, their actions and their opinions, and lastly their philosophical opinions as well. To be sure, History is, if you please, a long "discussion" between men. But this real historical "discussion" is something quite different from a philosophic dialogue or discussion. The "discussion" is carried out not with verbal arguments, but with clubs and swords or cannon on the one hand, and sickles and hammers or machines on the other.' Schiller's maxim is invoked in Fukuyama 1993, p. 137.
[39] See 'Note to the Second Edition', in Kojève 1980, pp. 159–62.
[40] Anderson 1992b, p. 324.
[41] Anderson 1992b, p. 332.
[42] Anderson 1992b, p. 336.
[43] Anderson 1992b, p. 336.
[44] Anderson 1992b, pp. 336–7. Anderson writes: 'Fukuyama's cool refusal of certain kinds of conventional wisdom is nowhere more striking than in his

socialist phoenix from the Communist ashes – was no more availing.[45] This last strategy of refutation took two mainstream forms. One – the positive social-democratic variant represented by Michael Mann – affirmed that socialism

> was alive and well as the most advanced form of democracy of our time – the variety that calls itself social. In Western Europe, temporary setbacks may have checked its progress in the eighties, when international capital increasingly outflanked national governments; but the proportion of the national product absorbed by public expenditure has not qualitatively fallen, and the coming of a Federal European Union will create the conditions for renewing a forward march.[46]

In other words, a scenario of the sort imputed to Anderson himself by Gray. An alternative – the negative social-democratic variant represented by Paul Hirst – disputed the uniformly capitalist reality of advanced liberal societies. Both proposals met with a courteous refusal:

> Progressive loyalty and analytic clarity are ... two different things. Western Europe as a zone is ... distinct in its Social-Democracy ... from the USA or Japan. ... But the economies of the Community are ... capitalist on any definition ... of the term, structurally driven by competition between enterprises hiring wage-earners to produce profits for private owners. ... The wish to drape a softening veil over this reality ... is idle. The attempt to quit the realm of concepts altogether, by denying the very existence of capitalism ... is equally fruitless. ... What such postures really represent is a strategy of intellectual consolation. Fukuyama's inventory of the world appears unpalatable: but if it is difficult to find forces capable of altering the world, why not change the inventory? With a wand of redescription, we can dispose of capitalism or reassure ourselves of socialism.[47]

Weltgeist and Zeitgeist

If the rational – empirical – kernel of Fukuyama's essay survived inspection unscathed, what of the expansion of its mystical – teleological – shell in his non-Communist Manifesto? In *The End of History and the Last Man*, the mechanisms of historical transformation

---

judgement of this issue. The conflict in the Gulf which excited so many of his critics, igniting enthusiasm on Right and Left alike for the battle to uphold the cause of national independence and democracy in the Middle East against the menace of a new Hitler, he was to compare with the quarrel between a fifteenth-century condotterie and a thirteenth-century clerical seigneurie' (p. 337).
[45] Anderson 1992b, p. 338–9.
[46] Anderson 1992b, p. 339–41.
[47] Anderson 1992b, pp. 340–1.

were elaborated as the material 'desire' for the satisfaction of needs, and the 'spiritual' struggle for recognition; and a fully fledged philosophy of history developed, offering an account of the overall direction and meaning of the historical process – *le sens de l'histoire* – in its laborious progress towards a liberal-capitalist end-state. Turning from essay to book, Anderson tracked a series of 'oscillations' in Fukuyama's prioritisation of the causal mechanisms of his universal history; and a consequent torsion of his narrative, 'tilt[ing] the outcome of the enquiry towards the stark dichotomy between a rational hedonism and an elemental agonism with which Fukuyama's reflections conclude'.[48] But however problematic Fukuyama's project at the metahistorical level, the plausibility of its principal empirical contention – 'the prospectus of universal capitalist democracy', presaged by the ongoing liberal economic and political revolutions of the late twentieth century – was the main bone of contention. In picking it over, Anderson came to the point at once:

> The enormous change in the world that gives its central force to Fukuyama's case has been the collapse of the USSR. ... Without this global turning-point, the other parts of his story ... would remain scattered episodes. ... If the end of history has arrived, it is essentially because the socialist experience is over. ... But the dissolution of Stalin's empire still leaves a great question unanswered. It is clear that the primary cause of its downfall was its failure to compete in productivity with the major capitalist powers surrounding it – a fate envisaged by Stalin's opponent over half a century ago. ... The fall of communism has brought liberal democracy [to the population], and is bringing capitalism. What levels of consumption can they expect from the change?[49]

Here was the Achilles heel of Fukuyama's projection of a global liberal-capitalist cornucopia, in which a significant proportion of the world would have been levelled up to OECD living standards. Implacable ecological constraints, of which Cournot had had due premonition, told against any such erasure of the current 'staggering inequality' between North and South and East: '[i]n the global ecology of capital today, the privilege of the few requires the misery of the many'.[50]

According to Anderson, the condition of the political term of Fukuyama's democratic-capitalist couplet was no more tonic:

> The inadequacy of ... [his] response to the devitalizing of modern liberty is all too evident. That process is the outcome

---

[48] Anderson 1992b, pp. 349–50.
[49] Anderson 1992b, pp. 351–2. Anderson cites Trotsky 1980, chapter IV, 'The Struggle for Productivity', p. 78. In Trotsky 1982, Trotsky had averred that 'it is impossible to build a socialist paradise, like an oasis in the hell of world capitalism' (p. 68). Three years later, 'socialism in one country' was execrated as a 'reactionary, national-socialist utopia' (quoted in Deutscher 1979, p. 102).
[50] Anderson 1992b, p. 353. Readers are referred to 'a fundamental map of our time' (p. 353 n. 153): Arrighi 1991.

> not just of the power of money and waning of choice within nation-states, but also of their surpassal by international markets and institutions that lack any semblance of democratic control. The European Community, so far the only attempt to transcend national forms for a higher collective sovereignty, still remains yet less accountable to its people than the states that compose it. But just as environmental balance cannot be achieved, social equity furthered, nuclear safety assured, so too popular sovereignty cannot acquire new substance, without a different international settlement. The Hegelian problems – poverty, community, war – have not gone away, but their solutions have moved to another plane.[51]

The existence of these global problems, and Fukuyama's failure to address them convincingly, did not refute his denial of any alternative to liberal capitalism. Only 'a credible alternative' – 'a different international settlement' – could secure that.[52]

The traditional name for the Left's alternative 'international settlement' – the Marxist solution to the Hegelian problems – was 'socialism': the proposal interrogated in the concluding, if not conclusive, section of Anderson's essay. Minus the extravagant philosophical framework of *Weltgeist*, Fukuyama's vision was fully in tune with the *Zeitgeist*: '[w]hat the end of history means, above all, is the end of socialism'.[53] Anderson's stock-taking of the cause which he had championed for more than three decades commenced, and continued, bleakly. In the last essay published before his death in 1961, just as Anderson's career was beginning, Merleau-Ponty remarked that '[t]he whole of human history is, in a certain sense, stationary.'[54] Thereafter, of course, it underwent an extraordinary acceleration. If, today, it was not rearrested, but might be thought to have culminated, it was because the forces 'making it' were the converse of those predicted.

Lukács's sometime Fichtean defiance – 'so much the worse for the facts' – was not available to Anderson.[55] Social-democratic, communist, and national liberation movements alike were seemingly spent, from First to Second and Third Worlds: '[n]one of the political currents that set out to challenge capitalism in this century has morale or compass today'.[56] The 'common disarray' could be explained by the erosion of each of the corner-stones of what Anderson called 'the classical conception of socialism'. These were (1) its 'historical projection' of a

---

[51] Anderson 1992b, p. 356. Anderson proceeds (pp. 356–7) to criticise Fukuyama's silence on inequalities between the sexes in flagrant contradiction of the official ideology of liberal societies: '[t]he end of history may see the last men, as they now are. Women willing to see themselves as the ultimate exemplars of their sex are likely to be fewer' (p. 357).
[52] Anderson 1992b, pp. 357–8.
[53] Anderson 1992b, p. 358.
[54] 'The Eye and the Mind', quoted in Jay 1984, p. 377.
[55] See 'What is Orthodox Marxism?' (1919), in Lukács 1972, pp. 19–27 (here p. 27).
[56] Anderson 1992b, p. 358.

socialisation of the forces of production which permitted supersession of the crisis-ridden capitalist mode of production; (2) its 'subjective agency' – the organised industrial working class, endowed with the structural capacity to abolish existing relations of production; (3) its 'political objective' of the replacement of the anarchic market mechanism by planned production for historical needs in a 'free association'; and (4) its 'ethical ideal' of complex equality, beyond what Marx had called 'the narrow horizon of bourgeois right', attainable in an advanced communist society. 'Today', Anderson regretted,

> all of these elements of the socialist vision have fallen into radical doubt. The secular trend towards increasingly social forces of production ... continued from the industrial revolution to the long boom. ... Technological advances in transport and communications have since broken up manufacturing processes and decentralised plants. ... Meanwhile the industrial working class ... has ... gradually declined in size and social cohesion [in the metropolitan countries]. On a world scale, its absolute numbers have grown. ... But since global population has risen much faster, its relative size as a proportion of humanity is steadily shrinking. Centralised planning achieved remarkable feats in conditions of siege or war. ... But in peacetime conditions, the command-administrative system in the communist countries proved quite unable to master the problem of coordination in increasingly complex economies. ... Equality ... is now widely discounted as either possible or desirable. Indeed, for the commonsense of the time, all the ideas that once made up a belief in socialism are so many dead dogs.[57]

In point of fact, the 'popular verdict' was wanting in nuance. Integration of the productive forces; expansion of waged labour; capitalist planning; legal equality – these spreading post-war phenomena dictated significant qualification of the consensus: '[t]he sources of socialism, as it was traditionally conceived, have not simply dried up'. Nevertheless, given that they had not flowed into the stream of a feasible socialism in the past, '[t]he test for [its] validity ... as an alternative to capitalism lies in whether it retains a potential for solutions to the problems confronting the latter in its hour of historical triumph'.[58]

The intellectual culture of the Left did retain vitality, so Anderson reckoned, referring to *After the Fall* and awarding a special merit to Blackburn's account of the Marxist legacy.[59] Two common themes were discernible in reconstructive proposals: 'socialization of the market', as opposed to its 'impossible abolition'; and a more 'developed democracy' than the standard parliamentary-capitalist fare. As to the practicability

---

[57] Anderson 1992b, p. 359.
[58] Anderson 1992b, p. 360.
[59] Anderson 1992b, pp. 361–3, cf. Blackburn 1991.

of these theoretical avenues, Anderson was less sanguine. The classical socialist economic case against capitalism – its reproduction of social inequalities within and between societies – remained valid; and was even strengthened by its production of 'ecological crisis', which indicated its long-run unsustainability as a global mode of production. But socialist silver linings were not glimpsed in acid-rain clouds. For the inviability of capitalism did not prove the viability of socialism. Indeed, the vices of the former compounded the quandaries of the latter, dramatising its programmatic and strategic deficits: 'the paradox is that the terrain on which the socialist economic critique of capitalism has most contemporary power also poses it with even more difficult tasks [of planning] than those it failed to acquit in the past'.[60]

Similarly, at the political level, proposals for socialist advance via supra-national institutions, now that capital could readily circumvent nation-states, ran into difficulties of scale:

> Western Europe contains the one significant start towards such a federation. The European Community was created principally by Christian Democrats, and the Treaty of Rome was expressly designed as the framework for a robust continental capitalism. It took a considerable time for many socialists to see it as an opportunity for long-term advance in another direction. Today that awareness is much more widespread. On any realistic reckoning, it is clear that a major task of the Left will be to press towards the completion of a genuine federal state in the Community, with a sovereign authority over its constituent parts. That ... will require a democratically empowered European legislature. ... Such a Union is the only kind of general will that can contest the new power of the invisible hand as the arbiter of collective destinies. But realism also dictates an awareness that, just as the larger an economy the more difficult it is to plan, so the greater the territory and population of a state, the less subject it tends to become to democratic control.[61]

Intimations that socialism had, by classical Marxist criteria, become utopian again were amplified in Anderson's scrutiny of the fortunes of its 'scientific' fulcrum: the social agency of the 'collective labourer'. Contemporary capitalism had impaired socialist strategy and goal. If it had not buried its allotted grave-diggers, it had prepared their obsequies. With greatly reduced numbers of peasants and enhanced numbers of female waged workers, 'the human potential of opposition to the dictates of capital has become more truly universal than it was at the height of the traditional labour movement'.[62] Yet the result of this

---

[60] Anderson 1992b, p. 363–4.
[61] Anderson 1992b, p. 365. This passage precedes the statement that 'the construction of effective supranational sovereignties is the obvious remedy to the loss by national states of so much of their substance and authority' (p. 365).
[62] Anderson 1992b, p. 366.

massive, ongoing recomposition of the world's labour-force was highly ambivalent, for

> The new reality is a massive asymmetry between the international mobility and organization of capital, and the dispersal and fragmentation of labour, that has no historical precedent. The globalization of capitalism has not drawn the resistances to it together, but scattered and outflanked them. ... [F]or the moment no change in this unequal balance of forces is in sight. The potential extension of social interests in an alternative to capitalism has been accompanied by a reduction in social capacities to fight for one.[63]

The inference was stark – and unflinchingly drawn in a summarising judgement:

> All these difficulties have a common origin. The case against capitalism is strongest on the plane where the reach of socialism is weakest – at the level of the world system as a whole. ... [T]he future belongs to the set of forces that are overtaking the nation-state. So far, they have been captured or driven by capital – as in the past fifty years, internationalism has changed sides. So long as the Left fails to win back the initiative here, the current system will be secure.[64]

By way of conclusion, various historical paradigms were envisaged for the possible fate of socialism. An 'oblivion' comparable to that into which Jesuit egalitarianism in Paraguay had lapsed; a 'transvaluation' equivalent to that undergone by the ideals and idiom of the English Revolution; a 'mutation' similar to that which bred socialism out of the principles of 1789; or a 'redemption' commensurate with that experienced by liberalism itself, once the Red Army had assured the defeat of its European fascist rival in the Second World War – these were the 'analogies' that presented themselves.[65] Anderson's own intuition as to which eventuality was most probable is an imponderable. But if it is safe to infer his predisposition to the last, the nadir from which it would occur was immitigable: '[b]y the end of the [1980s], communism was everywhere in crisis or collapse, and social democracy was rudderless'.[66] As Nicholas Tredell remarked in a fine review of *English Questions* and *A Zone of Engagement*, by Anderson's own submission, 'evidence constrains emplotment: and it is hard to see how the history of socialism could be written as anything but tragedy'.[67]

---

[63] Anderson 1992b, p. 366.
[64] Anderson 1992b, p. 367.
[65] Anderson 1992b, pp. 367–75.
[66] Anderson 1992b, p. 374.
[67] Tredell 1992, p. 70. He is alluding to Anderson's essay 'On Emplotment–Andreas Hillgruber' (1990), in Anderson 1992b, pp. 169-81 (especially p. 180).

After the Fall

In his calibration of the *fin-de-siècle* 'potential of socialism at large', Anderson registered 'the lesser discredit (but also lesser weight) of social democracy'.[68] The weightiest factor in his own revaluations – most evident in his second thoughts on the market and representative democracy – was not the degradation of social democracy, but the destruction of its *frère ennemi*. '[W]ith the collapse of the Soviet bloc', he wrote two years later, 'the rationale of descent from the October Revolution has all but disappeared'.[69] Made with specific reference to West European Communism, this assertion equally implicated the Far Left to which Anderson, for all his organisational aloofness, had been affiliated. To borrow the terms of his Foreword to *A Zone of Engagement*, the 1984 Ali anthology on *The Stalinist Legacy* in which his Trotsky text figured, pertained to 'the intellectual world of the revolutionary Left, from a particular standpoint within it':[70] the world of Trotsky, Deutscher, Mandel, and their successors, whose house journal had been *NLR* under Anderson's editorship. By contrast, the 1991 Blackburn symposium on the future of socialism commended by Anderson featured not a single one of these successors, and inhabited a different universe. No peremptory inconsistency was involved here. In accordance with Deutschero-Trotskyist perspectives, the implosion of actually existing socialism was construed as the definitive historical verdict on formerly existing revolutionary socialism, descended, like Stalinism, from the October Revolution.

In 1917 Trotsky had conceived the Russian Revolution as 'the prologue to world revolution'. A decade later, making his stand against 'socialism in one country' while awaiting the main action in the metropolitan theatre of the world, he conceded that 'if capitalism were to flourish and if its economy and culture were to be on the ascendant that would mean that we had come too early'.[71] After the outbreak of the Second World War, an even more 'onerous' prospect than Bolshevik prematurity was contemplated by him:

> if the world proletariat should actually prove incapable of fulfilling the mission placed upon it by the course of development, nothing else would remain except only to recognise that the socialist programme, based on the internal contradictions of capitalist society, ended as a Utopia.[72]

Given the refutation of Trotsky's interpretation of Stalinism in the East, and notwithstanding the misfortunes of socialism in the West, Anderson could in 1976 postulate 'the descendant position of capitalism on a

---

[68] Anderson 1992b, p. 374.
[69] 'Introduction', Anderson and Camiller (eds) 1994, p. 7.
[70] Anderson 1992b, p. xii.
[71] Quoted in Deutscher 1979, p. 301.
[72] 'The USSR in War' (1939), in Trotsky 1990, pp. 3–21: here p. 9.

global scale, in an epoch which despite everything saw a third of the world wrested from it'.[73] Furthermore, although eschewing talk of the proletariat's historical 'mission', with the destabilisation of imperialism he could anticipate a resumption of 'socialist advance' in the metropolis. This, rather than Deutscher's scenario of an 'obliterati[on]' of 'the old antithesis between backward Russia and the advanced West' via de-Stalinisation from above, and a consequent 'regeneration of the Russian Revolution',[74] was the Andersonian wager of the time – a time which he measured much like Trotsky, who in 1932 estimated the intervening fifteen years as 'a minute on the clock of history'.[75] A little less than four minutes on, the Bolshevik past was not prologue, but epilogue. Western prospects had evaporated; and the Eastern results with which they were inextricably bound up, had been overturned. The 'heavy artillery' of capitalist commodities – more potent than any imperialist ordnance in Korea or Vietnam – had levelled Russian, and mined Chinese, walls.[76] As the bourgeoisie set about 'creat[ing] a world after its own image', putatively post-capitalist societies were rendered pre-capitalist overnight.

The conviction that events in the East have not infirmed the classical Marxist theory of historical trajectory underpinning 'scientific socialism' led Alex Callinicos to object that there was a systemic alternative to liberal capitalism scouted in Anderson's sense of an ending: precisely revolutionary socialism.[77] But even were we to endorse his opposing interpretation of the 'key empirical issue', accept that Stalinism was in fact 'a particular variant of capitalism' ('bureaucratic state capitalism'), therewith reconceive the 'great contest' as one between competing capitalisms, and thus retrieve an unvanquished socialism from a Western capitalism victorious only over its Eastern alter ego, this consolation would furnish cold comfort. For if the USSR and the Second World were not in any sense socialist, then there never has been socialism; and hence its feasibility as a systemic alternative to capitalism remains undemonstrated: an inviolate ideal, rather than a proven potential.[78]

Citing John Stuart Mill on the choice between capitalism and communism, Anderson at one point posed the question of whether socialism had as yet received 'a fair trial': 'have we seen it, not as it

---

[73] Anderson 1976, p. 56.
[74] Cf. Deutscher 1979, pp. 521–2: here p. 522.
[75] Quoted in Deutscher 1979, p. 185.
[76] See 'Manifesto of the Communist Party' (1848), in Marx and Engels 1969, p. 112.
[77] See Callinicos 1995, chapter 1, 'Sympathy for the Devil? Francis Fukuyama and the End of History', pp. 15–43 – especially pp. 17–22, which criticises the Deutscherite reactions of Anderson, Halliday, and myself. Callinicos cites (pp. 215 n. 23, 218–9 n. 92). Anderson's response to his criticisms during a seminar held at the Center for Social Theory and Comparative History, University of California, Los Angeles, in April 1993. On the Marxist theory of historical trajectory, see Wright 1993.
[78] Cf., however, Callinicos 1991, for an argument to the contrary.

actually existed, but as it might exist?'[79] More or less in the spirit of Schumpeter's admonitions about comparing 'a given reality with an *idea* ... [or] with an *ideal*',[80] he stressed that 'real conditions' – not 'utopian circumstances' – were the requisite test-bed. Those conditions exhibited a fearful asymmetry, according to him, between capital and the forces disarrayed against it. In what Blackburn termed a 'prophetic article', C. Wright Mills had regretted the New Left's subscription to the 'labour metaphysic'.[81] In the Introduction to *Mapping the West European Left* (1994), Anderson resumed his apprehension of the quasi-dystopian circumstances faced by the Left at the end of the twentieth century – 'a time when hopes of socialism have been struck off its agenda'.[82] A 'double change in its strategic situation' obtained. First there was the dispersion of its 'constituencies' with the waning of the 'centrality' of the manual working class, as wage-labour increasingly disaggregated along lines of occupation, income and job security, generation, gender, and ethnicity. Having outlined the materialist analysis of class recomposition which had been alluded to in *In the Tracks of Historical Materialism*, but whose implications for working-class politics had been minimised,[83] Anderson rescinded the Marxist commonsense of the 1960s and 70s for a moderate version of the sociological consensus of the 1980s: the result of this recomposition bordering upon discomposition was to 'make the task of subjective mobilisation for any radical change inherently harder'.[84]

The second alteration was a circumscription of 'the objective space' for the governmental Left's habitual policy instruments, fiscal and monetary, by national and international exigencies – especially 'the globalization of capital'.[85] In these conditions, Anderson foresaw 'a farewell to the substance of social democracy ... [without] a disappearance of the term'.[86] The supra-national light previously glimpsed at the end of the national tunnel was itself being extinguished, as the European Union gradually conformed to neoliberal canons of economic correctness. Inveighing against the Maastricht Treaty, Anderson maintained that:

> Reclamation both of the basic principles of representative democracy, and of any prospects of effective macroeconomic policy, requires the construction of a true federal framework in Europe. The left has on the whole been no more clear-sighted or imaginative about this than the centre or right. Indecision and confusion are still the norm. ... Purely national

---

[79] Anderson 1992b, pp. 360–1.
[80] Schumpeter 1994, p. 200.
[81] See 'Letter to the New Left', *NLR*, 5, September/October 1960: 18–23; cited in Blackburn 1992, p. vi.
[82] Anderson and Camiller (eds) 1994, p. 11.
[83] Anderson and Camiller (eds) 1994, pp. 11–14, and cf. Anderson 1983b, p. 105.
[84] Anderson and Camiller (eds) 1994, p. 14.
[85] Anderson and Camiller (eds) 1994, pp. 14–15.
[86] Anderson and Camiller (eds) 1994, p. 16.

> strategies are vanishing for every part of the political
> spectrum. The West European left will acquire new contours
> only when this crux is resolved.[87]

Meanwhile, the roll-call of dishonour with which Anderson's survey opened, dramatised not simply the political debilitation, but the moral degeneration, of leading sectors of the Second International. With dwindling rationale, social democracy was incontestably 'at an impasse' – reduced to appealing to a '[m]odernity voided of any content beyond market adjustment',[88] implementing 'Reaganomics' under the antipodean rubric of 'Rogernomics'. Contemplating the possibility of an Americanisation of West European politics less than a decade earlier, Anderson had averred: '[t]here is still a long way to go before such a scenario is realised'.[89] By 1994 it seemed alarmingly close at hand. At all events, the corrosion of the Second International – the 'rusty brake' from whose inhibition Trotsky had wished to release 'the masses', and hence 'the locomotive of history'[90] – had not redounded to the benefit of the non-social-democratic Left, to whom a solitary paragraph was devoted. It bluntly concluded that:

> Nowhere ... does it have any chance of forming a
> government: its only hope of office is in coalition with a
> dominant social democracy. Nor, for all the greater sharpness
> of its rejection of post-Reaganite capitalism, is its stock of
> solutions much richer. For the moment ... the existence of
> this political area does little to modify the programmatic
> dilemmas of the left.[91]

Disconcerted in government by the disintegration of the post-war conditions that had facilitated it, social democracy was disorientated in opposition, in signal contrast to the record of the New Right in its wilderness years.[92] Anderson did not emulate the sentiment of Horkheimer's manifesto for Critical Theory in 1937: 'truth has sought refuge among small groups of admirable men'.[93] It was, however, to 'the margins of day-to-day politics' that he looked for 'creative reflection', reprising proposals canvassed in 'The Light of Europe'[94] – including 'lines of attack' on existing capitalist property relations that seem conspicuously exposed to the exact objection of political utopianism

---

[87] Anderson and Camiller (eds) 1994, p. 22.
[88] Anderson and Camiller (eds) 1994, p. 11.
[89] Anderson 1986b, p. 28.
[90] See 'What Next? Vital Questions for the German Proletariat' (1932), in Trotsky 1975, p. 122.
[91] Anderson and Camiller (eds) 1994, p. 7. Cf. the very pertinent reflections by a leading member of one of the organisations to which Anderson refers, Lucio Magri, of Rifondazione Comunista in Magri 1991.
[92] Anderson and Camiller (eds) 1994, p. 19.
[93] 'Traditional and Critical Theory' (1937), quoted in Jay 1984, p. 209.
[94] Anderson and Camiller (eds) 1994, pp. 19–21; and see 'The Light of Europe' (1991) in Anderson 1992a, pp. 302–53.

raised by him against Nove's *Economics of Feasible Socialism* a decade before.[95]

If, according to Anderson, social democracy 'appears to have lost its compass', 'un monde déboussolé' – a world which has lost both its bearings and its compass – was the all-embracing verdict on the era of 'globalitarianism' offered by one French commentator.[96] In a review of a work which concluded on a similar note – Hobsbawm's *Age of Extremes* – Anderson tactfully demurred at its catastrophist intimations: if not the socialism or barbarism of the century's outset, then a 'changed society' or 'darkness' at its close. Underlining the 'reversal of verdicts' operated in Hobsbawm's account of the twentieth century, Anderson queried the depiction of 1945–73 as a 'golden age', succeeded by a 'landslide'. Where Hobsbawm foregrounded the globally deleterious effects of the collapse of Communism and the diffusion of deregulated capitalism, Anderson wondered 'how far [the latter] have ... been offset by the extraordinary improvement in Chinese living standards, a phenomenon of the last 20 years – a much larger historical fact than the temporary decline of Russia'.[97] Whilst Anderson's summary of Hobsbawm's 'sombre prospectus for the millennium' coincided, in essentials, with his own in 'The Ends of History', his inference differed. Contrary to the title under which his review appeared, darkness had gathered; it had not fallen.

Reflection and resistance

In Hobsbawm's characterisation of the post-1973 period as a 'landslide', Anderson observed, 'the vision of the historian and the passion of the politician are one'.[98] In the case of the late Anderson, we might vary the attribution: the vision of the historian and the dispassion of the politician are one. An earlier *Guardian* notice of Martin Bernal's *Black Athena* had advanced 'a world-historical perspective' as the necessary corrective to its audacious revisionism, and counselled that 'lively contemporary sympathies tend to be most fruitful in studies of the past when also most guarded against'.[99] Now practising what he here preached, Anderson has extended the protocol to his own studies of the present, in remarkably temperate overviews of Brazil, a long-standing and passionate interest;[100] and of South Korea, a new departure.[101] Such

---

[95] Anderson 1983b, pp. 102–3.
[96] See Ramonet 1997.
[97] Anderson 1994a.
[98] Anderson 1994a.
[99] Anderson 1987.
[100] Anderson 1994b.
[101] Anderson 1996b. If Anderson's report registered the pressures that were shortly to ignite massive labour unrest in South Korea, his encomium to the convenience and cleanliness of Seoul (p. 28) suggests a somewhat sheltered experience. According to a 1996 UN report, it is one of the most expensive and polluted cities in the world, tap-water there rarely being drinkable on account of contamination by heavy metals. See Carroué 1997.

redoubtable analytical sobriety betokens no fraying of progressive loyalties, on the part of a contributor to the *London Review of Books* who positions himself on 'the far left of its spectrum'.[102] Yet as Anderson remarked in *Mapping the West European Left*,[103] just as the *appellation mal contrôlée* of 'social democracy' could outlast the evacuation of its substance, so 'a "left" could survive within an all-capitalist system that was to the right of anything now considered in the centre' – a general theory of political relativity which presumably encompasses a 'far left'. Such a scenario has been repeated in Anderson's most recent text, at time of writing – a review of Bobbio's *Left and Right*.[104] In what sense is Clinton's Democratic dispensation in health and welfare more progressive than that of the Republican administration of Nixon? Or, to take the argument a stage further, who could seriously argue that today's British Labour Party is actually to the left of the official party of the Centre, the Liberal Democrats? Mitterrand, Gonzales, Blair and their sort in Europe; Lange and Hawke in Australasia – shaking the invisible hand, these men of 'the left' have converted executive alternation into 'un jeu à risque nul' for capital.[105]

In his letter of 12 December 1988 to Bobbio, Anderson had confided 'a deep conviction' to his correspondent:

> I ... do not believe that the listless and manipulated semi-liberty of today will be humanity's last historical word. ... Who can really imagine the present order will just be reproduced ... till the end of time? Things will eventually either get much worse or much better. The one safe prediction is that they will not remain the same. Of course, one is speaking of centuries rather than decades – far 'too late' for someone like me as well. But given the road covered so far, I think there are grounds for a rational optimism about the direction of this future ...[106]

A few short years later, such 'rational optimism', grounded in a secular historical perspective, was but dimly discernible: stoicism, rather than optimism or pessimism, had become the predominant temper of Anderson's writing. And his failure, to date, to complete the expanded version of 'The Ends of History' promised some years ago is perhaps symptomatic. If the role of reality-instructor is the one to which Anderson currently seems most attuned, resistance to that reality is not abandoned in the act of reflecting it.

> A purely axiological defense of the idea of the Left, bereft of any historical theory or institutional attack capable of shaking the status quo, will not pass muster. Bobbio once looked to

---

102 Anderson 1996a, p. ix.
103 Anderson and Camiller (eds) 1994, p. 17
104 Anderson 1998.
105 See Halimi 1997 p. 10.
106 Letter of 12 December 1988 in Anderson 1989.

liberal socialism for such a challenge. Today he redescribes social democracy as liberal socialism, in a notable lowering of expectations. ... The lesson of his book ... is that the opposition between Left and Right has no axiomatic guarantee. If the Left is to survive as a meaningful force, in a world overwhelmingly dominated by the Right, it will have to fight for a real alternative to it.[107]

Anderson too has notably lowered his expectations. But aside from 'A Culture in Contraflow', he has mostly declined the consolations of redescription. Philosophers – and historians – have to interpret the world aright. The point, however, remains to change it.

References

Ali, Tariq 1988, *Revolution from Above: Where is the Soviet Union Going?*, London: Hutchinson.

Anderson, Perry 1976, *Considerations on Western Marxism*, London: New Left Books.

Anderson, Perry 1980, *Arguments Within English Marxism*, London: New Left Books.

Anderson, Perry 1983a, '*NLR* Charter', unpublished document, no date.

Anderson, Perry 1983b, *In the Tracks of Historical Materialism*, London: New Left Books.

Anderson, Perry 1984, 'Trotsky's Interpretation of Stalinism', in *The Stalinist Legacy: Its Impact On Twentieth-Century World Politics*, edited by Tariq Ali, Harmondsworth: Penguin.

Anderson, Perry 1986a, 'Agendas for Radical History', *Radical History Review*, 36 :32–7.

Anderson, Perry 1986b, 'Social Democracy Today', *Against the Current*, 1, 6: 21–8.

Anderson, Perry 1987, 'The Myth of Hellenism', *Guardian*, 13 March.

Anderson, Perry 1989, 'Un Carteggio tra Norberto Bobbio e Perry Anderson', *Teoria Politica*, V, 2–3: 293–308.

Anderson, Perry 1991, 'August in Moscow', *London Review of Books*, 26 September, pp. 5–8.

Anderson, Perry 1992a, *English Questions*, London: Verso.

Anderson, Perry 1992b, *A Zone of Engagement*, London: Verso.

Anderson, Perry 1993, 'Diary', *London Review of Books*, 21 October 1993, pp. 24–5.

Anderson, Perry 1994a, 'Darkness Falls', *Guardian*, 8 November, p. 12.

Anderson, Perry 1994b, 'The Dark Side of Brazilian Conviviality', *London Review of Books*, 24 November, pp. 3–8.

Anderson, Perry 1996a, 'Reader's Note', in *London Review of Books: An Anthology*, edited by Jane Hindle, London: Verso.

---

[107] Anderson 1998.

Anderson, Perry 1996b, 'Diary', *London Review of Books*, 17 October, pp. 28–9.

Anderson, Perry 1998, 'Review of Norberto Bobbio, *Left and Right*', *New Left Review*, forthcoming.

Anderson, Perry and Patrick Camiller (eds) 1994, *Mapping the West European Left*, London: Verso.

Arrighi, Giovanni 1991, 'World Income Inequalities and the Future of Socialism', *New Left Review*, 189: 39–64.

Blackburn, Robin 1991, 'Fin de Siècle: Socialism after the Crash', *New Left Review*, 185: 5–66; reprinted in Blackburn (ed.) 1991, pp. 173–249.

Blackburn, Robin (ed.) 1991, *After the Fall: The Failure of Communism and the Future of Socialism*, London and New York: Verso.

Blackburn, Robin 1992, 'A Brief History of New Left Review 1960–1990', in *Thirty Years of New Left Review: Index to Numbers 1–184 (1960–1990)*, London: Verso.

Bobbio, Norberto 1989, 'The Upturned Utopia', in Blackburn (ed.) 1991, pp. 3–5.

Callinicos, Alex 1991, *The Revenge of History: Marxism and the East European Revolutions*, Cambridge: Polity Press.

Callinicos, Alex 1995, *Theories and Narratives: Reflections on the Philosophy of History*, Cambridge: Polity Press.

Carroué, Laurent 1997, 'Les travailleurs coréens à l'assaut du dragon', *Le Monde Diplomatique*, February, pp. 1, 18–19.

Debray, Régis 1989, *Que vive la République*, Paris: Editions Odile Jacob.

Deutscher, Isaac 1979 (1963), *The Prophet Outcast–Trotsky: 1929–1940*, Oxford: Oxford University Press.

Elliott, Gregory 1998, *Perry Anderson: The Merciless Laboratory of History*, Minneapolis: Minnesota University Press.

Fukuyama, Francis 1989, 'The End of History?', *The National Interest*, 16: 3–18.

Fukuyama, Francis 1993 (1992) *The End of History and the Last Man*, Harmondsworth: Penguin.

Gray, John 1992, 'Enlightenment Projects', *Times Literary Supplement*, 14 August, pp. 4–5.

Halimi, Serge 1997, 'La Nouvelle-Zélande éprouvette du capitalisme total', *Le Monde Diplomatique*, April, pp. 10–11.

Halliday, Fred 1990a, 'The Ends of Cold War', *New Left Review*, 180: 5–23.

Halliday, Fred 1990b, 'A Reply to Edward Thompson', *New Left Review*, 182: 147–50.

Harman, Chris 1990, 'Criticism Which Does Not Withstand the Test of Logic', *International Socialism*, 49: 65–88.

Hobsbawm, E. J. 1990, 'Goodbye to All That' in Blackburn (ed.) 1991, pp. 115–25.

Hobsbawm, E. J. 1994, *Age of Extremes: The Short Twentieth Century 1914–1991*, London: Michael Joseph.

Jay, Martin 1984, *Marxism and Totality: The Adventures of a Concept from Lukács to Habermas*, Cambridge: Polity Press.

Kojève, Alexandre 1980 (1947), *Introduction to the Reading of Hegel: Lectures on The Phenomenology of Spirit*, edited by Allan Bloom, Ithaca: Cornell University Press.

Lukács, Georg 1972, *Political Writings 1919–1929: The Question of Parliamentarism and Other Essays*, London: New Left Books.

Magri, Lucio 1991, 'The European Left between Crisis and Refoundation', *New Left Review*, 189: 5–18.

Mandel, Ernest 1989, *Beyond Perestroika: The Future of Gorbachev's USSR*, London: Verso.

Mandel, Ernest 1990, 'A Theory which has not withstood the test of the facts', *International Socialism*, 49: 43–64.

Marx, Karl, and Frederick Engels 1969, *Selected Works*, Vol. 1, Moscow: Progress Publishers.

Marx, Karl, and Frederick Engels 1976, *Collected Works*, Vol. 1, London: Lawrence and Wishart.

McCarney, Joseph 1993, 'Shaping Ends: Reflections on Fukuyama', *New Left Review*, 202: 37–53.

Medvedev, Zhores 1986, 'Innovation and Conservatism in the New Soviet Leadership', *New Left Review*, 157: 5–26.

Niethammer, Lutz 1992 (1989), *Posthistoire: Has History Come to an End?*, London and New York: Verso.

Ramonet, Ignacio 1997, 'Régimes globalitaires', *Le Monde Diplomatique*, January 1997, p. 1.

Schumpeter, J. A. 1994 (1943), *Capitalism, Socialism and Democracy*, London: Routledge.

Thompson, E.P. 1990, 'The Ends of Cold War', *New Left Review*, 182: 139–46.

Tredell, Nicholas 1992, 'Modern Tragedy', *P. N. Review*, 19, 1: 66–70.

Trotsky, Leon 1975 (1971), *The Struggle Against Fascism in Germany*, Harmondsworth: Penguin.

Trotsky, Leon 1980 (1936), *The Revolution Betrayed: What is the Soviet Union and Where is it Going?*, New York: Pathfinder Press.

Trotsky, Leon 1982 (1929), *The Third International After Lenin*, New York: Pathfinder Press.

Trotsky, Leon 1990 (1942), *In Defense of Marxism: The Social and Political Contradictions of the Soviet Union*, New York: Pathfinder Press.

Wright, Erik Olin 1993, 'Class Analysis, History and Emancipation', *New Left Review*, 202: 15–35.

DOXA
CUADERNOS DE CIENCIAS SOCIALES

A Quarterly Review of Social and Political Theory and
Criticism, from Buenos Aires

Papers, interviews, book's reviews, conference reports on
Sociology, History, Philosophy, Economy, Politics, Labour Studies,
Cultural Studies
(in Spanish)

DOXA no 18, Year IX, Summer 1998
DOSSIER: MARXISM and CULTURAL STUDIES

Forthcoming!
Stuart Hall: *Marxism and the problem of ideology*
Raymond Williams: *Notes on Marxism in Great Britain since 1945*
Silvia Delfino: *Differences and inequality: 'identity' in cultural criticism*
Edgardo Lander: *Modernity, colonisation and postmodernity*
Gabriel Nardaccione: *The social meaning of citizenship: decline or
re conceptualisation?*
Edgardo Logiudice: *Copyright and the left*

Jacques Bidet: *John Rawls and the theory of justice*
Interview
Ana Dinerstein: *Conversation with Sol Picciotto: The political and
economic forms of the new phase of internationalisation of capital*

SUBSCRIPTIONS AND BACK ISSUES

Annual Subscription Rates for 3 issues (includes postage)
Individual: £ 24
Libraries and Institutions: £ 40
Back issues (includes postage)
Single issues: £ 6
Back issues: nos. 13-16: £ 5

Name:	
Address:	
City:	Country:
Postcode:	Sub-amount:
Back issues:	Tot. Amount

Please start my subscription with No.16   17   18

Postal orders or cheques to Tesis 11. Grupo Editor SRL
Send to: Av. de Mayo 1370 - Piso 14 - Of 355/56
(c.p.1362) Capital Federal Buenos Aires - Argentina

Recognition and Social Relations of Production

Andrew Chitty

'Social relation of production' is a key term in Marx's theory of history, for the social relations of production of a society give that society its fundamental character and make it, for example, a capitalist rather than some other kind of society.[1] In Marx's words:

> The social relations within which [humans] produce, the social relations of production [*gesellschaftliche Produktionsverhältnisse*] ... in their totality form what are called social relations, society, and specifically a society at a determinate historical stage of development, a society with a peculiar, distinctive character. Ancient society, feudal society, bourgeois society are such totalities of relations of production, each of which at the same time denotes a special stage of development in the history of mankind.[2]

For Marx the major institutions of a historical epoch – specifically its legal and political systems – are deeply conditioned by its social relations of production. In his metaphor from the 1859 *Preface*, the social relations of production form a 'base' and these institutions a 'superstructure' which arises out of it.[3] Accordingly his general strategy for explaining these institutions is to show how the relations of production give rise to them. The base is *explanans* and the superstructure is *explanandum*, and to say that some aspect of social life belongs to the base or the superstructure is simply to say what its role is in this conditioning process, and so in Marx's explanation of social institutions.

However Marx never says in so many words just what social relations of production *are*, and the concept has been strongly criticised by non-Marxists. In some places Marx appears to equate them with property relations: in *Moralising Criticism and Critical Morality* he

---

[1] I shall use 'relation of production' as a shorthand for 'social relation of production'. I am grateful to Alison Stone for discussions that helped me develop some of the ideas in this article, and to Joseph McCarney, Chris Arthur and the editors of *Historical Materialism* for their valuable comments on earlier drafts. This piece is dedicated to the memory of Justin Fashanu.

[2] Marx and Engels 1956–71 (hereafter MEW), Vol. 6, p. 408; Marx and Engels 1975– (hereafter CW), Vol. 9, p. 212. This and most other translations have been modified. In the translations as modified 'relation' always stands for the German *Verhältnis* unless I mention otherwise.

[3] MEW, Vol. 13, p. 8; Marx 1970, pp. 20–1. The metaphor of a 'base' is unfortunate since it confuses the idea of 'that which determines the character of' with that of 'that which is the necessary condition for the existence of'. The notion of a 'core' or 'kernel' would be less misleading.

states that *'private property ...* consists in the totality of the *bourgeois* relations of production',[4] and in the 1859 *Preface to the Contribution to the Critique of Political Economy* he says that property relations are 'only a legal expression for' relations of production.[5] Yet if property relations are legal relations – and this is the most obvious way to understand them – then they cannot be identical with social relations of production, for the legal system is meant to be part of the superstructure of society, the character of which is explained by the relations of production. Legal property relations would have to make up the base and yet also belong to the superstructure. This difficulty has been called the 'problem of legality'.[6] Problems like it have given rise to the criticism that the very idea of 'social relations of production' in Marx is incoherent, or as Plamenatz put it, that it is 'a phrase used not to express thought but to cover up its absence, and is therefore not to be rendered into meaningful English'.[7]

The best-known Marxist response to the problem of legality is G.A. Cohen's in *Karl Marx's Theory of History: A Defence.* Cohen distinguishes social relations of production from legal property relations by interpreting them as relations of *de facto* power over means of production and labour-power (human labouring capacity).[8] Legal property relations are then assigned unambiguously to the superstructure, and are explained from given relations of *de facto* power by the fact that they are functional for maintaining those relations.[9]

Another response, proposed by Derek Sayer, and also by Ellen Meiksins Wood (in a recent interpretation of E.P. Thompson), is to understand social relations of production as that 'core' set of moral, legal, customary or other relations within which the process of production takes place in a given society, and which makes that process possible.[10] This means that legal property relations, as well as perhaps

---

[4] MEW, Vol. 4, p. 356; CW, Vol. 6, p. 337.
[5] NB not 'only a legal expression *of*': Marx's words are 'nur ein juristischer Ausdruck dafür'. MEW, Vol. 13, p. 9; Marx 1970, p. 21. His meaning seems to be that 'property relations' is simply a legalistic way of describing relations of production. In *The Poverty of Philosophy* (1846–47) he first differentiates and then appears to identify property and relations of production. 'In each historical epoch, property has developed differently and under a set of entirely different social relations. Thus to define bourgeois property is nothing else than to give an exposition of all the social relations of bourgeois production.' CW, Vol. 6, p. 197.
[6] The problem is suggested in Plamenatz 1954, pp. 24–5, and briefly articulated in Plamenatz 1963, Vol. 2, pp. 280–81. It is named, and stated as I have presented it here, by Cohen 1978, pp. 217–8.
[7] Plamenatz 1954, p. 21.
[8] That is, over what Cohen collectively calls 'productive forces'. The initial definition is at Cohen 1978, pp. 34–5, and the idea of *de facto* or 'effective' power is elaborated in Chapters 3 and 8. In the initial definition Cohen adds that any relations 'presupposing' such relations of *de facto* power also count as relations of production, and gives some examples. However he ignores this extension when he defines and exemplifies relations of production again at pp. 63–5. In Cohen 1988, pp. 5–6, he reproduces the more restricted definition and set of examples. I conclude that the restricted definition is his official one.
[9] See Cohen 1978, Chapter 8.
[10] Sayer 1987, Chapter 3; Wood 1995, Chapter 2. Godelier 1982 advances a similar view of relations of production.

other parts of law, are explicitly assigned to the base rather than the superstructure.

In this paper I shall propose an alternative view, by trying to understand the idea of social relations of production as a development of the accounts of right (*Recht*) given by two of Marx's immediate philosophical predecessors, Fichte and Hegel. I begin by elucidating Fichte's account of the 'relation of right' (*Rechtsverhältnis*) as a relation of mutual recognition between self-conscious subjects through which they mutually constitute each other as self-conscious. I then show how Hegel's account of right (*Recht*) can be understood in terms of a plurality of such relations of mutual recognition. Then I outline an interpretation of Marx's notion of social relations of production as a transformation of this idea of relations of recognition. At the end I return to the problem of legality and suggest that this interpretation of social relations of production solves the problem in a more satisfactory way than either Cohen's or Sayer's and Wood's does, as well as fitting Marx's usage of the term better.[11]

1. Fichte's account of Recht

The German *Recht* is sometimes translated as 'law' or 'justice', but I shall translate it by the generic word 'right'. Broadly, *Recht* is the generic equivalent of *ein Recht*, a right. It is that which unites, is common to, or underlies, all particular rights and the laws that enforce those rights and their correlative duties.[12] So in translating it by the English word 'right' we need to keep in mind the usage of that word in which it is specifically tied to the idea of rights. This is our usage of 'right' when we talk about 'being in the right' or 'having right on your side', as opposed to the broader usage of it to mean what is morally correct, as when we talk about 'knowing the difference between right and wrong'. This is how I shall use the generic term 'right' here.

It is important to notice, however, that the German *Recht* is ambiguous between a 'natural' sense in which it means that which underlies all 'natural rights' (rights that are thought of as universally valid, independently of whether they are embodied in the institutions of any particular society) and a 'positive' sense in which it means that which is common to a given set of 'actual rights' (the rights actually defined and enforced by the legal and other institutions of some existing society). The two senses are distinguished in German by speaking of *Naturrecht* (natural right or natural law) and *positive Recht* (positive law) respectively. The English terms 'a right' and 'morality' are similarly ambiguous between natural and positive senses, but the generic 'right' has an exclusively natural sense, and the generic 'law' an almost

---

[11] I should say that in developing this interpretation I have benefited greatly from Cohen's and Sayer's work, in particular.

[12] See the somewhat similar account of *Recht* given in Hart 1955, Section 1A.

exclusively positive sense; they provide the nearest English equivalents to *Recht* when that word is used in the natural and positive senses respectively. This helps to explain why *Recht* is usually translated as 'right' in translations of Kant, Fichte and Hegel (who generally use the word in the natural sense) but as 'law' in translations of Marx (who generally uses it in the positive sense). So in using 'right' as a single translation for *Recht* we need to extend its meaning mentally to allow for the possibility of a positive as well as a natural sense.

Fichte, in his 1796 *Grundlage des Naturrechts* (Foundation of Natural Right), attempts to give a philosophical account of right by relating it closely to the kind of being that we are: specifically, beings that are self-conscious, or have 'I-ness', or are rational (three terms he uses as equivalents).[13] His account takes the form of a 'transcendental deduction' of the concept of right from that of self-consciousness: that is, an argument to show that a being can only be self-conscious if it acts in accordance with right. The argument provides at once a philosophical account of right (a statement of what right essentially consists in) and a philosophical justification of it (an explanation of why right must exist in the world, of why it must be the case that people act in accord with it). The argument's main stages are as follows. I can be self-conscious only if I am conscious of myself as engaging in free but limited practical activity.[14] But this is possible only if I experience myself as being required to act freely by another being outside myself, which I must think of as a self-conscious being like myself.[15] So to be self-conscious I must think of myself as one self-conscious being amongst others.[16] In Fichte's terminology, I must think of myself as an *individual* (*Individuum*).[17] In turn this is possible only if I think of the other, and the other thinks of me, as free, where to think of another as free is not just to see the other as self-determining, but to think of that self-determination or freedom as to be respected in some way.[18] But I can think of the other as free and the other can think of me as free only if, respectively, the other *treats* me as free and I *treat* the other as free, where treating another as free is somehow respecting the other's freedom in one's overt actions, as an expression of thinking that this freedom is be respected. For Fichte, treating another as free specifically means restricting one's own actions so that one does not invade a sphere of activity thought of as belonging to the other.[19] In the first instance this sphere is the individual's own body, but later he extends it to a sphere of private property. Now right, according to Fichte, consists fundamentally in this relation of mutually thinking of each other as free, and treating each other as free, and in what necessarily follows from it,

---

[13] Fichte n.d. (hereafter GNR), trans. as Fichte 1869.
[14] GNR §1, pp. 17–23; Fichte 1869, pp. 31–40.
[15] GNR §3, pp. 30–9; Fichte 1869, pp. 48–60.
[16] GNR §3, pp. 39–40; Fichte 1869, pp. 60–2.
[17] GNR pp. 8, 42; Fichte 1869, pp. 17, 64.
[18] GNR §4, pp. 42–4; Fichte 1869, pp. 65–7.
[19] GNR §4, pp. 44–7; Fichte 1869, pp. 67–72.

namely private property and the other legal institutions that he goes on to derive in the *Grundlage des Naturrechts*.

Fichte describes both the act of thinking of another as free, and the act of treating another as free that expresses such thinking, as 'recognition' (*Anerkennung*).[20] I shall distinguish his two senses of the word by using 'cognitive recognition' for the first and 'practical recognition' for the second, reverting to 'recognition' alone when not differentiating between the two. It is important to notice that both cognitive and practical recognition involve the thought of the other's freedom as 'to be respected'. As a result they are both normative ideas.[21]

Using this terminology, we can then say that Fichte's account of right is that it consists fundamentally in the relation of mutual cognitive and practical recognition between self-conscious beings, and in the further kinds of thinking and action that follow from it. In fact he calls this relation of mutual recognition the 'relation of right':

> The deduced relation between rational beings – namely one in which each individual restricts its freedom through the concept of the possibility of the freedom of the other, under the condition that the other simultaneously restricts its own through that of the first, is called the relation of right [*Rechtsverhältnis*], and its formula, stated here, is the principle of right [*Rechtsatz*].[22]

He goes on immediately to summarise his whole argument:

> This relation has been deduced from the concept of the individual ... Furthermore the concept of the individual has been proved to be a condition of self-consciousness. Therefore the concept of right is itself a condition of self-consciousness. Hence this concept has been properly deduced a priori, that is, from the pure form of reason, from the I.[23]

An awkward result of Fichte's argument is that it seems to make it literally impossible for one self-conscious being to infringe the freedom of another. I shall not look into this or other difficulties with the argument. Instead I want to draw out two points from his account.

---

[20] At GNR §4, p. 44; Fichte 1869, p. 67 he describes thinking of the other as free as 'recognition'. At GNR p. 47; Fichte 1869, p. 71 he at first describes treating the other as free as 'commonly valid recognition', but then simply calls it 'recognition'.

[21] By contrast the ideas of recognising a banknote as Swiss, recognising a figure in the street as one's sister, or recognising the law of gravity imply no such respect and are not normative. In English, the normative content of the idea of recognition appears to depend on what the object of recognition is. In German, the term *Anerkennung* is standardly used only where some kind of respect is implied. See Inwood 1992, pp. 245–7.

[22] GNR §4, p. 52; Fichte 1869, pp. 78–9. Kroeger's translation here omits a major part of the sentence.

[23] GNR §4, pp. 52–3; Fichte 1869, p. 79. 'Condition' in this passage should be understood as 'necessary condition'.

The first is that Fichte's relation of right is an 'interactional relation', that is, one that consists in two (or more) individuals thinking of and acting towards each other in complementary ways over some period of time.[24] I shall argue below that Hegel's relations of recognition and Marx's relations of production are also interactional relations.

The second is that the argument for the relation of mutual cognitive and practical recognition implies that this relation is partially 'interconstitutive' of self-consciousness. That is, any self-conscious being is constituted as self-conscious only through engaging in this relation with others while these other self-conscious beings are in turn constituted as self-conscious only by engaging in the same relation, although of course there is more to being self-consciousness than just engaging in this relation.[25] It follows that self-consciousness is only possible as a feature of members of a group of mutually recognising beings. In so far as self-consciousness is an essential characteristic of being human, the same goes for humanity: humanity can only exist 'in the plural'. Fichte draws this conclusion explicitly:

> A human (like any finite being)[26] becomes a human only
> among humans; and since he cannot be anything else but a
> human and would not be at all unless he were this, *if humans*
> *are to be at all, there must be many of them*. This is not an
> arbitrary assumption, or an opinion based on past experience
> or on other reasons of probability. It is a truth to be proved
> strictly from the concept of a human. As soon as one
> determines this concept fully, one is driven from thinking a
> single [human] to the assumption of a second, in order to be
> able to explain the first. Hence the concept of human is not at
> all the concept of a single one, for such a one is unthinkable,
> but of a species [*Gattung*].[27]

It would not be far-fetched to say that in this passage Fichte anticipates Feuerbach's and the early Marx's accounts of humans as species-beings (*Gattungswesen*).[28]

---

[24] It is only with regard to interactional relations that one can talk about individuals 'engaging' in a relation, as I do frequently below, for this is the collective equivalent of a single individual engaging in a course of action. The term 'interactional relation' (or 'relation of interaction') is from Elster 1985, p. 95. There Elster defines such a relation more briefly than I do, as one in which 'two individuals actually interact with one another'.

[25] In more technical terms, to say that a relation is partially interconstitutive of self-consciousness is to say that engaging in this relation is constitutively necessary but not constitutively sufficient for being self-conscious. I say that Fichte's argument 'implies' that mutual recognition is such a constitutively necessary condition of self-consciousness, because all that strictly follows from the argument is that it is a necessary condition of some sort.

[26] The phrase in parentheses is omitted in Kroeger's translation. I am not able to explain it satisfactorily. Fichte 1869, p. 60.

[27] GNR §3 p. 39; Fichte 1869, pp. 60–1. Here and below I have, where possible, translated *Mensch* by the nouns 'human' or 'human being', rather than the traditional 'man', since *Mensch* has no particular association with the male gender.

[28] It should be mentioned that the passage I have quoted is inserted part of the way through the argument from self-consciousness to right, at the point where

2. Hegel's argument

In this section and the following I shall argue that Hegel, in the *Encyclopaedia, Philosophy of Mind* and the *Philosophy of Right*, takes up but also transforms Fichte's account of the connection between self-consciousness and right, and his conception of relations of mutual recognition as interconstitutive.

Hegel's dialectical derivation of right in the *Philosophy of Mind* provides both an account and a justification of right, just as Fichte's deduction of right does, and the pattern of the two arguments is very similar.[29] It is true that Hegel does not simply begin like Fichte with self-consciousness (which Hegel anyway divides into his two concepts of 'consciousness' and 'self-consciousness'), since this in turn is derived from soul, animal, plant and so on back through the *Encyclopaedia*. But in the movement from Hegel's 'consciousness' and 'self-consciousness' up to 'right' there are strong structural parallels, for each of the main stages of the argument corresponds to a stage in Fichte's. Thus Hegel's argument leads from 'consciousness' to 'self-consciousness', to 'desire' (corresponding to Fichte's 'free practical activity'), to 'particular or related self-consciousness' (corresponding to Fichte's 'individuality'), to 'mastery and servitude', to 'universal self-consciousness' (corresponding to Fichte's 'relation of right'), to 'intelligence', to 'will' and finally to 'right'.

However the detail of Hegel's argument is very different from that of Fichte's. For example there is no equivalent in Fichte's argument to the master–servant relation. Furthermore, there is a fundamental difference in the form of the argument. Whereas Fichte's argument is transcendental, and proceeds from self-consciousness by successively uncovering the necessary conditions for its existence, Hegel's argument is dialectical and phenomenological, by which I mean that it works in the following way. It understands consciousness, self-consciousness, and so on as distinct 'forms of subjectivity' (my own term), that is, as distinct basic ways in which a subject conceives itself and the main elements of its world and which constitute it as one kind of subject or another. For each of these, the argument shows how a contradiction internal to each form of subjectivity forces the subject to conceive itself

---

Fichte has reached the conclusion that self-consciousness is only possible if one experiences oneself as required to be free by (what one thinks of as) another self-consciousness. So at this point the relation that has been shown to be necessary for self-consciousness is only the relation of one self-consciousness being required to be free by another. However Fichte goes on to argue that this relation in turn requires a relation of mutual recognition, so it follows that this relation will also be necessary for self-consciousness, and so for humanity.

[29] The derivation is in Hegel 1986b (hereafter E3), §§418–86, pp. 205–305; Hegel 1971, pp. 158–243. It is greatly clarified in lectures that Hegel gave in 1825 on §§413–439 of the *Philosophy of Mind*. Students' notes from the lectures are published in German and English as an appendix to Hegel 1979, Vol. 3. This section of the *Philosophy of Mind* is republished, with the 1825 lecture notes appended to the relevant paragraphs of the text, as Hegel 1981.

and the elements of its world in a new way, that is, to transform its form of subjectivity into a new one.

Thus the argument begins by defining 'consciousness' as that elementary form of subjectivity in which the subject conceives of itself merely in contradistinction to independent objects outside it. The argument then shows how a contradiction internal to consciousness forces the conscious subject to transform its form of subjectivity into 'self-consciousness', in which the subject conceives itself not just as counterposed to objects outside it, but also *as* an object, and conversely conceives other objects as somehow imbued with subjectivity. In turn self-consciousness as a form of subjectivity suffers from an analogous contradiction, so that the subject is forced to change its form of subjectivity again, to 'particular self-consciousness'. This is a collective form of subjectivity consisting in each of two subjects attributing self-consciousness both to itself and to the other. In turn particular self-consciousness has to give way to the next form of subjectivity, and so on.

The argument is 'dialectical' in that it proceeds by uncovering and resolving contradictions, but also 'phenomenological' in that it re-enacts the process through which a conscious subject is forced to successively reconstitute itself in the light of its discovery of these contradictions.[30] This means that Hegel can avoid the difficulty that I mentioned with Fichte's account of right. For Hegel, right is not a necessary condition of consciousness. His argument is rather only that a conscious subject, in so far as it successively becomes aware of and resolves the contradictions inherent in its forms of subjectivity, must eventually be driven to establish with others the form of subjectivity called right. For Hegel, that faculty in me that makes me become aware of contradictions and try to resolve them is my rationality, so if I as a conscious being fail to establish relations of right with others, this is a failure of rationality on my part, but such a failure of rationality does not mean that I am not conscious.

3. From particular to universal self-consciousness

To understand Hegel's account of right, it will be necessary to trace the part of his argument that runs from 'particular self-consciousness' through to 'right' itself.[31] In particular (or related) self-consciousness each of two subjects sees both itself and the other as an object which is

---

[30] It cannot be denied that some of Hegel's statements in the *Philosophy of Mind* suggest a transcendental interpretation of his dialectical argument. My view is that only a phenomenological interpretation makes sense of this section of the *Philosophy of Mind* as a whole. The phenomenological interpretation is inspired by Hegel's account of dialectical derivation in the Introduction to his *Phenomenology of Spirit* (Hegel 1977).
[31] What follows is a condensed and revised version of my reconstruction of this section of Hegel's argument, in Chitty 1996, pp. 190–203. My understanding of Hegel's usage of 'recognition', in particular, differs in the present version.

self-conscious and so free, so that each conceives the other as 'another I'.[32] The subject, says Hegel, 'counterposes itself as a *distinct I* to itself'.[33] As a result, in confronting this other 'I see in it, as an I, me myself, but also an immediately existing other object as an absolute I opposite me'.[34]

This form of subjectivity is contradictory, for on the one hand the first subject conceives the second as a self-related (because self-conscious) physical entity outside it, and yet on the other hand it sees the other not just as 'another being just like me', but as quite literally itself, as 'I'.[35] It sees at the same time two distinct subjects and a single subject: at once difference and identity.

According to Hegel, this contradiction can only be overcome, for each subject, through that subject displaying itself as free to the other, and being recognised by the other as free:

> This contradiction gives the drive to *show* oneself as a free
> self and to exist [*da zu sein*] as such for the other – the
> process of *recognition* [*Anerkennung*].[36]

Since it was part of the definition of particular self-consciousness that each subject sees the other as free, Hegel must be distinguishing recognition from simply seeing the other as free. Presumably, like Fichte, he conceives recognition, whether cognitive or practical, as involving a conception of the freedom of the other as to be respected.[37] His argument then appears to be as follows. If the other cognitively recognises me as free then it in some way identifies with me as a decision-maker, for in thinking of my freedom as to be respected it conceives my decisions as somehow to be deferred to, and therefore as partly authoritative over its actions – in just the same way as I think of my decisions as authoritative over my own actions. Hegel expresses this identification by saying that when I am recognised by another then I have given myself an existence (*Dasein*) in the 'ground' or 'soil' (*Boden*) of the other's consciousness.[38] When the other expresses this cognitive recognition practically, the practical recognition will provide me with

---

[32] Hegel calls this form of subjectivity 'particular' self-consciousness at E3 §430, p. 219; Hegel 1971, p. 170. For Hegel 'particular' means 'one amongst others of the same kind', so it has a similar sense to Fichte's 'individual'. Hegel also says that at this stage there are two selves 'relating to each other' (*sich aufeinander beziehenden*) at E3 §430Z, p. 219; Hegel 1971, p. 171, so 'related self-consciousness' is an alternative way to describe it.

[33] E3 §429Z, p. 219; Hegel 1971, p. 170.

[34] E3 §430, p. 219; Hegel 1971, p. 170.

[35] It sees the other as not just qualitatively but numerically identical to itself. Hegel thinks that the primordial experience of another self-conscious entity must take this form, perhaps on the grounds that one can only ever think of another self-conscious entity on the model of oneself, and therefore through initially construing it *as* oneself.

[36] E3 §430, p. 219; Hegel 1971, p. 170.

[37] His difference from Fichte would then be that Fichte fails to make the distinction between simply seeing the other as free and thinking of that freedom as to be respected.

[38] Hegel 1979, Vol. 3, p. 333. Cf. 335. *Boden* is translated there as 'basis'.

the proof of the cognitive recognition behind it. Only then will I be able to reconcile my sense that the other is both distinct from and identical to myself, for I will then be able to conceive the other as distinct from me in that it is a self-conscious physical being outside me, yet as identical to me in that it shows through its actions that it somehow *conceives* itself as identical with me as a decision-maker. So in order to resolve the contradiction of particular self-consciousness I must be cognitively and practically recognised as free by the other.[39]

Of course this is a demand that each of the subjects must make of the other. But these two demands are incompatible, because Hegel claims that at the stage of particular self-consciousness subjects have an individualistic conception of freedom. That is, in their eyes to be free means to be, as an individual, a completely self-originating source of decisions and actions. They do not yet have a sense of freedom as a single autonomous decision-making activity shared by a plurality of self-conscious beings. From this individualistic point of view, for me to recognise the other as free (to respect the other as free in my thinking and action) means for me to take the other's arbitrary individual decisions as partly authoritative over my own actions, and to act accordingly. But to do this would be to partly lose my own freedom, again in the individualistic sense of the complete self-origination of my own decisions and actions. In fact it would be to lose my freedom completely, for Hegel assumes that freedom is an all or nothing affair, in the sense that to be unfree in any of one's actions is to be completely unfree. It follows that I cannot recognise the other as at all free without becoming completely unfree in my own eyes. Therefore while I must demand that the other (cognitively and practically) recognise me as free, I must refuse to recognise the other as free at all. Furthermore, I must demand that the other become completely unfree in its own eyes in order that it be able to recognise me, and thus that it take my decisions as not just partly but absolutely authoritative over its actions. I must demand a recognition that has an 'absolute' or 'self-surrendering' character: one in which the other identifies not just 'in some way' but absolutely with me as decision-maker, seeing itself as nothing but an agent of my decision-making. By the same reasoning, the other must demand the same absolute recognition from me.[40]

The result is the well-known 'struggle for recognition' and its resolution one way or the other in a master–servant relation. This relation can best be described by introducing the term 'assertion' to mean the same thing as 'recognition', but referred to oneself rather than to another, so that is, to assert oneself cognitively as free is to see oneself as free and to think of that freedom as to be respected, and to assert oneself practically as free is to act accordingly. The master–

---

[39] Hegel's construal of 'recognition as free' as involving not just a sense of how one should act towards the other, but also an identification with the other, is crucial to the transition that he makes here from ontology to ethics.
[40] The argument summarised in this paragraph is given at Hegel 1979, Vol. 3, pp. 333–7.

servant relation is then an interactional relation consisting in one-sided recognition combined with one-sided assertion. In it, both cognitively and practically, one subject (the servant) recognises a second as free and does not assert itself as free, while the second subject (the master) asserts itself as free and does not recognise the first as free. The relation is 'fully interconstitutive' of mastery and servitude, in that simply by engaging in it they constitute themselves respectively as servant and master: being a master or servant consists in nothing but engaging in this relation.[41] As a result of the all-or-nothing character of freedom, the recognition and the assertion in question are absolute. So the servant's cognitive recognition and the master's cognitive assertion both take the form of taking the master's arbitrary decisions to be absolutely authoritative over the servant's actions. The servant's practical recognition then takes the form of obeying the master unconditionally, while the master's practical assertion takes the form of giving the servant orders at will.

Because of the dual cognitive and practical character of Hegel's recognition and its correlative assertion, mastery and servitude is a form of subjectivity that is not only collective but also *practical*, for it consists in two subjects not only conceiving but also acting towards each other (and other elements of their world) in a certain way. But this form of subjectivity in turn fails to resolve the contradiction of particular self-consciousness, even for the master who has won the struggle for recognition. The master aimed to resolve the contradiction through the servant somehow identifying itself with the master as a decision-maker, since in so doing the servant would become, in a sense, identical with but at the same time distinct from the master. In fact the all-or-nothing character of freedom forced the master to demand more from the servant: an absolute identification with the master as decision-maker. The servant's unconditional obedience would give the master the assurance that this identification had taken place. But in the process of bringing about this identification, the servant has surrendered its authority over its own decisions and the master has not. This means that the master now sees in the servant a being of a quite different kind itself. Thus the servant's recognition of the master fails after all to enable the master to think of the servant as identical to itself.[42]

The master–servant relation cannot solve the contradiction of particular self-consciousness because of its asymmetry. It must therefore give way to an interactional relation consisting in *mutual* recognition and assertion, in which each of two (or more) self-conscious subjects cognitively and practically recognises the other, and asserts itself, as free. In such a relation each 'knows itself recognised in

---

[41] Engaging in the relation is constitutively sufficient as well as constitutively necessary for being a master or a servant (see note 25 above). Obviously Hegel is giving his own special meanings to 'master' and 'servant' here.
[42] The explanation of the failure of the master-servant relation given in this paragraph is based on hints given by Hegel at E3 §433Z, p. 223; Hegel 1971, p. 174, and at E3 §436Z, p. 226; Hegel 1971, p. 176.

the free other, and knows this, in so far as it recognises the other and knows it as free'.[43]

This relation forms a new collective and practical form of subjectivity, which Hegel names 'universal self-consciousness'. The relation is fully interconstitutive of universal self-consciousness, in that by engaging in it individuals constitute each other as universally self-conscious beings. It is made possible by their giving up the individualistic conception of freedom mentioned above, one in which freedom consists in the individual's self-origination of its own actions. Instead freedom is now thought of as something like 'acting *with* others', or the collective self-origination of action. Here to be free is to be the representative and agent of a single decision-making activity, one which is no longer identified with the arbitrary decisions of any one individual, as in the case of the master–servant relation, but which is universal or common to all. This single free decision-making activity is something like Rousseau's general will, although Hegel reserves the actual term 'will' for its successor, discussed below.[44] Given such a conception of freedom, each can recognise the other as free, in the 'absolute' sense of recognition described above, without ceasing to think of itself as free.[45] In recognising the other as free, and being recognised as free by the other, each identifies with the other as decision-maker, and knows that the other identifies similarly with it, and since the decision-making in question is a free decision-making that is common to all of them this does not lead to the division of statuses that characterised the master–servant relation. In recognising each other as free, they do not simply think of each other as having the same property of being free, any more than in particular self-consciousness they simply thought of themselves as sharing the common property of being self-conscious. Rather they think of themselves as representatives of a single 'freedom': a single free decision-making activity. Thereby they experience themselves as identical, as literally a single I:

> the self-conscious subjects related to each other have through
> the supersession of their *dissimilar particular singularity* risen
> to the consciousness of their *real universality*, of their *freedom*
> which belongs to *all*, and thereby to the intuition of their
> *determinate identity with each other*.[46]

---

[43] E3 §436, p. 226; Hegel 1971, p. 176.

[44] In Hegel's German 'universal self-consciousness' (*das allgemeine Selbstbewußtsein*) and 'the general will' (*der allgemeine Wille*) have a verbal similarity. For the latter, see for example Hegel's discussion of Rousseau in Hegel 1986c (hereafter PR), §258R, p. 400; Hegel 1991, p. 277.

[45] For Hegel recognition continues to have an 'absolute' or 'self-surrendering' character even when it becomes mutual, apparently because freedom is still thought of as an all-or-nothing possession even when it is no longer conceived in an individualistic way. The absolute character of his recognition is what enables Hegel to synthesise ideas from Fichte and Rousseau in his idea of universal self-consciousness.

[46] E3 §436Z, p. 226; Hegel 1971, p. 176.

Yet while as representatives of a single 'freedom' they experience themselves as a single 'I', still as separate self-conscious physical entities they continue to experience themselves as distinct 'I's (thus as a 'we'). Just as in particular self-consciousness, they simultaneously experience themselves as identical and different, a double experience captured in the phrase 'universal self-consciousness', but this identity now takes a form in which it no longer contradicts their difference. Universal self-consciousness therefore finally resolves the contradiction of particular self-consciousness.

The 'universal reflecting'[47] of mutual recognition and assertion in universal self-consciousness not only involves individuals thinking of and treating each other as possessing a common freedom. It also, Hegel implies, constitutes them as actual possessors of such a freedom. Likewise it not only produces a sense on the part of the individuals that engage in it of themselves as a single I. It also actually constitutes them as a members of a common 'substance',[48] a substance that is at once unitary and plural because it is constituted by nothing but the relations of mutual assertion and recognition between its own members. This substance is the immediate precursor of Hegel's mature concept of 'spirit', the common freedom its members possess, which we could now call 'substantial freedom', immediately anticipates the freedom that for him is the essential property of spirit.[49]

4. From spirit to right

In universal self-consciousness a plurality of individuals see themselves as representatives of a single 'freedom' and thus as identical to each other. So one individual confronting another conceives itself as at root identical to an object outside itself. According to Hegel such individuals will generalise this attitude to the object from the special case where the object is another self-conscious being to the general case of the objective world as such. The resulting perception of oneself as at root identical with the objective world outside one is what Hegel calls 'reason', and insofar as a community of individuals possess it they become 'spirit' (or 'mind').[50] In that they see themselves as everywhere

---

[47] E3 §436, p. 226; Hegel 1971, p. 176.
[48] E3 §436, p. 226; Hegel 1971, p. 176.
[49] In the *Phenomenology of Spirit* (1807) Hegel describes spirit as 'this absolute substance, which, in the complete freedom and independence of its opposites, namely distinct self-consciousnesses which are for themselves, is their unity: *I* that is *we* and *we* that is *I*'. Hegel 1986d, p. 145; Hegel 1977, p.110. By the time of the *Philosophy of Mind* his concept of spirit has altered slightly, but this definition perfectly fits its precursor, universal self-consciousness.
[50] E3 §§437–9, pp. 227–9; Hegel 1971, pp. 177–8. 'Spirit' and 'mind' are alternative translations for the German *Geist*. The 'intersubjective' conception of spirit argued for here is clearest in the *Phenomenology of Spirit* and the Jena lectures which preceded it. In the *Philosophy of Mind*, the *Philosophy of Right* and the introduction to the *Philosophy of History* Hegel often speaks of spirit as if it was a universal substance or I that is ontologically prior to (although revealed

related only to that which is at root identical to them, they see themselves as self-determining or free with regard not only to each other but also the objective world, and thereby according to Hegel for the first time they become properly free.[51] So at this point the substantial freedom constituted by mutual recognition and assertion becomes true freedom, the freedom of which Hegel can say that 'freedom is the one authentic property of spirit'.[52]

Yet spirit in turn suffers from a contradiction. On the one hand, 'it is confident that in the world it will find its own self'.[53] Yet on the other, the objective world still appears as physically other to and distinct from it. Although Hegel does not spell it out, more specifically the contradiction seems to be that the universal freedom constituted by the general relation of mutual recognition and assertion lacks any determinacy, since to speak simply of 'mutual recognition and assertion as free' is not yet to say anything about what determinate kinds of thinking and action this involves, whereas by contrast the objective world is an extensively determinate one.

In order to overcome this contradiction individuals are driven to make the identity between themselves and the world explicit by progressively 'evaporating' the determinate detail of the objective world, and discovering a universality inherent in it which will be identical to the universality of their own freedom. This universality is that of the regularities of nature. Hegel calls the effort to discover it 'intelligence', or 'theoretical spirit'. Yet even when successful, this effort to discover universality in nature does not overcome the tension between the indeterminacy of universal freedom and the determinacy of the objective world. So individuals are in turn driven to overcome the difference by progressively realising that freedom in that world, by giving it a determinate objective existence there. Hegel calls this effort 'will', or 'practical spirit', and the freedom that they attempt to realise the 'free substantial will', the free will of their substance.[54]

Accordingly objectifying freedom, giving it a determinate existence (*Dasein*), will consist in elaborating *specific* relations of mutual recognition and assertion which will give a determinate content to the bare idea of 'mutual recognition and assertion as free'.[55] These

---

by) mutual recognition, rather than one which is constituted by it. Some writers have concluded that by this time he had abandoned an intersubjective conception of spirit. See Habermas 1973. I take the opposite view, defended most recently in Williams 1998; especially pp. 13–16.
[51] E3 §440Z, p. 230; Hegel 1971, pp. 179–180. See also Hegel 1979, Vol. 3, p. 357: 'In self-consciousness we saw the beginning of freedom, but spirit is concretely free.'
[52] Hegel 1975, p. 48. See also pp. 54–55 *passim*.
[53] E3 §440Z, p. 230; Hegel 1971, p. 179.
[54] E3 §486, p. 304; Hegel 1971, p. 242.
[55] In this context I think it is significant that *Philosophy of Right* Hegel says that *Dasein*, existence, is 'essentially being for another'. PR §71, p. 152; Hegel 1991, p. 102. See also E3 §431Z, p. 220; Hegel 1971, p. 171 and the sections on *Dasein* – there translated as 'determinate being' or 'being there' – in Hegel's two Logics. The specific way in which freedom 'is for another' is by one individual's freedom being practically recognised by another.

interactional relations will take the form of shared practices and social institutions, sustaining which will then be the means whereby individuals objectify and so realise their own freedom. In the *Philosophy of Right* Hegel successively derives the various practices and institutions that he thinks can objectify this freedom, through the same process of discovering and overcoming contradictions that has led him up to this point. Their totality, the objectification of freedom or the free will as a whole, is what he calls 'objective spirit' or 'right':

> [T]he *existence* [*Dasein*] of the free will is *right*, which is to be taken comprehensively, not just as limited juristic right, but as the existence of *all* the determinations of freedom.[56]

Or as he puts it in the *Philosophy of Right*:

> The system of right is the realm of actualised freedom, the world of spirit brought forth from itself, as a second nature.[57]

We can therefore summarise Hegel's account of right as follows: right consists in that set of specific relations of (cognitive and practical) recognition and assertion which is required in order to resolve the contradiction of spirit, by giving a determinate content to the bare idea of 'mutual recognition and assertion as free' and thereby giving an objectivity to the substantial freedom that individuals constitute through such recognition and assertion.

We can call each of these specific relations a 'form of right'. Their most general principle is that of asserting one's own freedom, and recognising that of others, in all its aspects. So whenever one individual claims a particular kind of right and another respects it, at root the first is simply asserting, and the second simply recognising, a particular aspect (or 'determination') of their substantial freedom.[58] Thus in the case of the first form of right, which Hegel calls 'abstract right', the principle of right is *'be a person and respect others as persons'*.[59] Being a person turns out to mean claiming property rights over some piece of nature, while respecting others as persons means respecting the corresponding claims of others, specifically through contract. In turn, this claiming and respecting is the way in which individuals respectively assert and recognise, and thereby objectify, the most elementary or 'immediate'[60] aspect of their freedom.

Similarly each of the further forms and sub-forms of right described in the *Philosophy of Right* – morality, the family, civil society and so on – should be understood as consisting essentially in a specific relation of

---

[56] E3, §486; Hegel 1971, p. 242. See also PR §29, p. 80; Hegel 1991, p. 58.
[57] PR §4, p. 46; Hegel 1991, p. 35.
[58] The polarity of master (pure asserter) and servant (pure recogniser) is in a certain way preserved within the microstructure of the system of right, as the correlation between every right and its associated duties.
[59] PR §36, p. 95; Hegel 1991, p. 69.
[60] PR §40, p. 98; Hegel 1991, p. 70.

mutual recognition and assertion as free between individuals, which is required according to Hegel in order to objectify a specific aspect of their substantial freedom. Together, he claims, they objectify that freedom as a whole.[61]

We said that for Fichte right essentially consists in a relation of mutual cognitive and practical recognition as free. If what I have said so far is correct, then Hegel's analysis of right is similar. The difference is that for him right consists in a relation of assertion as well as recognition, and in fact in a series of such relations. Furthermore, in Hegel these specific relations are the means of objectifying a substantial freedom which is constituted by 'mutual recognition and assertion as free' as such.

Despite these differences, Hegel's specific relations of recognition and assertion are, like Fichte's relation of recognition, interconstitutive. Each relation of recognition and assertion is a collective and practical form of subjectivity, consisting in a number of different subjects both conceiving and acting towards each other in a certain way, and thereby constituting each other as a certain kind of subject: as a person, a moral subject, a family member, a bourgeois (a member of civil society), a citizen and so on. So the relations are fully interconstitutive of personhood, moral subjectivity and the rest:

> In right [that is, abstract right – AC] the object is the person,
> in the moral standpoint the subject [that is, moral subject –
> AC], in the family the family-member, in civil society in
> general the burgher (as bourgeois).[62]

At the same time personhood, moral subjectivity and the rest are only single aspects of objective freedom, so the totality of the specific relations of recognition and assertion is fully interconstitutive of objective freedom as a whole, just as Fichte's relation of recognition is (partially) interconstitutive of self-consciousness. Individuals constitute each other as objectively free by engaging in the totality of the relations of recognition and assertion that make up right.

However, where Hegel goes decisively beyond Fichte is in historicising his account of right. In the *Philosophy of Mind* and the *Philosophy of Right* he derives, from the idea of substantial freedom as such, a set of basic forms of right, an 'outline of natural right' as he calls it in the subtitle of the latter book. This turns out to approximate to a description of the actual social and political institutions of post-French-revolutionary Europe. But in the *Philosophy of History* he attempts to

---

[61] The claim that the specific set of practices and institutions described in the *Philosophy of Right* could be the objectification of freedom (as Hegel conceived it) is of course controversial. It was almost immediately disputed by the Young Hegelians. Two accounts of the *Philosophy of Right* that focus on the role of mutual recognition within it are Theunissen 1991 and Williams 1998, Part 2. Neither of them supplements recognition with assertion in the way that I have done here.

[62] PR §190, p. 348; Hegel 1991, p. 228.

describe historical sets of social and political institutions as earlier, less adequate, attempts to objectify spirit and the substantial freedom that is essential to it. Thus there were earlier forms of property, morality, the family, civil society and the political state. So we can speak not only of the system of 'natural' or 'true' forms of right described in the *Philosophy of Right* but also of an ancient Oriental set of forms of right, making up what Hegel calls the 'Oriental state' or the 'Oriental world', and similarly for the ancient Greek world, the Roman world and the 'German' (ie. medieval and modern Christian) world.[63]

Each of these historical systems of right, on the interpretation proposed here, consists in a system of interactional relations: relations of mutual recognition and assertion. Each system is organised around some aspect of freedom and of spirit that it realises best, the 'spirit of a people' (*Volksgeist*) that animates the system, and accordingly in each of them one particular form of right dominates and colours the rest. Oriental right is dominated by the family, Roman right by property, and so on. Although they are all inherently restrictive in some way and so do not realise substantial freedom in full, they all realise it in part. Even the first and most despotic system of right, the Oriental world, where only the emperor is thought of as properly free, is still in some way a system of *right*: a partial realisation of spirit. So the emperor is free as the unique embodiment of the substantial freedom constituted by a system of mutual assertion and recognition. By contrast in the master–servant relation, which in its pure form can only have existed in a pre-historical period prior to the foundation of states there is recognition and assertion but no such system of mutuality, and the master has no genuine freedom. Furthermore, we can think of each of the historical relations of mutual recognition and assertion as interconstitutive of the identities of the individuals that engage in it, just as those of the *Philosophy of Right* are. Emperor and subject, citizen and slave, are constituted as such by the relations of mutual recognition and assertion between them and the rest of their society.[64]

In short, the *Philosophy of Right* provides the key to Hegel's philosophy of history. The different historical 'worlds' described in the latter are systems of right which are partial realisations of substantial freedom. Because each is only a partial realisation, it is eventually felt by the people that sustains it as restrictive, and has to give way to a system

---

[63] Here there is a nice fit between Hegel's theory and the ambiguity between natural and positive senses of the German *Recht*. It should be noted that Hegel often uses 'state' and 'world' in narrower or broader senses than the ones I attribute to him here.

[64] It is true that in the theoretical introduction to the *Philosophy of History* Hegel speaks of history as a succession of national spirits and states, but not of systems of mutual recognition. He also says that it is only in the 'German world' that all members of society finally come to think of themselves as free. See Hegel 1975, pp. 51–6, 129–31 (on national spirits and the emergence of the consciousness of freedom) and pp. 93–7, 131–8 (on states, history and pre-history). My claim is that nevertheless the systematic derivation of spirit in the *Philosophy of Mind* forces us to understand every national spirit as constituted through a system of mutual recognition of some kind.

which realises freedom more adequately. The resulting succession ends only with the emergence of a system of right that fully embodies substantial freedom, and this is the system set out, according to Hegel, in the *Philosophy of Right*. So that system is in effect the ideal towards which the successive historical systems of right move. The movement is a teleological one, even though none of the actors in history has a conception in advance of the final point towards which they are all moving.

5. Humanity and social relations of production

In Hegel's mature system, and even more so in his *Phenomenology of Spirit*, relations of recognition and assertion are often bound up with 'economic' relations: interactional relations of producing, transferring and acquiring goods capable of satisfying human needs. Specifically, Hegel frequently portrays an economic relation as the form that a relation of practical recognition and assertion takes. To take two examples: the master–servant relation is a relation of recognition and assertion whose practical aspect takes the form of the servant not just obeying but *working* for the master, producing material goods to satisfy the master's desires; and abstract right is a mutual relation of recognition and assertion of individuals as persons whose practical aspect takes the form of individuals possessing, working on and contracting to sell material goods to each other. In this and the next sections I outline how we can see Marx as 'inverting' Hegel by giving such economic relations, under the heading of 'social relations of production', the central place in his account of history that Hegel gives to relations of recognition and assertion, while relegating relations of cognitive and practical recognition to a closely related but derivative position.

I begin by looking at Marx's early concept of 'humanity' and the social ideal associated with it, for it is in articulating his idea of the human that he first uses the term 'social relation'. In his 1844 writings Marx conceives humans in their essence as 'species-beings', that is, beings who are constituted as the kind of being that they are by virtue of creating products to satisfy the needs of, and satisfying their own needs with the products of, other beings of the same kind.[65] The activity of creating, exchanging and enjoying such products (with the emphasis on the first two) is therefore fully interconstitutive of the human essence. In the *Notes on James Mill* Marx calls this activity as a whole 'species activity':

---

[65] For this account of species-being, see Chitty 1993, and especially Chitty 1997. In what follows I do not mention the important role of Feuerbach as a stepping stone between Hegel and Marx. Feuerbach's and Marx's conceptions of species-being are contrasted in Arthur 1986, pp. 118–20.

The *exchange*, both of human activity within production itself and also of *human products* with each other, equals *species-activity* and species-spirit, whose actual, conscious and true existence [*Dasein*] is *social* activity and *social* enjoyment.[66]

Elsewhere Marx describes this collective activity as 'the social relation' (*das gesellschaftliche Verhältnis*).[67] In *The Holy Family*, speaking of the product, he and Engels say that:

> the object, as being for man, as the objective being of man, is at the same time the existence [*Dasein*] of man for the other man, his human relation [*Beziehung*] to the other man, the social relating [*das gesellschaftliche Verhalten*] of man to man.[68]

The close association between 'relation', 'activity' and 'relating' in these passages make it clear that the social relation Marx has in mind is an interactional one.[69] Through engaging in it individuals constitute each other as possessors of the human essence, so that the terms 'social' and 'human' are effectively equivalent, and in passages from this period Marx often treats them as such.[70]

However, in a society of private property, this activity or relation has an 'alienated' form, and so is not a *genuinely* social relation and does not constitute individuals as properly human.[71] In a well-known passage at the end of the *Notes on James Mill*, Marx describes the ideal form of this activity, the form in which it would be properly social (would be what he calls in this period 'socialism'), and would properly constitute its participants as human. If we had produced as humans, he says:

> ... (2) In your enjoyment or use of my product I would have
> the *direct* enjoyment, both of being conscious of having

---

[66] Marx and Engels 1971 (hereafter MEW Erg.1), pp. 450–1; CW, Vol. 3, pp. 216–17. By 'exchange' (*Austausch*), Marx here means the interchange of human products and activities in general, rather than specifically the conditional exchange of privately owned products in the market.

[67] For example in MEW Erg.1, p. 453; CW, Vol. 3, pp. 218–9.

[68] MEW, Vol. 2, p. 44; CW, Vol. 4, p. 43. The extensive italicisation in the original is omitted. In quotations in this article I have translated *Beziehung* as 'relation' or 'connection', adding the German in brackets. Marx sometimes contrasts *Beziehung* to *Verhältnis* to emphasise the associations of the latter with property, for example in *The German Ideology* (1845–46), MEW, Vol. 3, p. 213; CW, Vol. 5, p. 231. But often he simply uses *Beziehung* as an equivalent for *Verhältnis*, as here and in the quotation in note 71 below. 'Man' translates *Mensch* (see note 27 above).

[69] *Verhalten* (relating) can also be translated as 'conduct' or 'behaviour'. The translation 'relating' brings out its close connection with *Verhältnis* for Marx, exemplified further below.

[70] For example in the *Notes on James Mill* at MEW Erg.1, p. 446; CW, Vol. 3, p. 212, and in the *Economic and Philosophical Manuscripts* (1844) at MEW Erg.1, pp. 536f; CW, Vol. 3, pp. 296f. See also the tenth of the *Theses on Feuerbach* (1845) at MEW, Vol. 3, p. 7; CW, Vol. 5, p. 5.

[71] See MEW Erg.1, p. 453; CW, Vol. 3, pp. 218–9, where 'The *social* connection [*Beziehung*] or *social* relation between two property owners' is described as 'the relation of alienation on both sides', as 'the *alienated* species-act', and therefore as 'the opposite of the *social* relation'.

satisfied a *human* need in my work, and thus having
objectified *human* nature, and of having thereby created an
object corresponding to the need of another *human* essence.
(3) I would have been for you the *mediator* between you and
the species, and would therefore have been known and felt by
you yourself as a completion of your own essence, and as a
necessary part of yourself ...[72]

What distinguishes such genuinely social production and enjoyment
from this activity as it has existed until now is that it is uncoerced. In it,
individuals do not produce and consume in ways that are somehow
imposed on them from outside, but instead in ways that freely express
their own needs for activity and enjoyment, needs which are ultimately
expressions of their own urge to realise themselves as fully human
beings. Such uncoerced mutual production and enjoyment, I suggest, is
Marx's 'materialist' version of the relation of mutual recognition and
assertion as free that underlies the *Philosophy of Right*.[73] Just as for
Hegel individuals objectify freedom, and constitute each other as
objectively free, by mutually asserting themselves to each other and
recognising each other as free, so for Marx individuals realise humanity,
and constitute each other as fully human beings, by mutually enjoying
each other's products and producing for each other's needs.[74]

Furthermore, just as Hegel understood historical systems of right as
inadequate attempts to do what the system of right in the *Philosophy of
Right* does, namely objectify freedom in all its determinations, so in the
same way Marx could now understand historical systems of production
as inadequate attempts to do what the production described in the
passage from the *Notes on James Mill* finally does, namely genuinely
realise humanity. Thinking in this vein, we could suggest that Marx's
idea of 'social relations', 'relations of production' or 'social relations of
production', as formulated in *The German Ideology* and *The Poverty of
Philosophy*, is conceived as just such an historical precursor to the
genuinely social form of mutual production and enjoyment described in
the *Notes on James Mill*, making it analogous to the idea of a set of
historical relations of recognition and assertion that I have attributed to
Hegel.[75] Just as Hegel's historical relations of recognition and assertion

---

[72] MEW Erg.1, p. 462; CW, Vol. 3, pp. 227–8.
[73] It is 'materialist' in that it is based on production, and the early Marx tends to
assume that production is the production of material objects, although in fact we
also produce, say, symphonies, football matches or scientific discoveries, and
enjoy those produced by others.
[74] Hegel had already seen production for each other's needs as constituting
individuals as human beings in the *Philosophy of Right*, saying that in the sub-
form of right called the 'system of needs', the object is not the person or the
family-member but 'the concretum of representation that one calls the *human
being*'. PR §190, p. 348; Hegel 1991, p. 228. However by 'the system of needs'
Hegel means the modern market economy based on private property, rather than
the system of free production and enjoyment of the *Notes on James Mill*. Also,
for Hegel being human is a relatively minor aspect of being objectively free.
[75] Marx's terminology is not settled at this stage. In *The German Ideology* he and
Engels use the terms 'relations of production', 'social relations', 'form of
intercourse' and 'relations of production and intercourse' as well as various

consist in more or less adequate approximations to relations of genuine mutual recognition and assertion, so Marx's social relations of production would consist in more or less adequate approximations to the uncoerced relations of producing-for and using-the-product-of sketched in the *Notes on James Mill*. Such relations would be interactional and interconstitutive of humanity, but by engaging in different social relations of production individuals would constitute each other as human in more or less adequate ways. Only by engaging in the genuinely social relations of uncoerced mutual production would they constitute each other as properly human.

However there is an immediate problem with this way of seeing Marx's concept of social relations of production. For in *The German Ideology*, which develops the theory of history in which the concept plays a central part, he and Engels appear to reject the ideal of a realised humanity which had informed the 1844 writings. There they see the idea of 'the human' or 'the human essence' as itself nothing but a philosophical expression of prevailing social relations:

> The conditions, independent of them, within which [people] produced their life, the necessary forms of intercourse connected therewith, the personal and social relations given therewith, had to take the form – insofar as they were expressed in thoughts – of ideal conditions and necessary relations, i.e. they had to gain their expression in consciousness as determinations arising from the concept *of* man, from the human essence, from the nature of man, from man *as such*. What men were, what their relations were, appeared in consciousness as ideas of man *as such*, of his modes of existence or of the immediate determinations of his concept.[76]

More succinctly, '[t]he positive expression 'human' corresponds to the determinate *dominant* relations appropriate to a certain stage of production and to the way of satisfying needs determined by them'.[77]

Accordingly, Marx and Engels no longer describe their social ideal (now called communism) in terms of the realisation of humanity. Instead they describe it simply in terms of democracy and particularism: as a society in which individuals collectively take control of the social

---

others. These suggest a distinction between relations associated with producing goods and relations associated with transferring them. In *The Poverty of Philosophy* (1846–47) Marx settles on the unified terminology of 'social relations of production' (eg. at CW, Vol. 6, pp. 165, 183), with 'economic relations', 'social relations' and 'relations of production' as alternative terms (eg. at respectively CW, Vol. 6, p. 145, 159, 160). This usage remains more or less stable thereafter.

[76] MEW, Vol. 3, p. 167; CW, Vol. 5, pp. 183–4. Here 'man' translates *Mensch* (see note 27 above).

[77] MEW, Vol. 3, pp. 417–8; CW, Vol. 5, p. 432. Marx's statement on 'the human essence' in the *Theses on Feuerbach*, that 'in its actuality it is the ensemble of social relations', can be read as making the same point, although it could also be construed as expressing the ideal of realised humanity described above. MEW, Vol. 3, p. 6; CW, Vol. 5, p. 7.

process of production, and in which their individual production, and enjoyment of each other's products, expresses their own individual particularity rather than being imposed on them by that social process.

It is true that the content of this ideal remains very close to that of the *Notes on James Mill*, and it may be that it remains covertly informed by the ideal of a realised humanity of the 1844 writings.[78] However we can avoid committing ourselves to a view on this by reformulating the suggestion above as follows: social relations of production should be understood as relations that are interconstitutive of humans as the kind of humans that they are in any given society.[79] To return to the above quote, 'what men were' in any historical period is 'what their relations were'. Hence people's concept of 'the human' indirectly reflects their own social relations. This much can be said without claiming either that there is or is not such a thing as a genuine humanity which is constituted by genuinely social relationships in communist society.

Furthermore, even if there is no such thing, with this suggestion the equation of 'human' and 'social' remains. For as Marx says in the quote with which we began, the relations of production 'in their totality form ... society' and specifically 'a society with a peculiar, distinctive character'. So it is the same relations that constitute society as one kind of society or another, that also – I suggest – constitute humans as one kind of human or another.[80]

6. Social relations of production and property ownership

The idea that humans are constituted as 'what they are' by their social relationships is a recurrent one in *The German Ideology*. To take one example:

> [Feuerbach] does not conceive humans in their given social interconnection [*Zusammenhänge*], under their existing conditions of life, which have made them *what* they are.[81]

---

[78] Another possibility is that it is now informed by a different ideal of realised humanity, in which this realisation is defined by the full development and satisfaction of the needs for activity and enjoyment that humans have as natural beings, rather than by the establishment of free producer-enjoyer relations.

[79] The idea of social relations as 'internal relations', that is as relations that are interconstitutive for those who engage in them, is advanced in Ollman 1971, Chapter 2, and also (using formulations closer to my own) in Gould 1978, pp. 30–9.

[80] The constitution has a different character in the two cases, for in Marx's view a society is nothing but a set of relations of production, whereas an individual exists and has various properties independently of being (fully) constituted *as* a certain kind of human by relations of production. See note 92 below.

[81] MEW, Vol. 3, p. 44; CW, Vol. 5, p. 41. Marx and Engels's formulations on these matters are often, as here, ambiguous between a constitutive claim (by definition people in certain relations count as a certain kind of being, for that is what it *is* to be that kind of being) and a causal one (people in certain relations tend, through causal processes, to turn into a certain – independently defined – kind of being). I interpret the claims as constitutive.

However to say that social relations of production constitute people in general as what they are in any particular historical epoch is not yet very informative. Over and above that, I shall claim that for Marx, relations of production constitute the individuals who engage in them as owners (or non-owners) of different kinds of property, and thus as members of one class or another.

This claim does not come through as clearly as it might in *The German Ideology*, where the concept of 'social relations' or 'relations of production' has an unclear connection to that of 'the division of labour'. In this book it is the division of labour which is credited with constituting people as property owners. For example:

> The various stages of development in the division of labour are just so many forms of property, i.e. the existing stage in the division of labour determines also the relations of individuals to one another with reference to the material, instrument and product of labour.[82]

However social relations are described as having the independence and intractability to the will of individuals which would be necessary to constitute them as property owners:

> How is it that ... the personal relating [*Verhalten*] of the individual is bound to be reified [*sich versachlichen*], estranged, and at the same time exists as a power independent of him and outside him, created by intercourse, and is transformed into social relations [*Verhältnisse*], into a series of powers which determine and subordinate the individual ... ?[83]

Furthermore this formation of independent and 'thinglike' social relations is directly associated with individuals' own positions vis-à-vis each other gaining a 'thinglike' character, that is, a character impervious to the individual will, as when the authors speak of:

> the pious wish that [individuals] *should* relate [*Verhalten*] and distinguish themselves *in such a way* that their relating does not acquire independence as a social relation [*Verhältnis*] independent of them and their differences do not assume the thinglike [*sachliche*] (independent of the person) character that they daily do.[84]

The fact that Marx conceives social relations as composed out of individual 'relating' shows that he continues to think of them as

---

[82] MEW, Vol. 3, p. 22; CW, Vol. 5, p. 32.
[83] MEW, Vol. 3, pp. 227–8; CW, Vol. 5, p. 245. See also the reference to 'the transformation of individual relating (*Verhalten*) into its opposite, a purely thinglike relating (*sachliches Verhalten*)' at MEW, Vol. 3, p. 423; CW, Vol. 5, p. 438.
[84] MEW, Vol. 3, p. 423; CW, Vol. 5, p. 437.

interactional relations, even if what now makes an interactional relation between individuals into a 'social relation' is that, on a social scale, it has become independent of the will of any individual. Presumably what this means is that its mere existence on such a scale exerts pressure on each individual to continue to relate to others in the same way, thus to continue to occupy the same position vis-à-vis others, so that the relation as a whole is self-sustaining, independently of the will of any one individual.

From saying that such self-sustaining social relations impose social positions on individuals it is a short step to stating that they constitute individuals as owners of particular types of property, conferring on them ownership statuses which they cannot change at will. In his later descriptions of capitalist society Marx takes this step explicitly.

For Marx, capitalist (or bourgeois) society, like every other, is characterised not by just one relation of production, but by a set of distinct relations, even if he thinks of one of these as the most fundamental.[85] He describes money, capital, credit (interest-bearing capital), and so on, as relations of production of capitalist or bourgeois society.[86] These relations are interconnected into a single system: 'The relations of production of every society form a whole.'[87] Each capitalist relation of production is expressed by one of the categories used by political economists, for 'economic categories are only the theoretical expressions, the abstractions of the social relations of production'.[88] Marx's project in *Capital*, as he makes clear in the introduction to the *Grundrisse*, is to give a systematic exposition of the capitalist system of relations of production using for the most part the same categories, although in such a way as to make clear for the first time the historically transient character of that system.[89] It follows that the best guide to Marx's understanding of the social relations of production of capitalism is *Capital* itself. We should understand the sections on 'commodity', 'money', 'capital' and so on in that book as expositions of the different relations of production of capitalism, in which each is shown as

---

[85] For Marx, 'relation of production' is generally a type-term rather than a token-term, so that for example if two different workers are hired by two different capitalists then the two particular relationships established, as two tokens of the same type, would not be two different relations of production but two different instances of the same relation of production, namely the capital relation. In this article I follow this usage, using 'relation' (and 'specific relation') as type-terms, and 'particular relationship' as a token-term referring to an individual instance of a relation.

[86] On money, see *The Poverty of Philosophy*; CW, Vol. 6, p. 145. On capital, see the next quote in the text. On credit, see CW, Vol. 6, p. 162. In *The Poverty of Philosophy* Marx also describes the division of labour and the modern workshop as capitalist relations of production. See CW, Vol. 6, p. 162, 183 respectively.

[87] CW, Vol. 6, p. 166.

[88] CW, Vol. 6, p. 165. Marx says the same thing at CW, Vol. 6, p. 162, and also in the letter to Annenkov of 8 Dec 1846, Marx and Engels 1965, p. 39; in the letter to Schweitzer of 24 Jan 1865, Marx and Engels 1965, p. 154; and in the introduction to the *Grundrisse*, Marx 1953, pp. 25, 26–7; Marx 1973, pp. 105, 106.

[89] Marx 1953, pp. 21–8; Marx 1973, pp. 100–8.

necessitated in some way by the previous one, so that they form an interconnected whole.[90]

Each relation of production constitutes the human products that are involved in it as a distinct kind of entity: the kind of entity after which Marx names the relation. Thus, roughly speaking, a human product is constituted as a commodity by virtue of being produced for exchange and then exchanged for other such products in the market. A commodity is constituted as money by virtue of being used exclusively for buying other commodities from other people. Money and commodities are constituted as capital by being used in a process of repeatedly buying labour-power and other commodities from others at one price and selling them or what is made with them to others again at a higher price. What Marx says most often of capital is just as true of commodities, money and the rest:

> [C]apital is not a thing, it is a determinate social relation of production belonging to a determinate historical social formation, which presents itself as a thing and gives this thing a specific social character.[91]

What is more, though, I claim that the relations also constitute the individuals who engage in them as owners or non-owners of certain types of property: as commodity-owners, as owners of capital, and so on.[92] Thus what makes working-class individuals the owners of their own labour-power as a commodity (and of nothing else) is that they work for employers to whom they sell that labour-power (and that they do not engage in certain other particular relationships).[93] Here Marx says explicitly what he only suggested in his general account of social relations in *The German Ideology*:

> The worker's propertylessness, and the ownership of living labour by objectified labour, or the appropriation of living labour by capital – both merely expressions of the same

---

[90] It may seem strange to treat the commodity relation or the money relation as relations of production, rather than say of exchange or transfer, but doing so follows the logic of the statements by Marx quoted in this paragraph, as well as that of his unified conception of social relations of production (see note 75 above).

[91] MEW, Vol. 25, p. 822; Marx 1981, p. 953. Marx says the same thing in *Wage-Labour and Capital* at MEW, Vol. 3, p. 411; CW, Vol. 9, p. 212; and also (emphasising that capital is a social relation 'between persons') in MEW, Vol. 23, 793; Marx 1976, p. 932.

[92] Of course one's being an owner of a certain type of property is not all that one is as an individual, just as something's being a commodity or capital is not all that it is as a particular thing (see note 80 above). From *The German Ideology* onwards Marx consistently contrasts the 'inherent' properties of an individual, thing or process with the characteristics that it has due to the relations of production that 'subsume' it. With regard to individuals, see for example *The German Ideology* at MEW, Vol. 3, p. 76, pp. 210–13; CW, Vol. 5, p. 78, pp. 229–30.

[93] Roughly speaking, to own something 'as a commodity' is for it to be yours to sell: to do what individuals do with things when they engage in the commodity relation. Likewise for other types of property or property.

relation from opposite poles – are fundamental conditions of
the bourgeois mode of production, in no way accidents
irrelevant to it. These modes of distribution are the relations
of production themselves, but *sub specie distributionis*.[94]

7. Factual recognition

It is tempting to think of these relations as presupposing property of
some kind: to think for example that unless individuals are first
recognised by each other as owners of their respective products they
cannot engage in the relation of commodity exchange with one another.
But Marx is emphatic that this kind of recognition arises *through* the
relations in question rather than being presupposed by them. Thus in
the *Notes on Wagner* he says of the relation of commodity exchange:

> With [Wagner] there is first right and then intercourse; in
> reality it is the other way round: first there is *intercourse* and
> then a *legal order* [*Rechtsordnung*] develops out of it. In the
> analysis of the circulation of commodities I have
> demonstrated that in developed trade, the exchangers tacitly
> recognise [*anerkennen*] each other as equal persons and
> owners of the respective goods to be exchanged by them; they
> *do* this even while they are offering each other their goods
> and agreeing to trade with one another. This *factual*
> [*faktische*] relation, which first arises through and in
> exchange itself, later obtains *the form of right* [*rechtliche
> Form*] in the contract etc.; but this form creates neither its
> content, the exchange, nor the *relation* [*Beziehung*] *of persons
> to one another present* in [the form], but vice versa.[95]

The notion of 'tacit' or 'silent' (*stillschweigend*) recognition is an
obscure one. What Marx may have in mind is an analogue of the
practical recognition of something as belonging to another. My practical
recognition of something as yours would be respecting your possession
of it (your power over it) in my actions, where this respect is based on
my thinking of your possession as 'to be respected', in other words on
an underlying cognitive recognition. My 'tacit recognition' of the thing
as yours would be my acting towards you in just the same way, but *with
or without* any underlying cognitive recognition. It would be my
behaving towards you exactly as if I cognitively recognised the thing as
yours, but without necessarily having the corresponding thoughts. This
would be an 'effective', or (to adopt Marx's term in the quote) 'factual'

---

[94] Marx 1953, pp. 716–7; Marx 1973, p. 832. As I understand him, Marx says
here that capitalist relations of production constitute modes of distribution,
which in turn are a necessary condition for the capitalist mode (method) of
production. See also MEW, Vol. 25, p. 784; Marx 1981, p. 911.
[95] *Marginal Notes on Adolph Wagner* (1879–80) at MEW, Vol. 19, p. 377; Marx
1975, p. 210.

recognition.[96] Whereas the practical recognition would have a normative content, the factual recognition would not. Now my act of consensually exchanging goods with you, rather than simply trying to seize possession of your goods, is just such an act of 'factual' recognition, for doing so is doing what I would do if I thought of your possession as to be respected, regardless of whether as a matter of fact I do think of it in that way.

With this understanding of 'tacit recognition', we can see Marx as describing a two-stage process in the above quote. The relation of exchange is, in itself, a relation of mutual 'factual recognition' in the above sense; this is what Marx means when he says that such a relation 'arises through and in' exchange. In a first stage this recognition constitutes each of the parties as the owner of 'factual property', that is, as someone who is treated by another as if the other cognitively recognised its possession as 'yours'.[97] In a second stage such factual recognition, on a social scale, eventually gives rise to the publicly stated recognition of exchangers' possessions as 'theirs' by legal system – a system of (positive) right – and the enforcement by this system of their stated property rights over these possessions, making contracts possible. This legal recognition constitutes them as the owners of legal property or 'property by right'. Both kinds of property are distinct from *de facto* power over or 'possession' of a thing, for both are (fully) constituted by some form of recognition.[98]

If we generalise this account from commodity exchange to relations of production in general, the implication is that relations of production are in themselves relations of factual recognition, through which those who engage in them constitute each other as factual property owners or non-owners. Hence if we understand property in the sense of 'factual property' we can see how the different types of property ownership involved in capitalism – property in commodities, in capital, and so on –

---

[96] Marx may call it 'tacit' or 'silent' because from your point of view the paradigmatic case of it is when I act as if I cognitively recognised your possession but remain silent about whether this is why I am acting. For in that case you do not know whether any such cognitive recognition underlies my actions, and can only say that my act is an act of factual recognition.

[97] Hence Marx's reference to 'the relation of persons to one another': he has in mind Hegel's identification of recognising someone as a person with recognising them as a property owner.

[98] Marx distinguishes factual (*faktisch*) and by-right (*rechtlich*) property in MEW, Vol. 25, p. 805; Marx 1981, p. 933, and also in MEW, Vol. 25, p. 688; Marx 1981, p. 814 (this time calling the former *tatsächlich* – another term that means 'factual' or 'actual'). However he does not define the two kinds of property there. I have based my definition of 'factual property' on his use of 'factual' in the present quote, and that of 'property by right' on his normal usage of 'right' in the sense of positive right. The move from exchange to factual property is a purely constitutive one, while the move from there to property by right is causal and then constitutive. The whole two-stage process is described more succinctly in the *German Ideology*: '[t]he thing [*Sache*] only becomes a thing, actual [*wirklichem*] property, in intercourse, and independently of right'. MEW, Vol. 3, p. 63; CW, Vol. 5, p. 91. It is also described somewhat differently, and in my view less clearly, in a passage in *Capital* Vol. 1 that parallels that from the *Notes on Wagner*. There Marx says that commodity exchange *requires* mutual recognition, and calls this recognition a 'relation of right' that is then 'legally [*legal*] developed'. MEW, Vol. 23, p. 99; Marx 1976, p. 178.

are not presupposed by the relations of production but are rather constituted by them.[99] Relations of production would then be relations of producing-for and transferring-the-product-to between individuals by engaging in which they constitutively *confer* (factual) *property* on each other, factual property of a different type for each relation of production.[100] Thereby they constitute each other as certain types of humans. Thus the kinds of humanity which have existed, at least up until now, consist at root in kinds of property-ownership, and thus (given Marx's definition of class) of class-membership.

It might be said that it is all very well to say that relations of producing-for and transferring-to are in themselves relations of factual recognition and so constitute factual property, but this evades the issue of how such relations could ever get off the ground and sustain themselves without a prior legal recognition of property rights by a functioning legal system, or else a prior cognitive recognition of possessions by the participants.

To see what Marx might have in mind, imagine a number of people who set out to collaborate in producing goods and transferring them to each other to enjoy: to form, in Marx's terminology, a society. In order for them to succeed in this, they must somehow arrive at a way of dividing between them the various physical tasks involved. But they must also arrive at a way of dividing the *decision-making* over how and when these tasks are to be carried out: over who is to do what and who is to get what. Equally, they must find a way of allocating the 'second-order' decision-making over how and when such decision-making powers are to be acquired, lost, or transferred from one individual to another. However they initially arrive at this 'division of decision-making' – whether by agreement, by the imposition of force by some over others, or by falling into it through a process of piecemeal adjustment – every act of producing and transferring goods in accordance with it will be, in itself, an act of factual recognition of the decision-makers as having authority over their respective areas of (first- or second-order) decision, and every act of decision-making by them will be an act of factual assertion of that authority. So the system of production and transfer will be at the same time a network of relations of factual recognition and assertion. The most natural way of delineating an area of decision is by reference to some entity which enters into the production process, be it a piece of land, a tool, a building, a person, or a person's labour-power. So this network of

---

[99] There is an early adumbration of this idea in the *Economic and Philosophical Manuscripts*, MEW Erg.1, p. 520; CW, Vol. 3, pp. 279–80, where Marx says that 'analysis of [the] concept [of alienated labour] shows that although private property appears as the reason, the cause of alienated labour, it is rather a consequence of it'. Alienated labour is that form of producing for another which is in itself factual recognition of the worker's labour-power, and product, as another's.

[100] They confer the property constitutively rather than causally, in that factual property just *is* recognition of something as mine by others, and such recognition is essentially involved in relations of production.

relations of factual recognition and assertion will in effect constitute a distribution of factual property in such entities.[101]

Furthermore, as soon as the system of production and transfer is established it will have some tendency to sustain itself. For if all the individuals meet certain needs as a result of the workings of the whole system, then they all know that if they continue to do as they have been doing until now they will at least continue to meet those needs, so they have at least that incentive to carry on as they have been doing. Also, over time the system will tend to give rise to cognitive recognitions corresponding to its factual recognitions. For the natural person to look to for a decision on some issue is the person who took the decision last time, and any individual who acts in contravention of the existing division of decision-making is likely to interrupt the process of production and provoke negative reactions from all those who are adversely affected. As a result, individuals are likely to come to *think* of the decision-makers as having an authority over their areas that is to be respected, instead of merely treating them as if that was what they thought. A normative consciousness will emerge in them which is 'consciousness of existing practice.'[102] In turn this cognitive recognition will tend to re-express itself in action, transforming merely factual recognition into genuine practical recognition. We could call the resulting jointly cognitive and practical recognition, when it is verbally articulated and shared across society, 'social recognition', and the kind of property it constitutes 'socially recognised property'. It will further help to sustain the distribution of decision-making, and so the system of production and transfer as a whole, although it would not be able to sustain that distribution by itself. (All the points made in this paragraph for recognition can also be made for assertion.)

Suppose finally that the property statuses of individuals do not vary continuously but fall into a small number of types. The individuals with each different type of property status would then form a class. At a certain point those with the most advantageous property status (those who derive most material benefit and economic power from the distribution of decision-making) might organise themselves to formulate explicitly the extent of the factually (and socially) recognised decision-making authority of each individual as the individual's property rights, and to establish a mechanism for punishing those who flout these rights. In other words they might institute themselves as a ruling class with a state. Factual property would then become legal property.[103] Such a

---

[101] In this paragraph I have silently introduced the idea of 'factual assertion' (as the equivalent of factual recognition), and expanded my definition of 'factual property' so that it is constituted by factual assertion as well as factual recognition.

[102] MEW, Vol. 3, p. 31; CW, Vol. 5, p. 45. This Hume-inspired sketch of how normativity might emerge out of the production process is necessarily extremely rough.

[103] Marx describes such a process of the solidification of factual property over time, and its subsequent 'sanctification' as legal property by the ruling class, in MEW, Vol. 25, pp. 801–2; Marx 1981, p. 929.

mechanism would again help to sustain the distribution of decision-making (and so the system of production and transfer), but it would not be able to maintain the distribution of decision-making by itself. It would only be able to 'ride on the back' of the process of production and transfer, and of the informal processes (including those that generate social recognition) through which it tends to maintain the distribution of decision-making.[104] For example, the mechanism might draw passive or active support for its punitive actions from those who depend most on the smooth running of the production process.

If the number of people involved in this society is small then it would be rather easy for a determined individual or group to change radically the existing distribution of decision-making. But if the number is large then the process of production and transfer might reinforce the existing distribution of decision-making so strongly that it became completely self-sustaining and 'thinglike', and impossible for any but the largest and most determined group to overthrow. In this way the social production process as a whole would sustain the systems of socially recognised and legal property, and so the economic and political power of the propertied over the rest.[105]

8. The definition of social relations of production

The plausibility of this story depends on a number of psychological and other assumptions. But if it *is* plausible, then it shows how relations of producing-for and transferring-to that constitute a system of factual property can be self-sustaining, and that they can give rise to and sustain corresponding systems of socially recognised and legal property, even if those systems in turn help to reinforce them. This makes possible the definition of relations of production that, finally, I would like to propose: social relations of production are those self-sustaining relations of producing-for and transferring-to that are at the same time relations of factual recognition and assertion of individuals as first and second-order decision-makers over entities involved in the production process, and thus that are (fully) interconstitutive of individuals as owners or non-owners of factual property.[106]

It might be tempting to include the relations of cognitive recognition that are generated by such relations in the definition of social relations

---

[104] Obviously in time the way that property rights were formulated by the legal system would also be likely to feed back into the ways that social recognition was expressed in everyday life.
[105] This story expands Marx's two-stage to a three-stage process: the stages are now from relations of producing and transferring to factual property, from there to socially recognised property, and from there to legal property.
[106] The definition leaves open the question of whether there can be relations of producing-for and transferring-to that are *not* simultaneously relations of factual recognition and assertion. The duality of 'producing-for' and 'transferring-to' in the definition reflects the duality in Marx's concept of social relations of production (see note 75 above).

of production, on the grounds that in practice such cognitive recognition is likely to be closely entwined with them, and that social concepts should reflect social reality. Marx himself may not have had a clear view on this issue, but one phrase in the 1859 *Preface* would support the narrower definition I have proposed. Introducing the base-superstructure metaphor, he says that the totality of relations of production form 'the real basis, on which a legal and political superstructure arises, and to which correspond determinate social forms of consciousness [*gesellschaftliche Bewußtseinsformen*].'[107] I suggest that the 'social forms of consciousness' that Marx has in mind here include attitudes of cognitive recognition. By saying that they 'correspond' to the totality of social relations of production, rather than saying that like the superstructure they arise on that totality, he would be signalling their close connection with relations of production, but he would also be distinguishing them from relations of production as such. This is what the definition proposed here does.

It should be added that this definition does not exclude 'forms of consciousness' in general from social relations of production. Relations of producing-for and transferring-to are relations that involve actions, and human action is always intentional, thus always imbued with thought and so with 'forms of consciousness.'[108] The only issue is whether the specifically normative thoughts that make up cognitive recognition should be thought of as a constitutive component of social relations of production. Marx's formulation, as I interpret it, suggests that they should not.

It may be objected to this account that individuals' property or propertylessness does not seem to them at all something which is brought into existence by their participating in relations like the commodity relation or the capital relation, but rather as something which is a precondition of such participation, and in fact which forces them into it. The response would be that for Marx each individual's factual property status is not determined by the particular relationships in which that individual engages, but it is determined by the totality of particular relationships in which the members of society as a whole engage, each of them an instance of one of the society's relations of production. This totality of relationships confronts the individual as 'thinglike', as something they can do nothing to change, but it consists in nothing but intentional activities of individuals directed towards each other:

---

107 MEW, Vol. 13, p. 8; Marx 1970, p. 20.
108 In his keenness to oppose a thoroughly materialist alternative to idealist explanations of social phenomena, Marx does sometimes seem to suggest that human practical activity as such is thought-free. But in *Capital* Vol. 1 he makes it clear that even the act of labour directed onto nature is governed by a conscious aim: '[the worker] not only effects a change of form in the natural; he also realises in the natural his own purpose, which he is aware of, which determines the kind and mode of his activity as a law, and to which he must subordinate his will'. MEW, Vol. 23, p. 193; Marx 1976, p. 284.

> it was, therefore, precisely the personal, individual relating
> [*Verhalten*] of individuals, their relating to one another as
> individuals, that created the existing relations [*Verhältnisse*]
> and daily reproduces them anew.[109]

In turn, of course, this totality gives rise to a system of socially recognised and legal property, and in standard cases the individual may feel that it is the system of social recognition (in whatever terms the individual describes it), or the legal system, that maintains the individual's property status. Marx's point would be that these systems in turn ride on the back of the system of relations of production.

It may also be objected that this account of relations of production does not tell us by what general criteria one relation of production is differentiated from another, that is, how in general one can tell whether a particular relationship between individuals counts as an instance of one relation of production or another.[110] The answer given above for capitalism, that each relation of production constitutes the human products that are involved in it as a distinct kind of entity (as a commodity, money, capital and so on), and its participants as owners of a distinct type of property (as commodity-owners and so on), is unhelpful in that we do not know, for example, what a commodity is or what commodity-ownership is until we know that the commodity relation is. The response is that the definition does not provide any general criterion beyond that of the 'kind of factual property' constituted by the relation. The only way to see how Marx differentiates one capitalist relation of production from another, and capitalist relations of production from feudal or slave ones, is to look at his accounts of the specific relations concerned. However this does not constitute a criticism of the definition: after all a definition cannot tell us everything about its object.

It might be said that to define relations of production as relations of producing-for and transferring-to is to make them into what Cohen calls 'work relations' or 'material relations of production', that is, relations defined and differentiated from each other by the physical characteristics of the production process or the product being transferred.[111] However this is not the case. Of course every particular relationship that is an instance of a relation of production involves some particular production process or product, which will have physical characteristics. But it is not these characteristics that make the particular relationship count as an instance of one relation of

---

[109] *The German Ideology*, MEW, Vol. 3, p. 423; CW, Vol. 5, p. 438. See also Marx 1953, p. 600; Marx 1973, p. 712: '[the] only subjects [of the direct production process] are individuals in relations [*Beziehungen*] to one another, which they equally reproduce and produce anew'; and CW, Vol. 6, pp. 165–6: 'these definite social relations [of production] are just as much produced by men as linen, flax etc.'
[110] For the contrast in this paragraph between 'relation' and 'particular relationship' see note 85 above.
[111] Cohen 1978, pp. 111–12.

production or another; rather it is the characteristics of the particular relationship as one of factual recognition and assertion that make it count as such an instance. To take as an example the commodity relation, a particular relationship between two individuals counts as an instance of that relation by virtue of fact that each transfers a good to the other by mutual consent, for it is in virtue of this aspect of the particular relationship that their actions count as acts of recognition and assertion. The technical aspect of the particular relationship, the fact that the exchange is of bricks for wine, say, is irrelevant. The relationship would be an instance of the commodity relation no matter what the particular goods exchanged were.[112]

On this account of Marx's social relations of production, they are akin to Hegel's historical relations of recognition and assertion in that they are themselves relations of recognition and assertion of a certain kind. Thereby like Hegel's, they are fully interconstitutive of different kinds of human beings. Furthermore, like Hegel's relations, although in a more indirect way, they underlie the system of (positive) right in a given society. Yet relations of production are distinct in that for Marx the recognition and assertion they constitute is not cognitive and practical but factual, and in that it is exclusively recognition and assertion of individuals as (factual) property owners. Furthermore, for Marx recognising another as a property owner is not a particular way of recognising the other as free; rather recognising the other as free is only a philosophical abstraction from recognising the other as a property owner.[113] Most importantly, relations of production are distinct from Hegel's relations of recognition and assertion in that they are not *merely* recognitive relations. They are relations of producing-for and transferring-to that as such are relations of factual recognition and assertion. This gives them a stability, rooted in the needs that human production supplies, that relations of recognition and assertion standing alone could never have.[114]

---

[112] The question of how such relations might affect, and be affected by, the technical relations between individuals in production, and so the development of the productive power of society as a whole, is a quite separate one. I shall not address it, except to claim that the present definition of social relations of production makes it plausible that there could be effects in both directions, as required by what Marx says in various places on this subject.

[113] For a clear statement of this, see Marx 1953, p. 156; Marx 1973, p. 245.

[114] Jürgen Habermas showed that he was aware of the recognitive dimension in Marx when he argued in the 1960s that Marx, 'under the unspecific title of social praxis' reduces relations of recognition between human beings to relations of producing between humans and nature: that he 'reduces ... communicative action to instrumental action', Habermas 1973, pp. 168–9. If by 'social praxis' Habermas has in mind the social practices that constitute Marx's relations of production, then the response to this criticism is that to define social relations of production such that they have both a productive and recognitive aspect is in no way to 'reduce' the latter to the former.

9. Sayer, Wood and Cohen on relations of production

Much more would need to be done to spell out properly the interpretation of social relations of production that has been sketched here, to show that it fits Marx's overall use of the term and renders his views on the structure of human societies coherent, and to assess the role it could play in a contemporary Marxist social theory. Here I will only briefly compare this interpretation to Sayer's and Wood's, and to Cohen's, in terms of how successfully they all deal with the problem of legality, and in terms of their faithfulness to Marx's usage.

Sayer and Wood construe social relations of production as whatever customary, moral, legal or other relations provide the necessary context of the production process.[115] Their implicit response to the problem of legality is straightforward. To recall, the problem stems from the fact that Marx seems to identify relations of production with property relations, yet if property relations are legal relations they would seem to belong to the legal superstructure. Sayer's and Wood's response must be to accept the identification of social relations of production with property relations, including legal property relations, and to deny that such relations belong to the superstructure. Yet this seems to divide the legal system into a 'basic' and a 'superstructural' part in a way that simply does not match Marx's way of talking about law. Furthermore if the identification of relations of production with property relations is taken seriously, as it is by Sayer, the result is that *any* relation that enables the production process to proceed counts as a property relation.[116] This stretches the meaning of 'property' beyond credibility.

Furthermore, Sayer's and Wood's definition of relations of production fails to match Marx's usage. Although they can point to many passages where Marx notes the role of moral, legal, political and even religious relations in enabling the production process to proceed, especially in his descriptions of pre-capitalist forms of society, I do not know of any which identify such relations with 'social relations of production', under that name or its shortened versions, or with specific relations of production such as the capital relation. The exceptions are those passages in which Marx appears to identify relations of production with property, which as just pointed out can be taken as evidence for the interpretation only if 'property' is given an unnaturally stretched meaning.

In Cohen's case his definition of social relations of production can be understood as a direct response to the problem of legality. For in effect he defines relations of production by beginning with legal property relations (which he understands as relations of legal ownership between persons on the one hand and things or human labour-power on the other) that are backed by force, and then stripping out the legal

---

[115] It is not possible to tell from Sayer's and Wood's accounts whether they think of these various kinds of relations as interactional or not. I assume that they do.
[116] See Sayer 1987, pp. 58–75.

rights and duties from them. What is left are simply the relations of bare power and lack of power over things or labour-power that such enforced rights and duties maintain, where 'power over a thing' just means the ability to use it in some way, or to transfer such ability to others. Each such power or non-power matches a corresponding enforced legal right or duty that maintains it.[117] But at the same time relations of production as so defined exclude legal relations, for they are defined quite independently of how their powers and non-powers are maintained.[118] So they are clearly distinguished from the legal superstructure. Cohen can explain why Marx apparently identified relations of production with property relations by arguing that he found it convenient to use the language of property in an extended way as a means of referring to the powers and non-powers that are the non-legal analogues of property rights and their correlative duties.[119]

However this neat solution to the problem of legality is bought at a high price. For it means that his relations of production in a society are standardly determined by its legal property relations. Yet legal property relations are supposed to be explained by relations of production. The only way of reconciling these two claims, Cohen says, is by construing the explanation of the superstructure by the base as a case of functional explanation: a given base is said to give rise to the superstructure *because* such a superstructure would maintain that base.[120] In principle Cohen is right to say that a functionalist explanation reconciles, indeed requires, such a double direction of explanation. Yet surely for relations of production to give rise to legal property relations that would maintain them, these relations of production must first exist independently of the legal property relations in question, and given Cohen's etiolated definition of relations of production it is hard to conceive how they could have any such independent existence.[121]

Furthermore, Cohen's definition of relations of production suffers from a major difficulty as an interpretation of Marx. I have argued above that Marx thinks of social relations of production as interactional relations between individuals. By contrast, for Cohen a relation of production consists only in the ability of an individual to use a thing, or

---

[117] Cohen implicitly allows for the possibility of relations of production that do not require a legal system to maintain them at Cohen 1978, p. 231, but in practice he always thinks of them as requiring such a system.
[118] '[O]ur definition of production relations does not stipulate how the powers they enfold are obtained or sustained ... The programme says what production relations are, not what maintains them.' Cohen 1978, p. 223.
[119] See Cohen 1978, p. 224. Note that here Cohen interprets Marx's 'factual property' as *de facto* power over things, whereas I interpret it as factually asserted and recognised power over them (see note 98 above).
[120] See Cohen 1988, pp. 9–10, 31–2.
[121] This criticism is made in Elster 1985, p. 403. Since Cohen thinks that relations of production are in turn functionally explained by their propitiousness for developing the productive forces, he could short-circuit the explanatory route and simply say that legal property relations are functionally explained by the propitiousness of the pattern of powers and non-powers they create for the development of the productive forces, in fact at Cohen 1978, p. 231, he does give such a formulation. But this would be tantamount to defining social relations of production as (enforced) legal property relations.

to direct another individual's actions, in various ways. For example, he understands the relation of production between a master and his slave in ancient slave society as consisting only in the master's power over the labour-power of the slave, that is, his ability to direct the actions of the slave (and perhaps his ability to transfer that ability). It does not consist in any actual pattern of interaction between the master and the slave that results from his exercising that ability.[122] Such an ability-based definition of relations of production flies completely in the face of Marx's usage of the term. In particular, it means that Cohen can give no plausible account of the capital relation, the single most important relation of production in Marx's thought, *as* a relation of production. For this relation can only be understood as an interactional relation.[123]

To turn to the interpretation that I have proposed here, in this interpretation social relations of production are relations of producing and transferring which, as at once relations of factual recognition, constitute *factual* property. But such property remains quite distinct from *legal* property, which can therefore be placed in the superstructure. This solves the problem of legality in a way akin to Cohen's, in that relations of production are defined in non-legal terms and yet are closely related to legal property. So they are clearly distinguished from the legal superstructure, and yet Marx's apparent identification of them with property relations can be explained by assuming that when he makes this identification he is thinking not of legal property but of something close to it. The difference is that here the 'something close' is not *de facto* powers but what I call factual property, that is, the property that is constituted by the factual assertion (by oneself) and factual recognition (by others) of possessions as 'one's own', and relations of production directly involve such factual assertion and recognition.[124] Relations of production are not thought of as the *de facto* powers conferred by property law, but are conceived independently, as interactional relations that are self-sustaining on a social scale. Thus they are not determined by the law, although of

---

[122] In fact strictly the relation is not even between the master and the slave, but between master and the slave's labour-power. Cohen makes the distinction between having a power and exercising it, expressed in terms of the contrast between the occupancy of a role defined by one of his relations of production and the performance of that role, in Cohen 1988, pp. 44–50.

[123] The critique of this paragraph applies to what I take to be Cohen's official conception of social relations of production (see note 8 above). However in Cohen 1978 a number of his examples of relations of production appear to be interactional relations. For example '... is hired by ...', '... hires ...', and '... leases his labour-power to ...' at p. 35, and '... works for ...' at pp. 35, 85. Since Cohen explicitly repudiates a definition of relations of production in terms of 'the kinds of actions performed in society' at Cohen 1988, p. 47, I assume that these examples are aberrations.

[124] This means that Cohen and I understand 'property relations' differently. He understands them essentially as relations between persons and things (or labour-power), whereas I understand them essentially as relations between persons. In the case of factual property they are interactional relations between persons of factual assertion and recognition, and in the case of legal property they are non-interactional relations between persons of 'having a legal right against' and 'having a legal duty towards'.

course they are typically reinforced by it. As a result, this interpretation does not force us to resort to a functional explanation of the legal superstructure by the base. As self-sustaining interactional relations, relations of production can serve as a base from which the character of the legal and political system can be explained in more straightforward ways, such as those exemplified in the story above.[125] This interpretation therefore solves the problem of legality, on Marx's behalf, in a more satisfactory way than either of the other interpretations does.

Finally, this interpretation has the virtue that it fits well with what Marx explicitly says about social relations of production, whether under their full name or its abbreviations. In particular, it understands such relations literally as relations *of* production, relations of producing-for and transferring-to, whereas Sayer, Wood and Cohen all understand them only as relations *necessary for* or *conducive to* production.[126] Unlike the other interpretations, this one makes it reasonably easy to see how Marx's central examples of relations of production, such as the capital relation, could count as relations of production under the interpretation. And finally, against Cohen's definition and in conformity with Marx's usage, this interpretation explicitly construes relations of production as interactional.

10. Conclusion

This article has been an exercise in Marx interpretation. I claim that its understanding of relations of production is closer to that implicit in Marx's usage than the other two I have discussed. But clearly all three are in the spirit of Marxism, and it is possible that one of the others would provide a better conceptual basis for a Marxist understanding of society than this one. Exegetical truth to Marx is unlikely to be the route to the best version of contemporary Marxism. Having said that, I will end by suggesting that the conceptualisation of social life suggested by the present definition can provide insights in two areas.

One is the explanation of social power. The traditional view of the power of some over others in society is that it 'grows out of the barrel of a gun': that it is always based on the threat of physical force. Although it is of the essence of Marxism that it refocuses social explanation and social criticism on the economy rather than the state, Marxist thought often fails to get much beyond this view of power. Power in capitalist society is thought of as wielded by the economically dominant class, the bourgeoisie, but only because it has the financial resources to pay for a

---

[125] The mere fact that the law *reinforces* (as opposed to determines) the relations of production which explain it does not require that the explanation of law by relations of production be functional: an alternative would be that the relations of production have a more powerful effect on the law than the 'back effect' of the law in reinforcing them.

[126] Marx's German term *Produktionsverhältnisse*, 'production relations', ties the relations even more closely to production.

state which in turn is able to organise overwhelming physical force. Yet the position of the bourgeoisie as economically dominant is in turn thought of as maintained only by the state's enforcement of property law. This means that the bourgeoisie comes to be seen as a class whose power resides essentially in control of the state. When this view seems untenable it is supplemented by the idea that the bourgeoisie uses the same financial resources to control the media, with which it then deluges society with an ideology that justifies its position and its actions. The problem is that in practice the capitalist class has looked much less united, and the links between the mass of its individual members and the state or the media have looked much weaker, than these views would imply. I suggest that the conception of relations of production offered here, under which the activities of production and transfer spontaneously tend to reinforce any existing distribution of property in the means of production, would help to provide an account of the power of an economically dominant class which does not need to rely so heavily on physical force or ideology. For its implication is that this class does not depend exclusively on the state to maintain its economically dominant position, since that position is constantly reinforced by the process of social production itself.

The other area is the relation between class movements and the 'new social movements' which are supposed to have supplanted them in the last few decades: specifically the feminist, ethnic, and gay movements (I shall not discuss the ecological movement, which is the other main example). In a recent article Nancy Fraser has argued that these movements are all motivated by a demand for 'recognitive justice', that is, for recognition and respect as equally human, or as the particular kind of person that one is, as opposed to the traditional demand for economic redistribution of working-class based movements.[127] Fraser argues that workers, ethnic minorities, women and gays suffer different combinations of the two kinds of injustice, from workers at one end of the spectrum who suffer (as workers) almost exclusively from economic injustice, to gays at the other who suffer (as gays) almost exclusively from recognitive injustice. Obviously, recognitive injustice can take many forms, from casually demeaning language and everyday judicial discrimination to the murder of individuals just because they are of a particular kind. Fraser's identification of a common demand for recognition in the different movements of 'identity politics' or 'the politics of difference' is insightful, but on the understanding proposed here of relations of production – that is, of economic relations – the conceptual dichotomy she draws between the economic and the recognitive is mistaken.[128] For economic relations like the capital relation and the commodity relation are themselves intrinsically

---

[127] Fraser 1995.
[128] I leave aside the point that Marxism's concerns with collective control over the social production process as a whole, and with the reorientation of that process to the specific needs of each individual, are both poorly captured by the idea of 'economic redistribution'.

recognitive. They are relations of producing and of transferring goods which are simultaneously relations of factual recognition and non-recognition. Accordingly the exploitation and economic exclusion that given social relations of production involve can themselves be seen as forms of recognitive inadequacy or injustice. In turn the implication is that the varieties of injustice uncovered by the new movements might themselves be understood as indirect products of these economic relations, or alternatively of a basic set of 'social relations of need satisfaction' conceived more broadly than Marx's relations of production but retaining the intrinsic connection with recognition that, I claim, his relations of production have.

These ideas cannot be pursued here. Nevertheless I hope they show that, by taking seriously the Fichtean and Hegelian ideas of mutual recognition and interconstitution, we can gain a better understanding not only of Marx's thought, but also of the social reality to which it was directed.

References

Arthur, C.J. 1986, *The Dialectics of Labour: Marx and his Relation to Hegel*, Oxford: Basil Blackwell.

Chitty, Andrew 1993, 'The Early Marx on Needs', *Radical Philosophy*, 64: 23–31.

Chitty, Andrew 1996, 'On Hegel, the Subject and Political Justification', *Res Publica* 2, 2: 181–203.

Chitty, Andrew 1997, 'First Person Plural Ontology and Praxis', *Proceedings of the Aristotelian Society*, 97, 1: 81–96.

Cohen, G.A. 1978, *Karl Marx's Theory of History: A Defence*, Oxford: Clarendon Press.

Cohen, G.A. 1988, *History, Labour and Freedom*, Oxford: Clarendon Press.

Elster, Jon 1985, *Making Sense of Marx*, Cambridge: Cambridge University Press.

Fichte, Johann G. [1796] n.d., *Sämtliche Werke: Volume 3, Grundlage des Naturrechts* [GNR], Leipzig: Mayer and Müller.

Fichte, Johann G. [1796] 1869, *The Science of Rights*, Philadelphia: J.B. Lippincott.

Fraser, Nancy 1995, 'From Redistribution to Recognition? Dilemmas of Justice in a "Post-Socialist" Age', *New Left Review* 212: 68–93.

Godelier, Maurice 1982, 'The Ideal in the Real', in *Culture, Ideology and Politics: Essays for Eric Hobsbawm*, edited by Raphael Samuel and Gareth Stedman Jones, London: Routledge and Kegan Paul.

Gould, Carol 1978, *Marx's Social Ontology: Individuality and Community in Marx's Theory of Social Reality*, Cambridge, Massachusetts: MIT Press.

Habermas, Jürgen [1967] 1973, 'Labour and Interaction: Remarks on Hegel's Jena *Philosophy of Mind'*, in *Theory and Practice*, Boston: Beacon Press.

Hart, H.L.A. 1955, 'Are there any Natural Rights?', *Philosophical Review*, 64, 2: 175–91.

Hegel, G.W.F. [1830] 1971, *Hegel's Philosophy of Mind*, Oxford: Clarendon Press.

Hegel, G.W.F. [1822–30] 1975, *Lectures on the Philosophy of World History. Introduction: Reason in History*, Cambridge: Cambridge University Press.

Hegel, G.W.F. [1807] 1977, *Hegel's Phenomenology of Spirit*, Oxford: Oxford University Press.

Hegel, G.W.F. [1830] 1979, *Hegel's Philosophy of Subjective Spirit*, 3 Volumes, edited by M.J. Petry, Dordrecht: D. Reidel.

Hegel, G.W.F. [1830] 1981, *The Berlin Phenomenology*, edited by M.J. Petry, Dordrecht: D. Reidel.

Hegel, G.W.F. 1986a, *Georg Wilhelm Friedrich Hegel Werke* in 20 Volumes, Frankfurt am Main: Suhrkamp.

Hegel, G.W.F. [1830] 1986b, *Georg Wilhelm Friedrich Hegel Werke 10, Enzyklopädie der philosophischen Wissenschaften III* [E3], Frankfurt am Main: Suhrkamp.

Hegel, G.W.F. [1821] 1986c, *Georg Wilhelm Friedrich Hegel Werke 7, Grundlinien der Philosophie des Rechts* [PR], Frankfurt am Main: Suhrkamp.

Hegel, G.W.F. [1807] 1986d, *Georg Wilhelm Friedrich Hegel Werke 3, Phänomenologie des Geistes*, Frankfurt am Main: Suhrkamp.

Hegel, G.W.F. [1821] 1991, *Elements of the Philosophy of Right*, Cambridge: Cambridge University Press.

Inwood, Michael 1992, *A Hegel Dictionary*, Oxford: Blackwell.

Marx, Karl [1857–8] 1953, *Grundrisse der Kritik der Politischen Ökonomie*, Berlin: Dietz Verlag.

Marx, Karl [1859] 1970, *A Contribution to the Critique of Political Economy*, Moscow: Progress Publishers.

Marx, Karl [1857–8] 1973, *Grundrisse*, Harmondsworth: Penguin.

Marx, Karl 1975, *Karl Marx: Texts on Method*, Oxford: Basil Blackwell.

Marx, Karl [1867] 1976, *Capital* Volume 1, Harmondsworth: Penguin.

Marx, Karl [1894] 1981, *Capital* Volume 3, Harmondsworth: Penguin.

Marx, Karl and Engels, Friedrich 1956–71, *Marx-Engels Werke* [MEW], 39 Volumes, Berlin: Dietz Verlag.

Marx, Karl and Engels, Friedrich 1965, *Selected Correspondence*, Moscow: Progress Publishers.

Marx, Karl and Engels, Friedrich [1843–4] 1971, *Marx-Engels Werke: Ergänzungsband, Erster Teil* [MEW Erg.1], Berlin: Dietz Verlag.

Marx, Karl and Engels, Friedrich 1975–, *Collected Works* [CW], London: Lawrence and Wishart.

Ollman, Bertell 1971, *Alienation: Marx's Conception of Man in Capitalist Society*, Cambridge: Cambridge University Press.

Plamenatz, John 1954, *German Marxism and Russian Communism*, London: Longmans.

Plamenatz, John 1963, *Man and Society*, London: Longmans.

Sayer, Derek 1987, *The Violence of Abstraction: The Analytical Foundations of Historical Materialism*, Oxford: Basil Blackwell.

Theunissen, Michael [1982] 1991, 'The Repressed Intersubjectivity in Hegel's *Philosophy of Right*', in *Hegel and Legal Theory*, edited by Drucilla Cornell et al, London: Routledge.

Williams, Robert R. 1998, *Hegel's Ethics of Recognition*, Berkeley: University of California Press.

Wood, Ellen Meiksins 1995, *Democracy Against Capitalism: Renewing Historical Materialism*, Cambridge: Cambridge University Press.

MA Modern European Philosophy
MA Aesthetics and Art Theory

Middlesex University, London

The well-established MA programme in **Modern European Philosophy** allows students to study areas of special interest within the field of nineteenth and twentieth–century European philosophy in a framework of intensive taught courses. The total duration of the programme is one year full-time or two years part-time. After studying several taught courses from a range of options, students write a research dissertation (15–20,000 words) on an approved topic of their choice, under close supervision.

Each taught modular unit on the MA Modern European Philosophy deals with the work of a single philosopher, normally within a single text. Modules are offered on Adorno, Derrida, Habermas, Hegel, Husserl, Kant, Gadamer, Kierkegaard, Marx and Wittgenstein. The module on Kant's *Critique of Pure Reason* is compulsory.

The new MA programme in **Aesthetics and Art Theory** is a response to the recent surge of interest in philosophy and aesthetics on the part of artists, art historians and art theorists. The total duration of the programme is one year full-time or two years part-time. After studying several taught courses from a range of options, students write a research dissertation (15–20,000 words) on an approved topic of their choice, under close supervision. Authors studied include Adorno, Benjamin, Danto, Derrida, de Duve, Duchamp, Greenberg, Heidegger, Kant, Kosuth, Krauss, Lippard and Merleau-Ponty.

The MA Aesthetics and Art Theory includes taught modular units on The Aesthetic Tradition, Modernist Aesthetics, Romantic Aesthetics, Phenomenological Aesthetics, and Postmodernism, Conceptualism and the End of Art. Options from the MA Modern European Philosophy are also available, and full-time students also take a course on Theories of Visual Culture.

Both the MA Modern European Philosophy and the MA Aesthetics and Art Theory fall within the **Centre for Research in Modern European Philosophy** at Middlesex University, which is the leading focus for graduate–level study and doctoral research in Continental Philosophy in London.

Core staff include Peter Osborne, Alexander Garcia Düttmann and Jonathan Rée.

Further information from Admissions Enquiries, School of Humanities and Cultural Studies, Middlesex University, White Hart Lane, London N17 8HR. Telephone (+44) (0)181 362 6722 Email: tmadmissions@mdx.ac.uk

Marx and the Magic of Money: Towards an Alchemy of Capital[1]

Michael Neary & Graham Taylor

We live in an age dominated by money. As capitalism has intensified and expanded as a social form, money has increasingly colonised the production and reproduction of the human condition. We live in an age of monetarism: an age in which social and political regulation are increasingly subordinate to the dictates of 'sound money'. We live in an age of national lotteries: an age where millions attempt each week to garner enough money to 'free' themselves from the grinding agony of wage labour. We live in an age in which people increasingly grasp the alienation inherent in the domination of society by money and attempt to reassert a sense of human community through the introduction of local currency and barter schemes. But we also live in an age where Marxism is supposedly dead; where we can only gaze in ironic postmodern wonder at the increasing domination of the human condition by money and its social forms. In this paper we go beyond this postmodern orthodoxy to suggest that it is not only possible to develop a historically materialist analysis of money and its social forms but also that this project is essential if we are to reclaim our humanity from the deadening alienation of money and its social forms. We explore the magical qualities of money, the qualities which have enthralled and transfixed bourgeois social science from the classical economy of Adam Smith to the present day postmodernists. We argue that the lasting legacy of Marx was to uncover the historical materiality underlying the magical appearance of money: a discovery of the alchemic properties of money capital through which money becomes more money and which involves the material subordination of living labour to the valorisation of money capital.

The secret life of money

Money is the chemical power of the modern world. And yet its existence as a supreme social being remains largely unrecognised. This invisibility demands an investigation into its secret life: *an alchemy*. The secret of money has transfixed science, metallurgy, astrology, astronomy, mythology, theology, philosophy, art and magic for thousands of years.

---

[1] This essay is based on material published in *Money and the Human Condition* by Michael Neary and Graham Taylor, published June 1998 by Macmillan, £40.00.

Alchemy was the science of the search for the secret of money: the way in which base (iron and copper) and noble (silver) metals could be used to create gold, or the process by which an original quantity of gold could be expanded or *multiplied*, to use an alchemic expression. But alchemy is more than a preoccupation with the transmutation of base metals into noble ones, it was also

> [a] grandiose philosophical system that aimed at penetrating and harmonising the mysteries of creation and of life. It sought to bring the microcosm of man into relation with the macrocosm of the universe. The transmutation of one form of inanimate matter into another, placed in this larger context, was merely an incidental aim of alchemy, designed to afford proof on the material plane of its wider tenets, in particular that of the essential unity of all things.[2]

The purpose of this paper is to reclaim that alchemic tradition for the modern world.

The history of alchemy is controversial and complex, containing the earliest examples of a fundamental theory of physical science. Thought to have originated in the ancient civilisations that made up the Egyptian, Arabic, Indian, Greek and Oriental world, it percolated into Western Europe in the twelfth century through Latin translations of Arabic texts: one of its earlier translations by Robert of Chester: *The Book of the Composition of Alchemy* (1144). Although it has a disparate history, alchemy is unified by its principle assumption of the unitary nature of matter; that is, transmutable into other substantial forms through a potent transmuting agent: the Philosopher's Stone – a *motive power*. Originally a substance for turning base metal into gold, the 'stone' later acquired additional properties: the curing of disease or the granting of immortality through 'the elixir of life'. For alchemy, all matter shares the same origin, appearing in various abstracted and separate forms as a manifestation of its essential derived nature. This natural condition is striving in the Aristotelian sense to express perfection and the Platonic sense to achieve the ambition of its inherent 'goodness'.

The theoretical framework of alchemy is organised within various adaptations depending on the tradition: for example, Five Elements (Wu-hsing) and Two Contraries (yin and yang) or four principles or qualities (earth, wind, fire and water). Alchemy maintains that all matter is comprised of these elements in various proportions depending on the tradition. Perfect matter is that within which its elemental form is not apparent: thus gold is the most perfect substance. According to the Aristotelian version these four elements were imbued with a *prima materia*: a quality that had no material existence until it became allied with its form, which allowed one element to transmute into another. Behind these four elements was another indistinct quality; for Aristotle

---

[2] Read 1961, p. 14.

it was 'ether', the element of the stars, for the neo-Platonists it was 'Logos', or the Word, or God, or Reason. Among medieval philosophy it was known as the 'quinta essencia': *the quintessence*.[3] Alchemy, then, is concerned with the synthetic or induced perfection of matter: the elaboration of a process that occurs naturally in the natural world.[4]

Although it has gained something of a disgraceful history – as a confidence trick, or delusion (eg. Ben Jonson's *The Alchemist* (1610)) – it has continued to hold an enduring fascination in philosophy and literature (Goethe, Shakespeare, Chaucer), and to be an inspiration for esoteric and exotic academic enquiry. It is also gratified by the quality (notoriety) of its various exponents, including all the major intellectual figures of the ancient world (Aristotle, Plato, Copernicus) and those who might be attached more comfortably to the modern (eg. Isaac Newton). Newton's interest in money extended to the practical administration of the Royal Mint between 1696–1726,[5] but he was also profoundly interested in alchemy. Newton's 'genius' was completely expressed in his integration of mathematics, physics and astrology, but he also attempted to integrate alchemic ideas with the contemporary mechanical philosophies.[6] So far as alchemy is concerned Newton is the last important alchemic adept: the last magician.[7] Newton is the culmination of the process for the search for the secret of money. After Newton alchemy disappears, or rather it becomes a much more limited endeavour: chemistry.

But this paper is not an investigation into the history of alchemy in all its esoteric exoticness, or even into the history of money. Rather, we take up the quest from the moment that alchemy disappears. When the search for the secret of money is to all intents and purposes abandoned. We shall suggest that this was no arbitrary moment or historical aberration, but that something changes in the nature of money itself that causes it to cease to be a subject for intellectual investigation. Alchemy is abandoned because the inheritors of the modern world, the world that begins with the accumulation of capital (the bourgeoisie), find a way to create money out of money itself. Thus, it is not that alchemy failed to find the secret of money and was, therefore, discredited, but that the search for the secret of money was solved, and in the nature of this practical success the explanation for this solution is obscured. Thus the discovery of the mystery and its mysterious disappearance as a subject for enquiry are connected.

Money is not ignored from this moment. Theories appear to explain this new phenomenon – the creation of money out of money – and the social upheaval it causes. In the seventeenth century John Locke, a close

---

[3] Read 1961, p. 3.
[4] Crosland 1962.
[5] Craig 1946.
[6] Dobb 1975, p. xi.
[7] Keynes was very interested in this aspect of Newton's work and collected his alchemic writings (he also bought his death mask for £34 and referred to him as the last magician).

friend of Isaac Newton, argued against the new world of money (laissez-faire), and that a just (Godly) society is possible only when money is absent. Money is unnatural, against the law of nature, leading to desire beyond need, ambition beyond morality, corruption and miserliness: 'for as to Money, and such Riches and Treasure... these are none of Nature's goods, they have but a Phantastical imaginary value: Nature has put no such upon them'.[8] The theories of money that came to dominate were invested with the naturalness (the rationality) that money seemed to contain, and were concerned not so much with money itself, but with the system of exchange that money appeared to facilitate: the market and its (dys)functionality. The new theories of money concentrated on monetary policy – the debasement of coin, the prohibition of export in an attempt to determine the real value of money and the control of the problem of price – including, in particular, a debate about the various quantity theories of money (for example, the debate between David Hume and Sir James Steuart).[9]

The most developed modern theory of the market appeared in the work of Adam Smith. The significance of this theory is that it has formed the enduring basis for subsequent economic analyses of money. On money, Smith claimed that 'it is not for its own sake that men desire money, but for the sake of what they can purchase with it'.[10] Writing against the mercantilists for whom the accumulation of money was the dynamic of economic activity – a conceptualisation of money which sought to justify trading and merchant activity – Smith sought to assert the instrumental rationality of money and the system it supports as a means of enhancing individual and collective material prosperity through a freely developing process of exchange. For Smith, consumption, not accumulation, was the dynamic of economic activity: 'consumption is the sole end and purpose of all production', a proposition 'so perfectly self-evident that it would be absurd to attempt to prove it'.[11]

Adam Smith naturalised production and consumption within an ideal model of reasonable exchange based around a claimed propensity in human nature 'to truck, barter and exchange one thing for another'. Money, the means through which one thing is exchanged for another thing, becomes a rational device facilitating a rational system, an instrument of exchange and account that enables a barter system to operate effectively and equitably. This system contains its own regulations through its own system of rewards for the thrifty and hard-working, and punishments for the indolent and greedy, with freedom of choice and equality of opportunity for all.

> If money is not an end in itself, but is merely a means of
> exchanging one thing for another, the powers attributed to

---

[8] Quoted in Tully 1982, p. 150.
[9] Clarke 1991, and Rubin 1979.
[10] Quoted in Clark 1988, p. 29.
[11] Quoted in Clark 1988, p. 29.

money are not inherent in money, but derive from its functions as a means of exchange. The rationality of money is the rationality of the system of exchange whose development it facilitates. Money is the means by which the hidden hand of the market achieves its ends.[12]

But within Smith there is no adequate account for the accumulation of money as profit: the process by which money makes itself into more money. Following his theory of value, where commodities exchange for the quantity of labour they embody, the cost of production or 'constant capital' (machinery, raw materials) resolves into revenue (wages, profit and rent). In this way, the entire product of society goes to the personal consumption of its members. Rubin called this an 'absurd conclusion'.[13] However, this became the dominant explanation of the classical school accepted by Ricardo, dogmatised by Say and repeated into the nineteenth century by J.S. Mill. The classical school was unable to deal with the consequences of the process, for in order to account for the expansion of money it had to abandon the naturalistic premise on which its assumptions were based. That is, it had to acknowledge that the natural equivalence of petty commodity production within which exchange is precipitated by the products of labour is undermined by a society taking on increasing regulatory and administrative forms in response to increasing injustice and disproportionality. Ricardo came close to making the point that profit equalled unpaid labour, but he failed to develop it. Thus, the classical school could not account for the continuing expansion of money as wealth and the creation of population into employed and unemployed.[14]

The shortcomings of this theory were revealed by the end of the nineteenth century when it became obvious that market rationalities (the hidden hand) did not benefit all sections of society. Poverty and its antagonistic forms – socialism – demanded a more convincing account. The new economic theory, marginalism, replaced the rationality of an economic system with the rationality of rational individuals as consumers making informed choices about their own needs as defined by their self-interest. The creation of the rational individual actor is derived out of the denial of the independent interest of the working class. This denial took the form of a political economy organised around subjectivist and individualist foundations. In economics this appeared as the marginalist revolution associated with Karl Menger in the Austrian school and Stanley Jevons in the UK. The accounts developed by these economists replaced the 'classic cost' of production theory of value with a subjective theory of value whereby distribution took place, not in terms of the laws of classical economics, but rather, according to moral and political judgement.

---

[12] Quoted in Clark 1988, p. 29.
[13] Rubin 1979, p. 212–13.
[14] Kay and Mott 1982.

J.M. Keynes: the magician of numbers.

A revolution in the theory of money appeared in response to the world crisis of money following the world's greatest economic disaster in the 1920s and 1930s. In this period J.M. Keynes was formulating an approach to money that was to have decisive importance for the modern world. We want to argue that this 'new' approach owed as much to alchemy as it did to classical economics. Keynes had been preoccupied with gold as a device for regulating economies, both as a supporter in the case of India in 1913 and as a strident critic against a return to the gold standard for the British economy following the First World War.[15] But his alchemic credentials are more interesting than that.[16] Keynes described Newton as 'the last magician'; for Skidelsky Keynes was the last magician of number.

> He was not the first of the modern statisticians, but the last of the magicians of number. For him the numbers were akin to those mystic 'signs' or 'clues' by which the necromancers had tried to uncover the secrets of the universe.[17]

This is the aspect of Newton that most attracted him.

> He regarded the universe as a cryptogram set by the Almighty. By pure thought, by concentration of mind, the riddle he believed, would be revealed to the initiate... For some purposes at least, Keynes thought that the distinctions between magic, science and art were less interesting than the similarities.[18]

While Keynes accepted the conventions of economics, especially the convention of rationality, scattered through his writings are clues to the fact that he regarded the intellectual technique he practised as a surface technique only. He recognised that public life was simply a world of appearance, and that beneath the knowledge in which he publicly dealt, there lay an esoteric knowledge open only to a few initiates, the pursuit of which fascinated him as it did Newton.[19] Arguing against the laissez-faire principles of classical economics, Keynes maintained that the market system was not self-regulating, it was not clockwork as it had been for Newton. The significance of that discovery is that the market ceases to be the motive power. It could not be the motive power because of difficulties within the nature of money itself. Following Aristotle and

---

[15] Clarke 1988, p. 204–5.
[16] Robert Skidelsky has noticed Keynes's interest in alchemy and Newton's experiments as a 'hobby'. Keynes did, indeed, talk about his interest in alchemy as a 'hobby', although for a hobby he was prepared to admit that it took up an inordinate amount of time: 'Newton still absorbs more time than it should; but that is a hobby' (16th August 1936 in a letter to his mother, quoted in Skiddelsky 1986, p. 626.).
[17] Skidelsky 1986, p. 414.
[18] Skidelsky 1986, p. 414.
[19] Skideslky 1986, p. 423.

Locke, Keynes recognised money as a means of exchange and as a store of value, but whereas they problematised these qualities as leading to an unnatural desire for conspicuous consumption or accumulation of more than one needs, Keynes recognised incipient problems within the relationship between these two functions of money which could only be resolved by extraneous interventions.

The significance of this understanding of the contradictory nature of money as a means of exchange and a store of value was that, because of the ignorance and uncertainty that characterised economic activity, it was rational for money to be withdrawn from circulation at times when the store could not be increased.[20] So if the hoarding of money could be prevented, production and profitability would ensue. This suggested not only that economic irregularities might not be resolved by market mechanisms and required intervention by the state, but more fundamentally, it pointed to the deeply problematic nature of money itself. In order to preserve itself as a store of value, money would evacuate the exchange process and thereby precipitate economic crises: the declining propensity to consume.

Keynes thus pointed to the influential nature of money itself: money as a means of social subjectivity, whose withdrawals or interventions had the capacity of a powerful social force to determine human life and the way in which it was lived. Keynes's alchemic importance, however, is that he discovered the *motive power*, the multiplicatory principle (the notion of the multiplier was an important one for alchemy) through which money could be produced. Through his theory of money, he established the link between the microcosm of man and the macrocosm of the universe; although for Keynes (wo)man was still the self-interested actor and his vision of a united universe was restricted to preserving the modern world of the bourgeoisie.

The basis of Keynes's magic formula for the expansion of money was labour. Keynes recognised the dangers inherent in attempting to reconcile the demands of the working class with the restrictions of the gold standard. Following war and the Bolshevik revolution he recognised that

> [t]he labouring classes may no longer be willing to forgo so largely, and the capitalist classes, no longer confident of the future, may seek to enjoy more fully their liberties of consumption so long as they last, and thus precipitate the hour of their confiscation. [21]

Keynes also realised the motive power of this antagonistic subjectivity. Since 1871 state intervention had been on the basis of the working class as the object of the process (as inertia): now to accommodate this revealed subjectivity the working class would have to be accommodated

---

[20] Keynes shared this observation with many earlier writers including Proudhon and Silvio Gessel (see Mattick 1941, p. 5.).
[21] From *The Economic Consequences of Peace* (1929), quoted in Mattick, 1971.

in its own terms.[22] In an attempt to prevent communism, and to reconcile the demands of the working class within the imperatives of profitable capitalist accumulation, Keynes developed a theory of macroeconomics. This entailed a concentration on money and its aggregate forms (savings, investment, balance of payments and, in particular, wages) as opposed to markets and prices. Orthodox economics argued that lower wages reduce unemployment and unemployment reduces wages, but Keynes maintained that wages were not flexible: workers had learned to defend them. Wages could be reduced more effectively than by trying to cut them. An increase in the quantity of money, linked to extra market policies to ensure 'effective demand' would raise prices and reduce real wages. This could be brought about through the management of mutually independent economic variables. For Keynes, these variables were the propensity to consume and the incentive to invest.

> [T]he wisest course is to advance on both fronts at once... to promote investments and at the same time, to promote consumption, not merely to the level which, with the existing propensity to consume, would correspond to the increased investment, but to a higher level still.[23]

Keynes's solution was profoundly alchemic. It involved the creation of money through a multiplication effect: loan-financed government investment and increased government spending which would be self-perpetuating and generate resources through taxation and saving to justify the initial deficit. Thus, in order to promote multiplication it involved the accumulation of induced effects through a manipulation (elaboration) of savings and investments. In this way, Keynes de-naturalised money and explained it as the means of articulating a particular system of social relationships.[24] But Keynes did not take this analysis of money any further, nor did he challenge the fundamental nature of capitalism. Thus, the nature of the regulation remains incidental to the purpose of regulation: to restore the essential unity of the bourgeois world.

While Keynes created the context within which the motive power of labour could be utilised as a potent catalyst in the expansion of money, his experiment could not control the reaction. The system went into melt-down: *inflation*. This appeared in the 1970s in the form of an economic crisis and the collapse of the boom.[25] Despite the importance of his work, Keynes had not fundamentally challenged the basic assumptions of bourgeois economics. The consequence of this was that Keynes was re-assimilated into neo-classical economics as a particular

---

[22] Negri 1988, p. 12.
[23] From *The General Theory of Employment, Interest and Money*, quoted in Mattick 1971, p. 13–14.
[24] Clarke 1988, p. 235.
[25] A logical and historical analysis of these developments is presented in Clarke 1988.

approach to economics rather than a revolution in economic thought. His alchemic approach was reversed, to emerge as bad alchemy, to become not an expansion in the supply of money, but an attempt to control the money supply and to discipline, rather than enhance, the motive power of labour. Alchemy dissolves into a preoccupation with mysticism and metallurgy – *monetarism*. This re-assimilation was associated with a denial of the idea that the state could regulate the harmonious development of capitalism. It was replaced with the notion that only the market had that capacity, and that barriers to the smooth operation of that market must be removed. This included the state itself, trade unions, popular democracy, a concentration of supply-side measures, deregulation and privatisation. The effectiveness of this model relies on the stability of money as an accurate means for the communication of information – as prices – and, therefore, demands a predictable and stable monetary policy. In the pursuit of 'sound money' all else must be sacrificed.

Sociology and the avoidance of money.

The space created by the demise of alchemy as a search for the secret of money was filled by theories of money concentrating on the market and prices: the formal and symbolic appearance of economic relationships. While this was sufficient to explain rational activity within the limits of the distribution of scarce resources based on individual subjectivity in conjunction with supply and demand, a gap was left that needed to be filled in order to explain behaviour that lay outside of this economic relation. This explanation was based on the same limited assumptions concerning the formal rationality of exchange as had been developed by marginalist economics and it took the form of modern sociology: the attempt to rationalise the rationality of money as the basis for social action based on non-rational activity. This is evident in classical sociology in Weber's protestant ethic, in Simmel's phenomenology of money and endures through to the structural functionalism of Talcott Parsons and Jürgen Habermas.

In the work of Parsons[26] we find the rationality of a fusion of value (object) and values (subject) in a sociological Keynesian utopia. Parsons articulates the Keynesian-inspired sociological notion of the subjectivity of money. According to Parsons, money is the rational symbol through which the goals and functions of the constituent sub-systems of society can be both represented and realised. Money ensures that the goods which an economy produces are those which consumers require and allows the state to reward productivity through the allocation of capital funds. Money also encourages entrepreneurial activity through the allocation of profit to innovative firms and individuals (cf. Schumpeter).

---

[26] See Parsons 1949a, 1949b and 1951.

In this way money constitutes a rational mechanism of communication between the 'economic' and political, ideological and cultural institutions of society.

Habermas attempts to deny this subjectivity. In Habermas we find the rupture of the unity between value (object) and values (subject) and an attempt to ground rationality on an inter-subjective denial of the object (value). This corresponds to the crisis of Keynesian money and money forms. In Habermas's system, power and money are divorced. Habermas rejected the labour theory of value and accepted Weber's theory of the state and political power.[27] It is this which allows the functional separation of economy, polity and socio-cultural spheres in Habermas's analysis of late capitalist society.[28] Money becomes merely an alienated form of 'steering mechanism' which prevents the development of 'communicative rationality'. Money, therefore, is reified as something outside the social relations which constitute the 'lifeworld' and which prevents rational communication. Habermas puts money in a box and allows it to escape only when it interferes with free and equal linguistic exchanges in the mythological sphere of civil society.

This was not a mistake of the classical sociology from which Habermas drew so much of his inspiration, particularly Georg Simmel. Simmel articulated the irrationality of money – although this was articulated alongside the formal rationality of capitalism. Simmel captured the phenomenological spirit of money in his seminal *The Philosophy of Money* (1906). Simmel argued that money constituted the essence of modernity, for it was through money that the modern spirit found its true expression. Simmel was concerned with the irrationality of a society dominated by money. This irrationality was attributed to a universal metaphysic or psychological process premised on the inversion of means and ends and evoked only because money is wrongly designated the supreme instrument of reason. Money facilitated the objectification of culture through the way in which the division of labour and the development of the money economy created a specific form of mutual impersonal dependence. The development of the money economy increased individual liberty and individualism, but in a way in which the subjective and objective aspects of life were torn apart. That is, money created a relationship between individuals whilst leaving individuality outside monetary relationships.

Whilst sociology has recognised the irrationality of money it has simultaneously avoided any confrontation with the content of this irrationality. This has been achieved through the invention of the 'lifeworld': a sphere in which social subjects are able to escape the objective impositions of money and the state. Sociology has thus tended to *avoid* the contradictions of money. However, as the crises and contradictions of Keynesianism intensified, sociological conceptions of money became increasingly abstract. In the historical context of bad alchemy, sociology

---

[27] Habermas 1971.
[28] Habermas 1988.

has retreated into hyper-abstraction – poststructuralist concerns to present money as merely a simulacrum. Money as simulacrum is the most developed form of the avoidance of the search for money. There is no real money. Therefore, there is no real secret. In postmodern social theory, as in all sociology, money is conjured out of *sheer intelligence* (speculation). Derrida, quoting Mallarmé, remarks on this process as constituting the death of alchemy, what he refers to as the victory of 'sheer intelligence':

> A certain deference, towards the extinct laboratory of the philosophers' elixir, would consist of taking up again, without the furnace, the manipulations, the poisons cooled down into something other than precious stones, so as to continue through sheer intelligence... The null stone, dreaming of gold, once called the philosophical: but it foreshadows, in finance, the future *credit*, preceding *capital* or reducing it to the humility of *money*.[29]

Money becomes a sign amongst other signs, but is more than a sign, a ghost. Its ghostly appearance is conjured out of the inability of sociology in its structural and poststructural forms to go beyond reciprocity in its analysis of money. Money is only true money when it emerges as the simulacrum of discourse: a sign or symbol. That is to say, there is no way of knowing what is or is not counterfeit, other than the discursive meaning that is imposed on money: '[A] true corpus is still perhaps counterfeit money; it may be a ghost or a spirit and of capital.'[30]

And Derrida adds that Marx too, who he regards as the chief wizard of money, fails to penetrate the ghostly apparition of money.

> Marx always described money, and more precisely the monetary sign, in the figure of appearance or simulacrum, more exactly of a ghost. The figural presentation of the concept seemed to describe some spectral *thing*... Gold or silver produces a remainder. This remainder is – it remains, precisely – but the shadow of a great name. "The body of money is but a shadow". The whole movement of idealisation that Marx then describes, whether it is a question of money or of ideologemes, is a production of ghosts, illusions, simulacra, appearances.[31]

According to Derrida, Marx was afraid of ghosts. Marx was not a magician content to drive away or exorcise the magic of ghosts with a counter-magic. Marx attempted to exorcise the ghost through a methodology which counterpoised the simulacrum with effective reality – life against death. Despite this, Derrida holds that Marx did not

---

[29] Derrida 1992, p. 116–7. Italics in original.
[30] Derrida 1992, p. 97.
[31] Derrida 1992, p. 37. Our italics.

actually transcend magic and counter-magic. In other words Marx was a magician:

> [Marx] tried to conjure away the ghosts, and everything that was neither life nor death, namely, the re-apparition of the apparition that will never be either the appearing or the disappeared, the phenomenon or its contrary.[32]

In other words Marx both invented and subsequently denied the simulacrum and the symbolic and ghostly existence of money. This theme has also been developed in the work of Jean Baudrillard who has been central in articulating the apparent pre-eminence of the sign and sign-value in the postmodern order. His work is instructive as his theoretical starting point is Althusserian structuralism. In his earlier works Baudrillard developed an essentially Althusserian Marxism in order to supplement orthodox Marxism's critique of capitalism with an assessment of the increasing domination of the objects of consumption over individual subjectivity.[33] According to this view, consumption had replaced production as the central mode of homogenisation, alienation and exploitation. Consumption constitutes a higher level of reification through which the 'signs' and 'symbols' attached to commodities result in the total death of the subject by the world of objects (the death of the individual and the social world). The most important form of labour becomes the labour of consuming commodities which allow one to differentiate oneself from others through the meaning, prestige and identity attached to commodities.

The ranking of commodities is achieved through a 'code of political economy' which links sign-value to exchange-value (money).

> [I]t is the code that is determinant: the rules of the interplay between signifiers and exchange-value. Generalised in the system of political economy, it is the code which, in both cases reduces all symbolic ambivalence in order to ground the 'rational' circulation of values and their play of exchange in the regulated equivalence of values.[34]

Money is the derivative of the code. The domination of capitalist society is symbolic. Money has no content except symbolic content: it is determined from the abstract as an abstract form. Money is alienating only in respect of the role it plays in the symbolic system of meaning represented by the economic logic of political economy.

The abstraction of money is mirrored in the abstraction of intellect: money and sheer intellect both serving the highest and most base needs and desires. The money economy creates an *abstract* structure or system which reflects back on the objects from which it has been

---

[32] Derrida 1992, p. 37.
[33] Baudrillard 1968, 1970.
[34] Baudrillard 1972, p. 146–7.

abstracted – the ghostly apparitions and spectral forms of money. This abstract structure is constituted by a metaphysical manifestation of objectified culture which, through the increasing rapidity of 'time-space compression'[35] associated with the money economy, creates an irresolvable tension between the totality of society and the totality of the individual. As we demonstrate in the next section it is through the 'real magic' of Karl Marx's methodology that the reified apparitions and ghosts of the world of money can be revealed and exorcised.

Marx, real magic and the critique of money.

Marx was a magician but his sorcery was of a different order of that outlined by Derrida. The reified and fetished nature of money is both abstract and real; between life and death – indeed a real abstract mediator between life and death. In denying the possibility of life out of death, poststructuralism articulates the death of money, the crisis of money – the death of the social – as the subject is objectified and the object becomes self-referential. The reassimilation of Keynes into classical economics denies money a subjectivity and so it becomes an object of itself – a ghostly apparition, a simulacrum. The possession of money becomes the most abstract and total expression of individualism, freedom and self-expression and, indeed, a differentiation within the individual: a fragmentation of the self along the myriad of fragmented monetary relations in a generalised money economy. These peculiar characteristics of money make money both a means and an end in (post)modern society linking all contents of life into a limitless teleological relationship and all relationships expressed in terms of objective exchange.

The problem with this sociology of money in both its modern and postmodern forms is that it both conceptualises money as a medium of communication (interaction) and reduces money to a harmless social device with no recognition of its 'orientation to pecuniary acquisition for its own sake'.[36] What Weber and Simmel alluded to but did not develop is the differentiation between money-as-money and money-as-capital. This distinction highlights the problem with poststructuralist conceptualisations of money which fail to recognise the existence of money as anything other than exchange (the spectre) and that 'it is only in the form of money as capital that the limitless drive for the enlargement of exchange-value can turn from a mere chimera into a living, actual reality'.[37] For Marx money is a symbol, but it is more than a symbol: it is a symbol of itself and, in that way, denies its symbolic life. Money is constantly becoming more than itself through its own self-expansion. It is a ghost of something that is not yet dead. Money is

---

[35] Harvey 1990.
[36] Weber 1968, p. 159.
[37] Rosdolsky 1977, p. 187.

living death. Money constitutes a loss of humanity as not-life; of living death. Money becomes the ultimate, supreme being.

> Through this *alien mediator* man gazes at his will, his activity, his relation to others as a power independent of them and of himself – instead of man himself being the mediator for man. His slavery thus reaches a climax. It is obvious that this *mediator* must be a *veritable* God since the mediator is the real power over that which mediates me. His cult becomes an end in itself. Separated from this mediator, objects lose their worth. Thus they only have value in so far as they *represent* him.[38]

Human activity (labour) is estranged and becomes the property of a material thing external to man – money. The cult of money becomes an end in itself. Man has a value only to the extent that he is represented by money – the anticipation of Simmel is startling, but now the important difference ... Man becomes money or becomes that which money can buy. Money has magical qualities. Money can conjure intelligence out of stupidity, beauty out of ugliness:

> The properties of money are my... properties and essential powers. Therefore what I am and what I can do is by no means determined by my individuality. I am ugly, but I can buy the *most beautiful* woman. Which means to say that I am not ugly, for the effect of my ugliness, its repelling power, is destroyed by money... I am a wicked, dishonest, unscrupulous and stupid individual, but money is respected and so is its owner... Through money I can have anything the human heart desires.[39]

Money therefore is a truly creative power. It transforms the contents of the imagination into sensual reality. Without money the demands, passions and desires latent in the imagination remain in the realm of ideas. Needs only exist if there is money to actualise them in reality. As Marx noted,

> money turns the imagination into reality and reality into mere imagination... real, human natural powers into purely abstract representations and tormenting phantoms, just as it turns real imperfections and phantoms... into real essential powers and abilities. Thus characterised *money is the universal inversion of individualities.*[40]

Man (the subject) becomes poorer as the mediator (the thing/object) becomes richer. Money is the omnipotent and ultimate mediator and objectification of human needs.

---

[38] Marx 1975a, pp. 260–1. Italics in original.
[39] Marx 1975b, p. 377. Italics in original.
[40] Marx 1975b, p. 387. Our italics.

> Money, in as much as it possesses the *property* of being able
> to buy everything and appropriate all objects, is the *object*
> most worth possessing... money is the *pimp* between need
> and object, between life and man's means of life. But *that*
> which mediates *my* life also *mediates* the existence of other
> men for me. It is for me the *other* person.[41]

Money is the universal confusion of an inverted world. Money is not
only contradictory but makes the contradictions embrace one another.
Money is therefore the primordial locus of alienation and reification in
bourgeois society. It is however the particular form that money takes
that allows us to see the distinctiveness of Marx's approach. The
ultimate achievement of Marx the magician was to unveil the
simulacrum of its mystical appearance and reveal the subjectivity of
labour beneath it. There is a difference between Marx's notion of the
abstract nature of money and the concept of simulacrum. A simulacrum
is the identical copy of an original that never existed, an abstract
abstraction; whereas Marx reveals the material content of the
abstraction. He did this through an analysis of labour.

Keynes, as we have seen, recognised the importance of labour as his
motive power. But this motivation and its possibilities were limited by
his vision of the united universe: the preservation of the bourgeois
world. In this sense Keynes was not a magician, but an illusionist,
preserving rather than challenging the mystification of capitalistic social
relations. Marx, on the other hand, was the real magician;
understanding the motive power (subjectivity) of labour and the
possibilities for social transformation. His alchemic importance was to
recognise that the motive power for the expansion of money lay in the
potential that is inherent in the contradiction between labour (as
rationality: the unity of need and capacity, ie. a world without money
capital) and labour-power (as the inability to exist other than through
money capital as the wage, the separation of need and capacity). The
expansion of money lay in the transmutation by labour of one form of
matter (nature) into another form (value).

> When man engages in production, he can only proceed as
> nature does herself, i.e. he can only change the form of the
> materials. Furthermore, even in this work of modification he
> is constantly helped by natural forces. Labour then is not the
> only source of material wealth. [42]

And in a profoundly alchemic moment Marx adds in a footnote:

> All the phenomena of the universe whether produced by the
> hand or indeed by the universal laws of physics, are not to be

---

[41] Marx 1975b, p. 375. Italics in original.
[42] Marx 1954, p. 134.

conceived of as an act of creation but solely as a reordering of
matter. Composition and separation are the only elements
found by the human mind whenever it analyses the notion of
reproduction of value... and wealth whether *earth, air* and
water are turned into corn in the fields, the secretions of an
insect are turned into silk by the hand of man, or some small
pieces of metal are arranged to form a repeating watch (from
Pietro Verri, *Meditazioni sulla economia politica* [1771] in
Custodi's edition of the Italians economists, Parte moderna,
vol. 15: 21–22).[43]

What this suggests is that the immanent energy of matter lay within
matter itself. Hence, while the social power of money appears outside
the process of commodity production, and is represented thus by the
economists, the motivating energy of this power lies immanently within
the money form itself: not as money as money, but money as capital.
Marx formulated the difference between money as money and money as
capital within the equations C–M–C and M–C–M', where C =
commodity and M = money. Capitalist production involves the
reproduction of capital or self-expanding value. The basis of this self-
expansion is labour-power. In this process money (the general form)
and the commodity (the particular form) function only as different
modes of existence of capital. Value is, therefore, the subject of this
process, changing from one form to another without becoming lost in
the movement, but in the process it changes its own magnitude,
throwing off surplus value from itself, and therefore valorising itself
independently:

> For the movement in the course of which it adds surplus-
> value is its own movement, its valorisation is therefore self-
> valorisation. By virtue of its being value, it has acquired the
> occult ability to add value to itself.[44]

In this process money is the independent form through which value
preserves itself and expands. Money provides value with an identity with
which to assert its dominant subjectivity through its process of self-
expansion (capital).

Marx discovered the occult nature of money's ability to expand
through itself. While money provides value in process (capital) with an
identifiable form through which it can expand, it does not imply any
change in the magnitude of the value. In the process of exchange
(circulation) money functions as the universal equivalent and, therefore,
a change of value cannot take place in the money form itself. The
change, therefore, can only occur in the use-value of the commodity, in
its consumption. It was Marx's major theoretical breakthrough that he
identified the commodity whose use-value possesses the peculiar quality

---

[43] Our italics
[44] Marx 1956, p. 255.

of being a source and creation of value. The commodity is the capacity to labour: labour-power.[45]

It was with the discovery of labour-power (the social form of labour) that Marx was able to postulate the source of surplus value (the social content ie. the alchemic principle). The separation theorised in Marx's early work (alienated labour) is now given a concrete material and socially specific reality and takes the form of the working class as a mass of people separated from themselves (labour and labour-power) and the means of their own survival (the means of production). The perpetuation of this separation is the absolutely necessary precondition for capitalist production.[46] It is this relationship of contradiction, antagonism and struggle over production, generalised through reproduction to the whole of human experience, and apparent in the struggle of everyday life that forms the social basis for the social relations of capitalist society and by which their contradictory nature can be understood.[47]

In this paper we have showed how in the world of money and self-expanding money (capital) it does appear that money changes everything. But as Marx exposed, the power of money is conjured out of the alienation of labour. The fifth element, the quintessence of money, is labour. Marx discovered what alchemy did not know: the secret of money. But Marx's discovery was not an esoteric achievement. Marx's magic was real magic. Ernst Fischer in *The Necessity of Art* defines magic as the domination of nature and the avoidance of work. Through his analysis of capitalist society Marx explained how the imposition of work through the commodity form (the separation of need and capacity of the working class) could be transformed into a state of abundance (ie. the unity of need and capacity) and capitalist work abandoned. Thus, the real importance of Marx's magic was to realise that money as money changes nothing, it is a ghost; and that the real 'spirit' of money is labour. But in the world of money capital labour is forced to exist as labour-power: as negative human capacity. In capitalist society money is the negation of human personality: the subjectivity of man denied by the objectivity of the thing (money). But this opens up an important gap in materialist investigation: the way the contradictory processes associated with money capital are lived as individuated biography and personality. Marx alludes to the importance of developing a materialist psychology but did not develop this idea further.[48] The poststructuralist escape into hyper-abstraction and hyper-individualism make such a project ever more essential. Through a reapplication of Marx's magic there is an urgent need to uncover the real abstractions through which money as capital moves and the way in which human life and individual

---

[45] Marx 1956, p. 270.
[46] Marx 1956, p. 716.
[47] Marx 1956, p. 724.
[48] See Marx 1975b, p. 354.

personality exist as institutional forms of this process as individuated
biography and personality.

References

Baudrillard, Jean 1968, *Le Système des objects*, Paris: Denoel-
Gonthier.
Baudrillard, Jean 1978, *La Société de consommation*, Paris: Gallimard.
Baudrillard, Jean 1981, *For a Critique of the Political Economy of the
Sign*, St Louis: Telos Press.
Clarke, Simon 1988, *Keynesianism, Monetarism and the Crisis of the
State*, Aldershot: Edward Elgar.
Clarke, Simon 1991, Marx, *Marginalism and Modern Sociology: From
Adam Smith to Max Weber*, London: Macmillan.
Craig, J. 1946, *Newton at the Mint*, Cambridge: Cambridge University
Press.
Crosland, M.P. 1962, *Historical Studies in the Language of Chemistry*,
London: Heinemann.
Derrida, Jacques 1992, *Given Time: Counterfeit Money*, Chicago:
University of Chicago Press.
Dobb, B. 1975, *The Foundations of Newton's Alchemy*, Cambridge:
Cambridge University Press.
Habermas, Jürgen 1972, *Knowledge and Human Interests*, London:
Heineman.
Habermas, Jürgen 1988, *Legitimation Crisis*, Cambridge: Polity.
Harvey, David 1990, *The Condition of Postmodertnity*, Oxford:
Blackwell.
Kay, G. & Mott, J. 1982, *Political Order and the Law of Labour*,
London: Macmillan.
Marx, Karl 1954, *Capital: A Critique of Political Economy Vol. One*,
London: Lawrence & Wishart.
Marx, Karl 1956, 'Comments on Adolf Wagner' in *Werke* Vol. 19, pp.
355ff. Berlin.
Marx, Karl 1975a, 'Excepts from James Mill's "Elements of Political
Economy" in *Early Writings*, Harmondsworth: Penguin.
Marx, Karl 1975b, 'Economic and Philosophical Manuscripts' in *Early
Writings*, Harmondsworth: Penguin.
Mattick, Paul 1971, *Marx and Keynes: The Limits of the Mixed
Economy*, London: Merlin.
Negri, Toni 1988, *Revolution Retrieved*, London: Red Notes
Parsons, Talcott 1949a, *Essays in Sociological Theory*, Illinois: Free
Press.
Parsons, Talcott 1949b, *The Structure of Social Action*, Illinois: Free
Press.
Parsons, Talcott 1951, *The Social System*, Illinois: Free Press.
Read, J. 1961, *Through Alchemy to Chemistry*, London: Bell & Sons.

Rosdolsky, Roman 1980, *The Making of Marx's Capital* Volume One, London: Pluto Press.

Rubin, Isaak I. 1979, *A History of Economic Thought*, London: Pluto Press.

Skidelsky, Robert 1986, *John Maynard Keynes: A Biography* Volume One, London: Viking.

Tully, J. 1982, *A Discourse on Property: John Locke and his Adversaries*, Cambridge: Cambridge University Press.

Weber, Max 1968, *Economy and Society* 3 volumes, Berkeley: University of California Press.

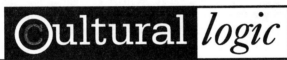

an electronic journal of marxist theory & practice

Internet: http://eserver.org/clogic   **E-mail:** clogic@eserver.org

Editors: David Siar, Gregory Meyerson, and James Neilson

Volume One, Number One:
Neil Larsen, "Poverties of Nation: *The Ends of the Earth*, 'Monetary Subjects without Money,' and Postcolonial Theory"; Teresa L. Ebert, "Quango-ing the University: The End(s) of Critique-al Humanities"; Gregory Meyerson, "Marxism, Psychoanalysis, and Labor Competition"; Adam Katz, "Postmodern Cultural Studies: A Critique"; Greg Dawes, "On the Textualization of History and Sexuality in Hispanism"; Carol A. Stabile, "From the Cold War to the Hot Zone: Nature, Capitalism, and the Postmodern Apocalypse"; Rich Gibson, "The Michigan Social Studies Standards"; Jeffrey Youdelman, "A Tribute to William S. Burroughs"; poetry by Amitava Kumar; reviews by Martha E. Gimenez, Imre Szeman, and Patricia Comitini

Surface mail:
P.O. Box 78032
Wichita, KS 67278-0382
US

A Critique of Neo-Malthusian Marxism: Society, Nature, and Population[1]

Paul Burkett

Introduction

Recent decades have seen a rethinking and renewal of Marxism on various levels, beginning in the 1950s and 1960s when New-Left movements in the developed capitalist countries combined with Maoist, Guevarist, and other Third-World liberation struggles to challenge the ossified theory and practice of Soviet-style communism and traditional social democracy. More recently, the rethinking of Marxism has been driven largely by the collapse of the Soviet Union and its official Marxist ideology, and by the movement toward neoliberal 'free market' policies on a global scale, which together have brought forth a tidal wave of frankly pro-capitalist as well as 'postmodern' left varieties of 'end of history'-type thinking. The contemporary challenge to Marxism, however, also has a positive side in the form of popular revolts against the neoliberalisation of the global economy – the Chiapas rebellion in Mexico, the December 1995 public sector upheavals in France, and many others, not to mention the heroic struggle of the Cuban people against the threat of recolonisation by US and global capital. Here the challenge is to incorporate the changing forms of working-class movement, and their new prefigurations of post-capitalist society, into the theory and practice of Marxian communism.

In this context, one of the most important forces encouraging the renovation of Marxism has been the growing popularity of environmentalist thinking in both mainstream and left intellectual circles, as well as the increasing emphasis on environmental issues in grassroots movements and struggles. The 'environmental justice' movements struggling against the selective concentration of ecological hazards in marginalised working-class areas, and the struggles of indigenous peoples world-wide against the capitalisation and degradation of their lands, are just two of the many indications that environmental concerns must be integral to Marxist theory and praxis.[2] The biospheric disruptions being produced by capitalist development, including global warming and reduced species diversity, also underline

---

[1] The author extends gratitude to John Bellamy Foster and the *HM* editorial board for comments and encouragement.
[2] Churchill 1993, Foster 1994, Chapter 7.

the need to incorporate ecological phenomena into Marxist analyses of capital accumulation and socio-economic crisis. It is therefore unsurprising that a new school of ecological Marxists (or 'eco-Marxists') has grown rapidly in recent years – a school whose work has centred largely on the correction of the ecological inadequacies of traditional Marxism. This development can only be welcomed by all Marxists interested in effectively grounding their theory and praxis in the material, social, and political reality of our times.

At the same time, any ecological renovation of Marxism should carefully recognise and utilise the intellectual resources that classical Marxism, as represented first and foremost by the work of Marx and Engels, can bring to bear on environmental issues – especially as these resources have often been downplayed if not ignored by Marxists themselves. Otherwise, the renovation process may be all too easily shifted onto the convenient road of uncritically transplanting 'ecologically correct' non-Marxist analyses into the main body of Marxism – the likely result being a watering-down of Marxism's materialist, class-relational, and human-emancipatory content. To be effective both analytically and politically, the critical incorporation of modern ecological knowledge into Marxist theory, and its application to concrete environmental issues and struggles, should be preceded by a full-scale inventory of the methods and categories with which Marx and Engels incorporated natural conditions into their analyses of capitalism and their projections of communism. The goal of the present work is to improve the accuracy of this inventory via a response to Ted Benton's influential 'ecological critique and reconstruction' of classical Marxism.[3]

Unlike most ecological critiques of Marx, Benton's tries to base itself on what Marx (and Engels) actually wrote about natural conditions under capitalism and communism. Moreover, Benton's argument encompasses a broad range of issues connected with the relations between Marxism and environmentalism – including Marx's critique of Malthus, the stance of Marxism on the natural limits to human production, and the Marxist conception of agricultural and other 'eco-regulated' production processes not reducible to transformative human labour. As a result, Benton's work uniquely encapsulates the most popular ecological criticisms of Marx, and this helps to account for the respect Benton's work has received from green theorists including many eco-Marxists.[4]

---

[3] Benton 1989.

[4] Benton's *New Left Review* piece was successful enough to warrant a summary version in a Verso collection on new directions in socialist thought as well as a reprint. (Benton 1991, and 1996). In the former volume, Kate Soper endorses Benton's 'pertinent indications of the conceptual inadequacies' of Marx from an ecological perspective (Soper 1991, p. 292, footnote 18). Benton's (1989) critique of Marx has not, however, been engaged in detail by any Marxist. Harvey's (1993) observations on Benton's views are highly general, while Grundmann (1991) limits himself mostly to a friendly juxtaposition of his own technological-determinist interpretation with the anti-ecological human 'domination' of nature that Benton purportedly detects in Marx. While Vlachou (1994) also detects a desocialised naturalism in Benton (1989), she does not

Most importantly, however, Benton motivates his reconstruction with a question as paradoxical as it is politically crucial: given that Marx and Engels embraced a materialist conception of history recognising the natural conditions of socio-economic life, how can one explain the history of 'bad blood' between Marxists and environmentalists, between the Red and the Green? Benton's answer to this question is equally challenging. He suggests that Marxists have too often over-reacted to Malthusian and other conservative natural limits arguments by asserting the historical contingency of environmental problems in 'social constructionist' ways which downgrade the role of natural conditions in delimiting, and shaping the material forms of, human production and development. Benton argues that Marxists can and should insist on the historical specificity of natural conditions and limits in terms of particular social relations of production, without downgrading nature's importance for human development. I would like to take this opportunity to endorse this element of Benton's argument. And although I disagree with his contention that Marx and Engels themselves fell prey to social constructionism, I still want to commend Benton for addressing the relationship between Marxism and environmentalism in such insightful terms. I hope he agrees that the questions I raise about his critique and reconstruction shed further light on the paradox of the materialist Marx versus anti-naturalist interpretations of Marxism.

Benton's analysis has two components: an ecological critique of *Capital*, based primarily on purported inadequacies in Marx's treatment of the labour process; plus an explanation of how these inadequacies came about.[5] The second component has two sub-arguments. First, Benton argues that *Capital's* environmental shortcomings derive largely from Marx's adoption, 'with important modifications', of the classical labour theory of value.[6] Second, Benton suggests that the 'crucial hiatus' between the 'naturalist and materialist' Marx and his ecologically inadequate 'economic theory' was rooted in a politically motivated 'Utopian over-reaction' to the conservative influence of Malthusian thinking. Specifically, Marx and Engels responded to Malthusianism by hastening a 'wholesale retreat into social constructionism' and 'productivist ideology', thus abandoning their ecologically correct but politically inconvenient 'materialist premises'.[7]

The present article focuses on the Marx/Malthus relationship, and Marx's *Capital* is discussed only insofar as is absolutely necessary to respond to Benton's charge of a social-constructionist reaction to Malthus.[8] I shall begin by showing that Benton's methodology centres

grapple with the details of Benton's ecological arguments. In addition, Vlachou (1989) confuses the issues by conflating material/social relations with thought/reality relations.
[5] Benton 1989.
[6] Benton 1989, p. 76.
[7] Benton 1989, pp. 55, 58, 77.
[8] Marx's value theory and the purported ecological shortcomings of *Capital* are treated in a forthcoming companion paper (Burkett 1998).

on a dichotomisation of the material and the social that is not found in Marx. I then demonstrate that this material/social bifurcation manifests itself in a series of additional dichotomies in Benton's critique: between Marx's principle of historical specification and Marx's applications of this principle to capitalism and communism, between the methodological and the empirical, and between analytical method and revolutionary praxis. Benton's material/social dichotomy is also manifested in the key role played by ahistorical notions of natural limits in his own conception of historical materialism. This Malthusianised Marxism is the vantage point from which Benton criticises Marx in order to 'facilitate the Red/Green dialogue', as when Benton appeals to Malthusian wage theory to criticise Marx's reserve army analysis.[9] Benton's analytical strategy thus leads to a dematerialisation of class and de-classing of the material in Marx's approach to human production, population, and capital accumulation – with potentially crippling analytical and political results.

Basic methodological characteristics of neo-Malthusian Marxism

Benton interprets 'historical materialism' as the view that 'human social life [is] dependent upon nature-given material conditions':

> The requirement that humans must interact with their natural environment in order to meet their needs is a transhistorical feature of the human predicament ... [T]he key to understanding the geographic *variations* and historical *transformations* in the form of human social and political life is to be found in the various ways in which these societies interact with nature.[10]

For Benton, what distinguishes the human metabolism with nature is that

> compared with other animal species, humans are exceptionally adaptable vis-à-vis their environmental conditions of existence, and also possess the capacity for a generation-by-generation cumulative augmentation of their transformative powers. These and other features define the *particularities* of human ecology, and also determine the enormous causal importance of human environmental impacts on the ecology of other species.[11]

---

[9] Benton 1989, p. 51.
[10] Benton 1989, p. 54.
[11] Benton 1989, pp. 54–5.

Benton should be applauded for pointing out the relevance of 'an ecological approach to ... human nature and history' for 'the basic ideas of historical materialism'.[12] The problem is that he recasts these basic ideas into a crude materialist form. While nominally endorsing the 'social and political' character of human life, Benton's conception does not explicitly recognise that 'the various ways in which societies interact with nature' are themselves socially constituted. There is no recognition of the material content of social relations, as in Marx and Engels's insistence that each 'mode of co-operation, or social stage ... is itself a "productive force"'.[13] Neither is there any perception of the social character of material conditions once these conditions are viewed as conditions of human *social* life. In short, Benton conceptualises human existence in terms of a spatial metaphor in which the social and the material are separate realms that interact with one another. Marx, on the other hand, treats human life as a contradictory unity (or unity-in-difference) of the *mutually constituted* social form and material content. Marx and Engels accordingly describe the 'sum of productive forces' as 'a historically created relation to nature *and* of individuals to one another'.[14]

Benton does not ground the exceptional human capabilities for adaptation to natural conditions, and for 'cumulative augmentation of their transformative powers', in the social character of human production. His desocialised specification of human ecology implies a dematerialised conception of social relations – placing severe analytical handicaps on any 'recognition that each form of social/economic life has its own specific mode and dynamic of interrelation with its own specific contextual conditions'.[15] Not surprisingly, then, the ascription of his own social/material dichotomy to Marx makes it easier for Benton to claim that Marx's 'historical/social relativisation' of natural conditions and limits involves a social constructionist retreat from ecologically correct 'historical materialism'.[16] It is only *after* submitting dematerialised renditions of Marx's analyses of the reserve army and labour-power reproduction, for example, that Benton subjects these analyses to his ecological critique.

Benton is right that Marxists should never downgrade the importance of material conditions in general and ecological conditions

---

[12] Benton 1989, p. 55.
[13] Marx and Engels 1976, p. 49.
[14] Marx and Engels 1976, p. 62, my emphasis. See also Marx 1933, p. 28, and 1973, p. 87, Rosdolsky 1977, p. 78, and Ollman 1993, Chapter 2. For Marx and Engels (1976, p. 37), the 'mode of production must not be considered simply as being the reproduction of the physical existence of the individuals. Rather it is a definite form of activity of these individuals, a definite form of expressing their life, a definite *mode of life* on their part'.
[15] Benton 1989, p. 77. Benton adopts this desocialisation of historical materialism despite his having quoted Marx's famous 1859 *Preface* explicitly specifying human life as a 'social production of ... existence', and the 'mode of production of material life' as occurring in and through 'definite social relations'. Marx 1970, p. 20.
[16] Benton 1989, p. 77.

in particular. The fact is, however, that the 'materialist premises' that Benton has Marx retreating from are not Marx's; they are rather the desocialised premises of Benton's Malthusian Marxism. Whence Benton's repeated appeals to natural conditions and limits not conceptualised in relation to historically specific social forms even in the general sense that all societies have specific social production relations. Among these Malthusian conceptions are 'ultimate natural limits to population, or to human transformative powers', 'nature-imposed limits to human potential', and 'the human predicament ... that humans must interact with their natural environment in order to meet their needs'.[17] Benton even offers up an empirical endorsement of Malthus's pseudo-naturalistic population theory. As shown below, it is only from the standpoint of such desocialised conceptions of human production and reproduction that Marx's historical specification of material conditions appears as a 'retreat from ... thoroughgoing historical materialism' into 'some form of social constructionism'.[18]

Marx and Malthus's population 'laws'

Benton describes Marx and Engels's critique of Malthus's law of population as

> double-pronged: first, a series of arguments against the universality and necessity of the law, and, second, a reconceptualisation and explanation of the phenomenon – a relative surplus population – which Malthus had addressed, as an effect not of the human predicament, but of the dynamics of capital accumulation ... This dual strategy against Malthus – denial of *naturally* imposed limits, but recognition of historically transitory *socially* imposed limits – has clear political consequences.[19]

Benton is right about Marx rejecting the notion of purely natural limits to human reproduction. What Benton leaves out, however, is the materialist *and* social-relational character of Marx's response to Malthus. To begin with, the above-quoted interpretation dichotomises the material and the social. Benton's stark contrast between naturally and socially imposed limits presumes that natural limits cannot themselves be socially imposed – a presumption contradicting Benton's nominal endorsement of the social specificity of human production's natural conditions and limits. Similarly, the counterposing of 'the human predicament' and 'the dynamics of capital accumulation' as alternative causes of the relative surplus population presumes that the latter dynamics are strictly non-material and the former predicament

---

[17] Benton 1989, p. 59, pp. 55–6, p. 54 respectively.
[18] Benton 1989, pp. 55, 77.
[19] Benton 1989, pp. 59–60.

strictly non-social according to Marx and Engels. Whence Benton's repeated assertions that when Marx and Engels criticise Malthus for not treating the conditions and limits of capitalist production in terms of capitalism's specific production relations, this itself constitutes a denial, or at least a downgrading, of natural conditions and limits; for example:

> Marx and Engels were disposed, especially through their critiques of Malthus, to reject as necessarily conservative 'natural-limits' arguments. Whilst they were firmly committed to the view that capital accumulation *was* subject to outer limits, these limits were theorised as *internally* generated by the contradictory social-relational structures of capitalist economies, and mediated through class struggles.[20]

This statement seems to presume that for Marx and Engels, capital accumulation and its outer limits are non-material phenomena, ie. that capital accumulation is not itself a form of (expanding) material production. Otherwise, Benton needs to explain how capitalist 'social-relational structures' can generate outer limits to production if these structures are not themselves material *and* social. In short, it is only his non-dialectical (internal/external) conception of social and material reality that forces Benton to conclude that Marx and Engels, when investigating capitalism's historical limits, had to choose between a transhistorical 'human predicament' *or* 'the dynamics of capital accumulation' – as if capitalism were not a specific form of human metabolic interaction with nature. This false problematic disappears once capitalist production is treated as a contradictory mutual constitution of historically specific social forms and the material content of these forms.[21]

Moreover, although Benton's 'double-pronged' interpretation of Marx and Engels's critique of Malthus is potentially insightful, his social/material dichotomy causes him to overlook the true relationship between the two 'prongs'. The first prong (denial of 'the universality and necessity of the law', ie, denial of *purely* natural limits), is a general principle of historical materialism, namely that human population phenomena must be treated in terms of specific social relations. As Marx says, 'every special historic mode of production has its own special laws of population, historically valid within its limits alone'.[22] The second prong of the critique, Marx's reserve army analysis, applies this general principle to capitalism. The intrinsic connection between the two prongs is clear from Marx's most detailed critique of Malthus, where Marx points out that Malthus's

---

[20] Benton 1989, p. 74.
[21] The commodity, for example, is a contradictory unity of exchange-value (social) and use-value (material), and the latter always has a natural basis and substance in Marx's view (Marx 1967, I, p. 43).
[22] Marx 1967, I, p. 632.

conception is altogether false and childish (1) because he
regards overpopulation as being of the same kind in all the
different phases of economic development ... and hence
stupidly reduces these very complicated and varying relations
to a single relation, two equations, in which the natural
reproduction of humanity appears on the one side, and the
natural reproduction of edible plants (or means of
subsistence) on the other, as two natural series, the former
geometric and the latter arithmetic in progression ... This
baboon thereby implies that the increase of humanity is a
purely natural process ... He would find in history that
population proceeds in very different relations, and that
overpopulation is likewise a historically determined relation,
in no way determined by abstract numbers or by the absolute
limit of the productivity of the necessaries of life, but by limits
posited rather by specific conditions of production ...; (2) He
stupidly relates a specific quantity of people to a specific
quantity of necessaries. Ricardo immediately and correctly
confronted him with the fact that the quantity of grain
available is completely irrelevant to the worker if he has no
employment; that it is therefore the means of employment
and not of subsistence which put him into the category of
surplus population.[23]

We see that the first 'prong' of Marx's critique merely recognises the
social specificity of natural conditions and limits, and that when Marx
emphasises the importance of specific conditions of production for
population dynamics, he is talking about conditions that are material
and social. Similarly, the second 'prong' of Marx's critique posits that
capitalist 'overpopulation' must be treated in terms of 'the social
mediation as such, through which the individual gains access to the
means of his reproduction and creates them; hence it relates to the
conditions of production and his relation to them'.[24] In Benton's
dichotomous reading, by contrast, the first prong is reduced to a denial
of all natural limits (even historically specific, social-relational ones) and
the second to a recognition of social limits (but not material or natural
ones).[25]

In this way, Benton severs the materialist connections between
Marx's principle of historical specification and its application to
capitalism, thereby creating an opening for the Malthusian
'reconstruction' of historical materialism. Hence, in Benton's
interpretation, Marx's reserve army analysis becomes a 'correctly
formulated' rendition of Malthus's law of population![26] We are told that
Marx and Engels not only admitted 'the actuality of the phenomena

---

[23] Marx 1973, pp. 605–7.
[24] Marx 1973, p. 607.
[25] The connection between Marx's general critique of Malthus's population law
and Marx's analysis of the capitalist surplus population is also clear in the
'Wages' manuscript of 1847, which contains Marx's first extensive critique of
Malthus (Marx 1976a, pp. 428–35).
[26] Benton 1989, p. 60.

which the law is intended to explain', but ascribed the status of 'economic law' to Malthus's law – now 'associated with determinate social conditions', ie., 'valid ... as a characterisation of the ... reserve army of labour'.[27] Benton thus sets up a dichotomy between Marx and Engels's historical specification of the surplus population (anti-Malthus) and their empirical understanding of the same surplus population (pro-Malthus). This methodological/empirical dichotomy occludes Marx's decisive rejection of Malthus's empiricist method. In Marx's view, Malthus merely

> *asserted* the fact of overpopulation in all forms of society. Proved it he has not, for there is nothing more uncritical than his motley compilations from historians and travellers' descriptions ... Malthusian man, abstracted from historically determined man, exists only in his brain; hence also the geometric method of reproduction corresponding to this natural Malthusian man. Real history thus appears to him in such a way that the reproduction of his natural humanity is not an abstraction from the historic process of real reproduction, but just the contrary, that real reproduction is an application of the Malthusian theory ... In this way he transforms the historically distinct relations into an abstract numerical relation, which he has fished purely out of thin air, and which rests neither on natural nor on historical laws.[28]

Clearly, Marx did not treat his own conception of surplus population as empirically equivalent to Malthus's, and the reason lies in the completely antagonistic paradigms underlying the two conceptions. An uncritical empirical endorsement of Malthus's law would implicate Marx in the empiricist, ahistorical methodology from which this law was derived. It would, in short, implicate Marx in a qualitative commensuration of the very different determinations and forms of population and overpopulation dynamics in different socio-economic systems. Unfortunately, while Marx avoids this trap, Benton does not; for the logic of the latter's argument dictates that Malthus's law be treated as *transhistorically* valid empirically. Benton fails to explain, for example, why *pre*-capitalist phenomena of 'widespread poverty and misery due to lack of availability of means of subsistence for a significant but fluctuating portion of the population' do not *also* provide an 'empirical basis for Malthus's laws'.[29]

The Malthusian bias in Benton's analysis becomes even more evident when he observes that for Marx and Engels, 'ultimate natural

---

[27] Benton 1989. Elsewhere Benton similarly asserts that 'Marx and Engels never denied the reality of the phenomena which constituted the empirical basis for Malthus's laws. They rather offered an alternative conceptualisation and explanation of them'. Here again, Marx's reserve army analysis is reduced to an historical specification of the evidently accurate 'empirical basis' of Malthus's laws (See 1991, p. 257).
[28] Marx 1973, pp. 605–6.
[29] Benton 1991, p. 257.

limits to population, or to human transformative powers vis-à-vis nature
... were certainly not responsible for the prevailing poverty and misery' –
a statement which seems to suggest that although such a view was
'understandable enough' in Marx and Engels's time, it is no longer true
today.[30] Benton's observation appears to downgrade the possibility –
one consistent with Marx and Engels's thinking – that poverty and
misery, including hunger and malnutrition, are not due to any absolute
national or global shortages in food or productive capacity, but rather to
what Sen calls failures in the entitlement systems of contemporary
economies, ie. to malfunctions in the relations of production, exchange,
and distribution from the standpoint of human-material reproduction.[31]
In short, to ascribe 'responsibility' for global environmental and
population problems to ahistorically defined 'ultimate natural limits' is
to blame nature for problems generated by a specific socio-economic
system.

Marx's reserve army analysis

As evidence that 'Marx and Engels take historical/social relativisation to
imply some form of social constructionism', Benton observes that:

> For them, 'relative surplus population', or 'the reserve army
> of labour', is a *consequence* of the dynamic tendency of
> capital accumulation. The form taken by the argument in
> Marx's *Capital* makes the surplus population an effect of the
> tendency of constant capital to rise as a proportion of total
> capital.[32]

The role of natural conditions in Marx's reserve army analysis is an
interesting question which can help reveal some important connections
between capital's exploitation of labour and capital's appropriation of
natural conditions. Unfortunately, Benton's investigation of this
question is crippled by its initial *presumption* that Marx's reserve army
analysis is social constructionist. This presumption forces Benton to
assume that Marx treated capital accumulation as a purely social, non-
material process. Moreover, since capital accumulation depends on the
exploitation of labour, Benton's criticism *presumes* that Marx also
treated this exploitation as a non-material process not dependent on
natural conditions. It is only these *presumptions*, along with an
occlusion of the class character of the reserve army process, that allow
Benton to bypass the connections Marx's analysis draws between the

---

[30] Benton 1989, pp. 59–60.
[31] See Sen 1981. Benton's observation also implicitly downgrades the
endogeneity of population growth with respect to specific socio-economic and
gender relations and material living conditions. (Also, Sen 1994)
[32] Benton 1989, p. 77.

class-exploitative character of capital accumulation on the one hand, and the material conditions of production on the other.

For Marx, capital accumulation and the reserve army process presuppose, first, the social separation of the direct producers from necessary conditions of their material reproduction which they can gain access to only by being employed by capital as wage labourers. This encompasses the producers' separation from any *natural conditions* which might allow them fully to reproduce themselves outside the wage labour relation.[33] Second, the rising value composition of capital is an expression of the rising productivity of social labour; as such, it manifests not only the natural basis of all labour productivity, but also the continuous revolutionisation of the material process of production, as capital scientifically appropriates natural conditions in order to transform material production so as to increase relative surplus value – ie, to increase surplus labour time *via* reductions in necessary labour time.[34] Third, once natural conditions of production are appropriated by capital, they acquire an alienated social power over the producers.[35] The constant creation of a pool of superfluous labour-power in the process of capital accumulation hinges upon this continuous alienation of socially developed natural forces vis-à-vis the producers – as 'cannot be otherwise in a mode of production in which the labourer exists to satisfy the needs of the self-expansion of existing values.'[36]

These social-material connections nullify any social constructionist reading of Marx's reserve army analysis. However, Benton offers the additional criticism that Marx's analysis is defective insofar as 'the tendency of constant capital to rise as a proportion of total capital ... only follows on the basis of implicit assumptions about the rate at which the working population reproduces biologically'.[37] Benton does not specify the implicit assumptions required to sustain Marx's analysis; nor does he explain how Marx's analysis would be invalidated by assumptions other than these implicit ones. In any case, Benton's criticism presumes that Marx's reserve army analysis hinges upon the rising value composition of capital.

In fact, Marx first establishes the necessity of a reserve army of unemployed for capitalism under the assumption of no technological change (zero growth in labour productivity). Here, the tendency of

---

[33] Marx 1967, I, pp. 714–6, 768, and 1973, pp. 471, 497.
[34] Marx 1967, I, pp. 621–2, III, pp. 213, 759, I, pp. 511–5, and 1976b, p. 34. Also Marx 1967, I, Chapter 15. The relationship between the value composition of capital and labour productivity helps explain how, in the *Grundrisse*, Marx was able to 'conceive of the industrial reserve army ... directly from the concept of relative surplus value ... without having first described the effect of machinery and capital accumulation on the development of the working population.' (Rosdolsky 1977, p. 250. See also Marx 1973, pp. 608–10). Benton's critique thus ignores the material content of the rate of surplus value *and* of the value composition of capital in Marx's view. Burkett 1998 provides further details on this point.
[35] Marx 1967, III, pp. 264, 745, and 1977, pp. 1054–5.
[36] Marx 1967, I, p. 621.
[37] Benton 1989, p. 77.

capital to maintain a reserve army of unemployed is based not on a rising value composition of capital, but on the unsustainability of any growth of capital accumulation beyond the point where the reserve army is depleted. As Marx indicates, if

> the quantity of unpaid labour supplied by the working class, and accumulated by the capitalist class, increases so rapidly that its conversion into capital requires an extraordinary addition of paid labour, then wages rise, and, all other circumstances remaining equal, ... a reaction sets in: a smaller part of revenue is capitalised, accumulation lags, and the movement of rise in wages receives a check [as the reserve army of unemployed is replenished].[38]

It is basic to Marx's argument that this dynamic: (1) continues to operate even when technological change is present;[39] (2) does not depend on any *particular* given rate of working-class population growth.[40]

This discussion incidentally shows that Benton's criticism of Marx's reserve army analysis is valid only if the rate of growth of the exploitable working-class population (hence the degree of downward pressure on wages exerted by the reserve army) is itself a positive function of the wage rate. In other words, Benton's criticism implicitly assumes a Malthusian relationship between wages and working-class population growth. By contrast, Marx not only rejects any socially unmediated conception of 'the rate at which the working population reproduces biologically',[41] but more specifically suggests that under most circumstances working-class population growth is likely to have an *inverse* relationship with workers' wages and living conditions. In his analysis of the stagnant faction of the reserve army, for example, Marx notes that:

> Its conditions of life sink below the average normal level of the working-class; ... It is characterised by maximum of working-time, and minimum of wages ... But it forms at the same time a self-reproducing and self-perpetuating element of the working-class, taking a proportionally greater part in the general increase of that class than the other elements. In fact, not only the number of births and deaths, but the absolute size of the families stand in inverse proportion to the height of wages, and therefore to the amount of means of

---

[38] Marx 1967, I, p. 620.
[39] Of course, once Marx allows for technological change and the rising technical composition of capital, capitalism's tendency to maintain a reserve army is augmented by a further 'apparently absolute increase of the labouring population' relative to 'the variable capital or the means of employment'. Marx 1967, I, p. 630.
[40] Emphasising this point, Marx states: 'Capitalist production can by no means content itself with the quantity of disposable labour-power which the natural increase of population yields', but rather 'requires for its free play an industrial reserve army independent of these natural limits' (Marx 1967, I, p. 635).
[41] Benton 1989, p. 77.

> subsistence of which the different categories of labourers dispose.[42]

Elsewhere, Marx suggests that

> the life-situation in which capital places the working class, its conglomeration, its deprivation of all the other pleasures of life, the utter impossibility of attaining a higher social standing and maintaining a certain decorum, the vacuity of their lives, the mixing of the sexes in the workshop, the isolation of the worker himself, all these things impel marriage at an early age. The curtailment and practically the abolition of the necessary period of apprenticeship, the early age at which children can themselves step forward as producers, the shortening therefore of the period during which they must be provided for, increases the stimulus to a more rapid production of human beings.[43]

The point here is not the exact accuracy of such statements, but rather that Marx's various discussions of working-class population growth approach a class-relational version of what is nowadays called demographic transition theory (under which rising per capita incomes tend to lower birth rates, ceteris paribus), with implications diametrically opposed to Malthus's so-called law. This throws further doubt on Benton's argument that Marx and Engels accepted Malthus's law as an empirically accurate description of capitalist reality. Stated differently, Benton conflates Malthus's naturally imposed limits to working-class population growth with the capitalistically imposed limits to working-class conditions posited by Marx. Benton treats the two kinds of limits as qualitatively the same, differing only in the way they are imposed (naturally or socially), which is evidently incorrect given that, for Marx, any tightening of capitalist limits on working-class conditions is more likely to raise than to lower population growth among workers.[44] Benton's material/social dichotomy is here manifested in the ascription of the same ahistorical conception of material limits to both Malthus and Marx.

---

[42] Marx 1967, I, p. 643.

[43] Marx 1988, p. 302. The passage just quoted is from a draft of *Capital*; in the published version Marx simply observes that capital's need for 'rapid renewal of the generations of labourers (this law does not hold for the other classes of the population) ... is met by early marriages, a necessary consequence of the conditions in which the labourers of modern industry live, and by the premium that the exploitation of children sets on their production'. (Marx 1967, I, p. 642).

[44] This observation may not hold in certain extreme situations, such as the Irish potato famine, where large numbers of workers are unable to obtain even means of physical subsistence, and where large-scale forced emigration and/or starvation may occur. However, even such famines should be analysed in class-relational fashion. See, in addition to Sen 1981, the interesting discussions in Marx 1978 and Braa 1997.

The reproduction of labour-power

Benton argues that Marx treats labour-power 'as the product of the prior labour of producing the labourer's means of subsistence,' and that this 'tendency ... to assimilate the processes of production and reproduction of the labourer to those of producing their means of consumption' was 'shared with other political economists'.[45] We respond to these claims here because, according to Benton, 'Marx's implicit assimilation' of domestic labour processes 'to productive processes complements his anti-Malthusian and more general reluctance to recognise "natural limits"'.[46] Benton does not clearly specify this complementarity, which is unsurprising seeing as how Marx never presumes that capitalist production of necessary means of subsistence ensures an unlimited exploitable labour force. Indeed, one of *Capital's* main concerns is to demonstrate capital's in-built tendency to enervate the labour force not only by keeping wages to the minimum and by poisoning and otherwise rendering unsafe the work and living conditions of the labouring class, but also by extensions of labour time which encroach upon the free time required for reproductive domestic activities.[47] In showing how this tendency elicits 'a reaction on the part of society, the very sources of whose life are menaced ... a struggle between collective capital ... and collective labour', Marx provides a model of class-based environmental analysis.[48]

Nonetheless, Benton does raise an important issue: the role of domestic labour and consumption activities in Marx's analysis of the value of labour-power. There are, moreover, certain parallels between the respective valuations of domestic labour and natural conditions under capitalism. This makes it all the more unfortunate that Benton bases his argument on the assertion that Marx assimilates labour-power reproduction to capitalist production. Actually, Marx insists that wages (variable capital) are paid in the form of money which is only converted into means of subsistence *outside* of the wage-labour relationship between capitalist and worker – as follows from the fact that 'what the capitalist consumes productively in the labour-process is the labour-power itself and not the labourer's means of subsistence'.[49] Indeed, as if responding to Benton, Marx states that

> the money which the capitalist pays to the labourer for the use
> of his labour-power is nothing more or less than the form of

---

[45] Benton 1989, pp. 71–2.
[46] Benton 1989, p. 72.
[47] Marx 1967, I, Parts 3 and 4. Even in this context, however, Marx emphasises that 'a quick succession of unhealthy and short-lived generations will [from the capitalist point of view] keep the labour market as well supplied as a series of vigorous and long-lived generations' – consistent with his view that working-class population growth is normally inversely related to working-class living standards. (Marx 1976b, p. 57).
[48] Marx 1967, I, p. 235. For further discussion see Burkett 1996b, pp. 350–1.
[49] Marx 1967, II, p. 165.

> the general equivalent for the means of subsistence required
> by the labourer. *To this extent*, the variable capital consists in
> substance of means of subsistence. But ... the capitalist does
> not buy the labourer's means of subsistence, but his labour-
> power. And that which forms the variable part of his capital is
> not the labourer's means of subsistence but his labour-power
> in action ... It is the labourer himself who converts the money
> received for his labour-power into means of subsistence, in
> order to reconvert them into labour-power, to keep alive.[50]

As observed by Fine and Leopold, this approach enables Marx to show
that

> one of the civilising effects of capitalism is to sharpen the
> distinction between human consumption and consumption
> for production, thereby removing the consumption attached
> to the production process away from the consumption
> attached to the worker ... Otherwise working-class
> consumption under capitalism would be treated as
> comparable to that obtaining under slavery, where
> reproduction of the worker includes the raising of children
> for sale.[51]

In short, Marx's view is that 'because final consumption involves the
exit of its value from continuing circulation, its role is no longer defined
by the internal logic of capital and its laws'.[52] By rigorously
distinguishing among money wages, means of subsistence, and labour-
power, 'Marx's analytical siting of consumption' avoids 'condemn[ing]
the working class to the role of an unresisting agent for capital in
effecting its own reproduction'.[53] Far from assimilating workers'
reproduction to capitalist production, Marx's approach clearly
recognises the importance of a relatively autonomous domestic sphere
of working-class consumption and labour-power reproduction under
capitalism.

A related problem with Benton's assimilation charge is its implicit
presumption that for Marx, all use values necessary for labour-power's
reproduction are purchased as commodities. Actually, all that Marx's
analysis of capitalist exploitation and accumulation requires is that a
significant share of such necessary use values can only be obtained as
commodities. One will search in vain through *Capital* for any assertion
that *all* necessary means of subsistence are commodities. True, when
theorising the value of labour-power, Marx states that the worker's
'maintenance ... requires a given quantity of the means of subsistence'
and that 'the labour-time requisite for the production of labour-power
reduces itself to that necessary for the production of those means of

---

[50] Marx 1967. My emphasis.
[51] Fine and Leopold 1993, pp.259–60.
[52] Fine 1994, p. 394.
[53] Fine and Leopold 1993, p. 260.

subsistence; in other words, the value of labour-power is the value of the means of subsistence necessary for the maintenance of the labourer'.[54] But since this entire analysis presumes a given value of labour-power, the labour time Marx is talking about is only the wage-labour time required to produce the commodified means of subsistence. Once one recognises this, it becomes quite clear that Marx is *not* saying that labour-power is the product of the labour producing the commodified means of subsistence, but only that these means of subsistence (and the wage-labour time required to produce them) are 'necessary' or 'requisite' for the reproduction of labour-power. Obviously, 'A is *necessary* for B' is quite a different statement from 'B is *the product of* A'.

Moreover, unlike Benton's interpretation, which conflates labour-power with its value, Marx points to 'a historical and moral element' in 'the determination of the value of labour-power' that is not reducible to the physical requirements of labour-power itself.[55] The necessary commodified means of subsistence are not just determined by workers' 'natural wants, such as food, clothing, fuel and housing, [which] vary according to the climactic and other physical conditions of the country' – although Benton's omission of the last variation is interesting in itself. Marx also insists that these necessary means of subsistence 'are themselves the product of historical development, and depend therefore to a great extent on ... the conditions under which ... the class of free labourers has been formed'.[56] In other words, the 'value of labour-power is in every country determined by a traditional standard of life ... not mere physical life, but ... *certain wants springing from the social conditions in which people are placed and reared up'*.[57]

We thus see that, far from treating labour-power as the product of commodity-producing labour, Marx's conception allows for an important influence of the 'conditions in which people are placed and reared up' – conditions clearly not reducible to produced commodities – on the value of labour-power, ie. on the value of commodified means of subsistence necessary for labour-power's reproduction. All Marx's analysis assumes is that the domestic processes of labour-power reproduction cannot themselves reproduce the working class in the absence of commodified means of subsistence obtained using money acquired via the sale of labour-power. From this perspective, the fact that Marx's analysis does not hinge on any particular specification of domestic reproductive processes is actually a plus, insofar as it jibes with the relative autonomy of working-class consumption and domestic reproduction from the circuits of capital referred to earlier. Benton's criticism, on the other hand, conflates use-value and value by failing to

---

[54] Marx 1967, I, p. 171.
[55] Marx 1967.
[56] Marx 1967.
[57] Marx 1976b, p. 57. My emphasis.

recognise that in Marx's view, domestic reproductive processes contribute to labour-power's use-value but not to its value.[58]

Marx's approach suggests that insofar as capitalism assigns a zero value to domestic activities that are individually and collectively useful, this is one important aspect of the fundamental contradiction between use-value and exchange-value. This is not to deny that the material forms and the distribution of undervalued domestic activities are largely determined in the context of gender and family relations; nor is it to deny that familial exploitation of women and children may be a necessary condition of said undervaluation. Indeed, given that the undervaluation of domestic activities goes hand-in-hand with the undervaluation of female time relative to male time, it would seem to follow that capitalism is an essentially patriarchal system.[59] In a similar way, capitalism's undervaluation of nature implicates its fundamentally anti-ecological character.[60] Rather than recognising these connections and the tough issues they raise, however, Benton's 'assimilation' charge is analogous to the error of faulting Marx's value theory for *capitalism's* reduction of the value of nature to the social labour time absorbed by capital's appropriation of natural conditions.[61]

Communism, population, and nature

Another crucial question Benton raises is the role of natural conditions and limits in Marx's vision of post-capitalist society. This question draws a special relevance from the threats to the quality of human development currently being posed by the biospheric effects of capital accumulation, ie. from the crying need for a more pro-ecological system of co-operatively planned production. Unfortunately, Benton's discussion does not consider how production might be qualitatively altered by the specific socio-economic relations Marx projects for communism. This causes Benton to interpret Marx and Engels's communist vision from the standpoint of ahistorical natural limits to human production and reproduction. Since this broad category of misinterpretations is addressed elsewhere,[62] the present section focuses on those elements directly connected with the Marx/Malthus relationship before commenting briefly on Benton's more direct distortions of Marx's projections. Consider, first, Benton's attempt to document how the founders of Marxism felt about 'ultimate natural limits to population' under communism:

> At most, Marx and Engels recognised "the abstract possibility" that limits would have to be set to the human

---

[58] Marx 1967, I, p. 40, and Carchedi 1991, p. 129.
[59] Schor 1992.
[60] Burkett 1996b.
[61] For further discussion see Burkett 1996a, pp. 64–6.
[62] Burkett 1996a, pp. 76–9, and 1997, pp. 170–3.

> population ... Engels goes so far as to say: "Thanks to [Malthusian] theory, as to economics as a whole, our attention has been drawn to the productive power of the earth and of mankind; and after overcoming this economic despair, we have been made *for ever secure against the fear of over-population.*"[63]

Benton's discussion does not address how the security from over-population referred to by Engels relates to Marx and Engels's social-relational method of specifying human-material reproduction.[64] This occlusion is facilitated by Benton's failure to link the 'for ever secure' passage to Engels's follow-up statement regarding Malthus's law:

> We derive from it the most powerful economic arguments for a social transformation. For even if Malthus were completely right, this transformation would have to be undertaken on the spot; for only this transformation, and the education of the masses which it alone provides, makes possible that moral restraint of the propagative instinct which Malthus himself presents as the most effective and easiest remedy for over-population.[65]

Interestingly, Benton does quote this passage, but not in its natural position immediately following the 'for ever secure' statement in Engels's text. Instead, Benton cites it separately as merely an example of how 'Engels made use of Malthus's recognition of the role of "moral restraint"'.[66] This textual splicing conceals how Marx and Engels's discussions of population were generally framed in historically specific, social-relational terms even prior to the maturation of their materialist conception of history.[67] Similarly, upon looking at the source of the 'abstract possibility' statement mentioned (but not referenced) by Benton, one finds the following:

> There is of course the abstract possibility that the human population will become so numerous that its further increase will have to be checked. If it should become necessary for communist society to regulate the production of men, just as it will have already regulated the production of things, then it, and it alone, will be able to do this without difficulties. It

---

[63] Benton 1989, p. 59–60.
[64] Note that Benton draws the 'for ever secure' passage from Engels's 1844 work, *Outlines of a Critique of Political Economy* – a very questionable source for an evaluation of Marx and Engels's applications of their mature conception of history to population problems (see Engels 1964, p. 221). Indeed, by 1851 Engels himself was referring to this early book's critique of Malthus as 'very CRUDE and not at all closely argued' (Engels to Marx, 29 January 1851, Marx and Engels 1982, p. 271).
[65] Engels 1964, p. 221.
[66] Benton 1989, p. 59.
[67] Similarly repeated in Benton 1991, pp. 257–9. The immaturity of Engels's 1844 critique of Malthus is shown by its failure to contest the empirical validity of Malthus's law.

> seems to me that it should not be too difficult for such a
> society to achieve in a planned way what has already come
> about naturally, without planning, in France and Lower
> Austria.[68]

Rather than flatly denying natural limits to population, this passage specifies these limits in historically specific social-relational terms. In Marx and Engels's view, the key to communism's ability to deal with the 'abstract possibility' of over-population would lie in its 'social transformation' of the people-nature metabolism, not in any total disconnection from, or overcoming of, natural conditions and limits. Compared to class-divided societies including anarchically competitive capitalism, communism's collective-democratic relations would more effectively 'regulate' human production and reproduction in environmentally sustainable fashion.

Benton's ecological critique of the young (1844) Marx is also based on an occlusion of the material and social specificity of Marx's communism.[69] We are told that Marx's reference to 'a "humanisation of nature" seems to suggest a potentially residue-less subjection of the natural world to human intentionality'.[70] The consistency of this suggestion with Marx's insistence that the human race 'is a part of nature ... with which [it] must remain in continuous interchange' is not explained by Benton – the question being how people can have a 'continuous interchange' with a 'residue-less' entity.[71] Here, Benton neglects two closely related aspects of Marx's 1844 projection: (1) the humanisation of nature as only one side of the communist resolution of the antagonism between people and nature – the other side being the renaturalisation of human beings;[72] (2) the social disalienation of the producers vis-à-vis their own labour and from each other as a necessary *condition and result* of human disalienation vis-à-vis nature.[73]

The material/social dichotomy also colours Benton's interpretation of Marx's mature projection. Benton describes Marx's communism as one where 'the possibility of human emancipation is premised upon the

---

[68] Engels to Kautsky, 1 February 1881, Marx and Engels 1975, p. 315.
[69] Here again, the relevance of Marx's early 1844 manuscripts to the issue at hand – purported ecological shortcomings in Marx's mature critique of political economy relative to Marx's materialist conception of history – is not clarified by Benton.
[70] Benton 1989, p. 76.
[71] Marx 1964, p. 112.
[72] See Marx 1964, pp. 137, 135. He thus refers to communism as 'the unity of being of man with nature – the true resurrection of nature – the naturalism of man and the humanism of nature both brought to fulfilment ... This communism, as fully developed naturalism, equals humanism, and as fully developed humanism equals naturalism; it is the genuine resolution of the conflict between man and nature and between man and man'.
[73] As Marx says: 'Every self-estrangement of man, from himself and from nature, appears in the relations in which he places himself and nature to men other than and differentiated from himself ... In the practical world self-estrangement can only become manifest through the real practical relationship to other men. The medium through which estrangement takes place is practical' (Marx 1964, p. 116).

potential for the transformative, productive powers of associated human beings to transcend apparent natural limits, and to widen the field of play for human intentionality'.[74] There is no recognition here of how the *qualitative content* of 'human intentionality' (eg. the social definition of what is useful) might be shaped by the specific forms of human association under communism. Instead, Benton interprets Marx's references to the producers' 'perfectly intelligible and reasonable relations ... to nature' and 'conscious rational cultivation of the soil' under communism, and to people being 'ruled by ... their interchange with nature' under capitalism, as manifesting some anti-ecological 'domination' of nature in Marx's vision of communism.[75] Grundmann pointed out the oxymoronic quality of this interpretation – the point being that it is a strange kind of 'domination' that erodes the natural conditions of its own reproduction.[76] As a matter of fact, Marx and Engels's mature projections often point to the need for the associated producers to adjust their plans in line with natural constraints and contingencies, and not only in agriculture.[77]

Benton's critique does not address the ecological significance of the most basic social characteristics of Marx's communism: (1) production for use rather than for profit; (2) the pre-positing of labour and production as directly social according to a collectively and democratically determined plan; (3) the non-commodity, non-market form of production and of products; (4) the complete decommodification of labour-power underpinned by the associated producers' 'individual property based on ... co-operation and the possession in common of the land and of the means of production'; (5) the progressive reduction of work-time and the use of free time as a measure of social wealth.[78]

Of these five basic characteristics, Benton considers only the reduction of work-time, and then only to argue that for Marx, 'the content of emancipation [is] given in the reduction to a minimum of the time taken up in [the] struggle' with nature.[79] Benton's interpretation ignores the potential pro-ecological role of increased free time in enhancing the productive capabilities and needs of the producers. This includes the reorientation of production and needs toward less material- and energy-intensive forms as well as the development of the producers' awareness (in both scientific and existential senses) of the natural conditions and results of their individual and collective labours.[80]

For Marx and Engels, production for use rather than for profit involves a transformation in the social conception of use-value to more

---

[74] Benton 1989, p. 76.
[75] Marx 1967, I, p. 79, and III, pp. 812, 820.
[76] Grundmann 1991, pp. 109, 111.
[77] See, for example, Marx 1966, p. 7, 1967; II, pp. 177, 469; III, pp. 117–8; and Engels 1939, pp. 125–6, 323–4.
[78] Marx 1967, I, p. 763; III, pp. 819–20; and Marx 1973, p. 708.
[79] Benton 1989, p. 76
[80] Marx 1973, pp. 172, 542, 612, 712; Mandel 1992, Chapter 5; and Burkett 1997, p. 171.

effectively incorporate social-environmental as opposed to private-pecuniary concerns.[81] What produces this transformation is the collective-democratic planning of the social-material metabolism of people and nature, not any overcoming of material constraints per se. In addition to increased free time for the development of the producers' capabilities and needs, communism's disalienation of the producers vis-à-vis nature and their own labour presumes a social (re)union of these producers with the social-material conditions of their reproduction, ie. the decommodification of labour-power. This contrasts with the situation in capitalist economy, where, instead of associated producers pre-positing their labour as social and thereby pre-positing an ecologically rational material interchange with nature, we see private owners of commodified labour-power anarchically ruled (in both social and ecological senses) by the products of their own labour and nature in the alienated forms of money, wages, commodity prices, profit, interest, and rents.[82]

The fact that Benton's interpretation is not grounded in the contrast between communist and capitalist social relations helps explain why he winds up injecting a questionable polarity between nature and human intentionality into Marx's projection. In this polarity, 'human autonomy' presupposes not only 'control over nature', but 'an underlying *antagonism* between human purposes and nature: either we control nature or it controls us!'[83] The crude materialism contained in this polarity (as if human autonomy and purposes could be reduced to control over nature apart from social relations) contradicts Benton's primary claim that Marx and Engels retreated to social constructionism when confronted with Malthus. Benton thus has Marx and Engels retreating into crude materialism and social constructionism at the same time – in line with the material/social dichotomy underpinning Benton's Malthusian Marxism.

Theory and praxis in Marx's response to Malthus

According to Benton, Marx and Engels opposed Malthusian thinking '[f]or political reasons,' ie. because of their 'perceptions of' the 'clear political consequences' of '"natural limits" epistemic conservatisms'.[84] These are serious charges deserving of a serious response – especially since Benton does not consider the possibility that Marx and Engels's research *method and agenda* were shaped by their revolutionary politics *and vice versa*. In other words, Benton conflates political opportunism (the concoction of analyses for the sake of political convenience) with the principled mutual constitution of theory and praxis (in which

---

[81] Marx 1967, III, p. 776; and Engels 1939, pp. 323–4.
[82] Marx 1967, I, pp. 72–9; and Marx 1973, pp. 171–2.
[83] Benton 1989, p. 75. My emphasis.
[84] Benton 1989, pp. 60, 77.

politics are analytically informed as much as analysis is politicised). That Benton's partial severing of the unity of theory and praxis complements his material/social dichotomy is clear from his response to the following observation by Marx:

> Labour is *not the source* of all wealth. *Nature* is just as much the source of use values (and it is surely of such that material wealth consists!) as is labour, which itself is only the manifestation of a natural force, human labour-power.[85]

Benton interprets this principle as one of the 'unequivocally naturalistic ... "threads" or "premises" of [Marx's] materialist view of history', ie. as being isolated from, and even opposed to, Marx's social-relational perspective.[86] Yet, in Marx's immediate follow-up, we find this:

> The bourgeois have very good grounds for fancifully ascribing *supernatural creative power* to labour, since it follows precisely from the fact that labour depends on nature, that the man who possesses no other property than his labour-power must, in all conditions of society and culture, be the slave of other men who have made themselves the owners of the material conditions of labour. He can work only with their permission, and hence only live with their permission.[87]

Marx's insistence that nature and labour both contribute to wealth is not simply naturalistic; it sheds crucial light on capitalism's class-exploitative alienation of the producers from necessary conditions of production. The notion that labour is the source of all wealth served (at this time) an important ideological function for capital: that of concealing the dependence of capitalist production on the alienation of natural conditions vis-à-vis the producers. In Marx's view, the two opposing conceptions of the *sources* of wealth reflect opposing conceptions of the *nature and purposes* of wealth itself.[88] From the standpoint of the producers, the idea that labour alone can produce wealth apart from nature is quite nonsensical, given the necessary role of natural conditions in their reproduction and development. In this sense, the insistence that nature and labour are both sources of wealth reflects the view of wealth as a means of realising the producers' evolutionary potential as natural and social beings. For capital, by contrast, wealth means simply the accumulation of value, of social labour time in the abstract as represented by money.[89]

---

[85] Marx 1966, p. 3.
[86] Benton 1989, p. 53.
[87] Marx 1966, p. 3.
[88] See Lebowitz 1992, pp. 98–100.
[89] This helps explain why capitalism (through its main theoretical representative, classical political economy) 'on the one hand proclaims labour to be the source of wealth, in both its material existence and its social form, as regards both use values and exchange values, [while] on the other hand it proclaims, just as much, the necessity for the worker to be in absolute poverty, a poverty which means

In sum, Marx's recognition that nature and labour are both sources of wealth is an essential element of his critique of capitalism as a system which places production at the service of value accumulation rather than human needs, including the need for a sustainable and fulfilling relationship with nature. It is from this materialist *and* class-relational standpoint that Marx considers the politics of Malthus's population theory. Marx argues that 'Malthus's theory' is 'significant ... because he gives brutal expression to the brutal viewpoint of capital' – a viewpoint in which 'the labourer exists to satisfy the needs of self-expansion of existing values, instead of, on the contrary, material wealth existing to satisfy the needs of development on the part of the labourer'.[90]

By contrast with Marx's effective integration of analytical and political concerns, Malthus's pseudo-naturalistic treatment of 'surplus population' is crassly opportunistic. Malthus's vulgar-empiricist exercises would never have drawn such acclaim or exerted such influence in ruling circles if they had not provided ideological justification for capital's treatment of human beings and their natural conditions as superfluous and disposable whenever they cannot serve as material vehicles of profitable accumulation. In the Malthusian story, unemployment, poverty, and malnutrition are not an endogenous outcome of capital accumulation, but rather of the producers' natural proclivity to multiply their numbers in excess of the means of subsistence which can be provided by capital under given natural and technological conditions. Similarly, Benton suggests that Marx's reserve army analysis holds only 'on the basis of ... assumptions about the rate at which the working population reproduces biologically'.[91] Benton's material/social dichotomy thus entraps him in the very kind of Malthusian thinking that he elsewhere rightly rejects as being inadequately historical.

The political consequences of any such Malthusianisation of Marx's reserve army analysis are reasonably transparent. As Marx says, 'it was, of course, far more convenient, and much more in conformity with the interests of the ruling classes, ... to explain this "over-population" by the eternal laws of Nature, rather than by the historical laws of capitalist production'.[92] Similar consequences follow from Benton's dichotomisation of the materialist and social-relational elements in Marx's analysis of the labour process and value production. These consequences, including the artificial de-classing of ecological politics, are analysed in the continuation of the present work.[93]

---

nothing else than that his labour capacity is the sole remaining commodity he can sell, that he confronts objective, real wealth as mere labour capacity' (Marx, 1988, p. 41). Even in his early *Outlines*, Engels observes that 'Labour – the main factor in production, the "source of wealth" ... comes off badly with the economist' (Engels 1964, p. 212).
[90] Marx 1973, p. 605, and 1967, I, p. 621.
[91] Benton 1989, p. 77.
[92] Marx 1967, I, p. 529.
[93] Burkett 1998.

References

Benton, Ted 1989, 'Marxism and Natural Limits: An Ecological Critique and Reconstruction', *New Left Review*, 178: 51–86.

Benton, Ted 1991, 'The Malthusian Challenge: Ecology, Natural Limits and Human Emancipation' in *Socialism and the Limits of Liberalism*, edited by Peter Osborne, London: Verso.

Benton, Ted (ed.) 1996, *The Greening of Marxism*, New York: Guilford.

Braa, Dean M. 1997, 'The Great Potato Famine and the Transformation of Irish Peasant Society', *Science & Society*, 61, 2: 193–215.

Burkett, Paul 1996a, 'On Some Common Misconceptions About Nature and Marx's Critique of Political Economy', *Capitalism, Nature, Socialism*, 7, 3: 57–80.

Burkett, Paul 1996b, 'Value, Capital and Nature: Some Ecological Implications of Marx's Critique of Political Economy', *Science & Society*, 60, 3: 332–59.

Burkett, Paul 1997, 'Nature in Marx Reconsidered', *Organization & Environment*, 10, 2: 164–83.

Burkett, Paul 1998, 'A Critique of Neo-Malthusian Marxism, Part II: Labour, Nature, and Capital', manuscript under review.

Carchedi, Guglielmo 1991, *Frontiers of Political Economy*, London: Verso.

Churchill, Ward 1993, *Struggle for the Land*, Monroe, ME: Common Courage Press.

Engels, Frederick 1939, *Anti-Dühring*, New York: International Publishers.

Engels, Frederick 1964, 'Outlines of a Critique of Political Economy' in *Economic and Philosophical Manuscripts of 1844* by Karl Marx, New York: International Publishers.

Fine, Ben 1994, 'Consumption in Contemporary Capitalism: Beyond Marx and Veblen – A Comment', *Review of Social Economy*, 52, 3: 391–6.

Fine, Ben and Ellen Leopold 1993, *The World of Consumption*, London: Routledge.

Foster, John Bellamy 1994, *The Vulnerable Planet*, New York: Monthly Review Press.

Grundmann, Reiner 1991, 'The Ecological Challenge to Marxism', *New Left Review*, 187: 103–20.

Harvey, David 1993, 'The Nature of Environment: The Dialectics of Social and Environmental Change' in *Socialist Register 1993: Real Problems, False Solutions*, edited by Ralph Miliband and Leo Panitch, London: Merlin.

Lebowitz, Michael A. 1992, *Beyond Capital: Marx's Political Economy of the Working Class*, New York: St. Martin's Press.

Mandel, Ernest 1992, *Power and Money: A Marxist Theory of Bureaucracy*, London: Verso.

Marx, Karl 1933, *Wage-Labour and Capital*, New York: International Publishers.

Marx, Karl 1964, *Economic and Philosophical Manuscripts of 1844*, New York: International Publishers.

Marx, Karl 1966, *Critique of the Gotha Program*, New York: International Publishers.

Marx, Karl 1977, *Capital*, Volumes I–III, New York: International Publishers.

Marx, Karl 1970, *A Contribution to the Critique of Political Economy*, New York: International Publishers.

Marx, Karl 1973, *Grundrisse*, New York: Vintage.

Marx, Karl 1976a, 'Wages' in *Collected Works, Karl Marx and Frederick Engels, Vol.6*, New York: International Publishers.

Marx, Karl 1976b, *Value, Price and Profit*, New York: International Publishers.

Marx, Karl 1977, 'Results of the Immediate Process of Production' in *Capital*, Volume I, New York: Vintage.

Marx, Karl 1978, 'Forced Emigration (etc.)' in *Ireland and the Irish Question*, Karl Marx and Frederick Engels. Moscow: Progress Publishers.

Marx, Karl 1988, 'Economic Manuscript of 1861–63, Third Chapter' in *Collected Works, Karl Marx and Frederick Engels*, Volume 30, New York: International Publishers, pp.9–346.

Marx, Karl and Frederick Engels 1975, *Selected Correspondence*, Moscow: Progress Publishers.

Marx, Karl and Frederick Engels 1976, *The German Ideology*, Moscow: Progress Publishers.

Marx, Karl and Frederick Engels 1982, *Collected Works*, Volume 38, New York: International Publishers.

Ollman, Bertell 1993, *Dialectical Investigations*, New York: Routledge.

Rosdolsky, Roman 1977, *The Making of Marx's 'Capital'*, London: Pluto Press.

Schor, Juliet B. 1992, *The Overworked American: The Unexpected Decline of Leisure*, New York: Basic Books.

Sen, Amartya 1981, *Poverty and Famines: An Essay on Entitlement and Deprivation*, Oxford: Clarendon Press.

Sen, Amartya 1994, 'Population: Delusion and Reality', *New York Review of Books*, 41, 15: 62–71.

Soper, Kate 1991, 'Greening Prometheus: Marxism and Ecology' in *Socialism and the Limits of Liberalism*, edited by Peter Osborne, London: Verso.

Vlachou, Adriana 1994, 'Reflections on the Ecological Critiques and Reconstructions of Marxism', *Rethinking Marxism*, 7, 3: 112–28.

Risk Society and its Discontents

Slavoj Zizek

Is tamagochi today's Satan?

Recent theory of ideology and art has focused on the strange phenomenon of interpassivity – a phenomenon that is the exact obverse of 'interactivity' in the sense of being active through another subject who does the job for me, like the Hegelian Idea manipulating human passions to achieve its goals (the 'cunning of Reason/*List der Vernunft*').[1] Perhaps the first explicit formulation of interpassivity was given by Lacan in his commentary on the role of the Chorus in Greek tragedy:

> When you go to the theatre in the evening, you are preoccupied by the affairs of the day, by the pen that you lost, by the check that you will have to sign next day. You shouldn't give yourselves too much credit. Your emotions are taken charge of by the healthy order displayed on the stage. The Chorus takes care of them. The emotional commentary is done for you ... Therefore, you don't have to worry; even if you don't feel anything, the Chorus will feel in your stead.[2]

In order to avoid standard contemporary examples of interpassivity like so-called 'canned laughter' (where laughter is included in the soundtrack, so that the TV-set laughs for me, ie. it realises, takes over, the spectator's very passive experience of the show), let me evoke a different example, that of the embarrassing scene in which a person tells a tasteless joke and then, when nobody around him laughs, himself bursts out into a noisy laughter, repeating 'that was so funny!' or something similar, that is to say, acting out himself the expected reaction of the audience. The situation here is in a way the exact opposite of that of the Greek Chorus: the Chorus feels for us, bored and preoccupied spectators unable to let ourselves go and experience the appropriate passive emotions, while here, it is the agent (the narrator of the joke) himself who also assumes the passive role, ie. who laughs (at his own joke) instead of us, his public.

Is not the ultimate example of interpassivity tamagochi, the new Japanese toy we all know: the virtual pet, a small round object with a screen that behaves like a child (or a dog, or a bird, or some other pet animal that needs care), making noises and posing demands on its

---

[1] Pfaller 1996; Zizek 1997.

[2] Lacan 1992.

owner? When it beeps, one has to look at the screen where the object's demand can be read – hunger, drink, or whatever – and push the proper button to satisfy the demand. The object can also demand that we play with it; if it is too wild, the proper thing to do is to punish it by, again, pressing the proper button; the number of small hearts on display even tells us the degree of the object's happiness. If one fails too many times to meet these demands, the object 'dies'; it possesses only one or two more lives, so that when we fail the third time, the objects dies definitely, ie. it stops functioning (there are, of course, already burial sites for the dead tamagochis). One of the common ways wicked children bully their peers immersed in their care for tamagochi is to meddle with the toy when it is briefly left unattended – for example, feeding it excessively, so that the virtual animal behind the screen chokes to death. Tamagochi is thus also breeding a number of virtual murderers among children, giving rise to the cyberspace counterpart of the sadistic child torturing a cat or a butterfly to death. Since tamagochi's ultimate death has caused nervous breakdowns and even suicides in the children who owned them, recent versions include the possibility of perpetual resurrection: after the object dies, the game is simply over and one can start it again... this, of course, already obfuscates what was so provocative about the original tamagochi, ie. the fact that its (third) death was final.

The 'other', our partner, is here purely virtual: no longer a true living being, but an inanimate screen, a stand-in for the non-existent pet animal, which just signals the animal's demands. The uncanny enigma, of course, resides in the fact that, although we are well aware that there is nothing beyond the screen, ie. that we are playing with signals with no referent, we fully feel the appropriate emotions. We can thus well imagine also a sex-tamagochi bombarding us with demands like 'Kiss me! Lick me down there! Penetrate me!,' to which we would respond by simply pressing the appropriate buttons and thus fulfilling our duty to enjoy, while in 'real life' we would put our feet up and have a nice lone drink... No wonder some conservative theologians have already proclaimed tamagochi the latest incarnation of Satan. In ethical terms, 'Satan' is also a name for the solipsistic self-immersion and utter ignorance of loving compassion for my neighbour. Isn't the faked compassion and care for a digital toy infinitely more perverse than a simple and direct egotistic ignorance of others, since it somehow blurs the very difference between egotism and altruistic compassion?

However, doesn't the same hold also for all kinds of inanimate objects with which we play games under the condition of the fetishistic disavowal, from children's dolls to inflatable sex-dolls with appropriate holes for penetration ('I know very well that this is just an inanimate object, but nonetheless I act as if I believe this is a living being')? Two features distinguish tamagochi from the usual inanimate plaything: first, in contrast to a doll, the tamagochi no longer aims at imitating (as realistically as possible) the contours of what it replaces, it does not 'look like' a small baby or a naked woman or a puppet – we are dealing with a radical reduction of imaginary resemblance to the symbolic level, to the exchange of signals; second, in contrast to a doll, which is a passive, pliable object with which we can do whatever we want, tamagochi is thoroughly active, ie. the whole point of the game is that tamagochi always has the initiative, that it controls the game and bombards us with demands.

Isn't the ultimate consequence of all this for a materialist that God Himself is the ultimate tamagochi, the virtual Other fabricated by our unconscious *Einbildungskraft* and bombarding us with inexorable demands? Does the fact that tamagochi no longer endeavours to resemble the pet it stands for not make it especially appropriate for the Judaic tradition with its prohibition of producing images of God? Again, no wonder that, for some theologians, tamagochi is Satan incarnated: it as it were lays bare the mechanism of the believer's dialogue with God, since it demonstrates how an intense and caring exchange of symbols is possible with an entity that is purely virtual, ie. that exists only as an interface simulacrum. In other words, tamagochi is a machine which allows you to satisfy your need to love thy neighbour: you have a need to indulge in the care for your neighbour, a child, a pet? No problem: tamagochi enables you to do it without bothering your actual neighbours with your intrusive compassion – tamagochi can take care of this pathological need of yours... The charm of this solution resides in the fact that (what traditional ethics regarded as) the highest expression of your humanity – the compassionate need to take care of another living being – is treated as a dirty idiosyncratic pathology which should be satisfied in private, without bothering your actual fellow beings.

The satisfaction of tamagochi is provided by our being compelled to care for the object any time it wants, by fulfilling its demands – don't we find here the ultimate exemplification of the obsessional object, insofar as the obsessional's object of desire is the other's demand? Things are the same in the obsessional's dealing with his psychoanalyst: when, in the course of the cure, the obsessional is incessantly active, telling stories, memories, bemoaning his fate, accusing the analyst, etc., he thereby endeavours to come to terms with the trauma of 'what does the analyst want from me,' with the dark spot of the analyst's desire, while the analyst is simply there in his impassive presence. The point is not just that I, the patient, am bothered and frustrated by the analyst's enigmatic silence, but, perhaps even more, that I am active in order to keep the other (analyst) silent: I am active so that nothing will happen, so that he will not proclaim the word (or accomplish some other gesture) which will disclose the nullity of my incessant babble and touch some of my repressed traumas.

This, perhaps, is the most succinct definition of false activity: when I am frenetically active not in order to achieve something, but to prevent something (that which really matters) from happening. Let us imagine a meeting of friends in which some underlying tension threatens to explode: the obsessional talks all the time, tells jokes, etc., in order to prevent the awkward moment of silence which would force the participants to tackle directly the uneasy topic. And does the same not go for the so-called postmodern politics? All the talk about new forms of politicisation focused on particular issues (gay rights, ecology, ethnic minorities...), all this incessant activity of fluid, shifting identities, of building multiple ad hoc coalitions, has something inauthentic about it and ultimately resembles the obsessional neurotic who talks all the time and is frantically active precisely in order to ensure that something – that which really matters, the free circulation of capital – will not be disturbed. Perhaps, therein resides the ultimate cause of tamagochi's success: it provides the best metaphor for what is fundamentally false and sterile in the frenetic activity in which we are caught in our daily lives.

Between Brassed Off and going The Full Monty

In what, then, resides the falsity of postmodern politics or, to use a more appropriate term, of what Jacques Rancière has called today's post-politics, the stance that emphasises the need to leave behind old ideological divisions and to confront new issues, armed with the necessary expert knowledge and free deliberation that takes into account concrete people's needs and demands? The best formula that renders the paradox of post-politics is perhaps Tony Blair's characterisation of the New Labour as the 'Radical Centre': in the old days of 'ideological' political divides, the qualification 'radical' was reserved either for the extreme Left or for the extreme Right. The Centre was by definition moderate: measured by the old standards, the term 'Radical Centre' is the same nonsense as 'radical moderation.' What makes New Labour (or Clinton's politics in the USA) 'radical' is its radical abandonment of the 'old ideological divides,' usually formulated in the guise of a paraphrase of Deng's motto from the sixties: 'It doesn't matter if a cat is red or white, what matters is that it effectively catches mice.' In the same vein, the advocates of New Labour like to emphasise that one should without any prejudice take good ideas and apply them, whatever their (ideological) origins.

And what are these 'good ideas'? The answer is, of course: ideas that work. It is here that we encounter the gap that separates a political act proper from the 'administration of social matters' that remains within the framework of the existing socio-political relations: the political act (intervention) proper is not simply something that works well within the framework of the existing relations, but something that changes the very framework that determines how things work. To say that good ideas are 'ideas that work' means that one accepts in advance the (global capitalist) constellation that determines what works (if, for example, one spends too much money on education or healthcare, that 'doesn't work,' since it infringes too much on the conditions of capitalist profitability). One can also put it in terms of the well-known definition of politics as the 'art of the possible': authentic politics is rather the exact opposite, ie. the art of the impossible. It changes the very parameters of what is considered 'possible' in the existing constellation. In this sense, even Nixon's visit to China and the ensuing establishment of diplomatic relations between USA and China was a kind of political act, insofar as it effectively changed the parameters of what was considered 'possible' (or 'feasible') in the domain of international relations – yes, one could do the unthinkable and talk normally with the ultimate enemy.

Two recent English films, both stories about the traumatic disintegration of the old-style working-class male identity, render two opposed versions of the act. *Brassed Off* focuses on the relationship between 'real' political struggle (the miners' struggle against the threatening pit closure legitimised in the terms of technological progress) and the idealised symbolic expression of the miners' community, their playing in the brass band. At first, the two aspects seem to be opposed: to the miners caught in the struggle for their economic survival, the 'only music matters!' attitude of their old band leader dying of lung cancer appears as a vain fetishised insistence on the empty symbolic form deprived of its social substance. However, once miners lose their political struggle, the 'music matters' attitude, ie. their insistence to go on playing and participating in the national competition, turns into a defiant symbolic gesture, a proper act of asserting fidelity to their political struggle. As one of the miners puts it, when there is no hope, there are just principles to follow. In short, the *act* occurs when the insistence on the empty form (we'll continue playing our brass band, whatever happens...) itself becomes the sign of fidelity to the content (to the struggle against the closures, for the continuation of the miners' way of life).

The Full Monty, my second example, is, like *Dead Poets' Society* or *City Lights*, one of those films whose entire narrative line moves towards its final climactic moment – in this case, the five unemployed men's 'full monty' appearance in the strippers' club. Their final gesture – 'going to the end,' disclosing the penises to the packed hall – involves an act which, although in a way opposite to that of *Brassed Off*, ultimately amounts to the same: to the acceptance of the loss. The heroism of the final gesture in *The Full Monty* is not that of persisting in the symbolic form (playing in the band) when its social substance disintegrates, but, on the contrary, in accepting what, from the perspective of male working-class ethics, cannot but appear as the ultimate humiliation – in readily giving away false male dignity. The tragicomic dimension of their predicament resides in the fact that the carnivalesque spectacle (of stripping) is performed not by the usual well-built dancing strippers, but by ordinary, middle-aged, decent and shy men who are definitely not beautiful – their heroism is that they agree to do the act, although they are aware that their physical appearance is not appropriate to it.

However, what one should bear in mind is that both acts, that of *Brassed Off* and that of *The Full Monty*, are the acts of losers, the two modes of coming to terms with the catastrophic loss: insisting on the empty form as fidelity to the lost content ('When there is no hope, only principles remain'); heroically renouncing the last vestiges of false dignity by way of accomplishing the act for which one is grotesquely inadequate. And the sad thing is that, in a way, this is our situation today: after the breakdown of the Marxist notion that capitalism itself generates the force that will destroy it in the guise of the proletariat, none of the critics of capitalism, none of those who describe so convincingly the deadly vortex that the so-called process of globalisation is drawing us into, has any determinate idea of how can we get rid of capitalism. Two attitudes thus impose themselves: either the Left nostalgically engages in the ritualistic incantation of old formulas, be it those of revolutionary communism or those of welfare-state reformist social democracy, dismissing the talk about new postmodern society as empty fashionable prattle obfuscating the harsh reality of today's capitalism, or the Left accepts global capitalism as 'the only game in town' and plays the double game of promising to the employees that the maximum possible of the welfare state will be maintained and to the employers that the rules of the (global capitalist) game will be fully respected and the 'irrational' demands of the employees effectively censored... So, in today's leftist politics, we seem effectively to be reduced to the choice between the 'brass' orthodox attitude of proudly, out of principle, sticking to the old (communist or social democratic) tune, although we know that its time has passed, or to the New Labour 'Radical Centre' attitude of going 'the full monty' in stripping, getting rid of, the last remainders of the proper left-wing discourse...

Risk society and its enemies

The paradoxes of this post-political logic of today's capitalism are the focus of the recently popular theory of the 'risk society.'[3] The paradigmatic examples of risks to which this theory refers are global warming, the ozone hole, Mad Cow Disease, the danger of using nuclear power plants as the source of energy, the unforeseen consequences of the application of genetics to agriculture, etc. All these cases are what is usually referred to as 'low probability–high consequences' risks: no one knows how great the risks are, the probability of the global catastrophe is small. However, if the catastrophe does occur, it will be really terminal. Biologists warn us that the increased use of chemicals in our foods and drugs can make the

---

[3] Beck 1992; Franklin (ed.) 1998; Giddens 1990

human race extinct not because of a direct ecological catastrophe, but simply by rendering us infertile – this outcome seems improbable, yet catastrophic. The next crucial feature is that these new threats are so-called 'manufactured risks': they result from economic, technological and scientific interventions into nature, which perturb natural processes so radically that it is no longer possible to elude the responsibility by letting nature itself find a way to re-establish the lost balance. It is also absurd to resort to a new-age turn against science, since these threats are, for the most part, invisible, undetectable, without the diagnostic tools of science. All of today's notions of ecological threat, from the ozone hole to how fertilisers and chemical additions to food are threatening our fertility, are strictly dependent on scientific insight (usually of the most advanced kind). Although the effects of the 'ozone hole' are observable, their causal explanation through reference to the 'ozone hole' is a scientific hypothesis: there is no directly observable 'ozone hole' up there in the sky. These risks are thus generated by a kind of self-reflexive loop, ie. they are not external risks (like a gigantic comet falling on Earth), but the unforeseen outcome of the very technological and scientific endeavour of individuals to control their lives and increase their productivity. Perhaps the supreme example of the dialectical reversal by means of which a new scientific insight, instead of simply magnifying our domination over nature, generates new risks and uncertainties, is provided by the prospect that, in a decade or two, genetics will not only be able to identify an individual's complete genetic inheritance, but even manipulate technologically individual genes to acquire the desired results and changes (to eradicate the tendency towards cancer, etc.). However, far from resulting in total predictability and certainty, this very radical self-objectivisation (the situation in which, in the guise of the genetic formula, I will be able to confront what I 'objectively am') will generate even more radical uncertainties about what the actual psycho-social effects of such knowledge and its applications will be (What will become of the notions of freedom and responsibility? What will be the unforeseen consequences of meddling with genes?).

This conjunction of low probability and high consequences makes virtually impossible the standard Aristotelian strategy of avoiding both extremes. It is as if it is impossible today to assume a moderate rational position between scaremongering (ecologists who paint impending universal catastrophe) and covering-up (downplaying the dangers). The downplaying strategy can always emphasise the fact that scaremongering at best takes for certain conclusions which are not fully grounded in scientific observations, while the scaremongering strategy, of course, is fully justified in retorting that, once it is possible to predict the catastrophe with full certainty, it will be, by definition, already too late. The problem is that there is no objective scientific or other way to acquire certainty about their existence and extent: it is not simply a matter of exploitative corporations or government agencies downplaying the dangers. There is effectively no way to establish with certainty the extent of the risk. Scientists and specialists themselves are unable to provide the final answer. We are bombarded daily by new discoveries which overturn previous common views. What if it turns out that fat really prevents cancer? What if global warming were effectively the result of a natural cycle and we should pour even more carbon dioxide into the air? There is *a priori* no proper measure between the 'excess' of panic-mongering and the indecisive procrastination of 'let us not panic, we do not yet have certain results.' For example, *à propos* of global warming, the logic of 'let us avoid both extremes, the careless further emission of carbon dioxide, as well as the quick shutting-down of thousands of factories, and proceed gradually' is clearly meaningless. And, again, this impenetrability is not simply a matter of 'complexity', but of reflexivity: the new opaqueness and impenetrability (the radical uncertainty as to the ultimate consequences of our actions) is not due to the fact that we are puppets in the hands of some transcendent global Power (Fate, Historical Necessity, Market); on the contrary, it is due to the fact that 'nobody is in charge,' that *there is no such power*, no 'Other of the Other' that pulls the strings – opaqueness is grounded in the very fact that today's society is thoroughly 'reflexive', that there is no Nature or Tradition providing the firm foundation on which one can rely, that even our innermost impetuses (sexual orientation etc.) are more and more experienced as something to be chosen. How to feed and educate a child, how to proceed in sexual seduction, how and what to eat, how to relax and amuse oneself, all these spheres are more and more 'colonised' by reflexivity, ie. experienced as something to be learned and decided upon.

The ultimate deadlock of the risk society resides in the gap between knowledge and decision, between the chain of reasons and the act which resolves the dilemma (in Lacanese: between S2 and S1): there is no one who 'really knows' the global outcome – at the level of positive knowledge, the situation is radically 'undecidable' – but we nonetheless *have to decide*. Of course, this gap was here all the time: when an act of decision grounds itself in a chain of reasons, it always retroactively 'colours' these reasons so that they support this decision – suffice it to recall the believer who is well aware that the reasons for his belief are comprehensible only to those who had already decided to believe... What we encounter in the contemporary risk society is, however, something much more radical: the opposite of the standard forced choice about which Lacan speaks, ie. of a situation in which I am free to choose on condition that I make the right choice, so that the only thing that is left for me to do is to undertake the empty gesture of pretending to accomplish freely what is in any case imposed on me. In the contemporary risk society, we are dealing with something entirely different: the choice is effectively 'free' and is, for this very reason, experienced as even more frustrating. We find ourselves constantly in the position of having to decide about matters that will fatefully affect our lives, but without a proper foundation in knowledge. What Ulrich Beck calls the 'second Enlightenment' is thus, with regard to this crucial point, the exact reversal of the aim of the 'first Enlightenment' – that is, to bring about a society in which fundamental decisions will lose their 'irrational' character and become fully grounded in good reasons (in a correct insight into the state of things): the 'second Enlightenment' imposes on each of us the burden of making crucial decisions which may affect our very survival without any proper foundation in knowledge. All the government expert panels and ethical committees etc. are here to conceal this radical openness and uncertainty.

And, again, far from being experienced as liberating, this compulsion freely to decide is experienced as an anxiety – provoking an obscene gamble, a kind of ironic reversal of predestination: I am held accountable for decisions which I was forced to make without proper knowledge of the situation. The freedom of decision enjoyed by the subject of the 'risk society' is not the freedom of someone who can freely choose his destiny, but the anxiety-provoking freedom of somebody who is constantly compelled to make decisions without being aware of their consequences. There is no guarantee that the democratic politicisation of crucial decisions, the active involvement of thousands of concerned individuals, will necessarily improve the quality and accuracy of decisions and thus effectively lessen the risks. One is tempted to evoke here the answer of a devout catholic to the reproach of the atheist liberal that they, catholics, are so stupid as to believe in the infallibility of the Pope: 'We, catholics, at least believe in the infallibility of *one* and only one person; does democracy not rely on a much more risky notion that the majority of the people, ie. millions of them, are infallible?' The subject thus finds himself in a Kafkaesque situation of being guilty for not even knowing what (if anything) he is guilty of: the prospect forever haunts me that I have already made decisions which will endanger me and all my beloved, but I will only, if ever, learn the truth about it when it will be already too late. Let us recall here the figure of Forrest Gump, this perfect 'vanishing mediator,' the very opposite of the Master (the one who symbolically registers an event by nominating it, by inscribing it into the big Other). Gump is presented as the innocent bystander who, by just doing what he does, unknowingly sets in motion a shift of historical proportions. When he visits Berlin to play football and inadvertently throws the ball across the wall, he thereby starts the process which brings down the wall; when he visits Washington and is given a room in the Watergate complex, in the middle of the night he notices some strange things going on in the rooms across the yard, calls the guard and sets in motion the events which culminated in Nixon's downfall. Is this not the ultimate metaphor for the situation at which the proponents of the notion of 'risk society' aim, a situation in which we are forced to make moves whose ultimate effects are beyond our reach?

Although the dissolution of all traditional links is the standard motif of nineteenth-century capitalist modernisation, repeatedly described by

Marx (the 'all that is solid melts into air' motif), the whole point of Marx's analysis is that this unheard-of dissolution of all traditional forms, far from bringing about a society in which individuals collectively and freely run their lives, engenders its own form of anonymous Destiny in the guise of market relations. On the one hand, the market does involve a fundamental dimension of risk: it is an impenetrable mechanism which can, in a wholly unpredictable way, ruin the efforts of an honest worker and enrich a sleazy speculator – nobody knows what the final outcome of a speculation will be. However, although our acts can have unforeseen and unintended consequences, the notion still persists that they are co-ordinated by the infamous 'Invisible Hand of the Market,' the basic premise of the free market ideology: each of us pursues his/her particular interests, and the ultimate result of this clash and interaction of the multiplicity of individual acts and conflicting intentions is global welfare. In this notion of the 'Cunning of Reason', the big Other survives as the social Substance in which we all participate by our acts, as the mysterious spectral agency that somehow re-establishes the balance. The fundamental Marxist idea, of course, is that this figure of the big Other, of the alienated social Substance, ie. the anonymous market as the modern form of Fate, can be superseded and social life brought under the control of humanity's 'collective intellect'. In this way, Marx remained within the confines of the 'first modernisation', which aimed at the establishment of a self-transparent society regulated by the 'collective intellect'; no wonder that this project found its perverted realisation in 'really existing socialism' which – in spite of the extreme uncertainty of an individual's fate, at least in the times of paranoiac political purges – was perhaps the most radical attempt to suspend the uncertainty that pertains to capitalist modernisation.

'Real Socialism's' (modest) appeal is best exemplified by the election-slogan of Slobodan Milosevic's Socialist Party in the first 'free' elections in Serbia: 'With us, there is no uncertainty!' – although life was poor and drab, there was no need to worry about the future, everyone's modest existence was guaranteed, the Party took care of everything, ie. all decisions were made by Them. In spite of their contempt for the regime, people nonetheless half-consciously trusted 'Them', relied on 'Them', believed that there was somebody holding all the reins and taking care of everything. There was effectively a perverse kind of liberation in this possibility of putting the burden of responsibility onto the Other: reality was not really 'ours' (of the ordinary people), it belonged to Them (the Party *nomenklatura*), its greyness bore witness to Their oppressive rule, and, paradoxically, this made it much easier to endure life; jokes could be told about everyday troubles, about the lack of ordinary objects like soap and toilet paper – although we suffered the material consequences of these troubles, the jokes were on Their account, we told them from an excepted, liberated position. Now, with Them out of power, we are suddenly and violently compelled to assume this drab greyness: it is no longer Theirs, it is ours... What happens today, with the 'postmodern' risk society, is that there is no 'Invisible Hand' whose mechanism, blind as it may be, somehow re-establishes the balance, no Other Scene in which the accountancy is properly kept, no fictional Other Place in which, from the perspective of the Last Judgement, our acts will be properly located and accounted for. Not only do we not know what our acts will effectively amount to, there is even no global mechanism regulating our interactions – *this* is what the properly 'postmodern' non-existence of the big Other means. Foucault spoke of the 'strategies without subject' that Power uses in its reproduction – here, we have almost the exact opposite: subjects caught in the unpredictable consequences of their acts, but no global strategy dominating and regulating their interplay. Individuals who are still caught in the traditional modernist paradigm are desperately looking for another agency, which one could legitimately elevate into the position of the Subject Supposed to Know and which would somehow guarantee our choice: ethical committees, the scientific community itself, government authority, up to the paranoiac big Other, the secret invisible Master of conspiracy theories.

So what is then wrong with the theory of the risk society? Doesn't it fully endorse the non-existence of the big Other and draw all ethico-political consequences from it? The problem is that, paradoxically, this theory is simultaneously too specific and too general: with all its emphasis on how the 'second modernisation' forces us to transform old notions of human agency, social organisation, etc., up to the most intimate ways of relating to our sexual identity, the theory of the risk society nonetheless underestimates the impact of the emerging new societal logic on the very fundamental status of subjectivity; on the other hand, in conceiving of risk and manufactured uncertainty as a universal feature of contemporary life, this theory obfuscates the concrete socio-economic roots of these risks. And it is our contention that psychoanalysis and Marxism, as a rule dismissed by the theorists of the risk society as outdated expressions of the first-wave modernisation (the fight of the rational agency to bring to the light the impenetrable Unconscious; the idea of a self-transparent society controlled by the 'common intellect'), can contribute to a critical clarification of these two points.

Bill Gates as an icon

Psychoanalysis is neither a theory which bemoans the disintegration of the old modes of traditional stability and wisdom, locating in them the cause of modern neuroses, and compelling us to discover our roots in old archaic wisdom or in profound self-knowledge (the Jungian version), nor is it just another version of the reflexive modern knowledge teaching us how to penetrate and master the innermost secrets of our psychic life. What psychoanalysis focuses on, what is its proper object, are rather the unexpected consequences of the disintegration of traditional structures that regulated libidinal life. Why does the decline of paternal authority and fixed social and gender roles generate new anxieties, instead of opening up a Brave New World of individuals engaged in the creative 'care of the Self' and enjoying the perpetual process of shifting and reshaping their fluid multiple identities? The problem with the theorists of the risk society is that they underestimate the radical character of this change: with all their insistence on how, in today's risk society, reflexivity is universalised, so that Nature and Tradition no longer exist, in all their talk about the 'second Enlightenment' doing away with the naive certainties of the first wave of modernisation, they leave intact the fundamental mode of subjectivity of the subject: their subject remains the modern subject, able to reason and reflect freely, to decide and to select his/her set of norms, etc. The error is here the same as that with feminists who want to do away with the Oedipus complex, and nonetheless expect the basic form of subjectivity that was generated by the Oedipus complex (the subject free to reason and decide, etc.) to survive intact.

Perhaps the ultimate example of the universalised reflexivity of our lives (and thereby of the retreat of the big Other, of the loss of symbolic efficiency) is a phenomenon known to most psychoanalysts today: the growing inefficiency of the psychoanalytic interpretation. Traditional psychoanalysis still relied on a substantial notion of the Unconscious as the non-reflected 'dark continent', the impenetrable 'decentered' Substance of the subject's being to be arduously penetrated, reflected, mediatised, by interpretation. Today, however, the formations of the Unconscious (from dreams to hysterical symptoms) have definitely lost their innocence: the 'free associations' of a typical educated analysand consist for the most part of attempts to provide a psychoanalytic explanation of their disturbances, so that one is quite justified in saying that we have not only Jungian, Kleinian, Lacanian... interpretations of the symptoms, but symptoms themselves which are Jungian, Kleinian, Lacanian... ie. whose reality involves implicit reference to some psychoanalytic theory. The unfortunate result of this global reflexivisation of the interpretation (everything becomes interpretation, the Unconscious interprets itself...) is, of course, that the analyst's interpretation loses its performative 'symbolic efficiency' and leaves the symptom intact in its idiotic *jouissance*. In other words, what happens in psychoanalytic treatment is similar to the paradox of a neo-Nazi skinhead who, when really pressed for the reasons for his violence, suddenly starts to talk like social workers, sociologists and social psychologists, quoting diminished social mobility, rising insecurity, the disintegration of paternal authority, the lack of maternal love in his early childhood – when the big Other *qua* the substance of our social being disintegrates, the unity of practice and its inherent reflection disintegrates into raw violence and its impotent, inefficient interpretation. This impotence of interpretation is also one of the necessary obverses of the universalised reflexivity hailed by the risk society theorists: it is as if our reflexive power can flourish only insofar as it draws its strength and relies on some minimal 'pre-reflexive' substantial support which eludes its grasp, so that its universalisation is paid for by its inefficiency, ie., by the paradoxical re-emergence of the brute Real of 'irrational' violence, impermeable and insensitive to reflexive interpretation.

The inability of the risk society theory to take into account all the consequences of the global reflexivisation is clearly discernible in its treatment of family. This theory is right to emphasise how the relationship of parents towards children in the traditional family was the last domain of legal slavery in our Western societies: a large part of society – underage persons – were denied full responsibility and autonomy and retained in a slave status with regard to their parents (who controlled their lives and were responsible for their acts). With reflexive modernisation, children themselves are treated as responsible subjects with freedom of choice (in divorce procedures, they are allowed to influence the decision of which of the two parents will retain them; they can start a court procedure against their parents if they feel that their human rights have been violated and so on) – in short, parenthood is no longer a natural-substantial notion, but becomes in a way politicised, it turns into another domain of reflexive choice. However, is not the obverse of this reflexivisation of family relations, in which the family loses its character of immediate-substantial entity whose members are not autonomous subjects, the progressive 'familiarisation' of the very public professional life? Institutions which were supposed to function as an antidote to family, start to function as surrogate families, allowing us somehow to prolong our family dependence and immaturity: schools, universities even, more and more assume therapeutic functions, corporations provide a new family home, etc. The standard situation in which, after the period of education and dependency, I am allowed to enter the adult universe of maturity and responsibility, is thus doubly turned around: already as a child, I am recognised as a mature responsible being, and, simultaneously, my childhood is prolonged indefinitely, ie. I am never compelled to really 'grow up,' since all institutions which follow the family function as *ersatz*-families, providing a caring surrounding for my narcissistic endeavours... In order to grasp all the consequences of this shift, one would have to return to Hegel's triad of family, civil society (free interaction of individuals who enjoy their reflexive freedom) and state.

Hegel's construction is based on the distinction between the private sphere of family and the public sphere of civil society, a distinction which is today vanishing, insofar as family life itself gets politicised, is turning into a part of the public domain, and, on the other hand, public professional life gets 'familiarised,' ie. subjects participate in it as members of a large family, not as responsible 'mature' individuals. So the problem here is not patriarchal authority and the emancipatory struggle against it, as most feminists continue to claim; the problem is rather the new forms of dependency that arise from the very decline of the patriarchal symbolic authority. It was already in the 1930s that Max Horkheimer, in his study of authority and family, drew attention to the ambiguous consequences of the gradual disintegration of paternal authority in modern capitalist society: far from being simply the elementary cell and generator of authoritarian personalities, the modern nuclear family was simultaneously the structure that generated the 'autonomous' critical subject able to confront the predominant social order on account of his/her ethical convictions, so that the immediate result of the disintegration of the paternal authority is also the rise of what sociologists call the conformist 'other-oriented' personality.[4] Today, with the shift towards the narcissistic personality, this process is even stronger and has entered a new phase.

When patriarchy is fatally undermined, so that the subject experiences himself as freed from any traditional constraints, lacking any internalised symbolic prohibition, bent on experimenting with his life and on pursuing his life-project, etc., we have thus to ask the momentous question of the disavowed 'passionate attachments' which support the new reflexive freedom of the subject delivered from the constraints of Nature and/or Tradition. What if the disintegration of the public ('patriarchal') symbolic authority is paid for (or counterbalanced) by an even stronger disavowed 'passionate attachment' to subjection, as seems to be indicated by, among other phenomena, the growth of sado-masochistic lesbian couples where the relationship of the two women follows the strict and severely enacted Master/Slave matrix: the one who gives the orders is the 'top', the one who obeys is the 'bottom', and, in order to become the 'top', one has to go through the arduous process of apprenticeship. While it is wrong to read this 'top/bottom' duality as a sign of direct 'identification with the (male) aggressor', it is no less wrong to perceive it as a parodic imitation of the patriarchal relations of domination; we are rather dealing with the genuine paradox of the freely chosen Master/Slave form of coexistence that provides a deep libidinal satisfaction precisely insofar as it delivers the subjects from the pressure of excessive freedom and from the lack of fixed identity. The standard situation is thus turned around: instead of the ironic carnivalesque subversion of the predominant Master/Slave relationship, we have social relations among free and equal individuals, where the 'passionate attachment' to some extreme form of strictly regulated domination and submission becomes the secret source of libidinal satisfaction, the obscene supplement to the public sphere of freedom and equality. In short, the rigidly codified Master/Slave relationship turns up as the very form of 'inherent

---

[4] Horkheimer 1995.

transgression' of subjects living in a society in which all forms of life are experienced as a matter of the free choice of a life-style.

As to the socio-economic relations of domination that go with the 'postmodern' constellation, the public image of Bill Gates is worthy of some comment; what matters is not the factual accuracy (is Gates really like that?), but the very fact that a certain figure started to function as an icon, filling in some fantasmatic slot – if the features do not correspond to the 'true' Gates, they are all the more indicative of the underlying fantasmatic structure.[5] Gates is not only no longer the patriarchal Father-Master, he is also no longer the corporate Big Brother running a stiff bureaucratic empire, dwelling on the inaccessible top floor, guarded by a host of secretaries and deputies. He is rather a kind of little brother: his very ordinariness functions as the indication of its opposite, of some monstrous dimension so uncanny that it can no longer be rendered public in the guise of some symbolic title. What we encounter here in a most violent way is the deadlock of the Double who is simultaneously like ourselves and the harbinger of an uncanny, properly monstrous dimension – indicative of this is the way title-pages, drawings or photomontages present Gates: as an ordinary guy, whose devious smile nonetheless points towards a wholly different underlying dimension of monstrosity beyond representation which threatens to shatter his ordinary-guy image. In the sixties and seventies, it was possible to buy soft-porn postcards with a girl clad in a bikini or wearing a proper gown; however, when one moved the postcard a little bit or looked at it from a slightly different perspective, the dress magically disappeared and one was able to see the naked body of the girl. Is it not something similar with the image of Bill Gates, whose benevolent features, when viewed from a slightly different perspective, magically acquire a sinister and threatening dimension?

In this respect, it is also a crucial feature of Gates as icon that he is (perceived as) the ex-hacker who made it – one should confer to the term 'hacker' all its subversive/marginal/anti-establishment connotation of those who wanted to disturb the smooth functioning of large bureaucratic corporations. At the fantasmatic level, the underlying notion here is that Gates is a subversive marginal hooligan who has taken over and dresses himself up as a respectable chairman... In Bill Gates, the Little Brother, the average ugly guy, thus coincides with and contains the figure of Evil Genius who aims for total control of our lives. In old James Bond movies, this Evil Genius was still an eccentric figure, dressed up extravagantly or in a proto-communist Maoist grey uniform. In the case of Gates, this ridiculous charade is no longer needed, the Evil Genius turns out to be the obverse of the ordinary guy next door. In other words, what we encounter in the icon of Bill Gates is a kind of reversal of the motif of the hero endowed with supernatural powers, but who is in his everyday life a common, confused guy (like

---

[5] Salecl 1998.

Superman who is in his ordinary existence a clumsy bespectacled journalist): here it is the bad guy who is characterised by this kind of a split. The ordinariness of Bill Gates is thus not of the same order as the emphasis on the so-called ordinary human features of the traditional patriarchal master. The fact that this traditional master never lived up to his mandate, that he was always imperfect, marked with some failure or weakness, not only did not impede his symbolic authority, but even served as its support, rendering palpable the constitutive gap between the purely formal function of symbolic authority and the empirical individual who occupies its post. In contrast to this gap, Bill Gates's ordinariness points to a different notion of authority, that of the obscene superego that operates in the Real.

There is an old European fairy-tale motif of diligent dwarfs (usually controlled by an evil magician) who, during the night, while people are asleep, emerge from their hiding-place and accomplish their work (set the house in order, cook the meals...), so that when, in the morning, people awaken, they find their work magically done. This motif is found from Richard Wagner's *Rhinegold* (the *Nibelungen* who work in their underground caves, driven by their cruel master, the dwarf Alberich) to Fritz Lang's *Metropolis* in which the enslaved industrial workers live and work deep beneath the earth's surface to produce wealth for the ruling capitalists.[6] This dispositif of the 'underground' slaves dominated by a manipulative evil Master brings us back to the old duality of the two modes of the Master, the public symbolic Master and the secret Evil Magician who effectively pulls the strings and does his work during the night. Are the two Bills who now run the USA, Clinton and Gates, not the ultimate exemplification of this duality?

When the subject is endowed with symbolic authority, he acts as an appendix to his symbolic title, ie. it is the big Other, the symbolic institution, who acts through him: suffice it to recall a judge, who may be a miserable and corrupted person, but the moment he puts on his robe and other insignia, his words are the words of Law itself. On the other hand, the 'invisible' Master (whose exemplary case is the anti-semitic figure of the 'Jew' who, invisible to the public eye, pulls the strings of social life) is a kind of uncanny double of public authority: he has to act in shadow, irradiating a phantom-like, spectral omnipotence. This, then, is the conclusion to be drawn from the Bill Gates icon: how the disintegration of the patriarchal symbolic authority, of the Name of the Father, gives rise to a new figure of the Master who is simultaneously our common peer, our fellow-semblant, our imaginary double, and for this very reason fantasmatically endowed with another dimension of the Evil Genius. In Lacanian terms: the suspension of the Ego Ideal, of the feature of symbolic identification, ie. the reduction of the Master to an imaginary ideal, necessarily gives rise to its monstrous obverse, to the superego figure of the omnipotent Evil Genius who

---

[6] Zizek 1996.

controls our lives. In this figure, the imaginary (semblance) and the real (of paranoia) overlap, due to the suspension of proper symbolic efficiency.

The disintegration of paternal symbolic authority has thus two facets. On the one hand, symbolic prohibitive norms are more and more replaced with imaginary ideals (of social success, of bodily fitness...); on the other hand, the lack of symbolic prohibition is supplemented by the re-emergence of ferocious superego figures. So, we have a subject who is extremely narcissistic, ie. who perceives everything as a potential threat to his precarious imaginary balance (see the universalisation of the logic of victim: every contact with another human being is experienced as a potential threat – if the other smokes, if he casts a covetous glance at me, he already hurts me); however, far from allowing him to float freely in his undisturbed balance, this narcissistic self-enclosure leaves the subject to the (not so) tender mercies of the superego injunction to enjoy. The so-called 'postmodern' subjectivity thus involves a kind of direct 'superegoisation' of the imaginary Ideal, caused by the lack of the proper symbolic prohibition; exemplary are here the 'postmodern' hacker-programmers, these extravagant eccentrics hired by large corporations to pursue their programming hobbies in an informal environment. They are under the injunction to be what they are, to follow their innermost idiosyncrasies, allowed to ignore social norms of dress and behaviour (what they obey are just some elementary rules of polite tolerance of each other's idiosyncrasies); they thus seem to realise a kind of proto-socialist utopia of overcoming the opposition between alienated business, where you earn money, and the private hobby-activity that you pursue for pleasure during weekends. In a way, their job is their hobby, which is why they spend long hours at weekends in their workplace behind the computer screen: when one is paid for indulging in one's hobby, the result is that one is exposed to a superego pressure incomparably stronger than that of the good old 'protestant work ethic.' Therein resides the unbearable paradox of this postmodern 'disalienation': the tension is no longer between my innermost idiosyncratic creative impulses and the Institution that doesn't appreciate them or wants to crush them in order to 'normalise' me: what the superego-injunction of the postmodern corporation like Microsoft targets is precisely this core of my idiosyncratic creativity – I become useless for them the moment I start losing this 'imp of perversity,' the moment I lose my 'countercultural' subversive edge and start to behave like a 'normal' mature subject. What we are dealing with here is thus a strange alliance between the rebellious subversive core of my personality, my 'imp of perversity,' and the external corporation.

So what is superego in its opposition to the symbolic Law? The parental figure who is simply 'repressive' in the mode of symbolic authority tells a child: 'You must go to grandma's birthday and behave nicely, even if you are bored to death – I don't care about how you feel, just do it!' The superego figure, in contrast, tells the child: 'Although you know how much grandma would like to see you, you should visit her only if you really want to do it – otherwise, you should stay at home!' The superego trick resides in this false appearance of a free choice, which, as every child knows, is effectively a forced choice that involves an even stronger order, ie. not only 'You must visit the grandma, whatever you feel!', but 'You must visit your grandma, and, on the top of it, *you must be glad to do it!*' – the superego orders you to enjoy doing what you have to do. The same goes for the strained relationship between lovers or a married couple: when a spouse says to his partner 'We should visit my sister only if you really want to!', the order given between the lines is, of course: 'Not only must you agree to visit my sister, but you must do it gladly, of your own free will, for your pleasure, not as a favour to me!' The proof of it resides in what happens if the unfortunate partner takes the offer as an effective free choice and says 'No!' – the spouse's predictable answer is then: 'How could you say that! How can you be so cruel! What did my poor sister do to you to make you not like her?'

It's the political economy, stupid!

The point of our insisting that we are dealing with Bill Gates as an icon is that it would be mystifying to elevate the 'real' Gates into a kind of Evil Genius who masterminds a plot to achieve global control over all of us. Here, more than ever, it is crucial to remember the lesson of the Marxist dialectic of fetishisation: the 'reification' of relations between people (the fact that they assume the form of phantasmagorical 'relations between things') is always redoubled by the apparently opposite process, by the false 'personalisation' ('psychologisation') of what are effectively objective social processes. It was already in the thirties that the first generation of the Frankfurt School theoreticians drew attention to how – at the very moment when global market relations started to exert their full domination, making the individual producer's success or failure dependent on market cycles totally out of their control – the notion of a charismatic 'business genius' reasserted itself in the 'spontaneous capitalist ideology,' attributing the success or failure of a businessman to some mysterious *je ne sais quoi* which he possesses. And does the same not hold even more today, when the abstraction of market relations that run our lives is pushed to an extreme? The book market is overflowing with psychological manuals advising us on how to succeed, how to outdo our partner or competitor – in short, making our success dependent on our proper 'attitude'. So, in a way, one is tempted to turn around the famous formula of Marx: in contemporary capitalism, the objective market 'relations between things' tend to assume the phantasmagorical form of pseudo-personalised 'relations between people'. No, Bill Gates is no genius, good or bad, he is just an opportunist who knew how to seize the moment, and as such the result of the capitalist system run amok. The question to ask is not 'How did Gates do it?' but 'How is the capitalist system structured, what is wrong with it, so that an individual can achieve such disproportionate power?' Phenomena like that of Bill Gates thus seem to point towards their own solution: once we are dealing with a gigantic global network formally owned by a single individual or corporation, is it not that ownership becomes in a way irrelevant to its functioning (there is no longer any worthwhile competition, profit is guaranteed), so that it becomes possible simply to cut off this head and to socialise the entire network without greatly perturbing its functioning? Does such an act not amount to a purely formal conversion that simply brings together what *de facto* already belongs together: the collective of individuals and the global communicational network they are all using, and which thus forms the substance of their social lives?

This already brings us to the second aspect of our critical distance towards the risk-society theory: the way it approaches the reality of capitalism. Is it not that, on a closer look, its notion of 'risk' points towards a narrow and precisely defined domain in which risks are generated: the domain of the uncontrolled use of science and technology in the conditions of capitalism? The paradigmatic case of 'risk,' which is not simply one among them but the risk 'as such,' is that of a new scientific-technological invention put to use by a private corporate company without proper public democratic debate and control, and then generating the spectre of unforeseen catastrophic long-term consequences. Is, however, this kind of risk not rooted in the fact that the logic of market and profitability is driving privately owned corporations to pursue their course and use scientific and technological innovations (or simply expanding their production) without effectively taking care of the long-term effects of such activity for the environment as well as for the health of humankind itself? Is thus – in spite of all the talk about a 'second modernisation' which compels us to leave behind the old ideological dilemmas of Left and Right, of capitalism versus socialism, etc. – the conclusion to be drawn not that, in the present global situation in which private corporations outside public political control are making decisions which can affect us all, including to the chances of our survival, the only solution resides in a kind of direct socialisation of the productive process, ie. in moving towards a society in which global decisions about the fundamental orientation of how to develop and use productive capacities at the disposal of society would be somehow made by the entire collective of the people affected by such decisions? Theorists of the risk society often evoke the need to counteract the reign of the 'depoliticised' global market with the move towards radical re-politicisation, which will take crucial decisions from the hands of state planners and experts and put them into the hands of the concerned individuals and groups themselves (through the revitalisation of the active citizenship, of the broad public debate, etc.).

However, they stop short of putting in question the very fundamentals of the anonymous logic of market relations and global capitalism, which imposes itself today more and more as the 'neutral' Real accepted by all parties and, as such, more and more depoliticised.

The big news of today's post-political age of the 'end of ideology' is the radical depoliticisation of the sphere of the economy: the way the economy functions (the need to cut social welfare, and the like) is accepted as a simple insight into the objective state of things. However, as long as this fundamental depoliticisation of the economic sphere is accepted, all the talk about active citizenship, about public discussion leading to responsible collective decisions, and all the rest, will remain limited to the 'cultural' issues of religious, sexual, ethnic and other lifestyle differences, without effectively encroaching upon the level at which long-term decisions which affect us all are made. In short, the only way effectively to bring about the society in which long-term risky decisions would ensue from the public debate of all concerned is some kind of radical limitation of capital's freedom, the subordination of the process of production to social control, in other words the radical repoliticisation of the economy. That is to say, if the problem with today's post-politics ('administration of social affairs') is that it increasingly undercuts the possibility of a proper political act, this undercutting is directly due to the depoliticisation of economics, to the common acceptance of capital and market mechanisms as neutral tools/procedures to be exploited. We can see now why today's post-politics cannot attain the properly political dimension of universality: because it silently precludes from politicisation the sphere of economy. The domain of global capitalist market relations is the Other Scene of the so-called repoliticisation of civil society advocated by the partisans of 'identity politics' and other postmodern forms of politicisation: as we have already emphasised all the talk about new forms of politics bursting out all around ultimately resembles the obsessional neurotic who is frantically active precisely in order to ensure that something – that which really matters – will not be disturbed, that it will remain immobilised. In short, today's post-politics is fundamentally interpassive. So, instead of celebrating the new freedoms and responsibilities brought about by the 'second modernity,' it is much more crucial to focus on what remains the same in this global fluidity and reflexivity, on what serves as the very motor of this fluidity: the inexorable logic of capital. The spectral presence of Capital is the figure of the big Other which not only remains operative when all the traditional embodiments of the symbolic big Other disintegrate, but even directly causes this disintegration. Far from being confronted with the abyss of their freedom, ie. loaded with the burden of responsibility that cannot be alleviated by the helping hand of Tradition or Nature, today's subject is perhaps more than ever caught in an inexorable compulsion that effectively runs his life.

The irony of history is that, in the Eastern European ex-Communist countries, the 'reformed' Communists were the first to learn this lesson. Why did many of them return to power via free elections in the mid 1990s? This very return offers the ultimate proof that these states have effectively entered capitalism. That is to say, what do ex-Communists stand for today? Due to their privileged links with the newly emerging capitalists (mostly members of the old *nomenklatura* 'privatising' the companies they once ran), they are first and foremost the party of big capital; furthermore, to erase the traces of their brief, but nonetheless rather traumatic experience with the politically active civil society, they as a rule ferociously advocate a quick de-ideologisation, a retreat from active civil society engagement into passive, apolitical consumerism – the very two features which characterise contemporary capitalism. Dissidents are thus astonished to discover that they played the role of 'vanishing mediators' on the way from 'socialism' to capitalism, in which the same class as before rules under a new guise. It is therefore wrong to claim that the return of the ex-Communists to power signals how people are disappointed by capitalism and long for the old socialist security – in a kind of Hegelian 'negation of negation,' it is only with the return to power of ex-Communists that 'socialism' was effectively negated, ie. what the political analysts (mis)perceive as the 'disappointment with capitalism' is effectively disappointment with the ethico-political enthusiasm for which there is no place in 'normal' capitalism. Retroactively, one thus becomes aware of how deeply the phenomenon of the so-called 'dissidence' was embedded in the socialist ideological framework, of the extent to which 'dissidence,' in its very utopian 'moralism' (preaching social solidarity, ethical responsibility, and so on) provided the disavowed ethical core of 'socialism': perhaps, one day, historians will note that – in the same sense in which Hegel claimed that the true spiritual result of the Peloponnesian war, its spiritual End, is Thucydides's book about it – 'dissidence' was the true spiritual result of the 'really-existing socialism'...

We should thus reassert the old Marxist critique of 'reification.' Today, emphasising the depoliticised 'objective' economic logic against the allegedly 'outdated' forms of ideological passions is THE predominant ideological form, since ideology is always self-referential, ie. it always defines itself through a distance from an Other dismissed and denounced as 'ideological.' For that precise reason, ie. because the depoliticised economy is the disavowed 'fundamental fantasy' of postmodern politics, a properly political *act* would necessarily entail the repoliticisation of the economy: within a given situation, a gesture counts as an *act* only insofar as it disturbs ('traverses') its fundamental fantasy.

Insofar as today's moderate Left, from Blair to Clinton, accepts fully this depoliticisation, we are witnessing a strange reversal of roles: the only serious political force which continues to question the unrestrained rule of the market is the populist extreme Right (Buchanan in the USA,

Le Pen in France). When Wall Street reacted negatively to the fall in the unemployment rate, the only one to make the obvious point that what is good for capital is obviously not what is good for the majority of the population was Buchanan. In contrast to the old wisdom according to which the extreme Right openly says what the moderate Right secretly thinks, but doesn't dare to pronounce publicly (the open assertion of racism, of the need for strong authority and cultural hegemony of the 'Western values', etc.), we are therefore approaching a situation in which the extreme Right openly says what the moderate Left secretly thinks, but doesn't dare to pronounce publicly (the necessity to curb the freedom of capital). One should, of course, fully acknowledge the tremendous liberating impact of the postmodern politicisation of domains which were hitherto considered apolitical (feminism, gay and lesbian politics, ecology, ethnic and other so-called minority issues): the fact that these issues not only became perceived as inherently political, but also gave birth to new forms of political subjectivisation, this fact thoroughly reshaped our entire political and cultural landscape. So, the point is not to play down these tremendous advances in favour of the return to some new version of the so-called economic essentialism; the point is rather that the depoliticisation of economy generates the populist New Right with its Moral Majority ideology, which is today the main obstacle to the realisation of the very (feminist, ecological...) demands on which the postmodern forms of political subjectivisation focus. In short, we plead for a 'return to the primacy of the economy' not to the detriment of the issues raised by the postmodern forms of politicisation, but precisely in order to create the conditions for the more effective realisation of these demands.

References

Beck, Ulrich 1992, *Risk Society: Towards a New Modernity*, London: Sage.

Franklin, Jane (ed.) 1998, *The Politics of the Risk Society*, Oxford: Polity Press.

Giddens, Anthony 1990, *The Consequences of Modernity*, Cambridge: Polity Press.

Horkheimer, Max 1995, 'Authority and the Family' in *Critical Theory*, New York: Continuum.

Lacan, Jacques 1992, *The Ethics of Psychoanalysis*, London: Routledge.

Pfaller, Robert October 8-10, 1996, Intervention at the Symposium: Die Dinge lachen an unserer Stelle, Linz, Austria.

Salecl, Renata 1998, *(Per)Versions of Love and Hate*, London: Verso.

Zizek, Slavoj 1996, '"I Hear You with My Eyes"; or, The Invisible Master' in *Gaze and Voice as Love Objects*, edited by Renata Salecl and Slavoj Zizek, Durham: Duke University Press.

Zizek, Slavoj 1997, *The Plague of Fantasies*, London: Verso, Chapter 3.

Adorno: A Critical Introduction
Simon Jarvis
Cambridge: Polity Press, 1998
Adorno On Music
Robert W. Witkin
London and New York: Routledge, 1998
Adorno's Aesthetics Of Music
Max Paddison
Cambridge: Cambridge University Press, 1993

Reviewed by Ben Watson

For those who believe that Marxism and academia can be productively combined, Theodor Adorno is a charismatic figure. Relentlessly on guard against anything that might ring of commercial duplicity, his convoluted, self-critical formulations – anti-slogans for intellectual integrity – give heart to anyone wishing to defend intellectual complexity, anti-spectacular obscurity or plain ornery resistance to the banality of everyday life under capitalism. Adorno's critique of bourgeois assumptions about the split between self and society – institutionalised by the separation between art and science – suggests something beyond academic time-serving. Further, over half his extant writings were on music; since the 1960s, music has been the pre-eminent medium for the circulation of subjective anti-authoritarianism. Adorno's materialist musicology promises much for the Left too.

However, when Adorno's arguments are theorised, they can lose their sting. Originally specific and partisan, his blows against Heidegger, Stravinsky and Donald Duck can become generalised defences of high-brow intellectualism versus vulgar communication. Adorno's left-Freudian insistence on fantasy and play crumbles into dry-as-dust 'radical philosophy'; with the epigones, demonstrations of familiarity with the Hegelian jargon replaces elucidation of concrete contradiction.

Simon Jarvis's survey exemplifies the problem. Hailed by J.M. Bernstein as 'absolutely splendid ... the standard introduction', it sifts Adorno's thought into a series of carefully-graded positions. Each contention is assessed next to Kant, Hegel, Heidegger, Husserl, Habermas, Derrida. Jarvis's colourless, pedagogic prose has none of Adorno's spark or outrage or bursts of expressionist vehemence. Whereas Adorno's phrases always target an antagonist – the inanity of the game-show host, the positivism of the sociologist, the philistinism of those who assume artists abhor analysis – for Jarvis, there is only Adorno's philosophy and the patience required to unravel it. His book reaches a climax of contradiction in concluding that Adorno reviled the academic division of labour – phrased in a terminology only students of philosophy will follow.

If there is an object of scorn in Jarvis's book, it is not bourgeois ideology, but those 'metaphysical' and 'dogmatic' materialists who believe Marxism supersedes philosophy. In other words, the active Left. This despite Jarvis's call for thinkers to become aware of the manual labour they live off. If the Marxist Left is dismissed, what material basis can there be for a critique of academic idealism? Jarvis apes Adorno's worst moments as he mobilises scholastic gibberish to justify ivory-tower inertia. Despite repeated genuflections to Adorno's claim that a genuine materialism will illuminate concrete particulars and not reduce actuality to examples, Jarvis keeps everything relentlessly abstract. Gottfried Benn, Samuel Beckett and Mark E. Smith figure as the sole literary exemplars, but they remain just that: their art has no impact on the theory before which they are called to testify.

Jarvis maintains that Adorno's negative dialectics can provide neither a method (a separation of thought from its object) nor a world-picture (a separation of the object from thought). Marxists who might hope to find in Adorno a musicology that understands capitalism have their hopes dashed. Jarvis ends up rehearsing the paradoxical interpenetration of despair and hope in Adorno's late essay 'On Resignation'. Though Jarvis acknowledges the materialism of *Negative Dialectics* – an aspect that encourages Marxist readings – he has a tendency to juggle subject/object back into equivalence (a process, according to Lenin's *Materialism and Empirio-Criticism*, that inevitably precedes philosophic reconciliation with the status quo):

> It is the nature of conceptuality as such for Adorno that the concept is always more and less than what can be subsumed under it, just as the object is always more and less than the concept which subsumes it. [Jarvis 1998, p. 205]

This easy balance – everything is 'more or less' accurate in the realm of epistemology, and simply requires more work – has a different tenor to Adorno's forthright 'the concept does not exhaust the thing conceived'. Jarvis supplies a general description of thinking, not criticism of a particular error. The author vanishes into the pseudo-objectivity of academic discourse. The priority of the world (object) to thought (subject) has been rescinded. Adorno's brave and self-revealing polemic against academic division of labour becomes its opposite: self-congratulatory expertise that leaves the world as it is.

The paradox is that the method Jarvis has chosen to explicate – dialectics – is indeed essential for thought about society. It was not for nothing that Lenin wrestled with Hegel's Logic just before he broke with the Second International, or that C.L.R. James wrestled with the same work as he broke with orthodox Trotskyism and formulated the concept of Stalin's Russia as state capitalist. Adorno's refusal of Kant's split between fact and value allowed him to make musical judgments that leap the divide between subjective response and objective analysis. Such dialectical interpenetration of opposites is crucial. However, for

Jarvis, the dialectical method becomes a fetish. Any categorical statement must be followed by rehearsing its opposite. The flexibility of thought required to perceive change in the world becomes a dogmatic flexibility that blurs the vision to non-change. Capital, class society, nation, fascism – pointing to such strangely intransigent features of the modern world is materialist 'dogma'.

In Jarvis's version of dialectics, a more complex and paradoxical sentence is always truer. Without Marx's grip on empirical facts, dialectical operations become obfuscation, and more nearly resemble what Marx criticised as the constituent principle of petit-bourgeois thought: 'on-the-one-hand and on-the-other-hand'. Whereas Adorno is necessarily shrill against both matter-of-fact positivism and wishful-thinking idealism, Jarvis positions him between Weber and Durkheim (pp. 44–8), as if it were all a matter of regal philosophical 'choice'. Necessary critique is degraded into a shopping-mall of options.

Elsewhere, Jarvis brings out Adorno's materialism more persuasively, but it is always a matter of 'difficulty', something won by strenuous, ever-fragile speculation. This is not the kind of materialism that can act collectively or build a picket-line (let alone organise a political party): for Jarvis, thought that holds to *any* position regarding the actual world is 'dogma'. Beneath this defence of thought's 'freedom' is of course a familiar and much more powerful dogma: the liberal belief that any conscious attempt to change the world is a crime.

In *Dialectic of Enlightenment* (1944), Adorno was forced into Aesopian language by Max Horkheimer's attempts to find American sponsorship for the Frankfurt School. Jarvis's reluctance to translate 'official materialism' into 'Stalinism' and 'reconciliation of identity and non-identity' into 'revolution' is likewise to be crippled by academic respectability – despite his claim to be investigating the material base of thought (p. 231), not a matter Jarvis wishes to bring to consciousness. Jarvis describes Adorno's thought as 'aporetic' – it 'admits to being contradictory, but claims that the contradiction is necessary rather than accidental' (p. 33). This mystifies elementary Marxism as Adorno's personal 'style'. As Marx said in *Capital*: 'If, therefore, such expressions... appear contradictory, this is only because they bring to the surface a contradiction immanent in capitalist production.'[1]

Although Jarvis expounds Adorno as a critic of invariant, history-transcending categories, he nevertheless understands him philosophically rather than politically: as a contribution to the timeless realm of philosophical ideas rather than as a source of truly 'determinate negations'. Adorno's arguments are torn from their moment. To many readers, *Dialectic of Enlightenment* comes across as a stirring left polemic. In expounding its thesis, Jarvis argues that domination preceded capitalism, so a mere overthrow of capitalism will not solve the problem of history (an anti-socialist argument derived

---

[1] Marx 1906, p. 238.

from 'patriarchy' theory). However, in order to attribute this reactionary brickbat to Adorno, Jarvis must suddenly switch to *Negative Dialectics* (1966), a stratagem only revealed by resort to the footnotes (p. 28, n. 15).

However, even here, in this more pessimistic and speculative work, Adorno is making distinctions Jarvis lacks the politics to appreciate. Though Adorno's text is rambling and obscure, it is clear he is defending Marx and Engels. Indeed, he describes them as he might describe himself, as 'enemies of Utopia for the sake of its realization'. Adorno is concerned to explain how reaction – West and East – gleaned sustenance from the failure of the Russian Revolution. Far from anticipating bourgeois feminism's scepticism about opposing capitalism, Adorno *criticises* bourgeois ideology for prophesying domination 'an infinite future', and thus fostering precisely the convenient despair of 'patriarchy' theory.[2] Jarvis has turned Adorno upside down.

Those wishing to establish the materialist basis of Adorno's thought – who would assess his responses to the revolutionary ferment of 20s Germany, to the disasters of Nazism, Stalinism and World War II, and to the consumer boom of the 1950s and 1960s – require keener attention to dates than this. Jarvis's attention to philosophical jargon is not carried through to details of history and politics.

Despite this, Jarvis's formula that Adorno's thought was a 'rebellion of experience versus empiricism' is telling. The closer to explaining his *oeuvre* as a 'Defence of Poetry', the better Jarvis's exposition. However, ignorance of left politics means that Jarvis cannot decide whether Adorno's poetical critique of both Western positivism and Soviet Marxism was liberal or revolutionary. In the logico-philosophical dream seminar, there is no judgment of ideas by reference to concrete political position. In Jarvis's account, socialist commitment ('metaphysical' or 'dogmatic' materialism) always implies Stalinism, a viewpoint Trotskyists, anarchists, situationists and unofficial strikers would all take issue with. The crunch-point of 1968, when Adorno reneged from revolutionary ideas he had successfully communicated to his students, is never mentioned.

Jarvis does provide some salutary reminders of Adorno's contributions to Marxism: the idea that the increased organic component of capital has a cultural and psychic impact (p. 71), for example, or that conceiving concepts as 'constellations' makes them as irreducibly specific as language (pp. 176–7). The former catapults an analysis generally restricted to the revolutionary Left into the cultural sphere; the latter could relate to V.N. Voloshinov's Marxist linguistics of 'concrete utterance', (or Peter Sloterdijk's return to materialist philosophy as polemic).

Jarvis says Adorno used Marx's *Critique Of the Gotha Programme* versus earlier 'mistakes', but once again misconstrues the relevant

---

[2] Adorno 1973b, p. 323.

passage in *Negative Dialectics*. True – a characteristic provocation – Adorno calls Marx's idea of practice Kantian and 'arch-bourgeois', but only then to point out Marx's dialectical 'recoil': having developed the productive forces, the actual historical development of capitalism lays the groundwork for a non-bourgeois and un-oppressive practice. Despite arguing thinkers should bring to the surface the material forces that sustain them (p. 231), Jarvis allows liberal scepticism – his equation of Stalinism and effective left action – to dictate his supposedly 'logical' deductions.

When Jarvis extends the discussion of Adorno to Heidegger, one misses the cruel laughter and breathless indignation of Adorno's polemic in *The Jargon Of Authenticity*. It is possible to read Adorno as refusing to grant Heidegger any intellectual merit at all – mocking his concept of 'Being' as clownish novelty, *ersatz* profundity, an outbreak of Black Forest kitsch – but Jarvis is insensitive to this aspect of Adorno's attack. Likewise, the weak distinctions Jarvis makes between Jacques Derrida's deconstruction and negative dialectics (pp. 222–4) fail to indict the imperial nudity: the charge that Heidegger and Derrida only illumine labyrinths of their own devising.

Jarvis ends up with an Adorno who provides us with no method and no world picture. He concludes with the consoling remark that a certain 'utopianism' is not liquidable from thinking – though there is no guarantee that thinking itself will survive. At this point, the lack of enlightenment we've achieved is glaring: we're being offered 'culture or barbarism' without even Rosa Luxemburg's advice about what to do about it. For those who agree with Susan Buck-Morss that Walter Benjamin and Theodor Adorno furnish us with the keenest insights into the cultural superstructure, such a conclusion is inadequate.

One retort to such 'philosophical' mystification is to examine music, the non-verbal experience to which Adorno's historical materialism was most hotly and strongly applied. Indeed, some would argue that it is because Adorno offers a materialist understanding of music that his ideas are relevant to the Left, however 'practical' or 'classical' activists may deem their Marxism, and however 'academic' they may consider Adorno. The term 'academic', after all, derives from the institution of the musical academy; by recalling Adorno's antagonistic stance on academic music, we release a noisy spirit, one the cloth ears of unmusical Adornians mummify in lettered wraps. Let Odysseus's crew open their ears to the sirens of both Varèse[3] and the street, and perhaps Adorno's texts can speak.

Robert Witkin's account of Adorno focuses on music. By admitting that there is an object for discussion, he avoids the defensive, tongue-tied purism of Jarvis's 'difficult' Adorno. However, insufficient dialectics

---

[3] Edgard Varèse (1885–1965), iconoclastic composer credited by Adorno as the sole follower of Stravinsky to inherit his 'aversion to the total syntax of music' (Adorno 1948, p. 153); *Hyperprism* (1922–3) used sirens. Most 'classical' music written this century has been a retreat from the hardcore modernism of Varèse's 1920s work.

means Adorno becomes unrecognisably middle-of-the-road. Complete absence of what Jarvis called 'non-liquidable utopianism' severs any connection to Marx. Witkin's account of bourgeois society manages to omit the working class. Placing Adorno within German romantic aesthetics – Hegel, Burckhardt, Panofsky – explains historical periodisations missed by Jarvis's analytical approach, but theorising Adorno's concept of the subject and forgetting economics miscontrues his polemic. Abstraction of Adorno from the Marxist context in which he argued does him a disservice; he was a polemicist, not a standalone moralist (one reason why the collection *Aesthetics & Politics*, which sets him in debate with Benjamin, Bloch, Lukács and Brecht, is so crucial).[4]

Witkin emphasizes Adorno's Weberian side, ending up with a history of the West as a climax of rationalisation rather than the victory of capital. Witkin claims Jean Piaget's contrast between assimilation (play) and accommodation (conformism) is an example of both Hegelian process and Kantian *a priori* categories, a grave confusion between dialectics and structuralism (Witkin, p. 54).

Jarvis's readings in sociology and anthropology at least save him from the idealist interpretation of Marx rampant in cultural studies. Not so Witkin. 'It is the evanescence of the modern subject which ensures that – to quote Marx – 'all that is solid melts into air'.' (p. 60)

Marx strenuously avoided tautologies like these (and delighted in pointing them out in his opponents). *The Communist Manifesto* insisted it was capitalist economic progress that did the melting, but Marshall Berman's current hegemony means that such agency has been forgotten. Witkin reduces the dialectic of subject and object in Adorno to a 'struggle against both these extremes', and emerges with an impeccably liberal politics: opposition to Anarchy on the one hand, and Fascism on the other (p. 66).

Marxist insistence on social totality – one that makes Marxists sceptical of movements for reform that only touch on spiritual and cultural issues – is paraphrased by Witkin thus: 'What is needed, Adorno argues, is for a spiritual regeneration of society to arise from genuine and rational co-operation in social production.' (p. 78)

Using such euphemisms to describe proletarian revolution is disastrous. It implies Adorno favoured the pipe-dreams of workers co-operatives and worker-management quality circles. In fact, his scorn for such reformist measures was as scathing as any revolutionary socialist's. Witkin's squeamishness about dealing with the economic base turns Adorno into a fluffy liberal.

Indeed, Witkin is so disciplined by postmodernist taboos about mentioning the 'real' that he coins a new word; abstract concepts are always contrasted to 'sinewy' social relations. His liberalism shows its callous side when he surmises that a Jewish account of the Holocaust perforce 'lacks objectivity'; a direct rebuttal of Adorno's Benjaminian

---

[4] Bloch *et al* 1977.

doctrine of the voice of suffering being the voice of truth. Antitheses currently sweeping sociology – 'intra-subjective' versus 'inter-subjective' – are deployed without upsetting commonsense truisms about the objectivity of social facts and the powerlessness of individual subjectivity.

Despite the liberal blinkers, Witkin evidently wants to use Adorno to explain music, and this provides an exit from the defensive, ivory-tower involution of Jarvis (whose Adorno is less a negative dialectic than a degenerated nihilectic). Witkin's account of Adorno's sympathy for the antiquated sentimentalities of Gustav Mahler is excellent (pp. 110–114). Whereas Jarvis has Adorno contrasting 'bad' twelve-tone[5] (Joseph Hauer's) to 'good' twelve-tone (Arnold Schoenberg's) (Jarvis, p. 135), Witkin understands Adorno's critique of twelve-tone's systematization in serialism as allergy to institutionalisation (Witkin, p. 131). Practical music criticism harbours insights denied to those who deem academia a meritocracy.

Witkin's nuanced discussion of jazz objects to Adorno's wholesale condemnation. He uses Max Paddison's writings on Frank Zappa[6] to argue that mass music can achieve critical consciousness, though he is too timid to broach any more up-to-date (or so-far unacademically approved) examples. His discussion would have been enlivened by considering the situational 'embarrassments' to the mass media engineered by artists like Malcolm McLaren, the KLF or Chumbawumba. Restriction to ratified examples blocks the discussion.

Witkin's conclusion – that mass and avantgarde are more 'mediated' than Adorno allows – simply ducks the gauntlet Adorno threw at class society. If his history of jazz had not finished with Zappa, he might have been able to show how Adorno's demolition of commonsense social categories is more than ever required to understand music today. Since the free jazz explosion of the 1960s, the 'high' aspirations of low jazz have fused with an exiled classical avantgarde now forced to slum it. At the productive cutting-edge, no-one can distinguish between genres. The music of John Zorn, for example – indistinguishably jazz, improvisation, classical, electronic and rock – is a self-conscious manifesto of this state of affairs. It is only when it comes to marketing – the appearance of the musical essence in class society – that 'high' and 'low' reemerge as categories and genre is reaffirmed. Witkin's exposition of Adorno on music remains unsatisfactory because it fails to emulate his courageous pronouncements on the contemporary

---

[5] Twelve-tone is the name given to the music pioneered by Arnold Schoenberg (1874–1951), who took Wagner's chromaticism to its conclusion by permutating notes so there is no discernible key. Vulgarly known as 'plink-plonk' or 'unlistenable torture', twelve-tone (later serialism) became the orthodox style in the musical academy of post-war Europe – partly due to Adorno's efforts – but has suffered an eclipse since the 70s due to the advent of minimalism in the States. Postmodernist music critics love minimalism and despise both twelve-tone and Adorno (both are routinely abused as 'male', 'modernist' and 'elitist').
[6] Paddison 1982, p. 215.

avantgarde. To do so would mean breaking with the Kantian precepts of 'objective' academic sociology.

Max Paddison is a musicologist, and perhaps this is why his survey of Adorno's thought retains its sting. His unwieldy title – *Adorno's Aesthetic of Music* – foregrounds the fact that Adorno was preeminently concerned with music (half his written output). Susan Buck-Morss showed how even Adorno's philosophical discourse used the retrogrades and inversions of twelve-tone composers to develop the initial tone row: Schoenberg's refusal of the home key corresponded to critical theory's refusal to affirm.[7] If Adorno's evaluation of twelve-tone is correct, it suggests an approach to blues, jazz, rock and rave very different from the simple high/low dichotomy used by sociologists for whom class is a positive fact rather than a dynamic contradiction.

Far from denying us the vistas of philosophy and social theory, restoring *music* as Adorno's primary focus accentuates his relevance to radical social critique. His materialism demands that, rather than his texts, we make *music and society* the objects of our study. In this he differs sharply from the Parisian philosophers currently setting the agenda in cultural theory, where the text is primary and the real problematic. For Adorno, music was a privileged site for the encounter between subjectivity and the social, between nature and history. In his attempt to adumbrate a dialectic in opposition to the state ideology of Stalinist Russia, music played a crucial role: like sexuality for Wilhelm Reich, Norman O. Brown and Mikhail Bakhtin, music allowed for a Nietzschean and anti-authoritarian revival of Marxist insights. Shocks to crack the monolith of Stalin's 'Dialectical Materialism' and dizzy the perspective that makes humanity a spectator of its own history. Radical art as the science of subjectivity 'personal politics' pretended to be. Anyone wishing to relate Marxism to a politics of experience will find in Adorno's aesthetics of music a rich series of propositions.

Max Paddison's book avoids anti-establishment postures. Cover, layout and imprint compound the image of Adorno specialists as difficult, even conservative, scholars and critics. This contrasts with, say, Sarah Thornton's *Club Cultures*, promoted in paperback with a cover of blurred 'rave' graphics, which began with the conventional condemnation of Adorno as a party-pooping mandarin: 'Theodor Adorno, an early theorist of mass culture, reserved some of his most damning prose for the "rhythmic obedience" of jitterbug dancers ...'[8]

However, in his conscientious working-through, Paddison lays the foundations for a materialist musicology, one with revolutionary implications undreamt by postmodernist apologists for consumer capitalism. In order to do so, Paddison will need to steer past some of Adorno's prejudices and ostensible judgments, and explicate his concept of music as historical process and material practice.

---

[7] Buck-Morss 1977, chapter eight, especially p. 131.
[8] Thornton 1995, p. 1.

Paddison rightly begins with the Frankfurt School's emphasis on totality, its conviction that only by relating specific social forms to the whole that anything may be explained (Paddison, p. 7). Adorno may have aphorised 'the whole is the untrue', but he does not thereby abandon the idea of the One. This is why the word for Adorno's interest in music needs to be *focus* rather than *specialism*: the leap from part to whole and contingent to universal is relentless and giddying. Paddison notes a synoptic quality to Adorno's thought that brings it closer to the imagistic constellations of poetry than to the straight-line logic of Aristotle. 'Adorno's work in many ways defies categorization over time because its underlying themes do not develop chronologically, but are all present to varying degrees at every point in his writings.' (p. 22)

However, because Paddison has a material object in view – namely music and its history – this does not lead to the timeless 'philosophised' Adorno of Simon Jarvis. Paddison translates Adorno's thought into sober musicology, setting up procedures comprehensible to the music departments for whom the book was written. Although this occasionally suggests the blind man and the elephant – particularly where Paddison seeks to summarise Adorno's arguments under forms as inimical to dialectical thought as the list – it at least becomes a thesis musicology cannot ignore.

In postmodernist cultural studies, Adorno's attack on jazz has become one of the most notorious examples of 'modernist' elitism. Indeed, his judgment is cited so often, and in such isolation from the rest of his thought, that students are given the impression that Adorno was simply a Sir Kenneth Clark or Roger Scruton, a reactionary defending 'high culture' versus democracy and populism. Paddison's concern with musical specifics breaks down such received notions, showing how deeply Adorno thought about oppression and imperialism. Having quoted Adorno on how Hitler and Stalin used folk music as 'false reconciliation', to 'foster a sense of national identity', Paddison explores Adorno's positive response to Béla Bartók. He considered that Bartók – like Janácek – was able to make use of folk music as a valid source of musical material because South-East Europe at that period remained largely untouched by the process of industrialization which had transformed Western Europe and North America. Because East European folk music had largely fallen outside the dominant process of rationalization it could be used critically by Bartók and Janácek for radical and progressive ends. (p. 38)

In other words, the 'folk' used by romantic composers in industrialised countries – Vaughan Williams in England, Jean Sibelius in Finland – was a bourgeois fantasy of class reconciliation, evoking a patriotic never-never land. In contrast, the music of the Transylvanian Gypsies researched by Bartók was a living tradition, an unsettling reminder of the marginalised and oppressed. Adorno's understanding of international relations – which followed Lenin on the national question

– becomes a way of articulating an aesthetic response. Instead of repression, Adorno's political correctness promises liberation.

In war-time Britain, Beethoven and Wagner were suspect because the Nazis promoted them as proofs of German superiority; the popularity of Sibelius in Britain today derives from his key position in the war-time repertoire. Adorno's awareness of modes of production cuts across such arbitrary legacies. He examines the social actualities that sustain musical traditions and ascertains their relative truth. Political distinctions emerge in the grain of the music: hence the contrasting tendency of the 'folk' component in Sibelius and Bartók (cloying nostalgia in the first, rhythmically-charged vertigo in the latter). Although Paddison does not choose to take the argument in this direction, this also suggests listening to jazz, R&B and rap as expressions of the oppressed.

It is easy to see why Adorno's virtues as a musicologist have fallen on stony ground in Britain. Not only does he proceed from an understanding of history that flies in the face of post-war liberalism – his analysis of imperialism did not accept a qualititative difference between German and British nationalism – he is also confident enough about his own aesthetic responses to treat them as empirical data. For Adorno, experience is not an illusion to be expunged by application of science, whether positivist or Althusserian, but a fact which requires explanation. It is difficult to know which of these virtues – his Leninist take on imperialism, or his conviction that aesthetic experience is a gateway to truth – offends most.

Paddison does not enter directly the prickly thicket of Adorno's relationship to Marx, or seek to explain the paucity of his references to Lenin or Trotsky. However, rather than comparing it to recent trends like schizoanalysis or deconstruction like Jarvis,[9] Paddison expounds Adorno's critique in Marxist terms.

> For Adorno, although he was certainly no vulgar Marxist reductionist, art, and indeed "cultural life" as a whole, cannot escape ideology because of "universal mediation". That is to say, all aspects of "culture" (taken in the sociological/ anthropological sense of "whole way of life", and not only as the "high arts") partake of the dominant ideologies of society through their participation in, and internalization of, social relations. This idea will be examined in more detail in Chapter 3. [p. 54]

For the Marxist, there is something unavoidably comic about calling class society an 'idea' and relegating its details to 'chapter 3'. It is as if

---

[9] Eg Jarvis, pp. 222–24. cf: 'The internal rupturing of a system by the technique of conceptual reversal upon which negative dialectics rests may sound extremely close to a limited form of Derridean deconstruction', Sweeney-Turner 1994, p. 716. Such a summary of negative dialectics is structuralist, implying that Adorno merely reshuffled elements of a semiotic code. In fact he was continually at pains to emphasize the inadequacy of concepts in the face of the real: for him, Auschwitz was no metaphysical fancy.

Paddison has rolled up the world we live and work in, and proposed to put this carpet-roll into storage!

Because Paddison subscribes to the idea of theory as passive description rather than active critique or polemic, his scepticism about the possibility of ever transcending ideology recalls Althusser:

> The distinguishing feature of ideology in this sense is that it is to be understood not as a consciously held system of beliefs, but instead as *a lived system of values of which we are largely unconscious*, which forms our sense of identity, and in relation to which we are normally unable to take a critical and self-reflective position. [p. 53]

The 'we' here rules out class analysis (understanding how different material relationships to capital determine different responses to ruling ideas). Paddison's 'we' assumes the abstract universalism of the seminar, and blocks comprehension of Adorno's antagonistic and polemical stance. Paddison lacks the revolutionary perspective that allowed Marx to point to concrete social movements and actions as manifesting ideology-critique. However, despite subservience to academic respectability, Paddison is conscientious enough as a musicologist to wax materialist every time music is raised as a point of issue. Fair enough. This is the most the Marxist can expect from bourgeois science: respect for empirical data.

In 1982 Paddison published an article called 'The Critique Criticised: Adorno and Popular Music'. He wanted to save Adorno's method from his prejudices. He argued that Adorno's appreciation of the critical nature of Kurt Weill's montage of cultural debris could be applied to the Mothers of Invention, the Velvet Underground, Carla Bley, Henry Cow and the Art Bears. His conclusion was that in so far as commercial music develops critical features, it will encounter the same resistance that greeted Schoenberg and Webern. Adorno was not fighting for 'high' art versus 'low', but attempting to posit the problems for true expression in a consumer society. This is basically the thesis of *Adorno's Aesthetics of Music*. Paddison has moved on from the gaucheness of naming actual musical forces that might embody critique. This new maturity/guardedness makes his argument more persuasive, or less suggestive, according to one's assessment of the uses of academic decorum.

Paddison proves the subtlety and power of Adorno's thought in a treatment of 'On the Social Situation of Music' (1932). Adorno's defence of avantgarde antagonism had more to do with criticising capitalism than belief in culture as a repository of higher values. Talking of modern music's alienation from its audience, Adorno said:

> Music, lacking proper knowledge of the social process – a condition likewise socially produced and sustained – blamed itself and not society for this situation, thus remaining in the illusion that the isolation of music was itself an isolated

matter, ie. that things could be corrected from the side of
music alone with no change in society.[10]

Paddison explodes the charge of snobbery, emphasizing Adorno's
mischievous up-turning of commonsense: the unashamedly commodity-
character of pop reveals the sexual and economic drives polite society
denies; the claims of high culture to be 'non-commercial' are an
ideological fig-leaf (p. 103). Paddison also stresses Adorno's hostility
towards integrity and stability, prize tenets for conservative aesthetics.
In theorising a potential surrealism of music, Adorno talked about
'permitting social flaws to manifest themselves by means of a flawed
invoice which defines itself as illusory, with no attempt at camouflage
through attempts at aesthetic totality' (cited in Paddison, p. 104).

This brings Adorno into the orbit of anti-art, rubbish theory and
punk. Adorno's impatience with Stalinist assumptions about the narrow
nature of workers consciousness strikes a chord with Marxists who wish
to wager on the working-class's capacity for revolution. Trotsky said:
'Not a single progressive idea has begun with a 'mass base', otherwise it
would not have been a progressive idea. It is only in its last stage that
the idea finds its masses.'[11]

And concluded: 'Art can become a strong ally of revolution only in
so far as it remains faithful to itself.' (Cited in Paddison, p. 101)

Adorno said: 'Music is under the same obligation as theory to reach
out beyond the current consciousness of the masses.'[12]

These statements are more congruent than received notions about
the gulf between Trotskyist activism and Adornoite aestheticism imply.

Paddison concludes his account of 'On the Social Situation of
Music' by pointing out that Adorno saw the split between 'light' music
and 'serious' music as a distortion, a product of alienation. Modern
music blamed itself for being incomprehensible to the mass audience,
but this was actually a social problem, not the 'degenerate' or 'anti-
working-class' wilfulness denounced by Hitler and Stalin. This is an
argument socialists would do well to take on board before entering
debates about contemporary music.

Paddison's argument has important lessons for those studying non-
classical music. Since it was via the backdoor of sociology that Simon
Frith and Dick Hebdige transformed their love of rock and pop into a
respectable discipline, the field has been dominated by value-free
approaches. Postmodern orthodoxy brands any aesthetic judgment
'elitist'. Adorno's heretical notion of art having a relation to social truth
explodes such sociological relativism. Because Paddison is more serious
about Adorno's musical judgments than either Jarvis or Witkin, his
version of Adorno is more abrasive and critical.

---

[10] Adorno, 'On the Social Situation of Music', 1932, quoted in Paddison, p. 99.
[11] Trotsky 1970, p. 112.
[12] Paddison 1993, p. 101.

Paddison's careful account of Adorno's terms reveals a central flaw – one that has provided Trotskyists and aesthetes ample material for unproductive quarrels. Because only the privileged have access to culture, only the super-educated can feel: all reflective thought is bourgeois. Paddison's run-through of Adorno's terms points to a dangerous slippage. He points to 'Adorno's potentially confusing identification of the "bourgeois individual" with concepts like the "historical Subject", "advanced consciousness", "critical self-reflection" and the "avant-garde"' (p. 119)

This confusion was prepared for by Lukács's reconciliation of high-brow philosophy and Leninist revolution in *History and Class Consciousness*. The sensitive bourgeois Hegelian could hail revolution as the solution to history without being transformed thereby in the process. Paddison is right to criticise the way Adorno slips from 'bourgeois individual' to 'historical subject'. Marxism is a political practice that challenges intellectul individualism. Benjamin had a clearer idea of what needed to be smashed in bourgeois aesthetics and what collectivity and engagement could offer the artist.

Paddison's brief is to expound Adorno's aesthetic, so he cannot make the turn towards Walter Benjamin possible for those who adhere to Buck-Morss's concept of the 'Königstein Programme', the revolutionary Marxist understanding of the superstructure that burst on a quartet of thinkers who holidayed together in 1929 – Gretel Karplus, Max Horkheimer, Benjamin and Adorno. Probably most indebted to Walter Benjamin's brain-storming, Königstein provided Adorno with his life's goal: a materialist philosophy and politics that would liberate rather than suppress aesthetic experience. Although Buck-Morss concedes that Adorno finally occluded the Königstein Programme in quietist pessimism, Paddison is concerned to ressurect the method, thus freeing the genie from the bottle.

Those who believe that classical Marxism is neither determinist nor reductionist will take exception to Paddison's explanation of how Adorno countered the 'Dialectical Materialism' sponsored by Stalin. Paddison contends that the very notion of base and superstructure is 'determinist'. Anyone familiar with treatments by, say, Franz Jakubowski[13] or John Rees[14] will demur. Though phrased in Aesopian euphemisms, Adorno's thought was too dialectical and – this writer would contend – too Marxist to be explained as a tempering of Marx's 'crude socio-economic determinism' with Freud's concept of the subject. This perpetrates the very duality – the eternal opposition of external facts to subjective feeling – that critical theory from Hegel and Marx through to Adorno has been intent on superseding.

Adorno used Marx and Freud because they were both *materialists*. They refused to countenance the idealist vision of ideas acting over the heads of humans as species- and political beings. Radical humanists,

---

[13] Jakubowski 1990.
[14] Rees 1998.

they both wished to ground thought in the sensuous, historically-produced body. Insufficiently convinced of the difference between revolutionary Marxism and Stalinist apologetics for state capitalism, Paddison implies Adorno diluted his Marxism with Freud. In fact, reading Adorno is an explosive reminder of the antagonism of dialectical thought to any and every intellectual compromise. As with the Trotsky of the *Notebooks*,[15] Freud provided Adorno with materialist viewpoints regarding consciousness that Stalinised versions of Marx couldn't handle.

Paddison's wide knowledge of music allows him to warm to Adorno's central argument – that genuine musical analysis brings to consciousness 'the sublimated content of traditional forms and genres' (p. 157). This is not Sarah Thornton's sociology, one that tramples judgment under the heel of 'objective' patterns of social consumption, an approach that has more to do with market research than scientific social analysis.[16] Nor does it propose the emphasis on traditional form that leads down the cul-de-sac of musical academicism and Schenkerian analysis.[17] On the contrary, like Marx, Adorno sees analysis as ineluctably implicated in process and revolution. He goes on from 'form is sedimented social content' to argue that music should be judged by the degree to which it *transforms* this latent content.

Let me improvise a concrete example of the kind of criticism the doctrine of 'form as sedimented content' suggests. The drum'n'bass troupe Roni Size Reprazent use singers and rappers, computer-generated beats and effects, trap drums and an upright bass. Whereas press-releases and reviews talk up Roni Size's 'talent' and 'originality' – abstract values forever required in the marketplace – the Adornoite could explain that the band's use of musical form articulates a social position. Refusing the rootless, ahistorical sublimity of E-culture rave music – ecstatic surrender to the simple options supplied by capitalist technology (Cubase programmes running on Sony equipment) – Roni Size programmes 'intelligent beats' that require vigilance on the part of dancers (who resort to cubistic dislocation). These recall the stop-and-start rhythms invented by Thelonious Monk and the Beboppers. An acoustic bass twang also evokes the legacy of jazz and its resistance to commercial homogeneity. However, computer effects, automatic beats and a reggae-tinged raps about the joy of volume-pumped loudspeakers ('step to the rhythm made out of brown paper') mock the upwardly-

---

[15] 'By itself the method of psychoanalysis, taking as its point of departure "the autonomy" of psychological phenomena, in no way contradicts materialism. Quite the contrary, it is precisely dialectical materialism that prompts us to the idea that the psyche could not even be formed unless it played an autonomous, that is, within certain limits, an independent role in the life of the individual and the species.' Leon Trotsky 1986, p. 106.

[16] An accusation that seems less wild now that Sarah Thornton has left cultural studies for advertising.

[17] Heinrich Schenker (1868–1935) argued that a single musical structure underlies classical masterpieces from Bach to Brahms, thus laying the basis for the 'strict' analyses ('formal description' is really a better word) familiar from classical concert-programmes and sleevenotes.

mobile fetish of acoustic instrumentation with which Wynton Marsalis's neoclassicism has surrounded jazz. The listener is further dis-oriented by whirring 'space noises' that go back to Miles Davis's *Bitches Brew*, and beyond that to Stockhausen's electronic serialism (when postmodernists decry twelve-tone as 'elitist', they demonstrate ignorance of such applications). The musical forms employed by Roni Size want jazz's antagonism to banality without its upwardly-mobile trappings. By looking at the way musicians work on the latent social content of their material, partisan criticism of the *music* (as opposed to the usual liberal/left moralism about career choices) becomes a possibility.

Paddison promises still greater insights once musical analysis – tempo, key-choice, instrumental timbre – is freed from the formalism of Schenker and unpacked to reveal social orientations. Against postmodern squeamishness about social provenance[18] – now revealed as sales patter, basking in the alienation of a commodified culture – Paddison's reminder that form is sedimented content looks for politics in the body of the sound. When Johnny 'Guitar' Watson said that when he was recording he was looking for the 'right *attitude* for each of the instruments', he intimated the kind of understanding of art as declaratory social judgment[19] required for a non-prescriptive Marxist criticism alert to subaltern expression. Paddison's version of Adorno helps us get there, which is why, despite its academic limitations, *Adorno's Aesthetics of Music* contributes towards Marxism.

Of all the humanities, music remains the most specialised and impenetrable. 'Gifted' pupils capable of co-ordinating the score's eye-to-finger symbols and its numerical exposition of rhythm are picked out for a specialised musical education that inhibits social maturity and even genuine musicality. Those rejected by this system gain revenge by involvement with informal musics – rock, rave, improvisation, record-buying – that allow them to participate outside official channels. On the other hand, they remain ignorant of musical syntax and history. Different genres – chart-music, classical, rave, rock, MOR – confirm social identity and cement ideology: class perceived as positive fact rather than dynamic contradiction. By bringing in a Marxist awareness of history, Paddison broaches a discussion about the role of music in a commodity society. Listeners sympathetic to this approach could aid

---

[18] The best example is David Toop 1995, a decadent trip through the universe of sound made 'available' by consumer capitalism that never mentions issues of solvency or commercial dilution. Ignorance about how music is actually made is taken to be a new 'freedom'.

[19] The phrase 'declaratory social judgment' combines two phrases that occur at the conclusion of Valentin Voloshinov's treatise on linguistics. It calls for the recognition of the 'categorical word, the word "from one's own mouth", the *declaratory* word... the word permeated with confident and categorical social value judgment, the word that really means and takes responsibility for what it says.' Voloshinov 1929, p. 159.

each other to understand their music of choice – both its functioning and its provenance – without being sabotaged by sectionalism.[20]

Despite Paddison's formal training, there is only one passage in his book this lay reader found impenetrable (pp. 163–8). There is also one puzzling moment of professorial tetchiness where he ticks off Adorno for his 'impatience with the process of detailed technical analysis' and 'rather old-fashioned motivic-thematic formal analytical approach', concluding that he 'represents the old-style musical dilettante whose knowledge of a work comes more from what he hears than from a detailed study of the score'. This is an extraordinary charge! It is *precisely* because Adorno analysed what he heard rather than what he read that his criticism is so potent. In an era in which recording has made music accessible and analysable by those who cannot read scores, Adorno's attention to aural fact is still more relevant. Despite his 'elitism', Adorno praised the gramophone record for the way it removed the auratic, ritual nature of concert attendance and allowed the listener to skip back and replay sections.[21]

Adorno opened up musical analysis to philosophy and politics, making him an embarrassment to musicology as a specialty. This is what makes him relevant to non-specialists: Adorno is a bridge between technical expertise and social sense-making.

Adorno was immensely influential on post-war classical music, especially in Germany, where his militant modernism was taken to be the correct medicine for the Nazi disaster (Hitler banned twelve-tone as a Jewish/Bolshevik conspiracy). Like Witkin, Paddison stresses Adorno was a left critic of such institutionalisation, suspicious of serialism as academic dogma. Adorno looked forward to twelve-tone emerging in 'spontaneous' free composition, which suggests free improvisation as conceived by guitarist and theorist Derek Bailey.[22] Further, Adorno considered that symmetry could be achieved via return to similar tone colours rather than a reprise of a pitch sequence, which sugggets abandoning traditional harmony for Varèse's contrasting 'blocks' of sound.[23] Neither Varèse nor Bailey have been embraced by the musical establishment: Adorno's scepticism about the 1960s counter-culture has delayed the application of his ideas to non-classical form, but they are highly suggestive for anyone seeking to understand later musical developments.[24]

Central to Adorno's aesthetic is the idea that music is not simply expressive of an individual's viewpoint, but represents a necessary

---

[20] Many well-meaning socialist debates about music degenerate as successive contributors merely declare allegiance to different musical genres.
[21] Theodor Adorno 1991. In other words, the mandarin was scratching half a century before hip hop.
[22] 'The amalgamation and absorption of twelve-tone technique by free composition – by the assumption of its rules through the spontaneity of the critical ear.' Adorno 1973, p. 115.
[23] Adorno 1984, p. 228, quoted in Paddison 1993, p. 179.
[24] Adorno's concepts have led to one of the most perceptive discussions of modern jazz: Radano 1995.

historical unfurling of potential. The crisis of music in the twentieth century – the bourgeoisie's regression to a fossilised classicism and the disconnection of creative music from any social role – becomes a classic example of the forces of production stymied by relations of production.

If Adorno's pessimism about the working class is abandoned, and mass music is understood as thwarted subaltern expression – a potential created by capitalism that its property relations deny – all kinds of processes become clearer: the reduction of collective music-making to the promotion of individual stars,[25] the royalty-system which rewards copy-rightable 'composition' rather than performance,[26] the fetishistic emphasis a profit-motivated music industry places on commodified, recorded sound as the 'real' experience.[27] Adorno's critique of pop culture came from the left not the right. The entertainment industry destroys the vitality and seriousness of low art by 'the civilisational constraints imposed on the rebellious resistance inherent within it'. This is not a manifesto for snobs, but a programme for punk and Reclaim The Streets.

Paddison concludes by examining Adorno's 1962 essay on Stravinsky. Having set the agenda for post-war music by a polemic against Stravinsky in *Philosophy of Modern Music*, Adorno criticised his own conclusions. Adorno now argued that Stravinsky's neoclassicism could become a form of surrealism and therefore transmit a critical sting. This is a far better basis for criticism than abstract prescriptions about twelve-tone versus tonality (or montage versus authenticity). Instead, it assesses the social positioning of the specific artwork (though naturally issues of tonality and coherence will still be paramount, though not as general 'laws'). Like Witkin, Paddison sees this essay, and Adorno's interpretation of fragmentation and burlesque in Mahler, as 'offering a possibility for going beyond the stalemate of serialism'. Adorno's notion of true music as antagonistic to social conformity 'has a relevance for the pluralism which characterizes music in the late twentieth century'.

The postmodernism of Foucault and Deleuze and Guattari – the abandonment of class struggle as a product of the old, bad 'binary' logic, and the adoption instead of a proliferating rainbow of liberal causes – has had as deleterious an effect on musical criticism as it has on politics. Anything which contradicts, which opposes, which negates, which shows up what surrounds it as illusions and kitsch is pilloried as old-fashioned, modernist, male and ill-mannered.[28] This suits a classical

---

[25] This point is brought home in a redneck, Adornoite-without-knowing-it fashion by Carducci 1994.
[26] This is the thesis of Tremlett 1990; the real money in rock is all made in securing rights to publishing, not in performance.
[27] Outlined in melodramatic, surrealist/anthropological terms by Attali 1985.
[28] Susan McClary argues that modernism 'masculinized' music (McClary 1991, p. 18). Though her discussion of Schoenberg's twelve-tone supersession of gender distinctions is brilliant, McClary's case for minimalism (loud and interruptive = male/bad; soft and repetitive = female/good) has been more influential. This has been abetted by fantasies about the 'primordial female will-to-chaos' celebrated by Gilles Deleuze and Sadie Plant (irrationalist philosophy

establishment assailed by cuts and desperate to find newly-composed music that will not alienate middle-class audiences wishing to re-live the era when bourgeois composition was integral, affirmative and full of lovely tunes.

Minimalism's patronising view of non-classical music as repetitive and unchallenging[29] is buttressed by a thousand programme-notes that celebrate the 'end of modernism'. Meanwhile, when there is musical advance – the New Complexity, Iancu Dumitrescu, drum'n'bass, lo-fi, Derek Bailey, John Zorn, Simon Fell, harmolodics, free improvisation – cries go up about 'noise', 'incomprehensibility' and 'arrogance'. Far from the dawn of a qualitatively new era, postmodern and debarbed, the catcalls that greeted Igor Stravinsky, Edgard Varèse and Charlie Parker are still very much in evidence. Musical truth is still offensive and negative; Adorno's links between aesthetics and politics still work.

Paddison acknowledges Adorno's mistakes and lacunae, but finishes with an impeccably dialectical observation. 'That his critical aesthetics of music cannot be understood, interpreted and reapplied to changing historical conditions without us actively entering that debate and, in the process, very likely changing its terms, is a sign of its authenticity.' (p. 278)

Paddison's Adorno is the opposite of the prescriptive mandarin vilified in the textbooks.[30] Founded on a materialist understanding of class society, Adorno's clashing, prickly, perverse and inspiring commitment to music as surprise and cataclysm – as experience which busts up reified categories and leads towards knowledge – rides again in Paddison's deceptively respectable treatise.[31] Adornians who believe his negative dialectic is an excuse for high-brow quietism are in for some noisy shocks.

References

Adorno, Theodor [1928] 1991, 'Needle Curves', *October*, no 55.
Adorno, Theodor [1949] 1973, *Philosophy of Modern Music*, translated by Wes Bloomster, London: Sheed & Ward.

---

supplies uncritical critics with beautiful phrases to 'describe' any music they are not up to analysing, a rerun of the pre-war vogue for Henri Bergson and Richard Wagner).

[29] A product of musical commodification, since it is only by turning down the volume on James Brown and failing to move to it, that it could be considered remotely unchallenging *or* repetitive.

[30] Which invariably restrict their quotes to Adorno's (hilariously) opinionated 1941 essay 'On Popular Music'. Actually, 1941 was a dismal year for radio music: the idea of 'pop' as an indivisible, trans-historical entity one is 'for' or 'against' provides occasion for innumerable misunderstandings and pseudo-debates.

[31] Paddison's book contains a *meticulous* bibliography of Adorno's writings on music in German. Since reference to the dates of Adorno's essays in English collections are frequently omitted by commentators, and the writing is so simultaneously politically-charged and allusive, Paddison's bibliography is essential if one wishes to tease out Adorno's concrete political positions.

Adorno, Theodor [1966] 1973, *Negative Dialectics*, translated by E.B. Ashton, London: Routledge & Kegan Paul.

Adorno, Theodor [1969] 1984, *Aesthetic Theory*, London and New York: Routledge & Kegan Paul.

Attali, Jacques [1977] 1985, *Noise*, Manchester: Manchester University Press.

Bloch, Ernst et al 1977, *Aesthetics and Politics*, London: Verso.

Buck-Morss, Susan 1977, *The Origin of Negative Dialectics: Theodor W. Adorno, Walter Benjamin, and the Frankfurt Institute*, New York: The Free Press.

Carducci, Joe [1990] 1994, *Rock and the Pop Narcotic: Testament for the Electric Church*, Los Angeles: 2.13.61.

Jakubowski, Franz [1936] 1990 *Ideology and Superstrucure in Historical Materialism*, London: Pluto.

Marx, Karl [1865] 1975, 'Letter to J.B. Schweitzer, 24 January 1865' in *The Poverty of Philosophy*, Moscow: Progress.

Marx, Karl [1867] 1906 *Capital*, New York: The Modern Library.

McClary, Susan 1991 *Feminine Endings: Music, Gender and Sexuality*, Minnesota, University of Minnesota Press.

Paddison, Max 1982 'The Critique Criticised: Adorno and Popular Music' in *Popular Music 2 Theory & Method* edited by Richard Middleton and David Horn, Cambridge: Cambridge University Press.

Radano, Ronald M. 1995 *New Musical Figurations: Anthony Braxton's Cultural Critique*, Chicago and London: University of Chicago Press.

Rees, John 1998 *The Algebra of Revolution*, London: Routledge.

Sweeney-Turner, Steve 1994 'Review of Ben Watson's *Frank Zappa: The Negative Dialectics of Poodle Play*', *The Musical Times*, November.

Thornton, Sarah 1995 *Club Cultures: Music, Media and Sub-cultural Capital*, Cambridge: Polity.

Toop, David 1995 *Ocean Of Sound: Aether talk, Ambient Sound and Imaginary Worlds*, London: Serpent's Tail.

Tremlett, George 1990 *Rock Gold: The Music Millionaires*, London: Unwin/Hyman.

Trotsky, Leon [1933-35] 1986, *Trotsky's Notebooks, 1933-1935*, New York: Columbia University Press.

Trotsky, Leon [1938] 1970 'Art & Politics in our Epoch', *Partisan Review*, edited Paul N. Siegel, *On Literature and Art*, New York: Pathfinder.

Volshinov, V.N. [1929] 1986 *Marxism & the Philosophy of Language*, Cambridge: Harvard University Press.

Watson, Ben 1994 'Interview with Johnny "Guitar" Watson', *The Wire*, no 126.

Watson, Ben 1994, *Frank Zappa: The Negative Dialectics of Poodle Play*, London: Quartet.

ART, CLASS & CLEAVAGE

Ben Watson

Q Quartet Books

If this book is not available from your local bookshop please ring Quartet Books on 0171 636 3992

£14.00

Ben Watson's *Frank Zappa: The Negative Dialectics of Poodle Play* set out 'to rewire everything we know about the politics of culture'. In *Art, Class & Cleavage*, he pursues this lead and starts digging up cables in the street.

A defence of poetry
A rediscovery of Trotsky
A polemic versus Deleuze & Guattari
A manifesto of Humanist Marxism
A satire on the Popsicle Academy
A materialist theory of immortality
A theoretical grounding for scientific criticism of pop music
A meditation on schizophrenia
A resurrection of Radical Thought

'*ART, CLASS & CLEAVAGE* IS A FUNNY AND BRILLIANT BOOK. IT PROVIDES EVIDENCE THAT RADICALISM SURVIVES IN ITS MOST EXCITING AND EXACTING FORMS' Peter Ackroyd

The Debate on Popular Violence and the Popular Movement in the Russian Revolution

A literature review by Mike Haynes

One of the great ironies of Cold War writing on the Russian Revolution of 1917 was that the views expressed on both sides of the iron curtain tended to be mirror images of one another. Since the existing Soviet regime claimed part of its legitimacy from 1917 it had to define the essence of the revolution in terms consistent with its own position. Thus the revolution was presented as having been led by an all-knowing and benevolent leader who led a willing and all-knowing party to direct a compliant working-class stage army in whose name power was taken. In the West this view was simply stood on its head. Here the argument was that a malign leader misled a malign party which in turn took power in the form of a *coup d'état* in the name of a misled working class. From the 1960s this essential consensus (which had always been disputed by the anti-Stalinist Left) came under attack in the West from a growing group of social historians inspired by the 'history from below' approach. Their work tried to restore a more autonomous working class and party to the history of 1917, and even, in a smaller number of cases, to unravel the political conflicts, decisions and indecisions of the leaders both on the revolutionary side and the side of order. To the extent that this view was accepted, it seemed to legitimise 1917 as a popular revolution, and most social historians were prepared to explicitly draw this conclusion. Much less clearly, it also posed the complex problem of the relationship between 1917 and what came later. If it was true that 1917 represented a genuine revolution then did the subsequent development of Stalinism in the Soviet Union also represent a betrayal of 1917 and, if so, how deep a betrayal was it? How should the claims of the Soviet Union to be 'socialist' be evaluated? Unfortunately many of this new generation of historians fudged this issue, either not treating it at all or implicitly accepting some form of qualified continuity. For some on the political right this represented the social historians' Achilles heel, enabling them to be depicted not only as justifiers of revolution but as historians who offered apologias, if not for Stalinism, then certainly for the post-Stalin regimes in Russia.

Already before the collapse of the Soviet Union, there was, therefore, room to doubt how consistent a new view of the revolution had been developed by the history-from-below school. And even without the events in Russia after 1985 these doubts were accentuated by the impact of the re-evaluation, inspired by François Furet, of the history-from-below approach to the French revolution as well as the beginnings of the development of so-called postmodernist approaches and the linguistic turn.[1] When, therefore, the hopes that many had that *perestroika* and *glasnost* would bring about a new golden age of 'socialism' in Russia began to turn sour in 1989, and when the Soviet state itself collapsed in 1991, it is not surprising that this created a turmoil amongst historians that has fed back into the re-evaluation of 1917.

Those on the Left who saw 1917 as a genuine revolution and Stalinism as 'counterrevolution' explained this retreat from the hopes and aspirations of 1917 in terms of the objective circumstances that the revolutionaries found themselves in after October. Although the Bolsheviks were victorious in the Civil War, its effect was catastrophic in three ways. Firstly, the Bolsheviks effectively had to fight the Civil War alone. The expected international revolution did not occur and by 1921 the revolution was left isolated. Hopes of permanent revolution, through which backward Russia would be linked up with the advanced West, were at first postponed and then, with the development of the doctrine of 'socialism in one country', abandoned. Secondly, the Civil War destroyed Russian society, especially the working-class base of the revolutionary regime, forcing power upwards. The Bolshevik Party substituted itself for the working class, not because there was an inherent substituionist logic in the revolution, but because the working class was destroyed by the crisis of 1918–22. Thirdly, as this substitution occurred, so Bolshevik ideas themselves began to change and to accommodate to the new situation. At first, this was only in subtle ways, as during the Civil War much of the emancipatory vision of 1917 survived alongside the more brutal practice forced by events. But this gap could not be sustained indefinitely, and despite attempts by Trotsky and the Left to maintain the original vision of what 1917 had been about, despite their attempts to develop a revolutionary politics that would help to lead back to it, ideas at the top accommodated to reality and Stalin and his supporters were able to use the growing bureaucratisation to consolidate their social, political and ideological grip. Ideological continuity was therefore not a real continuity but an illusion created by the peculiar fact of the organisers of counterrevolution having arisen from within the degenerating party, and seeking to maintain the rhetoric even as its original content was being thoroughly evacuated following their victory in 1928–29.

Historians of continuity could, of course, accept much of this, but they have also had to find evidence of the seeds of Stalinism in the revolution itself. Traditionally the most obvious way to do this has been to put the stress on the ideological and organisational characteristics of Bolshevism which were supposed to predispose it towards dictatorship – what might be called 'the logic of *What Is To Be Done?*'. But if social history had successfully demonstrated genuine support from below based on mass democratisation, then such accounts would no longer be

---

[1] Furet 1981.

adequate by themselves. Essentially there were three ways of responding to this challenge.

One was to argue that, while the Bolshevik revolution was a mass uprising, it was one that the Bolsheviks appropriated for their own purposes, either by design or miscalculation. This could happen because, although the revolution did reflect a growth in class consciousness, the level achieved was not sufficient to enable the working class to hang onto power. This argument is essentially a variation of that offered by the Mensheviks in late 1917–18. According to this view, the working class was not properly ready for revolution. Centre-left Mensheviks did recognise the radicalism of the time, but saw its extent as due to a temporary swing to the Left that would be difficult to sustain. To seize power on this basis, as the Bolsheviks had done, was therefore to risk the tide of support falling away, so forcing the revolutionary regime to rule over the working class rather than through it. In its modern form, this critique has perhaps found its sharpest exponent in Vladimir Brovkin who self-consciously identified with the Menshevik case (although over time his hostility to the Bolsheviks has become more strident and generalised).[2] But, in this critique, the problem still tends to lie with Bolshevism rather than the popular movement, which is primarily convicted of immaturity in orthodox (Second International) Marxist terms.

A more damning critique is possible if it can be shown that the worm in the bud was to be found not only in Bolshevism but in the popular movement itself. If this was the case, then the argument for the emancipatory character of the revolution can be more completely undercut. One way of doing this has been to focus on the organised movement. Marc Ferro, for example, claimed to detect oligarchical tendencies in the soviets and factory committees of 1917.[3] After the initial mass mobilisation of February-March, rank-and-file participation failed to maintain its early levels, allowing the committee leaderships to reproduce themselves. More recently, Shkliarevsky has used the 'labour bureaucracy' concept to argue that there was a tension between the soviet and factory committee elective bureaucracy and the rank-and-file movement. Ferro's account of the revolution is eclectic (though not at times without great insight), so his discussion of this problem can hardly be called strategic. In the hands of Shkliarevsky, however, we almost have an attempt to combine social history from below with the perspectives of Pareto and Michels.[4] In contrast to libertarians like Brinton, Shkliarevsky appears to see oligarchy and the circulation of elites as a virtually inevitable part of history.[5] Bolshevism was thus simply the expression of this underlying law, rather than the cause of the degeneration.

---

[2] Compare Brovkin 1987 with Brovkin 1994, 1997.
[3] Ferro 1985.
[4] Shkliarevsky 1993.
[5] Brinton 1970.

But another way of approaching the problem is to argue that the popular movement itself was the cause of much of the violence and terror of the time. On the right, this is not a new argument – the 'tricoteuse' approvingly watching the falling blade of the guillotine is for many the stock image of the French Revolution, in particular, and revolution, in general. But in the older conservative accounts, the popular movement is the audience for the sanguinary excesses of the elite actors. Now, however, some historians who would locate themselves in the social history tradition have begun to develop arguments that converge with this older view but which locate the excesses in the movement from below. Here the criticism of Bolshevism is that it legitimised and encouraged this violence rather than held it back. Again, elements of this view can be found in Ferro's earlier account. But, especially since the late 1980s when the general attack on revolutionary historiography has become more open, this critique has come much more to the fore in discussion of both the French and Russian revolutions.

This article will explore this latter approach through an analysis of the way in which the link between the popular movement and violence is dealt with in three accounts which cover the broad range of writing on the Russian revolution in the wake of the collapse of the Soviet Union. The positions reflected in these works can be described as right, centre (or centre-right) and left although, as we shall see, at important points they converge, which, we argue, reflects less the nature of 1917 than a pessimism about the potential for change from below that prevails in the late twentieth century.

On the right, the Soviet collapse has led to a resurgence of condemnatory writing which triumphantly asserts the traditional view of the revolution, bolstered to some extent by the Furet-type critique from France. This can be seen in Martin Malia's general history of Russia, but most notably for us in Richard Pipes's huge history of the revolution.[6] Viewing the revolution from the top down, Pipes makes the challenge from below appear as little more than indiscriminate violence. The February Revolution was underpinned by a soldiers revolt, 'a typical Russian *bunt* [riot], with powerful anarchist overtones'. He happily reports the views of the Empress writing to the Tsar that his throne was threatened by the 'hooligan movement' in Petrograd, as well as Vasillii Rozanov's attack on 'base people'.[7] This hostile view was perhaps best expressed by Shul'gin in his notorious comment on the crowds of February,

> no matter how many they were, they all had a kind of stupid,
> even devilish appearance. God, how ugly they looked! So ugly
> that I gritted my teeth. I felt pained and helpless and bitterly
> enraged. Machine guns! That's what I wanted, I felt that only

---

[6] Malia 1994; Pipes 1992, 1995.
[7] Pipes 1992, p. 281.

> the tongues of machine guns could talk to the mob, and that
> only machine guns and lead could drive back into his lair the
> frightful beast. The beast was no other than His Majesty the
> Russian people.[8]

As Pipes proceeds with his history the negative evaluation of the popular
movement does not improve – indeed at one point he has recourse to
Gustav Le Bon to assist his analysis. The culmination is therefore the
assertion that 'October was a *classic coup d'état'* riding this wave of
violence and anarchy. Steve Smith can with justice define him as 'the
Hippolyte Taine of the Russian Revolution'.[9] The problem with the
Bolsheviks was not only that they seized power but that they endorsed
and encouraged this violence from below; 'the result was instant nation-
wide anarchy: anarchy that the new government liked to blame on the
old regime but that was, in fact, largely of its own doing'. And
liberalism, too, has to take part of the blame, since

> the tacit premise that man could and ought to be remade ...
> links liberalism and radicalism and helps to explain why, for
> all their rejection of the violent methods employed by
> revolutionaries, when forced to choose between them and
> their conservative opponents, liberals can be counted on to
> throw their lot in with the revolutionaries.[10]

More in the centre, or perhaps better, a right-liberal account, is
provided by Orlando Figes in *A People's Tragedy: the Russian
Revolution, 1891–1924* (1996). Figes's earlier work placed him in the
social history school, but here we see a major re-evaluation which
consciously echoes Simon Schama's attempt to demolish the popular
view of the French Revolution by showing how brutality from below,
rather than political consciousness, compromised 1789. For Figes, the
Russian Revolution was a similarly negative event. It was a tragedy that
could not be resisted and which consumed all of its participants, a
tragedy in no small part driven from below. Here Figes, like Schama
before him, tries to turn 'social history' against itself by appearing to use
its 'bottom-up' techniques to demonstrate the brutality and violence of
the popular movement and its complicity in the destructiveness of the
time.

On the left we can locate a third new history, by Christopher Read,
*From Tsar to Soviets: the Russian People and Their Revolution,
1917–1921* (1996). Read self-consciously tries to continue the history-
from-below approach in the tradition established by E.P. Thompson at
the University of Warwick where Read works. In sharp contrast to both
Pipes and Figes, he describes his objective as being 'to restore the

---

[8] Read 1996, p. 62.
[9] Smith 1992, p. 332.
[10] Pipes 1992, pp. 281, 298, 386, 398. As a number of critics have pointed out,
Pipes offers a very inaccurate view of liberalism, which became increasingly
antagonistic to the Left after 1905.

autonomous revolutionary activity of the ordinary population to its rightful place in the overall interpretation of the revolution'. He insists that ordinary workers, soldiers and peasants were 'rational participants' and that therefore the revolution is capable of rational analysis.[11]

Our intention here is to explore these different approaches by concentrating on one concern that they all share and which is central to the hostile interpretations of both Pipes and Figes – the issue of the link between the popular movement and popular violence. This is a problem that has also been illuminated by studies like that of Joan Neuberger in her account of pre-war 'hooliganism' in St. Petersburg, as well as other discussions that straddle both sides of the revolutionary period.[12]

1. The double standard

The issue of what is legitimate and illegitimate violence has always been debated more clearly on the left than amongst liberals and conservatives who prefer to close their eyes to the extent to which existing society and the state rests upon violence of all kinds. Tom Paine made this point powerfully in his reply to Edmund Burke when Burke charged the French revolutionaries with 'outrages':

> everything we see or hear offensive to our feelings and derogatory to the human character should lead to other reflections than those of reproach. Even the beings who commit them have some claim to our consideration. How then is it that such vast classes of mankind as are distinguished by the appellation of the vulgar, or the ignorant mob, are so numerous in all old countries? The instant we ask ourselves this question, reflection feels an answer. They arise, as an unavoidable consequence, out of the ill construction of all old governments in Europe. It is by distortedly exalting some men, that others are distortedly debased, till the whole is thrown out of nature. A vast mass of mankind are degradedly thrown into the background of the human picture, to bring forward, with greater glare, the puppet show of state and aristocracy. In the commencement of a revolution, those men are rather the followers of the camp than of the standard of liberty, and have yet to be instructed how to reverence it ... outrages were not the effect of the principles of the revolution, but of the degraded mind that existed before the revolution, and which the revolution is calculated to reform. Place them to their proper cause, and take the reproach of them to your own side.[13]

---

[11] Read 1996, p. 5.
[12] Neuberger 1993; Phillips 1997.
[13] Paine 1937, pp. 22–3.

If we are to understand popular violence we have therefore to look not only at the revolution itself but at the society from which it came. Tsarist Russia was characterised by the enormity of poverty set against the wealth of the few. There are any number of ways of measuring this but we might point to the cull measured as infant mortality that occurred every year, not to mention the famines and epidemics that erupted periodically. Pre-war infant mortality in Russia as a whole was some 260 per 1000 live births, compared to 130 in England and 80–90 in Sweden and Norway. By the age of five child mortality was around 400 per 1000 in Russia. Infant and child mortality are fascinating precisely because they are some of the most sensitive indicators of inequality both between and within classes. In St. Petersburg, for example, infant mortality in families where the husband earned 20 roubles a month was 280 per 1000 on the eve of the war. But where the husband's wages were 50 roubles a month it was only 110 per 1000. Culture was a variable too. Where both parents were illiterate infant mortality averaged 250 per 1000 amongst the city's industrial workers, but where both were literate it was 160 per 1000.[14] Thus the material and cultural poverty of the majority within Russian capitalism was built into their daily lives in the most heart-rending way possible – through the survival chances of their children.

At the top, by contrast, we find a court run, in the words of the pre-war *Times* correspondent 'on a lavish and gigantic scale, and in a setting of luxury and splendour such as cannot be surpassed, or perhaps even equalled, by any other court in Europe'.[15] Under capitalism these problems appear as the product of apparently 'abstract forces' and are therefore sometimes labelled as examples of 'structural violence'. On the right, on the other hand, it is often suggested that it is illegitimate to call such suffering violence at all, as the resulting harm does not arise from human agency. But the distribution of resources and the indifference to suffering that allows this to exist does involve human choice and therefore human agency. The system that creates such inequalities does not appear out of the air, and its reproduction requires policies that accept and perpetuate the problems. Thus the issue here is not so much that of whether or not social problems could be eliminated by a simple redistribution, as the fact that there was a systematic relationship between the wealth, privileges and power of the few and the poverty of the masses in both town and country. If historians have been reluctant to see this, some at the bottom understood it more clearly. In March 1906, for example, we find the Bakers' Union in St. Petersburg complaining about what lay beneath the whirl of bright lights and parties in that city.

> Petersburg society does not know that, in the basement under
> the floor of beautiful pastry shops and attractive bread stores,

---

[14] Vigdorchik 1914.
[15] Dobson 1910, p. 106.

> truly penal labour is going on ... Where else do people work
> eighteen to twenty hours a day? Nowhere; only we do. Where
> else are holidays unknown? Nowhere; only among us. We
> know neither Easter, nor Christmas, nor New Year's day.
> Where else do people sleep in crowded, filthy housing?
> Where do they sleep in shifts, with no time for the cots to cool
> off? Here, among us bakers.[16]

Indeed we can go further and argue that the Tsarist system was based
to an extent on the conscious perception of the need to maintain
ostentatious display and a callous social distance at whatever the cost.
The Tsar, for example, has been defended by a number of historians on
the grounds that he did demonstrate human responses to the disasters
that befell people in his reign but that he was continually urged not to
show this more human face by his close advisors in the court. But their
motive was often precisely to defend the majesty of the regime, to
defend what James C. Scott might call 'the public transcript' of its
power, by keeping from its public face the display of normal human
emotions lest they reduce the awe in which Tsarism was held.[17]

The issue of the cultural level of Russian society provides a clear
indication of the priorities of those at the top. The 1897 census showed
that Russia had an urban literacy rate of 54 per cent for men and 35.6
per cent for women, while the rural rate was 25.2 per cent and 9.8 per
cent respectively. In each case the record was one of the worst in
Europe. We now know that there was something of an educational
revolution in late Tsarist Russia so that the numbers in elementary
education rose from around 1.1 million in 1880 to 8 million in 1914,
but even this is only just over 50 per cent of the potential school age
group. Thus, although the revolution was underpinned by a growing
formal literacy and wider formal education, it also carried forward the
marks of that reluctance to admit the mass of the population into full,
political and socio-cultural, membership of Russian society. Anxious to
preserve their privileges, Russia's rulers remained torn between holding
down the populace and trying to raise its cultural level and integrate it.[18]
Stolypin told a petitioner,

> you don't know for whom you are interceding. All of them
> are mad brutes and can only be ruled by fear. If we give them
> liberty, they would massacre all of us – you, and everyone
> wearing a suit.

---

[16] Quoted in Freeze 1988, pp. 265–6.
[17] See Massie 1968, for the Tsarist family; Scott 1990, *passim*.
[18] Brooks 1985. At the time of the 1905 revolution, one liberal critic of Tsarism
said that 'the illiteracy of the peasants was treasured as the most precious jewel
of the Imperial crown.' (Quoted Meyendorff 1929, p. 95.) Phillips (1997) points
out that cultured, sober workers were often treated as suspicious by the
authorities, and a good way for a working-class activist to avoid discovery was to
feign the role of an uncultured drunkard.

Later Miliukov would reflect very similar views, 'if the Revolution should come, it will not be so much an uprising as a hateful mutiny. The rabble will be let loose'.[19]

This highly pejorative view of ordinary Russians reinforced the comparatively more open use of direct physical violence in social and political relations before 1917. The use of the fist by the master against the servant, the employer and foreman against the worker, and the landlord against the peasant was something that perhaps survived to a greater extent and was thought more acceptable in Russia than the rest of Europe. The semi-official endorsement of pogroms and anti-semitism is well known, including the support of the Tsar for the Black Hundreds. In the light of this we should perhaps be surprised at how little response there was from below, even in times of the greatest tension. To the extent that the lower classes bore the weight of the brutality of the system, it might seem that they turned their violent reaction against themselves too much and not enough against their masters. As some of Pipes's critics have pointed out, for example, despite his hostile view of the popular movement, even he is forced to admit that in the countryside in 1905–06 there is only one authenticated instance of a landlord being killed.[20]

Yet it is just those actions from below directed against society above that provoke the concern of historians like Pipes and Figes before and during the revolution. But the inadequacy of their response when faced with this problem was pointed out by Barrington Moore Jnr. three decades ago:

> the way nearly all history has been written imposes an overwhelming bias against revolutionary violence. Indeed the bias becomes horrifying as one comes to realise its depth. To equate the violence of those who resist oppression with the violence of oppressors would be misleading enough. But there is a great deal more. From the days of Spartacus through Robespierre down to the present day, the use of force by the oppressed against their former masters has been the object of nearly universal condemnation,. Meanwhile the day to day

---

[19] Quoted Liebman 1970, pp. 23, 82.
[20] Figes 1996, p. 138 offers a no less startling judgement. Quoting the estimate of 17,000 *dead and wounded* in 'terrorism' in Tsarist Russia, he says that this is 'more than five times the number *killed* in Northern Ireland during the twenty-five years of "the troubles".' The comparison is clearly meant to be to the disadvantage of Tsarist Russia, showing the extent to which the revolutionary movement was prepared to engage in terror, so prefiguring the later pattern of revolution. But the comparison is completely fallacious. Note firstly that it is between *dead and wounded* and *dead*. Secondly, no regard is had to the composition of the victims (in Northern Ireland the nationalist community, the loyalists, and the army and police, the composition of the Russian figures are unclear). But thirdly, and most importantly, whereas the Russian Empire had a population of over 160 million in 1914, the population of Northern Ireland is a mere 1.5 million. Crudely applying the Northern Irish rate of 'death in terror' to Russia would therefore give over 300,000 dead. Equally, applying the Russian rate of '*death and wounding in terror*' to Northern Ireland would give not 3,000 dead but a mere 160 *dead and wounded*. In other words the level of 'terror' is enormously higher in Northern Ireland than Tsarist Russia.

repression of 'normal' society hovers dimly in the background
of most history books. Even those radical historians who
emphasise the injustices of pre-revolutionary epochs generally
concentrate on a short time span preceding the immediate
outbreak. In that way, too they may unwittingly distort the
record.[21]

But the point of this argument is not to suggest that one type of violence
can simply be offset by another, but to show that in terms of both its
structure and policies the existing society rested on brutality and
violence in such a way as not only to undercut claims to moral
superiority but also to help explain why human beings in extreme
circumstances acted as they did. And when the war broke out this drive
to violence of 'normal society' became even more pronounced. The First
World War was simply the greatest concentration of violence, organised
and unorganised, that the world had yet seen. One aspect of this was 10
million or so war dead and the many millions more casualties. In
respect of Russia Hindenburg later asked,

> In the Great War ledger the page on which the Russian losses
> were written has been torn out. No one knows the figures.
> Five or eight millions? We, too, have no idea. All we know is
> that sometimes in our battles with the Russians we had to
> remove the mounds of enemy corpses before our trenches in
> order to get a clear field of fire against fresh assaulting waves.
> Imagination may try to reconstruct the figure of their losses
> but an accurate calculation will remain for ever a vain thing.[22]

But it is not just a question of dead and wounded but also of the vicious
circle of brutalisation and degradation that arises in any war. In theory
military discipline enables a distinction to be drawn between the
legitimate and illegitimate use of violence, but in practice the line is less
clear and the tendency of all armies is to have more or less hidden
records of atrocities, not simply because military discipline slips, but
because the very brutalisation of war makes this inevitable and at least
some degree of tolerance of this is necessary even in the best-run
armies. Indeed we can go further and argue that when positive human
impulses come to the fore, such as desertion to escape the killing or
fraternisation to stop it, then they invariably provoke organised violence
from above in the form of court-martials and executions or the

---

[21] Moore Jnr. 1966, p. 505.
[22] The accepted figures for Russia's part in the First World War are that 15.7
million men were mobilised, of whom 13.7 million saw active service. Some 2
million were killed or died of wounds. 0.7 million were killed or died of wounds
at the front. 5.1 million were wounded or sick, of whom 1.1 million died; 3.2
million returned to fight and the rest were invalided; 5.1 million soldiers were
missing in action or taken prisoner (of whom 118,000 are recorded as dying). In
addition, the fighting on the Russian side of the Eastern Front created some 10
million refugees whose condition was comparable to later refugee tragedies this
century. Account must also be taken of the impact of the war on civilian
mortality on the home front. See Davies 1994, pp. 60–62.

notorious deliberate shelling by their own artillery that Russian troops were reported to have experienced on the Eastern Front. The cycle of violence and degradation therefore works both below on the ordinary rank-and-file soldiers and above on their officers and generals. They have to commit tens of thousands to die – sometimes in a single day – and maintain the system that supports this. Moreover, in the Russian case, this even meant sending soldiers into line 'with a sword bayonet in one hand and a bomb in the other'. Trotsky pointed out how the consequences of this were felt above as well as below during the Russian Civil War when the pattern of atrocities continued

> during the [world] war there emerged form the ranks of the bourgeoisie – large, middle and small – hundreds of thousands of officers, professional fighters, men whose character has received the hardening of battle, and has become freed from all external restraints: qualified soldiers, ready and able to defend the privileged position of the bourgeoisie which produced them with a ferocity which, in its way, borders on heroism.[23]

2. Theorising popular violence

This need for perspective does not mean that we do not have to confront the issue of popular violence when it occurs. Here Neuberger's analysis of both the image and reality of hooliganism before 1914 offers us a number of interesting guideposts. Violent behaviour of all kinds amongst young people, especially in the lower classes, was real. In the interpretation of this Neuberger makes the obvious point that what appeared as upper-class 'horse play', in the lower classes seemed to be 'hooliganism', so that the double standard was carried over here too. But she also builds her analysis of the image of hooliganism around a more sophisticated theme. Concern with 'hooliganism' she argues reflected the problems of Russia's middle and upper classes in adjusting to the rapid growth of St. Petersburg; the fragmentation of the intelligentsia as it grew in size and diversity; doubts over the character and purpose of Russian culture; and the shock of 1905. These powerful forces led 'hooliganism' as a concept to emerge 'from the ranks of a simple moral panic to enter and remain in Russian national discourse as an evocative symbol of social disintegration and cultural difference and decay'.[24] The very fact that 'hooligan behaviour' appeared to grow with the political crises of 1905–7 and 1912–14 helped to unravel middle-class support for change from below.

By the eve of the First World War, save for a 'small optimistic wing', many in Russian society were affected by fear of what Blok called the 'mighty floods of popular resentment that were barely restrained by the

[23] Trotsky 1961, p. 67.
[24] Neuberger 1993, p. 4.

feeble dykes of civilisation and a decaying state'. This is a useful corrective to the simplistic view of the intelligentsia as uncritical sympathisers with the lower orders. Instead Neuberger emphasises the 'widespread contempt for the poor among Russian elites'.[25] The middle and upper classes in Russia came to see themselves as standing on the margins of civilisation. Defining themselves as 'respectable' against 'the hooligan' helped them to define their own class position, to allow themselves to be seen as a barrier against Asia and a civilising force in Russia – they were Europe's barrier against the barbarians within and without.

Neuberger provides extensive evidence for this view in her detailed analysis of the St. Petersburg press and so-called 'thick discussion journals'. But the argument can easily be extended to the countryside. Whereas earlier writers had tended to idealise the peasantry, at the turn of the twentieth century, increasingly hostile views could be found in literature. Chekhov's famous and unflattering short-story 'Peasants,' was typical of the shift.[26] Accounts like this are frequently thought to be more realistic but what is often missed is that they too incorporate a particular agenda set by the outsider looking in, without allowing us to really understand the inner dynamics of peasant life. This applies no less to a writer like Gorky, who is extensively used by Figes because of his negative evaluation of the brutality in both urban and rural lower-class culture before, during and after the revolution. But Figes simply reads off Gorky as an objective chronicler of reality, failing to see his writing as a product of the former insider now looking back, a complex amalgam of revolutionary ideas with elements of conservatism, not uncommon in similar writers in the West.[27]

Not surprisingly, then, it is difficult to measure 'hooliganism' since the very idea incorporates a particular agenda. Neuberger makes a sensitive attempt to tease out the reality, but even she can be criticised for the way in which too often she appears to turn 'hooligans' into a class, failing to fully explore the way in which what are talking about for most people is behaviour that they occasionally indulged in.[28] Insofar as she tries to explain this, she draws attention to what James C. Scott calls the 'hidden transcript' of hooligan action. Hooliganism is what, following Scott, we can call 'a weapon of the weak'. 'Hooliganism' says Neuberger, 'is the tactics of people without more powerful weapons at their disposal, so hooligans can act only when traditional authorities are already weakened', and this leads her to try to link hooliganism to crisis. It does not, of course, make aspects of it any more pleasant – she shows that women were targets of hooligans because they were in a sense even

---

[25] Neuberger 1993, p. 277. This is further evidence in refutation of Pipes's view that if forced to choose between left and right liberals would choose the left.
[26] Chekov 1984.
[27] Hare 1962.
[28] This raises a wider point in discussions of popular culture. It can be argued that the idea of 'respectability', so often used by social historians, was a role that workers used socially and politically depending on the circumstances they faced.

more vulnerable than the hooligans themselves. But this idea of 'weapons of the weak' does point to an interesting way forward. It both requires us to be more sensitive to the variation in types of hooliganism and, when we see things occurring that in any society would be unacceptable, to recognise that, insofar as they spring from weakness, then the solution lies in 'strength' – in encouraging people to acquire stronger and more disciplined weapons. This points to a fundamental conflict of interpretation. For the normal agenda of historians, the one at the root of Figes's and Pipes's accounts, is about top-down control – to hold the immediate line through the imposition of alienated state action, most notably the police and the law, and in the longer term to combine this with social control through education. But this does nothing to address the issue of the balance of power and the distribution of strength and weakness in a society. On the contrary, the top-down approach acts to maintain the fundamental inequalities that lie at the root of this issue. If this is true of pre-revolutionary Russia, it is even more true of 1917 itself.

3. The type, scale and timing of violence in 1917–18

It is not difficult to counterpose a low view of the revolution in 1917 to the heroic myth, and both Pipes and Figes in their different ways do this. Figes, if anything, attempts a more damning critique than Pipes. His is a revolution where women are raped in side streets as major demonstrations take place, objects of crowd hatred are set upon in the streets; the Winter Palace is ransacked with its defenders suffering uncertain fates and the wine cellars broken open in a drunken binge which, much more than political consciousness – the preserve of the few – represents the level of the many. Atop this bleak picture strut macho Bolsheviks clad in leather jackets, embodying a muscular masculinity (since women Bolsheviks presumably did not wear leather), a critical perspective on Bolshevism which he seems to think will enable him to demonstrate his credentials as a social historian capable of attracting feminist readers.[29]

---

[29] When it comes to demonstrating his 'feminist credentials', however, Figes falls flat on his face over his account of Alexander Kollontai, who has not been treated so misogynistically for several decades. Thus we encounter her (p. 480) taking up with Dybenko when she was 'old enough to be his mother' (he was 28 and she 45!); practising her 'free love philosophy' with a long succession of lovers before, as Soviet ambassador, she 'by all accounts' became the lover of the King of Sweden after 1930. Figes thus reports the puerile gossip of the 1930s as 'evidence'. Had he worked a little harder he could have added 'grandfather snatching' to the implication of 'child snatching' since (the respectable) King Gustav was 72 to Kollontai's 58 in 1930. He then rounds off his case by throwing in the old canard that the revolution led to the official nationalisation of women in some areas, thus falling for one of the greatest pieces of black propaganda of the time and apparently oblivious of the long discussion of this issue. See, for example, Velidov 1990.

It would be foolish to deny that an adequate history of the revolution should recognise that brutal incidents did occur. But the question is their scale, dynamic, and link to the overall nature of the popular movement. Was Tom Paine right when he said that 'outrages were not the effect of the principles of the revolution, but of the degraded mind that existed before the revolution, and which the revolution is calculated to reform. Place them to their proper cause, and take the reproach of them to your own side'?

Basic 'criminality' clearly existed. It seems, for example, that some 20,000 'criminals' were released in Petrograd by the February Revolution. Who these people were is an interesting question. Some no doubt were just bemused and unfortunate victims of the system. Perhaps some were Neuberger's hooligans who happened to be in the wrong place at the wrong time. Some possibly were 'criminals' in the more legitimate sense of the term, whose attitudes might have been transformed by the liberating experience of the revolution. A significant core, however, having been socialised on the margins of society, perhaps saw the revolution as providing new opportunities for their existing 'talents' and no doubt they were joined by others experiencing its contradictory force. Even John Reed's classic account drew attention to the fact that in September and October 1917 'robberies and housebreaking increased. In apartment houses the men took turns at all night guard duty with loaded rifles'.[30] But the argument of historians like Pipes and Figes goes beyond this to condemn the more organised popular movement for its brutality, violence and criminality.

It might seem that one way to deal with this would be to create some index of violence in 1917 but, as Neuberger's account of pre-war hooliganism makes clear, what can be counted depended on what was recorded, which in turn reflected the ideological prism through which 'violence' and 'crime' were defined. It is important to note here that while historians like Pipes and Figes stress violent behaviour, to many contemporary observers what was remarkable was the lack of it. Wilton, the notoriously anti-semitic *Times* correspondent, wrote of 'the astounding, and to the stranger unacquainted with the Russian character almost uncanny, orderliness and good nature of the crowds of soldiers and civilians throughout the city [Petrograd] are perhaps the most striking features of the great Russian revolution ...' No less for Harold Williams, the Russophile British commentator:

> It is a wonderful thing to see the birth of freedom. With freedom comes brotherhood, and in Petrograd today there is a flow of brotherly feeling. Everywhere you can see it in the streets. The trams are not yet running, and people are tired of endless walking. But the habit now is to share your cab with perfect strangers. The police have gone, but the discipline is marvellous. Everyone shares the task of maintaining discipline

---

[30] Reed 1966, p. 37.

and order. A volunteer militia has been formed ... Everyone is
happy in this sense of free order. The strong sense of
common responsibility for order has united all classes in one
great army of freedom ...

Williams's comments are especially interesting because even after
October he could write, on November 6 (old style), that 'there is no
government in Russia and yet Russia still exists by force of habit, by
virtue of some common, irrefutable, irrational belief. The Russians are
certainly at bottom a most extraordinarily law abiding people,
considering the continual opportunity for provocation to excess'. Yet he
was married to the Cadet politician Adriadna Tyrkova-Williams who,
within a year, had written an account of the revolution with mob
violence very much at the centre of it.[31]

What this reflects is less, perhaps, real differences in the level and
character of violence than a changing appreciation of it. In the spring of
1917 violence was seen as a necessary and legitimate way of getting rid
of Tsarism. It was therefore ignored or viewed benignly by upper- and
middle-class observers. The more the revolution turned in a radical
direction, however, the more hostile their views became. This shift can
be seen in the changing attitudes of individual contemporaries. Baron
Heyking, for example, was happy initially to explain to his British
audience that the role of the soldiers in the February Revolution was
anything but Pipes's *bunt*, in particular, 'the peasant co-operators in
Russia clad in khaki educated their fellow-soldiers as to the coming
Revolution and were instrumental in making the Army ready to
overthrow the autocratic regime'. But with October he quickly reversed
this position, arguing now that Russia's new rulers represented a thin
veneer of culture against a mass of ignorance, and by 1918 he was
insisting that 'loyal and well-intentioned elements in Russia' had to call
on the Allies to exercise 'a benevolent temporary guardianship on behalf
of civilisation', similar to the way in which the European powers had
joined together to support civilisation against the Boxer rebellion in
China.[32]

The gap between appearance and reality can be seen in the
'violence' of the famous ritual of 'carting out', where hated managers
and foremen were tied up and carted out of the factory in wheel
barrows before jeering crowds of workers. For Paul Avrich, in a
pioneering account of working-class radicalism, 'the rumble of the
wheel barrows – latter day tumbrils for a new class of oppressors –
became the sound of the proletarian revolution in the towns of Russia'.
Three things are of interest here. First the interpretative – to the victim
this was degrading and brutally violent treatment, to the workers it was

---

[31] Pitcher 1994, pp.44, 61, 252-3; Tyrkova-Williams 1919, chapter 10 *passim*.
[32] Heyking 1918, pp. 26, 51, 60, 81. Since it was difficult in itself to defend the
right of property against 'the class prejudice of Bolshevism', Heyking argued that
the attack on wealth was but the means to the greater end of putting down 'the
educated classes in Russia'.

an assertion of their own dignity in which they allocated just deserts to those who had oppressed them. Second, brutal though the treatment was, much of the 'violence' was in the form of ritual precisely because it had an organised element to it. While it is true that workers did use the threat of violence – something of which managements frequently complained, it is also important to recognise that violent language in the context of industrial relations only rarely led to violent action. What we have to analyse is direct action which both broke with the past passivity that had allowed employer abuses to go unchecked but which still depended on conceptions of legitimacy. But a third issue is the question of how common such action actually was? Much as we might like, with Avrich, to see carting out as a key feature of 1917, the evidence suggests that it is more of interest as a token of radicalisation than a common practice.[33] Rosenberg and Koenker could only find six recorded episodes of carting out in both Moscow and Petrograd. Whether this is a realistic evaluation of the scale of carting out remains an open question. Analysis of the experience of individual factories might suggest that it was more widespread.[34] But what is important for us is that the low reported figure suggests that carting out is better considered as a token of radicalisation rather than, *pace* Avrich, 'the sound of the proletarian revolution in the towns of Russia'.

If we look beyond this to other kinds of popular violence the picture is equally complicated. Read, in particular, argues strongly that its real extent has been exaggerated and he insists that, when popular violence did occur, it has to be seen in the context of a rational popular culture and custom. In the army, for example, the take-over from below was 'spontaneous, orderly and responsible'. Committee punishments, when used, reflected an accepted scale of values.[35] In the countryside he also disputes the picture of peasant 'anarchy':

> violent disturbances, in which landowners and their associates were seriously injured and killed, were few and far between. Less serious damage to property was rarer than legend would have it. After all, peasants were practical people who preferred to take over and use resources rather than destroy them aimlessly ... The peasants acted roughly and crudely but, as a rule, they were not wantonly destructive.

Peasant action was generally 'rational and co-ordinated', reflecting the peasants 'sense of legitimacy' and customary justice. When it took the form of attacks these usually had a clear logic, eg. the burning of a manor house meant that landowners could not return.[36] In the towns, too, similar forces were at work, and a struggle could be seen developing over the nature of popular culture. Tyrkova-Williams

---

[33] Avrich 1963, p. 172; Rosenberg & Koenker 1992, p. 304.
[34] This section has benefited from comments by Kevin Murphy, who has been working on the history of the Guzhon factory. The argument remains my own.
[35] Read 1996, pp. 123, 130.
[36] Read 1996, pp. 114–5, 117.

illustrated this in respect of women's rights before her view of the revolution turned sour. She reports how one middle-class activist congratulated a crowd of women in a bakery queue for the fact that they were now going to get 'their rights'. She was met with puzzlement until a soldier asked 'Does that mean I can't hit my wife?' The crowd shouted

> None of that. Just you try it. Nothing doing. Let ourselves be beaten any more? Not on your life. Nobody has the right now.[37]

Much is made of indiscriminate attacks on those who looked like 'a bourgeois' or 'an intellectual', but these were usually associated even before 1914 with the activities of the Black Hundreds (the attack on people with glasses as 'intellectuals' in the reaction in 1905–1906 is noted by Pipes). Moreover, violent language, which some followers of the 'linguistic turn' see as significant indictor, is not necessarily a good guide to practice. Photographs of revolutionary crowds and even the Red Guard show well-dressed figures. Bolshevik leaders were hardly known for dressing down, and when the first statue of Karl Marx was put up outside the Smolny Institute it was difficult to imagine a more bourgeois image as he stood there, in Arthur Ransome's word's with an 'enormous top hat like the muzzle of an eighteen inch gun'.[38]

When it comes to the question of who was involved, Read argues that 'the most violent elements of the working class were the unskilled labourers, the *chernorabochii* ... who were usually the most recent migrants', but these were also the people who faced the most extreme conditions. Smith also points out that greater popular violence appeared to take place after October in the context of the spiralling post-revolutionary crisis as food and raw material supplies dried up in the winter of 1917–18. But even then it is not clear how extensive it was. Arthur Ransome cabled his newspaper on December 29 (new style) that:

> reports of disorder ... are based mainly on wilful misrepresentation by the opposition newspapers here. The city is more orderly than it had been [sic] for some months before the Bolsheviks took control. For the first time since the revolution the government in Russia is based on real force. People may not like the Bolsheviks, but they obey them with alacrity.[39]

Far from welcoming indiscriminate violence, the revolutionary movement opposed it and condemned it. Organised workers were especially hostile to the idea of the *bunt* and saw the need to defend themselves against it. Read points out that this was one of the jobs of

---

[37] Quoted in Marsh 1991, p. 136.
[38] Ransome 1992, p. 66.
[39] Pitcher 1994, p. 266.

the Red Guards and workers' militias and, though their scale should not be exaggerated, he suggests that 'they constitute incontrovertible evidence that the popular movement was not simply a mob'.[40] Getzler makes the wider point that violence was inversely proportional to the number of politically active workers in a situation, since it was they who tended to argue for a more constructive approach. This was one reason why, despite the growing gap between the Provisional Government and the activists, the Provisional Government itself continued to want the support of such people in 1917. This determination to give direction to the popular movement applied just as much to the Bolsheviks. It is evident, too, in one of the most notorious cases – the murder by sailors of two former provisional government ministers, Shingarev and Kokoshkin, while they were sick in hospital. Most hostile historians note this as an example of the brutality of the revolutionary crowds, but few noticed that the campaign against such indiscriminate violence was taken up amongst the soldiers and sailors. Arthur Ransome said of Krylenko, for example,

> I remember hearing him speak in the barracks soon after the murder of Shingarev and Kokoshkin, urging class struggle and at the same time explaining the difference between that and the murder of sick men in bed. He referred to the murder and, while continuing his speech, talking of another subject, he went through the actions of a man approaching a bed and killing a sleeper with a pistol. It was a trick, of course, but the thrilling, horrible effect of it moved the whole audience with a shudder of disgust.[41]

Of course, these arguments were not always successful. Shingarev and Kokoshkin were killed. But this does not mean that we can ignore the battle going on for the soul of the popular movement to give it direction and to hold the line against the forces of chaos and disorder from above and below.[42] It is therefore not possible to simply counterpose patterns

---

[40] Read 1996, p.88.

[41] Ransome 1992, p. 117.

[42] Figes provides a crass example of the way this type of contradiction is ignored which sadly illuminates the all too cavalier approach to the treatment of problems and evidence that mars his whole account. This is the seizing of gold in 1918 from the safety deposit boxes of the banks in St. Petersburg. This was not simply an attempt to seize the assets of the rich but to get desperately needed foreign exchange. For Figes, however, it is the manner of the seizure that is important. He quotes from a contemporary account a vivid description of a sailor running his hands through the 'mountain of booty' interested only in the gold and apparently stupidly leaving behind the jewellery including a Fabergé egg. The autobiography from which he extracts his evidence however uses this episode to make the almost opposite point. The memoirs of Countess Meshcherskaya stresses the need for foreign exchange and the opposition of the property owners who refused to hand over their gold saying 'Let the bastards break in! Let them reduce the building to rubble!' Meshcherskaya's mother was one of the few who did willingly surrender the family gold. It was the sailor's duty to take only the gold and he was obliged to surrender the jewels to their original owners. He did so by painfully recording what was taken and then giving the Meshcherskaya's a receipt for what had been taken. 'What a pity that I, who was still a silly adolescent ... took no pains to preserve it! It was only years later that I realised

of behaviour in 1917. Getzler's analysis is especially interesting in this respect, for he argues that what was involved in 1917 was a huge democratic learning process which came not from the top down but the bottom up. Despite the incantation to the effect that the Constituent Assembly was Russia's one and only free election at this time, it is probably true to say that no other population anywhere in world history has had so many opportunities to vote as did Russians (and especially urban workers) in 1917 – elections for local councils, for trade unions, for co-operatives, for miscellaneous local organisations, for factory committees and most famously for soviets. 'Russia's soviets became a vast training ground in electoral practice, parliamentary procedure and political pluralism', writes Getzler. Accounts of the battle for 'soviet democracy' often seem to be based upon the assumption that whereas elections for the Constituent Assembly involved the many, elections for soviets and other organisations involved the few. In fact whereas 44 million voted in the Constituent Assembly elections, he suggests that as many as 20 million voted for urban soviets and 17 million for rural ones.[43]

This was an immensely constructive response from below, and one moreover where, as in the votes given to non-Russians (including Jews), we can see a breaking-down of some of the worst legacies of the old regime. The same is also apparent in the election of women. It is worth recalling that the popular faces of Bolshevism in 1917 were Trotsky and Kollontai. Account must also surely be taken of the policies that were pursued within revolutionary democracy, and the way in which they tried to transform beliefs and practices. This puts historians like Figes and Pipes in something of a dilemma. To the extent that they argue against and disparage popular democracy, then they argue against the creative forces of 1917. Much as they might (especially in Figes's more 'liberal' case) seek to deny it, they effectively swing behind order from above legitimating a top-down imposition of rule through what they imagine to be the benevolent civilising tendencies of those in charge of Russian society.

---

the value of this fascinating historical document.' Meshcherskaya 1990, pp. 19–23. For Figes, no less than for the 'silly adolescent girl', the significance of the episode is missed or perhaps more disturbingly, deliberately attenuated in his account to demonstrate the irrational mob violence of the time. Here we have the revolutionary sailor carrying into the episode all his contradictory feelings and consciousness, still including part of the muck of the old order as when he reacts with hostility to an Othello necklace in the family safe deposit box, 'Just goes to show how shameless these upper class women were! Going around with pictures of 'niggers around their necks.' But instead of grabbing the wealth for himself, instead of slipping the Fabergé egg into his pocket he carefully sets aside what the revolutionary state is claiming, writes out a receipt and returns the rest to its owners. In other words, the point of the story is almost the opposite of that which Figes attributes to it. Figes 1996, p. 527.
[43] Getzler 1992.

5. Class formation and the question of politics

Does this mean that we should prefer an account like that of Read to those Pipes and Figes? If this is the choice the answer has to be an unequivocal yes – his account is far more balanced, far more nuanced and shows a clearer understanding of all the aspects of the revolution. But this does not mean that his approach can be uncritically endorsed, for it can be argued that he has himself failed to overcome key weaknesses in the 'history from below' approach and this not only leaves him vulnerable to attack from the likes of Figes and Pipes but in key areas it allows him to come to conclusions that seem to echo their views.

Read, for example, shares the view that the working class was incompletely 'made' in 1917. This is for two reasons related to the sociology of the popular movement. The first is the view that the underlying process of class formation was still weak. 'The proletariat was not so much a stable class as a railway station with a constant stream of people coming into it from the village and returning to the village during bad times, or, in the case of women, to have families'. He suggests that this led to a greater concern with the 'narod', people, than class, leading to the conclusion that in what he calls 'the Thompsonian sense' the Russian working class in 1917 was 'an "unmade" working class, or a working class still in the making'. He then makes a second argument to the effect that when workers turned to the Bolsheviks they did so defensively, in pursuit of their original agenda of February that the other parties were failing to deliver. Thus, 'far from a rising tide of revolutionary enthusiasm taking hold of workers as the revolution unfolded, the atmosphere in which they lived was one of increasing threats to their livelihood'. The call for 'All Power to the Soviets' was 'a last defensive resort'; 'the popular agenda – a better deal for the workers, land redistribution, protection from the economic crisis, greater direct democracy and a just end to the war – remained a relatively stable programme in search of implantation'. 'The popular movement did not turn towards Bolshevism because they had become converts to its basic philosophy.' The Bolsheviks were supported he says, ironically, because they were 'better Mensheviks'.

The difficulty with this is that it leaves aside the whole question of politics. The consciousness of people in 1917 involved political choices, as John Marot has argued.[44] This is not a question of introducing politics from the outside or seeing it, as postmodernists do, as an autonomous force. It is a question of seeing the choices people make as political ones, requiring political argument. The fact that workers may have been driven defensively to reject the Mensheviks and (right) SRs does not mean that this did not involve a political transformation in their ideas. What Read does, however, is to bend towards the tendency

---

[44] Marot 1994.

in social history to suppress a political understanding of the popular movement by conceiving the stomach as ruling the head of people in protest, rather than exploring the relationship between them. This has a double effect. Instead of class consciousness being related to the material situation of workers as something that is simultaneously social and political, it becomes something that is more crudely social and therefore more crudely determinist. It also leads to the view that what happened in 1917 was but a temporary convergence between the popular movement and a Bolshevik politics which existed independently of the movement, hanging over it so to speak, and doomed to hang even more in the air as the same social forces which drove the popular movement up before 1917 turned in on themselves and dragged it down after October, creating a situation in which the Bolsheviks (and left SRs) were inevitably going to rule in the name of the working class rather than through it. This also leads Read to the familiar argument that there is a contradiction between Marx's emancipatory vision and that of Lenin in 1917, despite what Victor Serge later called the 'libertarian communism' of the time.

6. Revolutionary degeneration and violence, organised and unorganised

Once Read moves beyond October we find a further familiar set of difficulties. At the root of these is his ambiguity over the relationship between the politics of the time and the later development of Stalinism. This is the key issue of the Lenin-Stalin link. We say Lenin-Stalin link because to argue over *Leninism* versus *Stalinism* is in a sense to prejudge the argument in Stalin's favour since *Leninism* as an *ism* was very much a creation of the period immediately after Lenin's death, of the faction fights of the time. For Read, however, as for so many historians, the post-October, even the October air, is thick with portent about what is to come and this is reflected in his language. Thus in the course of rejecting the monolithic model of Bolshevism, he writes of it as a cluster of 'quarrelling sects' with Lenin as the Ayatollah and the Leninists as 'the arch fundamentalists fearful of potentially polluting contact between themselves and the infidels'. His own acceptance of conventional views about what is and is not socialism is even reflected in a number of throwaway references to Mao and even Pol Pot. At the end we have a nod in the direction of the failed Gorbachev reform programme whose best aspects, he suggests, 'represented the healthy heart of Russia's post-revolutionary experiences bursting through the dilapidated and thoroughly discredited remnants of Stalinist dictatorship'.[45]

---

[45] Read 1996, p. 294.

With this perspective, Read is inevitably led away from the argument that the revolution was forced off its original path by the horrific circumstances of the civil war towards the Furet view that revolutions (whether French or Russian) make their own future. As Read puts it,

> one can no longer use considerations of this kind to relieve Bolshevism of its own share of responsibility for the outcome. Ironically, a, possibly, *the*, key reason for the failure of the 'dream scenario' did not lie with the revolution's enemies on the right – who were marginalised with surprising ease and never looked likely to muster power to roll back the social revolution – but from its Bolshevik friends.

It is true that, unlike Figes and Pipes, Read still sees that qualified choices were available at the end of the Civil War ('Even in 1921 various "futures" remained open. "Proto-Stalinism" had certainly gained ground but its further evolution was by no means inevitable although Lenin did appear to pushing an uncompromisingly fundamentalist line at the Tenth Party Congress in that year'). But in this emphasis he still follows Furet on the French Revolution, at least to the extent of putting the emphasis on internal ideological dynamics rather than the external circumstances.

To conclude our discussion, we will draw attention to two of the many difficulties with this argument. The first is the way in which it leads to a misinterpretation of the early measures of revolutionary self-defence. Read is not unsympathetic to the general dilemmas of the new revolutionary state in the area of law and self-defence. He notes, for example, the problems of what law is to be enforced. But the weight of the future lies so heavily in his analysis of 1917–18 that it illegitimately makes the history of that time prefigure later events and therefore reduces the significance of the subsequent shift that occurred. The contradictions this produces are nicely illustrated in Read's comment on Antonov-Ovseenko's arrest of the Provisional Government ministers in October, 'in a gesture full of portent for the bureaucratic system that was being born that night, the first thing Antonov-Ovseenko did when he arrested the [Provisional Government] ministers was to write a docket and get all present to sign it'. This is a typical example of the no-win situation historians tend to put the Bolsheviks and their supporters in at this time. Had the ministers simply been bundled away, degraded and perhaps shot this would have been interpreted as a manifestation of a *bunt* but because an attempt was made to give some formality to their arrest this prefigures the future bureaucratic system. In fact, viewed in terms of 1917 itself, Antonov-Ovseenko's actions seem to make considerable sense. Here was a moment of historic significance – the assertion of the old over the new, a moment that needed in itself a document both to record and legitimise it, a document that in effect registered the *de facto* transfer of power to be later supported by *de jure* constitutional documents. It needed it, moreover, precisely because this was a conscious political act and not a politically unconscious *bunt*. It is difficult to see how a genuine revolution would have required anything else and it therefore makes little sense to see this as an expression of bureaucratic degeneration in itself.

But of course the revolution did fail ultimately to live up to its 1917 ideals. To explain this, however, regard has to be paid to the spiral of crisis which the revolutionaries faced after October. Here the promise of the social history approach has not been realised, in part because its followers have not sufficiently attended to the chronology of crisis. Rosa Luxemburg put this point well, 'everything that happens in Russia is comprehensible and represents an inevitable chain of cause and effects, the starting point and end term of which are: the failure of the German proletariat and the occupation of Russia by German imperialism'.[46] The crucial idea here is that of 'an inevitable chain of cause and effects'. If we think in terms of a spiral of crisis, it is easy to see how it is possible to connect a number of points on the spiral to get a straight line or to simply generalise across the downward path. Read's more analytical social history falls into this trap by generalising across the spiral rather than following it around and down. Pipes and Figes on the other hand, with a greater emphasis on narrative, do have some sense of movement, but they too are focused on connecting the straight line rather than analysing the complexity of the shifting perspectives. This approach is also being assisted by more detailed studies of the civil war which are tending to dissolve it into a mass of competing 'civil wars'. That opposition to the Bolsheviks was not all of a piece has long been known; much attention has been paid to, for example, the opposition of the peasant and so-called Green forces. But this does not mean that the war did not have a basic unity. Indeed it is in the nature of war that it narrows choices to the often brutally simple ones of 'for and against'. It does this partly because of what Clausewitz called the 'fog of war' – the confusion, both political and military, that comes with the smoke of battle and which it is part of the job of the historian to recreate. But it also narrows choices because it is in the nature of warfare to reduce what we can call the 'structure of choice' itself. In the aftermath of such terrible events it is often tempting to go back and rewrite history as if there were third ways. Military history is full of this kind of speculation. But if it neglects the central thrust of the choices available at the time it ceases to carry conviction, and much of the more recent writing on the civil war does precisely this.

Similarly, the three accounts of the revolution under discussion tend to side-step serious consideration of the 'structure of choice'. They fail to grapple with the extent to which the general process of social decay affected the working class and therefore undercut the basis of the regime after 1917. While they all recognise the decomposition of the urban population in much of Russia, they nevertheless tend to treat the

---

[46] Luxemburg 1980, p. 394.

working class as a static entity, especially when it comes to contrasting the policies of the regime with the 'interests' of 'the working class' during the Civil War. But this is to minimise the dilemma of the Bolsheviks and to break the chain of cause and effect that Luxemburg identified. Once this is done, however, it is then easy to attack the Bolsheviks for ruling over the working class instead of through it.

The real extent of the dilemma of the time can be seen if we inject a sense of cause and effect back into the account of 1918–21. The crisis, for example, can be seen at its deepest in Petrograd but since this was the crucible of the revolution its collapse was perhaps the most serious socio-political measure of the scale of the Civil War disaster.[47] While the population of Petrograd fell from 2.4 million in 1917 to 740,000 in 1920 (a fall of 70 per cent), the numbers in the industrial working class fell even more. Between January 1914 and January 1917 the number of factory workers increased from 242,600 to 384,600, a net increase of 142,000 and a gross one of nearer 180,000 when the mobilisation of some 15-17 per cent of the industrial work force for the war is factored in. In 1917 itself the numbers remained more or less stable until October. But by that time the economy was already in the beginnings of a vicious circle of collapse that in one sense the revolution was a desperate attempt to stop. Despite the best efforts of the new revolutionary government, two successive waves of crisis smashed the working class of the city. The first wave from October 1917 to the summer of 1918 involved the first recruitment of the Red Army, the

---

[47] Civil War deaths are horrific but fall into four categories. Firstly, an estimated 0.8 to 1.2 million died in fighting (including from disease and atrocities on both sides); secondly, there were executions behind the lines whose scale remains disputed; thirdly, there were the excess deaths from hunger and disease which perhaps number 2 million for 1918–21; fourthly, there were 5 to 6 million deaths in the horrific famine of 1920–21 in the Volga area. In total this gives 8–10 million depending on the precise estimates for each category. These figures, unlike those for the 1930s, have never been secret. They were published and discussed widely in the 1920s in Russia, when the official view was that, since most could be laid at the door of the counterrevolution, they were a tragic consequence of foreign intervention and the Whites' actions. The key category in terms of debates about revolutionary violence in the Civil War relates to executions behind the lines, and executions and atrocities as the fluid front changed in battle and areas were captured and recaptured. The Cheka gave a figure for its own executions of some 13,000 but this excludes deaths arising in the course of fighting and in areas outside of central Russia. William Chamberlin, the best early 'neutral observer' suggested that putting these together at a more realistic level would give 50,000 (Chamberlin 1987 pp. 66–84). Graham Leggett, in his history of the Cheka, more than doubled this figure, which may be justifiable but it is difficult to see that this is so in terms of the evidence he offers, and he unfortunately legitimates his new estimate by drawing attention to its closeness to Robert Conquest's estimates which he then believed accurate for the later periods of Soviet history. (Leggett 1981, pp. 463–8). In fact it is now largely accepted (though not by Conquest himself) that his later estimates both of deaths and the camps were more or less double what was actually the case. Other authors have inflated the figures even more. Less attention was paid to the White side – Chamberlin did not offer an estimate of these deaths, nor does Leggett, but those authors who have looked closely at this suggest figures as high as those Leggett gives for the Red Terror – if not higher. Much depends on the evaluation and classification of Jewish deaths in the south. The terror of the so-called 'third forces' was also extensive; Read notes of Makhno that 'those who resisted were treated without mercy'. Read 1996, p. 259.

despatch of workers to spread the revolution in the provinces, hurried attempts at disruptive factory conversion from the war effort, and most importantly the impact of desperate food shortages and the lack of raw materials. The combined impact of this was to cut the number of factory workers in work to 293,000 in January 1918, 159,000 by April and 115,000 in October 1918. By this time, a second wave of crisis, this time directly induced by the Civil War, was sweeping the city. In the next two years a further 40,000 workers joined the Red Army, 20,000 went on to other state work and perhaps as many as 20,000 died, as the death rate at one point hit a high of some 80 per 1000. At its lowest point the number of factory workers was reduced to around 80,000 – some 20 per cent of the 1917 level. But this figure was as high as it was because many new workers were pulled into the workforce in 1919 and 1920, often from other social classes. Of those in the factories in Petrograd in 1917 perhaps only 50,000 were left in 1920 – 12.5 per cent of the 1917 figure. This crisis was felt in the party too as workers gave up work to fight for the revolution in other ways. If in October 1917 the party had 45,000 members in the city then by March 1918 it had 36,000 and by August 1918, only 15,500. A survey in October 1918 found that only 41.2 per cent of the members had joined before October, so that within a year perhaps as much as 80 per cent of the October 1917 party had left the city to fight and help run the revolution elsewhere.[48]

These figures demonstrate two things. First they show clearly how the decomposition of the working class meant that the party had to substitute for the class, but also how, within the party, power inevitably gravitated upwards. Second, they show how wrong it is to imagine that one can simply counterpose the party to the 'class' during the Civil War or in the fraught days of early 1921 during the strikes in Petrograd and the revolt in Kronstadt. The 'working class' was simply not a meaningful entity at this point. This accounts for the great paradox that has never been fully dealt with by critics of the Bolsheviks: that even their 'workerist' critics of the time sided with them rather than the 'working class' in periods of political crisis, because to raise the banner of the working class at this time was to invoke a rhetorical entity rather than a really existing force.

The problem was, therefore, that during the Civil War the Bolsheviks had to react bureaucratically because there was no other way. Of course, Luxemburg in her account went on to point to the problems of this situation as she saw it in its very earliest stages, 'the danger begins only when they make a virtue of necessity forced upon them by fatal circumstances'. But to understand this it is necessary to appreciate the ideological change that occurred in this period, as virtues were made out of necessities. But precisely because Pipes and others like him envision history as a more or less straight line, they are also

---

[48] Shkaratan 1959, *passim.*

unable to measure fully the ideological shift that took place. This is a crucial issue because, perhaps with the exception of Lenin's *State and Revolution*, there is no single work written in 1917 that codifies the essence of the democratisation from below as it was seen at the time. On the contrary, when contemporaries set down their visions of what 1917 was about they were informed by the measures of the Civil War, although attention to some of the most sensitive writing of this period, such as that of Victor Serge, enables one to almost feel the shifting redefinition of the revolution that was taking place and the tensions it produced.[49]

Conclusions

Recalling the deaths in the Jacobin Terror, Thomas Jefferson wrote that

> these I deplore as much as anybody, and shall deplore some of them to the day of my death. But I deplore them as I should has they fallen in battle. It was necessary to use the arm of the people, a machine not quite as blind as balls and bombs, but blind to a certain degree.[50]

This is a judgement that still has power in regard to both the French and Russian Revolutions, even though it has recently earned even Jefferson the opprobrium of a writer like Conor Cruise O'Brien.

But 'using the arm of the people' is not popular today, in East or West. When historians reject it, however, they must beware the tendency to line up in support of the established order. Nothing is easier than to create what we can call the tyranny of two alternatives – the choice is either 'Lenin to Stalin' or 'democracy and the market'. But what if these are not the choices? What if Lenin did not lead to Stalin and what if 'democracy and the market' are not the end of history. In their different ways, the works of Pipes and Figes are direct political contributions. Pipes has been actively engaged in both American and Russian politics, and the account by Figes fits well into both the perspectives of the Western liberal intelligentsia and the Yeltsin camp in the West.[51] But Russia is undergoing a trauma of change whose human costs are enormous, and riding it are the class who benefited from the degeneration of the revolution, a class which came to power in its name but over its dead, stealing the memory for its own purposes. Now, dressed in new clothes, they proclaim their new commitments and are happy for 1917 to still be associated with the regime they once ruled, or with the remnants of the Stalinist communist parties that occasionally

---

[49] Serge 1997.
[50] Quoted in Liebman 1970, p. 338.
[51] In a debate on BBC Radio 3, held to remember the eightieth anniversary of the Revolution, the historian Boris Kolonitskii described Figes's history as one that Yeltsin would approve of.

demonstrate in Red Square as part of the Red-Brown Alliance. Historians, however, should beware falling into the trap of too easily lining up with these choices. When E.P. Thompson spoke of rescuing the past from 'the tremendous condescension of posterity', it was not just a question of trying to understand the attitudes of small sects in the past but of trying to rescue the nature of the real choices that were faced then. To do so is not only to do justice to the past but it is also to do justice to the present in a world in which there is still too little real justice and too many people whose comfort and position depends on a closed view of the past.

References

Avrich, Paul 1963, 'The Russian Factory Committees in 1917', *Jahrbücher für Geschichte Osteuropas*, 11.

Brinton, Maurice 1970, *The Bolsheviks and Workers' Control*, London: Solidarity.

Brooks, Jeffrey 1985, *When Russia Learned to Read: Literacy and Popular Literature, 1861–1917*, Princeton: Princeton University Press.

Brovkin, Vladimir 1987, *The Mensheviks After October. Socialist Opposition and the Rise of the Bolshevik Dictatorship*, Cornell: Cornell University Press.

Brovkin, Vladimir, 1994, *Behind the Front Lines of the Civil War, Political Parties and Social Movements in Russia*, Princeton: Princeton University Press.

Brovkin, Vladimir (ed.), 1994, *The Bolsheviks in Russian Society: The Revolution and the Civil Wars*, New Haven: Yale University Press.

Chamberlin, William Henry 1987, *The Russian Revolution. Volume 2 1918–1921. From the Civil War to the Consolidation of Power*, Princeton: Princeton University Press.

Chekhov, Anton 1984, 'Peasants' in *The Russian Master and Other Stories*, Oxford: Oxford University Press.

Davies, R.W. (ed.), 1994, *The Economic Transformation of the Soviet Union, 1913–1945*, Cambridge: Cambridge University Press.

Dobson, G. 1910, *St. Petersburg*, London.

Ferro, Marc 1985, *The Bolshevik Revolution: A Social History of the Russian Revolution*, London: Routledge.

Freeze, Geoffrey 1988, *From Supplication to Revolution. Documentary Social History of Imperial Russia*, New York: Oxford University Press.

Figes, Orlando 1996, *A People's Tragedy: The Russian Revolution, 1891–1924*. London: Cape.

Furet, François 1981, *Interpreting the French Revolution*, Cambridge: Cambridge University Press.

Getzler, Israel 1992, 'Soviets as Agents of Democratisation' in *Revolution in Russia: Reassessments of 1917*, edited by J. Frankel et al, Cambridge: Cambridge University Press.

Getzler, Israel 1992, 'Richard Pipes' "Revisionist" History of the Russian Revolution', *Slavonic and East European Review*, 70, 1.

Hare, Richard 1962, *Maxim Gorky. Romantic Realist or Conservative Revolutionary*, London: Oxford University Press.

Heyking, Baron A. 1918, *Problems Confronting Russia*, London.

Leggett, George, 1981, *The Cheka: Lenin's Political Police, the All Russian Extraordinary Commission*, Oxford: Clarendon Press.

Liebman, Marcel 1970, *The Russian Revolution: the Origins, Phases and Meaning of the Bolshevik Victory*, London: Cape.

Luxemburg, Rosa 1980, 'The Russian Revolution', *Rosa Luxemburg Speaks*, New York: Pathfinder Press.

Malia, Martin 1994, *The Soviet Tragedy. A History of Socialism in Russia*, New York: Free Press.

Marot, John E. 1994. 'Class Conflict, Political Competition and Social Transformation: Critical Perspectives on the Social History of the Russian Revolution', *Revolutionary Russia*, 7, 2.

Marsh, Rosalind 1991, 'The Birth, Death and Rebirth of Feminist Writing in Russia', in *Textual Liberation. European Feminist Writing in the Twentieth Century*, edited by Scott H. Forsås, London: Routledge.

Massie, Robert K. 1968, *Nicholas and Alexandra*, London: Gollancz.

Meyendorff, Baron Alexander 1929, *The Background to the Russian Revolution*, New York: Holt & Co.

Meshcherskaya, Ekaterina 1990, *Comrade Princess. Memoirs of an Aristocrat in Modern Russia*, London: Doubleday.

Moore Jnr., Barrington Moore 1966, *Social Origins of Dictatorship and Democracy*, Harmondsworth Middlesex: Penguin.

Neuberger, Joan 1993, *Hooliganism. Crime, Culture and Power in Saint Petersburg, 1900–1914*, Berkley: University of California Press.

Paine, Thomas 1937 *The Rights of Man*, London: Watts & Co.

Phillips, Laura 1997, 'Message in a Bottle: Working Class Culture and the Struggle for Revolutionary Legitimacy 1990–1929', *The Russian Review*, 56, 1.

Pitcher, Harvey 1994, *Witnesses of the Russian Revolution*, London: John Murray.

Pipes, Richard 1992, *The Russian Revolution 1899–1919*, London: Fontana Press.

Pipes, Richard 1995, *Russia Under the Bolshevik Regime 1919–1924*, London: Fontana Press.

Ransome, Arthur 1992a, *Six Weeks in Russia 1919*, London: Redwords.

Ransome, Arthur 1992b, *The Crisis in Russia 1920*, London: Redwords.

Read, Christopher 1996, *From Tsar to Soviets: The Russian People and Their Revolution, 1917–1921*, London: University College London Press.

Reed, John 1966, *Ten Days that Shook the World*, Harmondsworth, Middlesex: Penguin.

Rosenberg, William and Koenker, Diane 1992 'The Limits of Formal Protest: Worker Activism and Social Polarization in Petrograd and Moscow, March to October 1917', *American Historical Review*, 92 , 2.

Scott, James C. 1990, *Domination and the Arts of Resistance: Hidden Transcripts*, New Haven: Yale University Press.

Serge, Victor 1997, *Revolution in Danger. Writings From Russia 1919–1921*, London: Redwords.

Shkaratan, O.I. 1959, 'Izmeneniya v sotsial'nom sostave fabrichno-zavodskikh rabochikh Leningrada (1917–1928 gg.)', *Istoriya SSSR*, 5.

Shkliarevsky, Gennady 1993, *Labor in the Russian Revolution: Factory Committees and Trade Unions, 1917–1918*, New York: St.Martins.

Smith, Steven, 1992, 'Review Essay: Richard Pipes, *The Russian Revolution* (1990)', *Social History*, 17, 2.

Trotsky, Lev 1961, *Terrorism and Communism. A Reply to Karl Kautsky*, Ann Arbor: University of Michigan Press.

Tyrkova-Williams, Adriadna 1919, *From Liberty to Brest-Litovsk. The First Year of the Russian Revolution*, London.

Velidov, Alexei 1990, 'The "Decree" on the Nationalisation of Women: The Story of a Mystification', *Moscow News*, no. 8-9: 13.

Vigdorchik, N.A. 1914, *Destskaya smertnost' sredi petersburgskikh rabochikh (po dannuikh anketui)*, St. Petersburg.

Walter Benjamin; Selected Writings, Volume 1 1913-1926
Marcus Bullock and Michael W. Jennings (eds.)
Massachusetts, Harvard University Press, 1996
Walter Benjamin; A Biography
Momme Brodersen
London: Verso, 1997
Words of Light; Theses on the Photography of History
Eduardo Cadava
Princeton: Princeton University Press, 1997

Reviewed by Esther Leslie

At last it is here. Promised many years ago, the first volume of the three-volume *Selected Writings* of Walter Benjamin has arrived. The earliest piece in the volume stems from 1913, when Benjamin was an activist in the Free Student Movement and an undergraduate, influenced by the neo-Kantianism of Rickert and Cohen. The collection closes with Benjamin's intermix of aphorisms and surrealist philosophising, *One-Way Street*, completed in 1926, by which time Benjamin was established, if precariously, as a writer and had declared some sort of commitment to communism. There is no consistency across Benjamin's whole work – he noted once that his slogan was 'always radical, never consistent' – and yet despite that, while migrating from metaphysical anarchism to historical, dialectical or anthropological materialism over the thirteen years that germinate the writings here, many of his concerns are recurrent. He returns again and again to a clutch of questions concerning experience – queries about the quality of experience, about the expression of experience, and about revolt, in the name of intensified experience. The first volume of the *Selected Writings* opens with a short outburst called 'Experience', an attack on adult cynicism, jadedness and philistinism, against which Benjamin counterposes youth's dreaming, compassion and spirit. The final cogitation in the volume, a part of *One-Way Street*, is titled 'To the Planetarium' and it urges the regaining of ecstatic, cosmic experience of pre-bourgeois man, in the context of a high-technological age. Evoking the German revolutionaries of Spartakus as indications of a proletarian attempt to harmonise nature, technology and humanity, after the techno-bloodbath of world war, Benjamin writes: 'Men as a species completed their development thousands of years ago; but mankind as a species is just beginning his. In technology a *physis* is being organized through which mankind's contact with the cosmos takes a new and different form from that which it had in nations and families' (Bullock and Jennings, p. 487).

The *Selected Writings* has been a long time coming. It supplements the English anthologies of Benjamin's writings that detonated on the English-speaking Left scene in the 1970s – *Illuminations* (1968),

Charles Baudelaire; A Lyric Poet in the Era of High Capitalism (1973), *Understanding Brecht* (1973), *Reflections* (1978), *One-Way Street and Other Writings* (1979) (largely a reprint of the contents of *Reflections*). Amongst the longer pieces included in this new volume are Benjamin's doctorate, *The Concept of Criticism in German Romanticism* (1919), and an engagement with Georges Sorel titled *Critique of Violence* (1921), dealing with strike legislation and the higher morality of revolutionary violence in the proletarian general strike, indeed higher in a truly theological sense, given that Benjamin affiliates such proletarian violence with divine violence. Some of the pieces included here have appeared in English before, and where this is the case, no revised translations have been commissioned. But a good proportion of the book is new – most notably, the translation of 'Goethe's Elective Affinities' (1922), Benjamin's reckoning with academic literary criticism, as represented by the vitalist circle of critics around the symbolist poet Stefan George. 'Goethe's Elective Affinities' is a 60-odd page essay that has accrued mythical status for anglophones. It was included in Adorno's prominent 1955 two-volume Benjamin-assortment, *Schriften*, and in Suhrkamp's key German compilation *Illuminationen* from 1977. It was deemed to be one of Benjamin's finest theoretical expositions – indeed biographer Momme Brodersen suggests that it may be Benjamin's most important essay (Brodersen, p. 132) – but no-one had dared to publish an English translation of the notoriously difficult piece with its puns, conceptual contortions and supposed cryptic allusions to Benjamin's own life-circumstances at the time. Stanley Cornfold, the translator in this volume, acknowledges assistance from nine previous unpublished renderings. Now English readers can judge whether Benjamin succeeded in his aim, which he expressed thus: 'the reestablishment of the power of the critical word, the renewal of dictum and verdict' (Brodersen, p. 124). The essay was written as a polemic against a set of attitudes in literary criticism of the time, and specifically against the practice of reading an author's work through the events of that author's life. Benjamin's philology reads Goethe's late novel immanently, divulging its carefully constructed weave of interlacing references. He discovers that, contrary to those interpretations that viewed the novel as a defence of the ethical sanctity of marriage and the dreadful consequences of adultery, the true meaning of the novel, discernible through microscopic reading of inner form, of symbols and language, is the denuding of monstrous mythic forces aroused once a relationship's basis has become purely legal and is no longer founded on substance. For Benjamin, Goethe's novel is an upbraiding of the bourgeois world that it seems at first glance to maintain. Benjamin's reading of *Die Wahlverwandtschaften* was not fundamentally concerned with being true to the historical moment of the novel and the novelist. In addition to re-interpreting the novel, Benjamin shows that what the interpreter finds in the work is not a timeless truth or a dead past, but the interpreter's own historical present. This task of 'actualisation' is found in Benjamin's subsequent work too. The essay did Benjamin few favours. Its uncompromising sweep against the grain contributed to Benjamin's freezing out from the intellectual community that held sway in many universities, journals, and publishing houses. It was largely ignored (Brodersen, pp. 129–32). Even greater then the irony that Benjamin appears so at home in these very zones today.

Thirty years after first being introduced to the anglophone world – in large part through the radical publishing house of New Left Books and on the basis of the Marxism-influenced, post-1925 writings – this latest edition of selected works re-draws the picture of Benjamin along the lines of the early writings. Four hundred of the four hundred and eighty pages concentrate on the period before Benjamin's part Lukács-inspired, part love-prompted Marxist epiphany on the holiday-island of Capri in 1924. These early writings are often concerned with the philosophy of language, with bizarre refractions of theology through history, sociology and linguistics, and with epistemology. Of course these same concerns are not abandoned later, but they are counter-balanced by the 'heavy weights' of commodity fetishism and class society, those irresistible conceptual pulls on Benjamin in the 'Stabilisation Years' and the Nazi Reich. The book's bent towards Benjamin's 1919-1923 writings makes clear the extent to which, in his twenties, Benjamin's eyes were fixed on a university career – and it reveals how this aspiration directed him to narrow his focus and attempt a working-through of traditional aesthetics. The doctorate on German romanticism and the *habilitation* thesis on German baroque tragedy are evidence of this, but they also disclose the extent to which, even when his eyes are fixed on the academy, Benjamin's concerns tug against traditional approaches and frustrate disciplinary boundaries. Indeed the university's hard policing of disciplinary boundaries in the mid-1920s scuppered Benjamin's career aspirations by rejecting his *habilitation* thesis. The methodology and concerns of *The Origin of German Tragic Drama* were deemed inappropriate for the Frankfurt University aesthetics department to which it was submitted. The material studied was too minor, the methodology too anti-systematic in a conventional academic sense, and the conceptualisation in the epistemo-critical prologue too complex for its reader Max Horkheimer, who protested that he could not understand it and so recommended that it should be failed (Brodersen, p. 149). Benjamin had blown it. Once the narrow channels of academic specialism had eliminated him, he was set loose to follow up the many threads of his eclectic interests, but had also to lead the chancy life of a freelancer. In those early years, in addition to working through the concepts presented by his tutors and the academic milieu of the time, he oscillates between philosophical study, graphology, art history and aesthetics, literary theory, the metaphysics of language, pedagogy, politics, the theory of love, and interpreting politically the hieroglyphics of everyday life. He never renounces this wide focus.

While this new volume reflects Benjamin's broad interests through its inclusion of fragments covering diverse themes, it does so without reflecting on its own selection and omission criteria. The book contains no chronicle of its own editorial history, no signals of the arguments and grounds behind its appearance, and no word of the bitter disputes about the editorial decisions that produced the German edition of the *Gesammelte Schriften*. Benjamin is smoothed into history. There is no introductory essay that contextualises the writings, or, more particularly, the selection of writings (for those contained here are but a small fraction of possible pieces). It does not provide the hundreds of pages of editorial commentary and analysis that come with the German edition. Editors Bullock and Jennings do not reveal the rationale underpinning the selection, or why there is a bent toward unpublished fragments on the philosophy of language and epistemology. Nor do they indicate absences, such as the lack of more political blasts like 'Weapons of Tomorrow', 'Peace Commodity' or 'Don't Knock the Illustrated Mags' or the curious first study of surrealism, or the essay on Paul Scheerbart and science fiction. Published essays mingle with unpublished notes. The status of unpublished fragments, notes, outlines is not probed – all jottings are, it would seem, equal before God. Unlike the thematic organisation and genre-based selections of the seven-volume *Gesammelte Schriften*, supplemented by myriad indices, this American venture is ordered chronologically. Readers get little sense of Benjamin as a creature with his tentacles curled around myriad forms of writing and address, and brushing multiple audiences. It is impossible to see just by glancing how many radio lectures for children and radio plays Benjamin wrote, how many journalistic reviews, and so on. Perhaps the editors will provide this type of analysis in the final volume. But as it stands at the moment, this book is large, spacious, not a scholarly edition, but a built-to-impress bookshelf slab. And because for the bourgeois intelligentsia the personality is infinitely more interesting than the work, a twenty-four page biography is appended covering the relevant years' trials and tribulations. Rather than biography, the editors might have produced a history of Benjamin-reception – for such an idea is more akin to Benjamin's own theoretical interest in the afterlife of works, and also because now, twenty-five years after the *Gesammelte Schriften* issued its first volumes and five years since the edition was completed, and after thousands of Benjamin books, articles and artworks have been produced in many countries, it could be said that the reception is now more fabulous, and politically fissured, than the oeuvre.

Towards the end of the period decked by this volume of the *Selected Writings* Benjamin experiences a remarkable realignment of his political and theoretical bearings. In 1924 he spends six months in Campania in Italy, a favourite destination for European intellectuals. There, when not reading Lukács's *History and Class Consciousness* or cavorting with Italian futurists, he spends hour after hour in discussion with leftists Ernst Bloch, Alfred Sohn-Rethel, and, most importantly, Asja Lacis, whom he calls 'a Bolshevist Latvian woman from Riga' and 'an outstanding female communist' (Brodersen, p. 137). On Capri, then, as he reveals to his horrified friend, the Judaic scholar Scholem, Benjamin first decodes 'communist signals', which, as the initial 'indications of a turnabout', had 'awakened in him the will not to mask the current and political elements of (his thoughts) in the old-fashioned way ... but to develop them by experimenting and taking extreme measures' (ibid.). Now begins Benjamin's arrogation of Marxism. This turnabout in 1924 was not the result of a sudden, unprecedented, encounter with Marxism, socialism and radical political theory. Around 1920 Benjamin read Luxemburg's *Letters from Prison*, Bakunin's *God and the State*, Landauer's *Call to Socialism*. Marx is mentioned in 'Critique of Violence'. And Marx also turns up in 'Capitalism and Religion', written the same year. Benjamin's politics had been attracted by radicalisms and anarchist forms of thought since his teenage years in the free-thinking German Youth Movement, but, in 1924, the combination of extensive discussions with communists and leftists, on the back of experience of extreme economic crisis in Germany in 1923, and the discernment of his own financial insecurities, drew him to a materialist critique of social life and social relations. This materialist turn leads him into adumbrating his version of materialist aesthetics, indeed what later, in 1935, in a letter to Werner Kraft introducing 'The Artwork-Essay', he will describe as an exemplary set of materialist axioms of art theory. The turn to materialism also necessitated denunciations of techno-worship and fetishized notions of history-making.

But Benjamin's appropriation of Marxism and materialism has stimulated argument: how Marxist is Benjamin? Has his 'historical materialism' anything in common with Marx's? Is his thought in actuality theological, as theological perhaps as Marx's own bet on redemption? This is an issue that Brodersen's very plainly written, unpretentious intellectual biography is keen to nail. His negatively accented version is that Benjamin's turn is not towards Marxism (he regards Benjamin as too inveterate an elitist for that), but away from esotericism (Brodersen, p. 141). Such an account produces a rather trembling balance, a Benjamin facing backwards, being swept away from metaphysics, yet keeping it still within his sights. Brodersen sees Benjamin's Marxism as grafted on, either by Benjamin himself, as he casts around for a language to legitimate his discomfort in his social world, or by the array of proselytisers that surround him, before and after death. Brodersen's vote is just another in a series of intonations whose accents are, of course, more often decided by the interpreter's own tendencies. Each of Benjamin's friends – most notably Brecht, Scholem and Adorno – took divergent cognisance of the significance of Benjamin's Marxism. Brecht, with whom Benjamin spent many days discussing the nature of the Soviet Union and Trotsky's critique of Stalin, appreciated Benjamin's sensitivity to the relations of aesthetic production, though he found traces of animism and mysticism in the idea of aura. Adorno accused Benjamin of a wide-eyed positivism, a sometimes crass materialism, and too credulous a faith in working-class rebellion. Scholem, anxious to de-Marx Benjamin, modelled him as Judaic mystic and promoted the line that Benjamin's historical materialism was nothing but a disruption, a blip, renounced shortly after the pose had been struck. These three positions bordered the perimeter of Benjamin-studies from the 1960s onwards, when Benjamin's academic rediscovery got underway. There were significant readings of Benjamin in the wake of 1968 – when occupying students at the Institute for German Studies at the University of Frankfurt renamed their block Walter-Benjamin-Institute (Brodersen, p. xvi). Studies of the 1960s and 1970s, written whilst the Left's star was glistening, often emphasised Benjamin's leftist 'production-aesthetics', his non-conformism – some were particularly inspired by his use of drugs, his critique of the philosophical basis of progress in bourgeois, social democratic and Stalinist thought. This Marxian Benjamin held ground in the New Art History of the 1970s and the cultural materialism that entered literary studies in England in the early 1980s, for example in Terry Eagleton's monograph on Benjamin, subtitled *Towards a Revolutionary Criticism*. But ever more representative these days are the writings of a scholarly school that takes its lead from poststructuralism and deconstruction. It is a body of work that, in abeyance to Derrida's meditation on 'Critique of Violence', deconstructs and, in effect, elides Benjamin and Heidegger, and Marxism and Fascism. Its action might be termed the production of a 'French Benjamin', but its current enthusiasts are Americans who 'got theory'. Eduardo Cadava is clearly one of these camp-followers.

Cadava's *Words of Light: Theses on the Photography of History* wordplays on the English title of one of Benjamin's last compositions, the series of theses on the philosophy of history. It is an essay-book, with the theses arrayed as snapshots. Each snapshot caption is a word or concept snatched from Benjamin – stars, heliotropism, reproducibility, danger, ghosts, lightning, mimesis, shocks, death. The theses pick up and twirl Benjamin's recurrent references to constellations, patterns, eternal return, reproduction. But they are also more generally interested in the fate and fatalism of technologies of vision in the twentieth century.

The book comes coated with praise on the back cover – where Judith Butler, Michael Jennings, Sam Weber and Homi Bhabha testify to its careful crafting, beautiful prose, elegance, subtlety, luminescence. It is full of that emphatic type of rhetoric that insists, for example, that 'there can be no thinking of history that is not at the same time a thinking of photography' (Cadava, p. viii). Cadava claims correctly that Benjamin recognised photography's decisive impact on the world, and that he was profoundly influenced by the invention of photography and the consequences this invention had. Cadava is also right to assert that photography's structure provided Benjamin with a filter through which to think history. With such a claim he stands in good company, for Adorno and Bloch also compared Benjamin's mode of writing and thinking to the process of taking snapshots and constructing photomontage. Benjamin thinks and writes in images. But his thinking and writing in images, what he calls his 'stereoscopic mode of seeing', results from an acknowledgement of the historicity of modes of vision. This means that he insists how, in each epoch, ways of seeing are augmented technologically, and that this augmentation is produced by, and works back on, human relations in quite specific ways. Cadava takes up this point, and yet, at the same time, discards it. For he also posits, by way of deconstruction's 'always-already' illogic, that there has never been a time without the photograph. Cadava's theses on photography tend towards a technological determinism. Citing Avital Ronell's work, Cadava insists that politics and history are to be understood as secondary, derivative forms of telecommunications. The world is only an image of itself. The universe is a giant photographic machine where everything is already imaged, already a copy of itself. Cadava reiterates again and again that the photograph predates the event, predates history, which is itself the emergence of images. Everything is already second order. There is only copy without origin, and so without fundament, reality or truth. The book is essentially morbid, concerned with the deadliness and deathliness of technologies of representation. Reproduction is severed from its conventional relation to life-making and generation, and aligned with the shadow-side. Cadava's book is peppered with the solemnity of mourning:

> Benjamin's "paper graveyard" – what I have wanted to call a photograph – tells us, if it tells us anything, that we must *regard* death. And it is there, in death, that Benjamin experienced what he had already experienced in life – death. The shock of his death – breaking in upon his own history and giving it, in this way, an end and a future – corresponds to the terrifying lucidity of his corpus. Death, corpse, decay, ruin, history, mourning, memory, photography – these are the words Benjamin has left for us to learn to read. These are the words that prevent his other words from being organized into a system, that prevent his writings and readings from being crystallized and frozen into a merely negative method. Words of light, they correspond to the cremation of his work, a cremation in which the form of the work – its suicidal character – reaches its most brilliant illumination, immolated in the flame of his own criticism. [Cadava, p. 130]

This is Benjamin for melancholics, for the successful who are peculiarly attracted to failure. A glance at Brodersen's biography dispels this mopy outlook, for we see there a figure who is at each stage of his life quickened, published, engaged, be that as leading student activist or, later, as discussant with key intellects of his day. The 'only real tragedy', as Brodersen's bookjacket underscores, is Benjamin's suicide at Portbou on the Franco-Spanish border in 1940. And that suicide was never predestined, not doomed to unfurl via a tragic logic foreshadowed in the writings. It was bad luck, and just maybe not even suicide, but a death brought on by the exertion of crossing the Pyrenees with a weak heart (Brodersen, p. 256). Still, a life projected through the filter of a suicide casts a more romantic, more tragic image. There is too much mileage in the maybe-myth to give it up. Cadava's bloodstained Benjamin is read through Derrida, Jean-Luc Nancy, Lacoue-Labarthe, Blanchot and Heidegger. Not just read through, rather read *as*. Cadava, mixing up a corpse and a corpus, slips and slides willy-nilly between conceits from Benjamin, Heidegger and fascist Ernst Jünger, fusing their often conflictive ideas on technology, shock, risk and history. Though Cadava suggests he will address Benjamin's analysis of fascism, he jumps straight into Jünger's techno-fetishism of fascism, with no comment on Benjamin's devastating attack on Jünger's mystical, aestheticised 'total mobilisation', written in 1930 and called 'Theories of German Fascism' (Cadava, p. xxii). The abrasiveness of conflictual positions is sanded down. Indeed rather than forming his philosophical and political opinions in the same spirit as Heidegger or Jünger, Benjamin explicitly forms them in contradistinction to these men whom he attacks as rightists and mystics. Of course Benjamin's lack of orthodoxy means that he does not sit easily with anyone, that he cannot be effortlessly assimilated to any one tradition. Untrammelled by Moscow-diktat, he criticises currents on the left, as well as on the right. For Cadava, though, this lack of card-carrying means that Benjamin can be made to represent an ambivalence or fatalism, whereby all positions collapse into their other, thus making charmed only the liberal centre-ground where ambivalence already reigns supreme. Cadava promotes the guiltlessness of the middle-ground and the privileging of thought over action, while perpetrating an imprecise understanding of the nature of revolution:

> There is no revolutionary discourse or situation, on the left or on the right (and, as Derrida has noted, "from 1921, in Germany, there were many of these that resembled each other in a troubling way, Benjamin often finding himself between the two" ...) that does not have recourse to technology, to the technical media, often in the name of progress. This is why so many of Benjamin's writings are directed against the rhetoric of progress, technological or otherwise. It is also why it is often difficult to distinguish between one revolution and another. As Jean-Luc Nancy notes, that "Fascism and Nazism were also revolutions, as were Leninism and Stalinism" means that "it is therefore also a question of revolutionizing revolutions ... . This requires something on the order of a revolution in thinking" ... . In the

instance of technology, it requires a manner of thinking that
emphasizes the unforeseeably mediated relations that prevent
the meaning of an event from ever being present. [Cadava,
pp. 133–4]

Cadava draws on Derrida's *Force of Law*. This allocates Benjamin's
'Critique of Violence' to a generalised wave of anti-parliamentarian and
counter-enlightenment criticism 'on whose surface Nazism emerges and
– in the '20s and '30s – even "surfs"'. Derrida ascertains an equivalence
of right and left discourse after the First World War and on into the
nazi regime. Both Left and Right 'contaminate' each other's categories,
he contends, aiming at a primary and state-grounding violent political
strategy. Benjamin's recommended violence of a general strike against
the state's monopoly of violence and law – a violence that is 'nihilating,
expiatory and bloodless' – is shown, by Derrida, to be carried out in
actuality, in the gas chambers. Derrida's super-attentive reading may
have uncovered something about the parallel motions of extremist
thought at a certain date, particularly when seen from the perspective of
the centre that feels squeamish about violence and considers it all as
commensurate. But Derrida's textual double-action – lurching forward
through a history of ideas on the horseback of hindsight – has also
established a precedent. Each deconstructing critic wishes to revolve
Benjamin into his political, theoretical opposite, always producing
readings that fetishize failure and end in stasis, impasse or collapse –
and that time and time again rebuild Benjamin as clone of his
antagonists, Heidegger and Jünger. The time between the wars is not
seen as the time of 'civil war' between critics, as Benjamin described it,
but as a time of intellectuals' common concerns, of generational
obsessions. Cadava draws back from fully endorsing the notion of
Benjamin as fascist. He strands Benjamin in the centre, 'between the
two', stressing his critique of the 'rhetoric of progress' as it emerges
from the mouths of nazis and communists. But Cadava's fuzzy
assimilation of Benjamin's insights to the dehistoricised ontology of
Heidegger or the fascistic officer-derring-do of Jünger promotes the
same ambivalence as Derrida, Jean-Luc Nancy and the rest, and
camouflages the intractable, political tensions of those years. It is as if,
seen down the telescope of time, all the detail fades to brown.
Positionings and arguments in real time do not even register on the
academic seismograph, as the instable words, in a world made of words,
are wobbled and wobbled till the historical actualities that weigh them
down drop off.

Justice, Nature and the Geography of Difference
David Harvey
Cambridge, Mass.: Blackwell Publishers, 1996

Reviewed by Elmar Altvater[1]

In his introduction, David Harvey pokes fun at one of those many 'sterile' conferences on globalisation, this time at Duke University, North Carolina. By chance, the author happens to witness a 'south-eastern regional meeting of evangelical Pentecostal preachers' which is taking place in his hotel in Durham. At the one conference, we find an aggregation of 'diverse people not only from many disciplines and walks of life but also from many different countries' (p. 1); at the other, a well-ordered gathering of nice families with well-bred and properly dressed children from America's south-east. Two worlds meet, hardly suspecting or being aware of the other's presence. Yet they are observed, and become Harvey's object of reflection on 'the geography of difference'. Towards the end of a book which is rich in both observations and ideas, Harvey concludes that 'if the languages of community and of globalisation are both to be rejected, then, where is there to go? We find ourselves stranded on a terrain where space/time, place and environment cannot be separated each from the other, or treated as mere abstractions outside of the concrete conditions of history and geography. The theory of historical-geographical materialism is therefore ripe for application. This mandates a shift from a language of globalisation or communitarianism to a language of uneven spatial-temporal development, or more simply: uneven geographical development' (p. 429). Here Harvey alludes to a fundamental difference in the system of co-ordinates between those who perceive the world through the lenses of globalisation, and the Pentecostal preachers of the American province; small wonder, then, that there are problems of communication between them and no reason to engage with each other. Precisely because both groups are separated by the geographical reach of their respective horizons of perception and action, a 'theory of geographical scale' (Harvey cites Neil Smith approvingly, p. 41)[2] is needed to be able to understand the very simultaneity and contiguity of what is temporally and spatially so different.

That is why the concept 'the geography of difference' appears in the book's title. It rejects notions of absolute time and absolute space, and substitutes a 'relational theory of space-time' (p. 4). When dimensions are no longer considered to be absolute, relations change or are changed. If one dimension changes, all other relations change with it. It

---

[1] Translated by Benno Teschke.
[2] Smith 1992.

follows that it is the processes rather than the products which are of interest. 'Flows', not 'stocks', are the object of inquiry. Harvey illustrates this very clearly with regard to the city: 'The thing called a city is the outcome of a process called urbanisation. A dialectical approach ... says that (a) processes are more fundamental than things, (b) processes are always mediated through the things they produce, sustain and dissolve and (c) the permanences produced (including ways of thought, institutions, power structures and networks of social relations as well as material objects) frequently function as a solid and immovable basis of daily material existence'(p. 418).

Consequently, Harvey's analysis of different geographical reaches of temporally parallel (synchronous) and successive (diachronous) processes is predicated on the dialectical method. It thus seems to be no accident, that '11 propositions' (the same number as in Karl Marx's *Theses on Feuerbach*) are advanced in the section on 'the principles of dialectics' (p. 48ff). Harvey starts with the analysis of processes, flows and relations. This is more important for an adequate understanding of the present than the analysis of elements, things, structures or of organised systems (p. 49). The 'self-evident world of things with which positivism and empiricism typically deals' has to be transformed 'into a much more confusing world of relations and flows that are manifest as things' (p. 49). The author is, of course, right to demonstrate this by way of Marx's concept of capital. For Marx, capital is not in the first place a quantity expressed in terms of money, but a social relation between classes, between the political and the economic, as well as an element of society's relation to nature.

Harvey's exposition of dialectics and historical actors should be read by those who run up against methodological difficulties in the analysis of capitalist relations. The first part, entitled 'orientations', contains a rich discussion of theories (that is, not narratives) with special regard to Raymond Williams – a discussion which struggles to adequately explicate a 'historical-materialist' conception of time and space. Dialectical principles are proposed and confronted with non-dialectical interpretations of social systems. At various points, Harvey has recourse to the so-called 'Leibnizian Conceit' which differs from the dialectical view of the world. According to this conception, man, endowed with Leibniz's binary numerical system, is a windowless monad, an absolute entity within a pre-established, harmonic world. It is the best out of the innumerable number of possible worlds. The monad is nothing else than the mirror of the universe. Now the isolated monad has a new mirror, being 'locked onto a computer screen connected by modem into a vast world of correspondence in cyberspace ... This in many respects is a fulfilment (repetition) of the Leibnizian dream' (p. 75). Harvey quotes Heim: 'Monads have no windows, but they do have terminals...'.[3]

---

[3] Heim 1995.

Ironically, the great majority of *windowless* monads at the terminal today is using a binary operating system called *Windows* (95 or 97). Leibniz's eighteenth-century conception of the monad has thus become reality in the late twentieth century – in the form of computer screens. Every monad mirrors the entire external world, steered by a *deus ex machina* as a perfect and harmonically functioning system. Social practices, which generate the whole in the first place and which themselves change as a consequence of the repercussions of their own effects, are hardly conceivable in this scheme of things. Processes of retro-action fall outside the purview of monads; the modern, dialectically oriented, social researcher (and social geographer), however, will put them at the centre of their inquiry. This points to the subterranean connection, alluded to by Harvey, which could be drawn between Marx's idea of dialectics and modern chaos theory. The conjunctive mode is here consciously chosen, for there are too many open questions for the indicative mode to be justifiable.

However, one thing is certain. We cannot talk of dialectical principles without incorporating 'historical agency' (p. 96ff.), that is, without thinking about praxis. Dialectical principles lead inevitably to a critique of social theories which have either ignored space and time or which have started from the assumption that spatio-temporal structures are stable and invariable. Neo-classical economics and widespread systems-theoretical approaches in sociology come to mind. Harvey concludes the section on historical-methodological-theoretical orientations with some pointers to a 'theory of historical, geographical materialism'. Curiously, although the space-time regime constitutes the central axis of his analysis, these pointers remain confined to space alone. '(1) The discursive activity of "mapping space" is a fundamental prerequisite to the structuring of any kind of knowledge ... (2) Mapping is a discursive activity that incorporates power ... (3) Social relations are always spatial ... (4) Material practices transforms the spaces ... (5) Institutions are produced spaces of a more or less durable thought (6) The imaginary (thoughts, fantasies and desires) is as fertile thought of all thoughts of possible spatial worlds that can prefigure ... all manner of different discourses ...' (p. 111ff.). We now start to understand that the emphasis on flows over and against stocks, of processes over and against results, of production over and against the product is intimately bound to the meaning of social praxis. Praxis is discursive. It encompasses material alterations as well as their appropriation in thought and modes of concept-formation. The process of comprehension (in its most developed and most abstract form as theory-building) is always related to space and time. Inversely, space and time are produced as dimensions of social relations.

Having laid these sound theoretical and methodological foundations, Harvey is now in a position to investigate the 'nature of environment' in the next chapter of his book. The nature of the environment, so runs Harvey's consistent claim, is generated by social praxis. It does not exist objectively; rather, 'it has been capital circulation that has made the environment what it is' (p. 131). Such a proposition does not only carry the critical and sceptical connotations of the present, but appears in the nineteenth-century literature too, and there it has cocksure and affirmative overtones. Claude-Henri de Saint-Simon and many others thought that it was nature, not humanity, which should be exploited. Until well into the second half of the twentieth century, this positive view of man's domination over nature provided the ideational raw-material for quite a number of socio-technical utopias as well as for serious social-scientific studies. Harvey turns against it.

Nature is no objective fact. As such, it carries no intrinsic limits as, for example, Robert Malthus maintained with conservative intent. However, Harvey also identifies the problematic Malthusian argument of 'ecoscarcity' in some strands of modern Marxism. For example, he challenges James O'Connor's proposal to integrate, alongside the contradiction between wage-labour and capital, a 'second contradiction' between society, economy and nature into the analytical core of critical social theory.[4] To be sure, in his attempt to refute objective conceptions of nature, Harvey far exceeds his goal. What would have been required to make his argument plausible is a prior distinction between scarcity and shortage of resources.[5] Resources always have to be scarce, if they are to be the object of economic calculation. Even if they are super-abundant, they have to be kept scarce in this specific economic sense. This differs from shortage. Shortage implies the acceptance of objective limits in the space and time of Earth, and thus acknowledges the irreversibility of material and energetic transformations. As such, it relates to the second law of thermodynamics. Clearly, Harvey is not interested in a thermodynamic interpretation of natural processes. He rebuffs it with the following argument: 'It is one thing to argue that the second law of thermodynamics and the laws of ecological dynamics are necessary conditions within which all human societies have their being, but quite another to treat them as sufficient conditions for the understanding of human history ...' (p. 140). Well, neither Nicolas Georgescu-Roegen nor those Marxist authors, which have dealt with the arguments of thermodynamics, have seen things quite as simply.[6] One might even go so far as to maintain that attempts to grasp social processes as temporally directed and spatially located will not be able to dispense with thermodynamic categories.

Furthermore, Harvey misunderstands the character of modern, that is, 'Fordist', capitalism. It might be feasible to start from the assumption that, in human terms, the universe is so vast and the supply of solar energy so inexhaustible that the second law of thermodynamics is irrelevant to human existence. However, the problem for the dynamics of modern capitalism consists in the fact that it is almost exclusively

---

[4] O'Connor 1988.
[5] Altvater 1993, pp. 70–1.
[6] Georgescu-Roegen 1971; Martinez-Alier 1987; Altvater 1992.

powered by fossil fuels. They are the fuel which keep capitalism in motion as a social system on a global scale. However, fossil fuels – even from a human perspective – are finite. This applies even more so to the capacity of those areas of the planet which are used as waste-bins for the combustion products of fossil resources of energy. Thus, the absolute historical limits of the capitalist mode of production have an ecological dimension which goes beyond discursive matters. This does not mean that these limits are not considered in social discourses before they manifest themselves objectively as catastrophes. The realistic anxiety of catastrophe (for example, climatic catastrophe) is an essential element of socio-ecological discourses. Sometimes, this anxiety is overplayed and thus appears in rather ludicrous guises. And it is this over-dramatisation of the issue, but only it, which make Harvey's objections justifiable.

In his discussion of 'sustainability', Harvey steadfastly adheres to his general line. He rejects the notion altogether. He is, of course, right to distrust a kind of sustainability discourse which receives its overall shape from the formulaic and anaemic compromise semantics of World Bank publications or from the texts of the Commission on Sustainable Development. However, this does not exhaust the current discourse on the subject. Since the implications of sustainability are today the object of social conflicts, it is only therefore correct to demonstrate, as Harvey does with reference to the 'Chipko-movement', that environmental movements are first and foremost social movements (p. 187). Undeniably, there are those conservationists which do not preoccupy themselves with the social dimension of the preservation of nature. However, at least in West European societies, conservative ecologists constitute an unimportant minority. So it is a grave misunderstanding when Harvey associates regressive, conservative and reactionary political visions with the German *Grünen* (p. 171). Ramachandra Guha and Juan Martinez-Alier have put forward much more subtle and sensitive arguments about this matter in their book *Varieties of Environmentalism*. The German discussion of the *Grünen* has also addressed this problem at great depth.[7] But this lacuna reflects a much broader problem in the globalisation literature, sadly hardly ever perceived but strikingly apparent in Harvey's book: there is a lot of writing on world politics and all the various social conflicts and movements, but due to a lack of linguistic ability, only a small fraction of what is rather randomly available in English provides the cognitive filter through which this world is understood. The notion of a windowless monad has been rejected, but there still exists a social subject observing the world through a window which is smaller than it might be.

The crudity of Harvey's arguments is arguably bound up with a failure to convincingly conceptualise the capitalist 'valorisation of

---

[7] Martinez-Alier and Guha 1997.

nature' (p. 150ff). His concept of money, which is crucial in this context, misses the point, both in terms of Marx's central determination of the money-form, as well as in the discussion of that important function of money, without which it is impossible to comprehend the transformation of money into capital, and capital's self-dynamic 'as self-valorising value': namely money as money, money as a self-referential (autoreflexive) medium, money as a means of payment. It is therefore not surprising that Harvey cannot retrace the logical sequence of stages in the valorisation of nature; that is, starting from the identification of valorisable resources, via their exploration and separation from those resources which are not amenable to valorisation, to their commodification and eventual transformation into money, or rather capital. It is only at this last point of the valorisation process that these resources become subjected to capitalist calculation. It is from this point of arrival that the entire sequence of valorisation is planned.[8]

This part of the book is disappointing, for the argument is put in such an extreme form as to be misleading. In discussing John Bellamy Foster's *The Vulnerable Planet: A Short History of the Environment*,[9] Harvey writes that 'it is crucial to understand that it is materially impossible for us to destroy the planet earth, that the worst we can do is to engage in material transformations of our environment so as to make life less rather than more comfortable for our own species being, while recognising that what we do does also have ramifications (both positive and negative) for other living species ... '(p. 194). Such a stance shows the limits of a discourse which does not recognise objective, that is, discursively non-modifiable, natural limits. In fact, today it is very well possible for us to destroy planet Earth to such an extent that life is no longer possible at our contemporary, historically achieved level of evolution. Chernobyl or Bhopal transcend discourses; they are ineluctable events which we can only talk about. The definition of the concept of discourse which Harvey proposes in the following chapter on space, time and place is doubtless correct and important: 'Discourses are ... internalised as beliefs, embedded within material practices and modes of social relating within institutionalised frames, and operate as forms of political economic power. By the same token discourses *internalise* events, experiences, structures and power relations, but not as a mere reflection. They act to constitute the world by virtue of the multiple translations and transformations which link them to these other domains of action understood as a whole ...' (p. 221ff). Here, decisive elements are mentioned which may suffice in many areas of social-scientific research, especially in dealings with space, time and place. However, they are insufficient when we debate the ecological limits of human action; for in this case, we have to take into account that it is precisely through 'discursive practices' which follow the logic of profit-

---

[8] This argument has been developed more in detail in Altvater and Mahnkopf 1996, pp. 373–83.
[9] Foster 1994.

maximisation, that those limits are objectively established – limits which no longer become reflexively visible in conventional social discourses.

This section on space, time, and place starts with the following incontestable assertion: 'Space and time, it is generally agreed, are social constructs' (p. 210). How, we may ask then, is the space-time regime socially constructed? The answer has to be: through social relations, through the forms of capitalist regulation and through social movements, which like the workers' movement, women's movement or environmental movements compete over the social definition of time and space. In the case of the processes behind the 'making' of the working class, this has been outlined meticulously, for instance by E.P. Thompson.[10] References to contemporary struggles on the shortening of labour-time should belong to these social constructions. To be sure, Harvey's construction of space and time through money – 'The Spatio-temporality of Moneys' (p. 234ff) – reiterates the deficiencies of his earlier determination of the money-form and the money-function. Harvey thinks that 'the diverse uses of money have not been well analysed' (p. 236). This may well be true; however, this statement is based on a highly restricted selection of relevant literature. He could have found other writings in which the shortcomings in the analysis of money, bemoaned by Harvey, are overcome.[11]

Consequently, Harvey also fails in combining his correct critique of the notion of time-space compression (p. 242ff) with an analysis of the form and function of money under conditions of globalisation. The spatio-temporal compression of the globe, as demonstrated in Harvey's examples, is essentially brought about by material infrastructures. It occasions the acceleration in time and the expansion in space, through which time and space are compressed. This is doubtless an important, if not decisive aspect. However, the spatio-temporal compression, which is caused by money largely independently of material flows, does not enter the horizon of reflection. So conceived, it then becomes difficult to understand the modern tendency towards a de-coupling of material and monetary accumulation.

It is only in the subsequent Chapter 10 on 'The Currency of Space-Time' that the meaning of the social construction of space and time becomes clearer. Places always contain a territorial dimension; placeless societies are non-existent. Relations of power emerge, reproduce themselves in places and achieve validity in space over and against other places. In the economic system, space signifies that place where 'interplace competition' (in German we might say *Standortkonkurrenz*) is carried out. Thus emerges a 'tension between place-bound fixity and spatial mobility' (p. 296), which has grown through the irrelevance of distances on a space-time-compressed globe. In those processes of

---

[10] Among the vast literature on the social conflicts over the historical introduction of a capitalist time regime, see the classical analysis by Thompson 1963.

[11] Backhaus 1969; Guttmann 1994; see also the literature quoted in Altvater and Mahnkopf, pp. 145–96.

competition over space, places turn not only into loci of collective memory but also into foci of place-related identity. The latter may degenerate, as Harvey puts it, into a chauvinism of place (p. 322).

The fourth part of the book turns to questions of justice. Justice is socially constituted. Its meaning is specific to respective forms of society. The introductory twelfth chapter starts therefore with the following statement: 'It is hard to discuss the politics of identity, multiculturalism, "otherness" and "difference" in abstraction of material circumstances and of political project. I shall, therefore, situate my discussion in the context of a particular problematic – that of the search for a "socially just" social order – within the particular material circumstances prevailing in the United States today' (p. 334). He opens up his discussion with a concrete case, viz. the burning of a chicken-farm, or rather, a chicken-factory in Hamlet, North Carolina. This case is shocking, not least because of Harvey's sober and distanced exposition. 25 out of a total of 200 workers died and 56 were seriously injured. The case is dissected as if viewed through a prism so as to clarify the various elements and dimensions of social justice: regional de-unionisation, robbing workers of their union protection; lowering of the workers' standards of living to those of the 'working poor'; the transformation of cities through increasing unemployment, and increases in the numbers of those in precarious occupations; de-regulation of labour-protection in the US since the 1980s; but also consumption patterns which have contributed to ecologically unsustainable mass livestock breeding at the lowest possible costs.

This concrete example serves as a spring-board to discuss different conceptions of justice. First of all, Harvey challenges the postmodern critique of universal rights and justice according to which the application of a concept of social justice has become generally problematic; secondly, he contests the belief in the creation of justice via market mechanisms; thirdly, he engages with the idea that dimensions of justice and injustice are dependent upon place and time. To be sure, the ensuing relativism of rights, justice, injury and injustice is situated outside those unifying tendencies which capitalist globalisation provokes in its train. This is seen by Harvey when he writes that 'in today's world, similarity largely resides in that realm of political-economic action so often marginalised in poststructuralist accounts, for it is in terms of commodities, money, market exchange, capital accumulation, and the like that we find ourselves sharing a world of similarity increasingly also characterised by homogeneity and sameness ... Only through critical re-engagement with political economy, with our situatedness in relation to capital accumulation, can we hope to re-establish a conception of social justice as something to be fought for as a key value within an ethics of political solidarity built across different places' (p. 360).

In a globalised world, the 'environment of justice' (p. 366ff) is likewise globalised, but not in the sense of its equal distribution. At the beginning of this chapter, Harvey cites a now rather infamous statement by Laurence Summers: countries with a low per-capita income are apparently 'underpolluted' and so waste imported from the industrialised countries will be beneficial for their development by raising the 'Wealth of Nations'.[12] Within the closed framework of neo-classical economics, Summers is certainly correct, and this points again to the strengths of neo-liberal discourses. However, the statement is, of course, only convincing and contradiction-free if it ignores the consequences of market action for society and nature. Harvey criticises this perspective and refers once more to his arguments in Chapter 6 where he denied objective ecological limits for human action – arguments to which I have already objected. However, one aspect which reveals the specificity of the US debate, is added here to his earlier reasoning: 'The severe recession of 1973–75, the subsequent slow-down in economic growth and the rise of widespread structural unemployment, made an appeal to some notion of natural limits to growth more attractive. Scapegoating natural limits rather than the internal contradictions of capitalism is a well-tried tactic ...' (p. 381). It is surely of merit to criticise green-tinted pretexts for economic abstentionism but also dangerous to negate ecological limits with well-meant arguments about ideology.

His reflections on 'justice, difference and politics' are summarised in the last chapter on 'possible urban worlds' (p. 403ff). Here Harvey refers again to Leibniz's understanding of the world as the best possible world, and here he comes into his own. Using as an example an analysis of Baltimore, Harvey shows convincingly that environmental justice does not exist in big cities (and in the world as a whole). The twentieth century is the 'century of urbanisation'. Here, Harvey could have drawn on Eric Hobsbawm's analysis of the century.[13] Today, urbanisation means not only the growth of mega-cities, but the emergence of a global network of urbanisation. This has been Saskia Sassen's subject of research, though Harvey does not mention her contribution.[14] Big cities enable 'space-time compression' across the globe. Spatial barriers are eliminated by cities at the price of a 'spatial fix'. The development of urbanisation has thus to be seen in the context of globalisation. Globalisation however, as Harvey says, has been around since the great discoveries at the end of the fifteenth century; what is new now are financial deregulation, the withering away of territorial borders to competition, changed forms of production and organisation in transnational corporations, a doubling of the world-wide proletariat, changes in the territorial structure of the globe and, finally, a loss of national sovereignty (p. 421). Is there a communitarian answer to globalisation? Harvey is, as already indicated, very sceptical. In this respect he supports Raymond Williams who wrote that 'the defence and advancement of certain particular interests properly brought together,

---

[12] *The Economist*, 8 September 1992.
[13] Hobsbawm 1994.
[14] Sassen 1991; Sassen 1996.

are in fact the general interest' (quotation by Harvey, p. 431). Harvey explicitly emphasises that this 'bringing together' should be the 'core task to be addressed' (p. 431). These passages resonate with Rousseauian ideas of a social contract. Unfortunately, Harvey does not elaborate on this point. Yet, such a discussion could have been of great interest, especially in the light of a frequently demanded 'global social contract' as a strategic goal (formulated, for example, by the Lisbon Group).[15]

The last few pages of the book are dedicated to the question of how this 'properly bringing together' might have to be achieved. Here Harvey is unable to overcome the fundamental distinction between the passage of time stretching from the past to the present – which he so lucidly analyses – and the passage of time stretching between the present and the future. For the latter, there are no analyses but merely forecasts, wishes, utopias, programmes and norms. Consequently, the book finishes with a series of 'musts': 'The work of synthesis and of bringing together the multiplicity of anti-capitalist struggle occurring on a variegated terrain of uneven geographical development must proceed a-pace. That is what avant-garde socialist political organisation must focus on. But it needs must arm itself with concepts and ideas, ideals and imaginaries fundamental understandings' (p. 434). Apparently, this is conceived by Harvey as a form of salvation. Curiously, his book ends with the following sentence: 'How to translate from this purely discursive moment in the social process to the realms of power, material practices, institutions, beliefs and social relations is, however, where practical politics begins, and discursive reflection ends' (p. 438). This formulation goes against the grain of what Harvey has said previously, precisely because discourses were defined as 'internalised as beliefs embedded within material practices and modes of social relating within institutionalised frames and operate as forms of political economic power' (p. 221). Consequently, discourses are practical, and practices are parts of discourses. This means that one should expect practical politics not to terminate discursive reflection but rather to open up opportunities for renewed reflexivity and strategic considerations. This is part and parcel of what Lelio Basso termed the 'collective process of research' in the development of a left political identity.[16]

For this project, Harvey's study is, despite various obscurities and contradictions, extremely important – perhaps even indispensable.

References

Altvater, Elmar 1992, *Der Preis des Wohlstands*, Münster: Westfälisches Dampfboot.

---

[15] Gruppe von Lissabon 1997.
[16] Pillitteri et al 1988.

Altvater, Elmar 1993, *The Future of the Market*, London: Verso.

Altvater, Elmar and Mahnkopf, Birgit 1996, *Grenzen der Globalisierung*, Münster: Westfälisches Dampfboot.

Backhaus, Jürgen 1969, 'Zur Dialektik der Wertform', in *Beiträge zur marxistischen Erkenntnistheorie*, ed. by A. Schmidt, Frankfurt am Main: Suhrkamp.

Foster, John Bellamy 1993, *The Vulnerable Planet: A Short Economic History of the Environment*, New York: Monthly Review Press.

Georgescu-Roegen, Nicholas 1971, *The Entropy Law and the Economic Process*, Cambridge and London: Cambridge University Press.

Gruppe von Lissabon, Die 1997, *Grenzen des Wettbewerbs. Die Globalisierung der Wirtschaft und die Zukunft der Menschheit. Mit einem Vorwort von Ernst Ulrich von Weizsäcker*, Neuwied: Luchterhand.

Guttmann, Robert 1994, *How Credit-money Shapes the Economy*, Armonk: Sharpe.

Heim, M. 1995, 'The Erotic Ontology of Cyberspace' in *Cyberspace* ed. by Michael Benedikt. Cambridge, MA: MIT.

Heinrich, Michael 1991, *Die Wissenschaft vom Wert*, Hamburg: VSA.

Hobsbawm, Eric 1994, *Age of Extremes: The Short Twentieth Century, 1914-1991*, London: Michael Joseph.

Martinez-Alier, Juan 1987, *Ecological Economics: Energy, Environment and Society*, Oxford: Blackwell.

Martinez-Alier, Juan and R. Guha 1997, *Varieties of Environmentalism: Essays North and South*, London: Earthscan.

O'Connor, J. 1988, 'Capitalism, Nature, Socialism. A Theoretical Introduction', *Capitalism, Nature, Socialism*, 1, pp. 11–45.

Pillitteri, P., Corbani, L. et al. 1988, *Ripensare il socialismo: la ricerca di Lelio Basso*, Milano: Mazzotta.

Sassen, Saskia 1991, *The Global City: New York, London, Tokyo*, Princeton: Princeton University Press.

Sassen, Saskia 1996, *Losing Control? Sovereignty in an Age of Globalization*, New York: Columbia University Press.

Smith, Neil 1992, 'Geography, Difference and the Politics of Scale', in *Postmodernism and the Social Sciences*, edited by Joe Doherty, Elspeth Graham and Mo Malek, London: Macmillan.

Thompson, Edward P. 1963, *The Making of the English Working Class*, London: Gollancz.

Writings on Psychoanalysis: Freud and Lacan
Louis Althusser, edited by Olivier Corpet and François Matheron
translated by Jeffrey Mehlman
New York: Columbia University Press, 1996

Reviewed by Martin Jenkins

If Spinoza was the philosophical detour which led Althusser to the distinctive Marxist philosophy of *Reading Capital* and *For Marx*, Lacan was also a vital and often ambiguous presence on the horizon of Althusser's thought. This collection of Althusser's writings, elegantly translated by Jeffrey Mehlman, brings together a number of texts on Freud and Lacan that demonstrate Althusser's constant attempt to force an encounter between psychoanalysis and Marxism. Drawing on the Stock/IMEC volume[1] published in 1993, these texts show us Althusser concerned with psychoanalysis as a subject vital to his project of a reconstruction of Marxism, and also provides us with a glimpse of Althusser the analysand and as protagonist in the involuted institutional politics that always surrounded Lacan.

The main texts are the well-known essay 'Freud and Lacan', and 'The Discovery of Doctor Freud'. The latter text was at the centre of the 'Tbilisi Affair'; an earlier draft (included in this book) was revised for an International Symposium on the Unconscious held at Tbilisi in 1979. Althusser did not himself attend the Symposium but the paper was published with several paragraphs missing; the paragraphs were those in which Althusser praised Freud as in some respects a superior practitioner of dialectics than Marx. The earlier draft was subsequently printed in 1984 without Althusser's permission. The resulting furore led some to hint darkly at Soviet censorship and lack of respect for intellectual property rights; others held that it was a simple confusion based on two similarly titled texts. Mehlman's resumé of the 'Affair' allows no simple conclusion.

Also included are Althusser's letters to his analyst René Diatkine which were written in 1966, two years after 'Freud and Lacan'. The letters combine theoretical ruminations with Althusser's attempt to browbeat Diatkine into a recognition of Lacan's importance ('... outside of Lacan, there is at present no one.' p. 49). Most interesting are Althusser's speculations on ideology and the unconscious that foreshadow the major essay 'Ideology and Ideological State Apparatuses' of 1969. Of less theoretical interest are Althusser's letters to Lacan, though they shed some biographical light. Althusser identifies with Lacan as a tragic outsider like himself, 'howling their loneliness' (p. 160), despairing of ever being heard. As befits the Father, Lacan's

---

[1] Louis Althusser, *Ecrits sur la Psychanalyse*, Stock/IMEC, 1993; revised edition, Le Livre de Poche, 1996. The edition reviewed here omits a short piece on transference and counter-transference and an interesting sketch of 'theories of discourse' of some 60-odd pages. The latter text's omission is to be regretted.

replies are of a perfunctory terseness. Finally there are two interventions that Althusser made at the time of Lacan's dissolution of his Ecole Freudienne in 1980. In 'An Open Letter' and 'Some Complementary Remarks' Althusser explains his bizarre appearance at a meeting called to ratify the dissolution; Lacan is characterised as an 'unfortunate and pitiful Harlequin' (p. 127) whom Althusser denounces in the name of the Holy Ghost (the libido). The sorry picture of two great thinkers, one senile, the other hypermanic, is both chastening and moving. What then do these texts tell us of Althusser's interest in psychoanalysis? The most basic concern is with a parallel between Marxism and psychoanalysis; such an affinity is at a high level of generality but is illuminating none the less. This affinity is two-fold: both are dialectical and materialist. 'If the minimal thesis defining materialism is the existence of reality outside thought or consciousness, Freud is indeed a materialist, since he rejects the primacy of consciousness not only within knowledge but within consciousness itself ...' (p. 107).

On the question of dialectic Althusser claims that Freud '... explored figures of dialectic very close to those of Marx but at times richer than them.' (p. 108). This richness lay in the distance from Hegel's notion of dialectic. While Marx was too close to Hegel, Freud 'shattered' the all too Hegelian category of contradiction. Althusser claims that Freud's use of the concept of overdetermination '... had the advantage of bringing into relief what separated Marx and Lenin from Hegel, for whom contradiction, precisely, is not overdetermined.' (p. 108) Althusser stresses that Marxism and psychoanalysis are both necessarily conflictual, not only by reason of their object but in their very constitution: 'The conflictuality of Marxism is constitutive of its scientificity, its objectivity.' (p. 110) Such 'conflictuality' is inevitable because both Marx and Freud made a radical break with bourgeois ideology in the founding of their sciences. In Althusser's lapidary formula regarding Marx and Freud he states '... for that truth is dangerous'. (p. 108).

Set against bourgeois hegemony, these sciences (Marxism and psychoanalysis) fall subject to resistance and attack from without, and this assault is reproduced within these very sciences themselves in the form of revision and scission. The dialectic of resistance/attack/revision/scission is the necessary condition of a conflictual science. It is worth stressing that 'conflictuality' is not purely internal to theoretical discourse but also refracts the contradictions with which History (*qua* class struggle) is riven, the History within which that science is inscribed. Althusser envisages his project as a struggle against the theoretical repression of such 'conflictuality' within Marxist theory and the concomitant historical amnesia; the consequence of which was an incorrect or impoverished practice. Most immediately this task of theoretical 'desublimation' was aimed at the policies adopted by the PCF; on the one hand, Althusser was engaged in a critique of theoretical Zhdanovism, and on the other, a critique of humanist 'dialogue' with all and sundry. In the case of the texts discussed here, the obstacle to be overcome was (as Althusser notes in his addenda to the English translation of 'Freud and Lacan') the official condemnation of psychoanalysis as a 'reactionary ideology' by the PCF in the 1950s. Althusser takes his stand defending, as crucial, the scientificity of psychoanalysis. Such a repression was not the preserve of the Communist movement alone; at the end of 'Freud and Lacan' Althusser forcibly raises the question of the 'theoretical silence' of psychoanalysis on the questions of its own history and practice and their imbrication (perhaps complicity) with the ruling politico-economic status quo. Aside from this basic shared status as conflictual sciences beyond the pale of bourgeois norms we can enumerate three levels at which Althusser approaches psychoanalysis. Firstly, Althusser is interested in psychoanalysis proper, as an exemplar of a science in the making. Psychoanalysis thus functions as a case study for Althusser's philosophy of science, informed as it is by the historical approach of Bachelard, Cavailles and Canguilhem. Secondly, there is Althusser's use of analogy. Psychoanalytic ideas are used as proto-concepts, which are not rigorously theorised, but rather tentative and exploratory. For example, Althusser speaks of the 'philosophical unconscious' and the 'philosophy-effect' of texts, by analogy with the psychoanalytic concept of the unconscious. Thirdly, Althusser imports psychoanalytic concepts that are rigorously theorised, which is to say that they are conceptually adequate to the new object they are applied to. One could mention for example 'overdetermination', or the use of Lacan's Mirror Stage in Althusser's theory of ideology. Such an importation implies a transformation rather than a simple, albeit suggestive transposition of concepts.

In the first case, psychoanalysis *qua* science, Althusser posits in the early text 'Freud and Lacan' that it is Lacan who has demarcated most rigorously for psychoanalysis its object: the unconscious. Moreover Lacan is the first to produce a theory adequate to that object, making of Freud's nascent science a science proper, rescuing psychoanalysis from the encroachments of psychologism, culturalism, biologism, etc. In Althusser's reading of Lacan the child, *qua* biological animal, passes through the 'aleatory abyss' to enter the realm of Culture, and the Law of Culture, whose 'first form is language, but [which] is not exhausted by language.' (p. 25) Language (in its materiality) is thus the privileged means by which we come to have knowledge of the unconscious, tracing its effects within the speech of the analysand. It should be noted that in his theory of ideology Althusser does not see language as the privileged key to its understanding; his theory of ideology is not a theory of 'discourses'. In the later texts in the book we can see how Althusser came to have doubts about Lacan's achievement. In 'The Discovery of Dr. Freud', Lacan is characterised as having produced nothing but a 'philosophy of psychoanalysis', rather than having established it as a science. At the conceptual level the most obvious use made of psychoanalytic ideas is in Althusser's theory of ideology. Notoriously, Althusser claimed that ideology has no history. Particular ideologies have histories but 'ideology in general' does not. This Althusser explicitly links to Freud's conception of the unconscious being eternal. There is no 'outside' of ideology, just as there is no escape from a measure of repression (in the psychoanalytic sense). Here the 'organic link' between ideology and the unconscious sets out the promise of a theory of ideology that Althusser was never able to honour fully. It is worth remembering that the ISA essay was merely a 'note towards an investigation'. The hope expressed in 'Freud and Lacan', echoed in the letters to Diatkine, that there is an affinity between the ideological imaginary and the unconscious imaginary was never satisfactorily conceptualised. However, we can here draw a line between Althusser's staging of the encounter between Marxism and psychoanalysis and those of other 'Freudo-Marxists'. Reich's full genitality, Marcuse's desublimated desire, and the surrealists' abolition of contradiction in the condition of surreality (the situationist project contains something of all these) rush all too swiftly to a 'resolution' which posits a subject beyond ideology; for Althusser this forecloses the question of class struggle and of politics as such.

Althusser's theory of the eternal and inescapable necessity of ideology would seem to militate against any rapprochement of his ideas with these other thinkers. Althusser's ideas, like Freud's, are too easily dismissed as 'pessimistic'; rather, they are the very condition for the subject and for any politics. The value of this book is to challenge those who would either lump Althusser in with an undifferentiated 'French ideology', or those who believe in a pure and closed Althusserianism. The encounter of Althusser and Lacan is still alive in the work of, for example, Zizek and Badiou; the full fruits of Althusser's project have still to ripen.

Marx and Non-Equilibrium Economics
Alan Freeman and Guglielmo Carchedi (eds.)
Cheltenham, UK and Brookfield US, Edward Elgar, 1996

Reviewed by Geoffrey Kay

In response to Engels's challenge in the preface to Volume 2 of *Capital* for theorists to anticipate Marx's treatment of values and prices, the debate about what became known as the transformation problem started even before Volume 3 was published. It was, however, Bortkiewicz's 'correction of Marx's fundamental theoretic construction' a dozen or so years later that proved most influential. It is still the reference point for discussion. In the collection of essays edited by Alan Freeman and Guglielmo Carchedi, Bortkiewicz is the author most cited.

At first sight Bortkiewicz's 'correction' appears an amendment of a detail Marx got wrong, albeit an important detail, but an essentially technical point of no great theoretical consequence in its own right. This, broadly speaking, was how it was viewed by Paul Sweezy who introduced it to an English speaking audience in *The Theory of Capitalist Development* in 1941, and this again broadly speaking was where matters rested for the next thirty years until they were reopened by economists drawing on the work of Piero Sraffa – *The Production of Commodities by Means of Commodities* (1960).

Sraffa himself was not primarily interested in Marx: his most important work aside from the *Production of Commodities* was the preparation of the collected writings of Ricardo and it was in a different field that his work had its first impact. In Cambridge in the 1950s a group of economists launched a scathing criticism of neo-classical theory, the prevailing orthodoxy. The original inspiration for this criticism was Keynes, but where Keynes had attempted to persuade his 'fellow economists' to look at things differently, the Cambridge School charged them with outright error and inconsistency. The problem was what to put in the place of the dilapidated orthodoxy. Sraffa's work was the obvious place to turn.

If it were necessary to single out the most important contribution Sraffa made to the development of economic thought, it would undoubtedly be his reinstatement of the concept of surplus which neoclassical theory had reduced to a hollow abstraction. The ideas, first that economies can produce more than they need to maintain themselves, and second that the extent and disposition of this net product is the critical variable for understanding how economies work, are the oldest and most fundamental ideas of economic thought. They lay at the centre of classical political economy but the leading members of this school, most notably Ricardo, were unable to integrate the concept of surplus with their conviction that the real price of things, their real value, was the labour needed to produce them. In economic terms they found it impossible to specify a set of prices which allocates surplus according to conditions laid down by the market (an equal average rate of profit in different branches of production) that is consistent with the labour theory of value as they understood it. Sraffa's way out of this impasse was to retain the concept of surplus but to reject the labour theory of value by defining prices simply as those ratios in which commodities must exchange to satisfy the conditions of reproduction, on one side, and the equalisation of the rate of profit, on the other.

The relevance of Sraffa's approach for Marxist theory became rapidly apparent but as soon as attempts to apply it were made Sweezy's compromise with Bortkiewicz's 'correction' fell apart. Bortkiewicz, it became clear, had not the followed the logic of his argument to its conclusion: had he not attempted to 'correct' Marx but concentrated instead on the problem of the prices which meet the requirements of reproduction and the equalisation of the rate of profit – the conditions he believed prices must satisfy but which Marx's transformed values could not meet – he would, like Sraffa, have seen that it was possible to dispense with the concept of value altogether. The lessons which the parties to the ensuing debate – the Sraffians and the Marxists – drew from this could not be further apart. The former, adopting Bortkiewicz as the precursor of Sraffa, drew the lesson that to correct the problem in Marxism which Bortkiewicz had demonstrated, it was necessary to substitute Sraffa's system for Marx's theory of value; the latter, taking the theory of value as an indispensable element of Marxism, saw no alternative to rejecting Sraffa and Bortkiewicz out of hand. This turned out to be a much bigger undertaking than it first appeared and the project is still far from complete.

The first difficulty facing Marxists in this project is that Bortkiewicz and Sraffa were not simply wrong; in their own terms their theories stand up and their criticisms of Marx cannot be discounted by identifying obvious errors in their formulations. It is the terms of their theory which must be confronted: do these represent Marx's theory accurately, or do they conjure up a version of the theory of value in their own likeness which bears little resemblance to the theory Marx advanced? A second difficulty is exactly what theory did Marx advance. It is possible that he would have said things differently had he anticipated the subsequent criticisms; as it is theorists have often to rely on the implications of passages which are not directly related to the issues in hand with the host of interpretative problems this creates. Connected to this is the possibility that *Capital* is not entirely consistent and that it is possible to find passages in the text which support quite disparate interpretations. A third difficulty is the problem of specifying the criteria by which a version of the theory of value which lies outside the range of the Bortkiewicz/Sraffian criticisms can be judged cogent.

These are the difficulties with which Freeman, Carchedi and the other contributors to *Marx and Non-Equilibrium Economics*, McGlone and Kliman, Ramos-Martinez and Rodriguez-Herrara, Naples, Saad-

Filho, de Haan and Giussani, have to contend. Except for the first piece by Freeman which gives a wonderfully clear account of the issues involved, though not everyone may appreciate the particular informality of its style, the articles are polished essays which presuppose a thorough knowledge of *Capital* and the 'transformation problem'. Each piece is closely reasoned and deserves more detailed comment than is possible here.

As the title of the collection intimates, the critique of equilibrium is central to the various arguments the authors develop. Marx employed the concept of equilibrium as a simplifying procedure to analyse two crucial conditions which prices must satisfy: exchange between the departments producing means of production and consumption (simple reproduction) and the movement of capital from one branch of production to another in search of the highest rate of return (the equalisation of the rate of profit). But he examined these conditions separately, recognising that while both operated on prices it did not follow of necessity that prices must satisfy them both simultaneously. It was Bortkiewicz and later Sraffa who adopted the standpoint of general equilibrium, arguing in effect that the economy must satisfy both these conditions at the same time. For them the simultaneous satisfaction of the two conditions was the overriding priority and the specification of the prices that achieves it was the criterion by which the theory of value must be judged.

The essays in this collection criticise this equilibrium approach on two grounds. The first is for diverting analysis down channels in which such essential features of the capitalist economy as class struggle and instability appear as unnecessary contingencies. As Lenin once remarked, examining the capitalist economy from the standpoint of equilibrium is equivalent to viewing the movements of a railway as interruptions of its natural state of rest in a station. The mathematical procedure for understanding how a variable (prices) is determined by two factors (reproduction and an equal rate of profit) at the same time, is simultaneous equations This is the procedure employed by Bortkiewicz and Sraffa. But as Freeman, Carchedi and the others show, the apparently self-evident validity of its results obscure the drastic unreality of the presuppositions its employment requires.

Consider one element of the process of reproduction – the use of iron (a shorthand for means of production) to produce iron. It is obvious that the purchase of iron as an input takes place before the sale of iron as an output and that there are two prices of iron – the input price and the output price – determined at different times. The output price is not determined until after production takes place, while the input price is determined in the previous cycle before current production is started. The simultaneous approach, however, takes these two prices as one. There is, of course, no way of justifying this supposition directly without denying time itself, but granting their determination at different moments while supposing them to be equal, which is what the mathematics of the simultaneous approach requires in this instance, leads to the same conclusion since the only circumstances in which they are equal are those in which the current cycle is identical to the previous one, ie. those circumstances in which time makes no difference and, for all intents and purposes, does not exist. The limitations of this approach are effectively exposed by the contributors to *Marx and Non-Equilibrium Economics* who show that once time is admitted into the analysis, the criticism that Marx failed to transform input prices, repeated for a hundred years like a mantra, falls apart. The essays by Carchedi, Freeman, Giussani, de Haan, Kliman, McGlone and Naples develop this argument and demonstrate in detail that once the simultaneous approach and its built-in supposition of general equilibrium are put aside the transformation of values into prices ceases to be a problem.

Alongside the quantitative relation of values to prices a number of contributors take up the qualitative relation. They show that the dualist notion which the equilibrium approach takes for granted is not what Marx had in mind: the transformation of a discrete set of values posited in terms of labour into a similarly discrete set of prices posited in terms of money is a problem imposed on Marxism and not really a Marxist problem at all. This line of argument dovetails neatly with the criticism of the simultaneous method but, while it is effective in cutting the ground from under the equilibrium approach, it falls short of a convincing account of Marx's concept of price as the form of value. This is a notoriously difficult subject, and remarks about dialectics and the contradictory unity of value and exchange-value which various authors fall back on do not come close to sorting it out. In the final analysis none of the essays convincingly escape the dualist trap. It would, however, be unhelpful to single this out as a particular shortcoming, for among those who have approached Marx philosophically, emphasising the Hegelian dimension of *Capital*, there can be found the complementary drawback of analyses of the value-form which pay little heed to its economic implications. The re-combination of 'economics' and 'philosophy' is a major task awaiting Marxists and this collection should be judged positively for making clear the theoretical conditions it must satisfy on the economic side.

A subsidiary theme developed by Freeman and Naples concerns the provenance of the simultaneous approach in neoclassical theory. Freeman cites Alfred Marshall, in turn approvingly cited by Bortkiewicz, who criticised Marx for thinking in chains of causation, ie. taking proper account of time, rather than stressing the mutual interaction of the elements of the economy upon one another. The idea that the consistency of a theory of value must be judged by its ability to specify a set of prices which simultaneously satisfy all the requirements demanded of them is a neoclassical conceit which is irrelevant to Marxism. The equilibrium critics of Marx performed a useful service in demonstrating that Marxism is inconsistent with neoclassicism, but this is not the same as proving Marxism is inconsistent in itself. Although mainstream economists do not recognise this point, it is their theory, not Marxism, which has lost the debate. If the essays in this collection did no more, their detailed demonstration of this point would alone make them worthwhile.

Perception and Experience in Modernity/ Wahrnehmung und Erfahrung in der Moderne: Walter Benjamin Congress, Amsterdam, 24–26 July 1997

Report by Henning Teschke

The International Walter Benjamin Association (IWBA) was founded in Amsterdam in April 1995. In July 1997 Amsterdam played host to its first Benjamin Congress *Perception and Experience in Modernity/ Wahrnehmung und Erfahrung in der Moderne*. The long delay was largely due to the unexpected death of Wil van Gerven, Assistant at the Institute of Comparative Literature at the University of Amsterdam, and the IWBA's driving force. The IWBA is based in the Dutch capital where it intends to publish its bilingual yearbook *Benjamin Studies/Benjamin-Studien*. It is to organise a Benjamin congress at different venues at three-yearly intervals. The IWBA, open to anyone, 'provides an international platform for two main activities: the study of the life and work of Walter Benjamin and cultural analysis and critique from the interdisciplinary and international perspective forged by Benjamin's groundbreaking initiatives in the field of the humanities.' (*Benjamin Bulletin*)

Organisational issues dominated part of the agenda of this constitutive meeting. The honorary members were chosen: Benjamin's two great-granddaughters Mona Jean Helga Benjamin and Kim Yvon Ingrid Benjamin, as well as Benjamin's former neighbour and friend from Ibiza, Jean Selz. The IWBA's advisory board is composed of Giorgio Agamben (Paris/Venice), Willi Bolle (São Paulo), Susan Buck-Morss (Ithaca), Jeanne-Marie Gagnebin (São Paulo), Klaus Garber (Osnabrück), Rodolphe Gasché (Buffalo), Werner Hamacher (John-Hopkins-University), Miriam Hansen (Chicago), Anselm Haverkamp (Frankfurt/O.), Martin Jay (Berkeley), Burkhardt Lindner (Frankfurt/M.), Michael Löwy (Paris), Winfried Menninghaus (Berlin), Stéphane Mosès (Jerusalem) and Sigrid Weigel (Zürich). The general assembly elected Helga Geyer-Ryan, Anselm Haverkamp, Kiernan Ryan, Sigrid Weigel, and Irving Wohlfarth to its executive committee.

The turbulent elections to the executive committee reflected the political and theoretical divergences in the international debate around Benjamin during the past decade. Substantially, the left-progressive continuation of Benjamin's work was confronted by Benjamin's postmodernist incorporation. Controversies also surrounded discussion importance which should be accorded to the German contribution to Benjamin-interpretation over and against the non-German one. In view of the many participants as well as the ninety contributors from fourteen countries, presenting their papers in five parallel workshops, there was some unease expressed over the exclusive choice of English and German as official Congress languages and the language of the bilingual Benjamin Yearbook *Benjamin Studies/Benjamin-Studien*. For it was, after all, the Parisian sky under which the Arcades spanned.

If the significance of the theme *Perception and Experience in Modernity* is not so much dependent upon the terrain it covers, but rather upon its new theoretical insights, then there was precious little that was substantially new in the nine main papers which set out the intellectual parameters of the Congress. Perhaps this was too much to expect. To be sure, this does not mean that the debate which has raged for three decades over Benjamin's philosophy of history, his messianism, Marxism, linguistic mysticism, and aesthetics, is bereft of new nuances. But these concern only selected parts of his work, not the overall (re-)interpretation of his thinking. Still, the conflicts surrounding Benjamin do not belong to the past, as Helga Geyer-Ryan wrongly asserted at the opening of the Congress. Neither the philological problems of the *Edition* (Rolf Tiedemann versus Klaus Garber) and the largely unpublished reply-letters of the Benjamin-correspondence, nor the conflicts which characterise a by now hopelessly segmented and mutually opaque Benjamin 'research-community' were openly voiced and discussed. These more general problems aside, *Perception and Experience in Modernity* was a broad enough title to allow for a whole range of new and heterogeneous perspectives on Benjamin in the workshops, and to continue or initiate the inter-disciplinary dialogue within those fragmented sub-fields.

George Steiner inaugurated the series of main presentations with a panoramic overview of central motives in Benjamin's life and work, ranging from the impact of bourgeois enlightenment embodied in Goethe, to linguistic mysticism and the influence of Wyneken, Scholem, Buber, and Rosenzweig, to Benjamin's writings on Baudelaire and on surrealism, and finally to his tragic relationship with Marxism. According to Steiner, however, no concept in Benjamin can be really understood without taking note of his Jewish background and no real insight can be gained in ignorance of his religion. From here, Steiner established the link to the future application of Benjamin. The collapse of 'really existing socialism' imposes an ever-increasing urgency on Benjamin's utopian socialism. At this point, the Tikkun idea which is found in Jewish mysticism enters into conjunction with the historical tasks of the present: 'making good what's left of this smashed world'. In conclusion, Steiner pointed sardonically to the gulf which has opened up between Benjamin's lifelong exclusion from the academic world and the insatiable academic voracity to which Benjamin subsequently fell prey.

Samuel Weber's exposition revolved around the *citability of gesture*. The opposition between traditional and modern art is replicated and rejuvenated in the position taken by epic theatre over and against

Aristotelian drama. The gesture, interrupting the action, de-dramatises the plot so as to neutralise the Aristotelian catharsis oriented towards empathy. The spatialisation of interruption transforms an aesthetic category into a political one. 'The podium of the epic theatre demonstrates the possibility that everything can happen differently.'

Gary Smith developed a Jewish theory of justice in the works of Benjamin, Scholem and Jonah, the prophet. Benjamin's distinction in his essay 'Zur Kritik der Gewalt' ('On the Critique of Violence') between mythical and godly violence, which is permeated by a two-fold relation to time and eternity, can be decoded with reference to Scholem's idea of human justice as an alienation of divine justice. If godly violence puts an end to mythical violence, then Jonah stands at the threshold of this process. Through his sermon calling for repentance in Niniveh, which the crowd unexpectedly obeys, Jonah prevents the execution of Jehovah's divine judgement over the city. Justice, in averting divine violence without succumbing to mythical violence, turns out to be a state of true suspension (*Aufhebung*).

Dissatisfied by the Anglo-American dominance in *Benjaminiana*, Sigrid Weigel recalled the intimate interrelatedness between image and language in Benjamin's thinking – a pictorial thinking, which inevitably gets lost in translations of his writings. Language, both for Karl Kraus as well as for Benjamin, is a genuine dimension of justice. The dialectic of lamentation and accusation (*Klage und Anklage*), witness and testimony (*Zeuge und Zeugnis*) takes on a theological dimension. The charges made at the Last Judgement put an end to lamentations about history. Drawing on Heidegger and Derrida, Weigel attempted a deconstructivist reading of Benjamin. As the dialectical image destroys the analogy which it sets up, so the metaphor obliterates the hierarchy of authenticity and non-authenticity. In this, however, Weigel overlooked the absence of the term 'deconstruction' in Benjamin's work, and the prominence, in contrast, of the term 'destruction'. Especially in view of Heidegger, the precarious handling of common concepts makes the establishment of their specific semantic differences pressing.

Irving Wohlfarth's talk revolved around 'The Idea of a Technological Eros'. The passage 'Zum Planetarium' in Benjamin's *Einbahnstraße* (*One-Way Street*) confronts the cosmic state of inebriation (*Rausch*) of antiquity with the modern optically oriented world-view. The new form of contact between collective physis and cosmos is organised by dint of technology. Against the fascist aestheticisation and eroticisation of technology (Jünger, Marinetti), which arose out of the bloody frenzy (*Blutrausch*) of the Great War, Benjamin sees the function of technology not so much in the mastering of nature, but rather in the mastering of the relation between nature and humanity. In Benjamin's anthropological materialism, the Revolution is entrusted to physically permeate a technology freed from its capitalist fetters and to organise the collective body for cosmic communication: to win over 'die Kräfte des Rausches', the powers of intoxication, for the Revolution.

Burkhardt Lindner's contribution focused on the constellation of time, space, and happiness in capitalist hell. In contradistinction to Blumenberg, Husserl, and Kant, Benjamin understands time concretely. Precisely because world-time is equated with one's own life-time, the personal horizon of time commences with the Creation and ends in the Apocalypse. That is why Benjamin, in his 'Thesen zum Begriff der Geschichte', can say that we have been expected on earth. Yet, the expectation which the dead have of us – Lindner referred here to Karl Kraus: 'The dead do not sleep, they do not sleep soundly and they do not sleep deeply' – has to remain unfulfilled, for Benjamin could neither hope for the advent of the Messiah nor for the arrival of the proletariat as the last avenging class. Both possibilities, the realm of freedom and the realm of Salvation, are historically blocked. The moment of happiness, which is associated with the act of stepping out of the fateful context of parasitic temporality, is denied. Towards the end of his presentation, Lindner elaborated on the contradictions in two phases in the reception of Benjamin's work. The politicisation in 1968 of Benjamin's work – when his critique of capitalism had to be clearly demarcated both from Adorno's seraphic paraphrase as well as from the dogmatic Marxism of the East-German SED – was replaced by the depoliticised reception of today. Textual work takes a dismantling form.

This last argument was taken up by Werner Hamacher in his presentation entitled 'Jetzt' (Now). For him, the very foundation of the IWBA is at one and the same time a reaction to and a manifestation of the political harmlessness of Benjamin scholarship today. Benjamin's insight that historical relations are not to be blindly accepted, but have to be critically analysed, applies *a fortiori* to that relation which enables Benjamin scholars to gain knowledge of the significance of their object of inquiry. As long as communication is nothing more than the decoupling of politics from morality, the incommensurable and asocial elements in Benjamin's thinking have to be emphasised so as to prevent its take-over by the hermeneutical tradition. Hamacher went on to unfold the aporias of Benjamin's philosophy of history which culminates in the historical *Jetzt*. On the one hand, the *Jetzt* belongs to the catastrophic continuum of time. As such, it is part of hell. On the other hand, the same *Jetzt* – as *nunc stans* – shall simultaneously put a stop to the chronological sequence of events of which it itself emerged. However, if the continuum of repression can only be momentarily suspended, the materialist historian is barred from writing a historiography of the repressed. Only the bourgeoisie – as demonstrated by the French Revolution – is able to cite the past. The proletariat has no memory. It is bereft of a *Jetzt*. In the *Passagenwerk* (The Arcades-Project), according to Hamacher, Benjamin sets out to construct this missing consciousness of history for the pre-revolutionary period.

Martin Jay's presentation elaborated on the relation between 'Remembrance and the First World War'. This epochal caesura came to present for Benjamin a decisive moment in his intellectual development. The exoteric gaze on contemporary issues displaced the esoteric gesture of his earlier work. Politics replaced metaphysics. The First World War constitutes the historical *a priori* for the *Passagenwerk*.

Susan Buck-Morss' 'Revolutionary Time: the Vanguard and the Avant-Garde' situated the dialectic between the political and cultural avant-garde in the young Soviet Republic. Benjamin's idea of revolutionary time as interruption is nothing other than the Soviet avant-garde conception of art. Together with socialist art, it forms a constellation against capitalism. The figure of Stalin, however, who judged Shostakovitch's work as 'rather a mess than a music', documents how quickly political consciousness fell behind aesthetic consciousness. Of general relevance for the future direction of the IWBA's Benjamin congresses were the concluding remarks by Buck-Morss which inquired into the political consequences of academic work. For obvious reasons, this nexus tends to be screened out by orthodox academia. 'And this, my friends, is problematic!'

Looking back at the Benjamin Congress, one thought comes to mind. Given today's new perspective, reading Benjamin with regard to the relation between theory and socially transformative praxis must remain faithful to the level of consciousness achieved by him. It is only then that the interdisciplinary dialogue with the most recent theoretical currents does not degenerate into postmodern additive arbitrariness. Only then can the study of Benjamin raise consciousness, only then does it acquire meaning. In the end, social transformation lies beyond that theoretical level on which the discussion is neatly divided into pros and cons.

Articles in Future Issues

Mark Neocleous Radical Conservatism, or, the Conservatism of Radicals
Werner Bonefeld The Politics of Novelty
David Harvey replies to Altvater
Robin Blackburn replies to Linebaugh
Chris Arthur The New Dialectics
Patrick Murray Abstract Labour
Emma Bircham on.the welfare state
Geoffrey Kay & James Mott On Labour
Geoffrey de Ste. Croix Democracy and class in Ancient Greece
Roy Bhaskar Critical Realism, Marxism and Dialectics
Simon Clarke Was Lenin a Marxist?
John Molyneux on Lenin
John Roberts on Adorno on Art
Kenneth J. Hammond on Gabriel Kolko
Howie Chodos & Colin Hay The Party Form and Class
Chris Bertram on Marcus Roberts
Julian Stallabrass Commodities and Cyberspace
An Interview with **Slavoj Zizek**
Hannes Lacher on Altvater on globalisation
China Miéville on Ben Watson
Sean Sayers on Dialectical Materialism
Gareth Dale on East Germany

and more...

Still Available: for £7 issue No.1, Autumn 1997. Including:
Ellen Meiksins Wood – The Non-History of Capitalism • **Colin Barker** – Reflections on Two Books by Ellen Wood • **Esther Leslie** – Walter Benjamin's Arcades Project • **John Weeks** – The Law of Value and Underdevelopment • **Tony Smith** – Neoclassical and Marxian Theories of Technology • **Michael Lebowitz** – The Silences of Capital • **John Holloway** – A Note on Alienation • **Peter Burnham** – Globalisation: States, Markets and Class Relations • **Fred Moseley** – The Rate of Profit and Stagnation in the US, plus reviews by **Linebaugh, Beaumont, Teschke**

For back issues and enquiries about future issues please write to us
The Editors, Historical Materialism,
London School of Economics,
Houghton Street, London, WC2A 2AE, UK

Email: hm@lse.ac.uk

Subscribe

Historical Materialism: research in critical marxist theory

Subscription Details

Name..

Address..

....

....

Email address..

I wish my subscription to start with issue No.1 / No.2 / No.3 (please circle)

```
Rates for two issue subscription
```

Individuals	UK	**£10**
	Europe	**£13 or US$20**
	Rest of World (surface)	**£13 or US$20**
	Rest of World (airmail)	**£16 or US$25**
Institutions	UK	**£30**
	Europe	**£38 or US$60**
	Rest of World (surface)	**£38 or US$60**
	Rest of World (airmail)	**£41 or US$65**

Methods of Payment

Cheques, Eurocheques or bank drafts should be made payable to Historical Materialism and should be drawn in pounds sterling or US dollars.

Charge credit card: Visa ☐ Mastercard ☐ Delta ☐ Eurocard ☐ (please tick)

Amount:...

Card no:..

Expiry Date:..

Signature..

Please send subscriptions to:
The Editors, Historical Materialism,
London School of Economics,
Houghton Street, London, WC2A 2AE, UK.
Email: hm@lse.ac.uk

Notes on Contributors

Elmar Altvater is Professor of Political Economy in the Department of Political Science at the Free University of Berlin, and a member of the editorial board of *PROKLA, Zeitschrift für kritische Sozialwissenschaft*. He is author of *The Future of the Market* (Verso, 1993); and *Grenzen der Globalisierung* (with Birgit Mahnkopf, 1997). His current research looks at European integration, transformation in Central and Eastern Europe, and ecological and financial aspects of globalisation.

altvater@zedat.fu-berlin.de

Paul Burkett teaches Economics at Indiana State University, Terre Haute, Indiana, USA. His research focuses on Marxism and ecology, and the political economy of finance, inflation, and economic crises. A member of the Conference of Socialist Economists and the Union for Radical Political Economics, his work has appeared in such journals as *Science & Society, Capital & Class, Organization & Environment* and *Studies in Political Economy*.

ecburke@scifac.indstate.edu

Andrew Chitty teaches Philosophy at the University of Sussex. He is co-editor of *Has History Ended?: Fukuyama, Marx, Modernity* (Avebury, 1994), and has published articles on Hegel and Marx. He is currently working on a book on the ontological basis of Marx's social thought, with particular reference to the ideas of 'nature' and 'human being'.

a.chitty@sussex.ac.uk

Gregory Elliott teaches at the University of Brighton. His publications include *Labourism and the English Genius: The Strange Death of Labour England?* (Verso, 1993); *Althusser: A Critical Reader* (ed., Blackwell, 1994); and *Perry Anderson: The Merciless Laboratory of History* (University of Minnesota Press, forthcoming).

Mike Haynes is a comparative economic and social historian who lectures in European Studies at the University of Wolverhampton. His published essays have primarily been on the pattern of long-run economic development, especially in Eastern Europe, and working-class history in Britain and Russia. He is a member of the Socialist Workers Party.

le1958@wlv.ac.uk

Martin Jenkins is writing a book on Paul Virilio, to be published by Routledge. His research interests include psychoanalysis, Althusser, Alain Badiou and the Situationist International.

Geoffrey Kay taught Economics at City University, London 1966–94. His books include (with Stephen Hymer) *The Political Economy of Colonialism in Ghana; Development and Underdevelopment: A Marxist Analysis* and (with James Mott)

Political Order and the Law of Labour. He is currently working with James Mott on labour.

gbkay@gbk.prestel.co.uk

Esther Leslie writes about Walter Benjamin, Marxism and aesthetics. She hopes to see her book on Benjamin and technology appear soon. She is currently writing a book on critical theory, the avant-garde and animation. She is a member of the Socialist Workers Party.

e.leslie@uel.ac.uk

China Miéville is studying for a PhD in International Relations at the London School of Economics. His research interests include Pashukanis and legal theory, science fiction and Middle East politics. His novel *King Rat* is forthcoming from Macmillan in November 1998. He is a member of the Socialist Workers Party.

c.t.mieville@lse.ac.uk

Michael Neary is a lecturer in Sociology at the University of Warwick. Publications include (with Graham Taylor) *Money and the Human Condition* (Macmillan, 1998) and *Youth, Training and the Training State: The Real History of Youth Training in the Twentieth Century* (Macmillan, 1997).

Syrbs@csv.warwick.ac.uk

Graham Taylor is a lecturer in Sociology at the University of the West of England, Bristol. Publications include (with Michael Neary) *Money and the Human Condition* (Macmillan, 1998) and *State Regulation and the Politics of Public Service: The Case of the Water Industry* (Mansell, forthcoming).

Graham.Taylor@uwe.ac.uk

Henning Teschke received his PhD from the Freie Universität Berlin and is a researcher at the Maison des Sciences de l'Homme, Paris. He has published a number of essays on Benjamin, Baudelaire and Proust and is the author of *Französische Literatur im 20. Jahrhundert – Ein Überblick* (1998) and *Proust und Benjamin: Unwillkürliche Erinnerung und Dialektisches Bild* (forthcoming).

Ben Watson writes about contemporary music in *The Wire* and *Hi-Fi News*, and is the author *of Frank Zappa: The Negative Dialectics Of Poodle Play* (Quartet, 1994) and *Art, Class & Cleavage: Quantulumcunque Concerning Materialist Esthetix* (Quartet, 1998). He is currently researching a book on guitarist Derek Bailey and the history and theory of free improvisation. He is a member of the Socialist Workers Party.

Slavoj Zizek is a philosopher and psychoanalyst, senior researcher at the Institute for Social Sciences, University of Ljubljana, Slovenia. His main publications include *The Indivisible Remainder: An Essay on Schelling and Related Matters* (Verso, 1986); *The Plague of Fantasies* (Verso, 1987) and *The Ticklish Subject: The Absent Centre of Political Ontology*, (forthcoming from Verso, 1998).